Cross-Cultural Collaboration

Cross-Cultural

Edited by Jordan E. Kerber

With a foreword by Joe Watkins

Collaboration

Native Peoples and Archaeology in the Northeastern United States

University of Nebraska Press • Lincoln and London

© 2006 by the Board of Regents of the University of Nebraska
All rights reserved
Manufactured in the United States of America

Set in Minion by Kim Essman.
Designed by R. W. Boeche.

Library of Congress Cataloging-in-Publication Data
Cross-cultural collaboration : Native peoples and archaeology in the northeastern
United States / edited by Jordan E. Kerber ; with a foreword by Joe Watkins.
p. cm.
Includes bibliographical references and index.
ISBN-13: 978-0-8032-2765-1 (hardcover : alk. paper)
ISBN-10: 0-8032-2765-5 (hardcover : alk. paper)
ISBN-13: 978-0-8032-7817-2 (pbk. : alk. paper)
ISBN-10: 0-8032-7817-9 (pbk. : alk. paper)
1. Indians of North America—Northeastern States—Antiquities.
2. Indians of North America—Material culture—Northeastern States.
3. Archaeology—Northeastern States—Methodology. 4. Archaeology—Moral
and ethical aspects—Northeastern States. 5. Human remains (Archaeology)—
Repatriation—Northeastern States. 6. Cultural property—Repatriation—
Northeastern States. 7. United States. Native American Graves Protection
and Repatriation Act. 8. Northeastern States—Antiquities.
I. Kerber, Jordan E., 1957–
E78.E2C76 2006
974'0101—dc22
2005036079

For my parents, Sidney Kerber and the late Pauline Kerber
and
In memory of James B. Petersen (1954–2005)

Contents

Foreword   xi
JOE WATKINS

Acknowledgments   xvii

Introduction   xix
JORDAN E. KERBER

Map   xxxi

Part One: Collaboration and Regulatory Compliance
Burials and Repatriation

1. Making a Final Resting Place Final
A History of the Repatriation Experience of the Haudenosaunee   3
RICHARD W. HILL SR.

2. Tradition, Sovereignty, Recognition
NAGPRA *Consultations with the*
Iroquois Confederacy of Sovereign Nations of New York   18
NINA M. VERSAGGI

3. Consulting with the Bone Keepers
NAGPRA *Consultations and Archaeological Monitoring*
in the Wampanoag Territory   32
RAMONA L. PETERS

4. Collaboration between Archaeologists and Native Americans
in Massachusetts
Preservation, Archaeology, and
Native American Concerns in Balance   44
BRONA G. SIMON

5. "The 368 Years' War"
The Conditions of Discourse in Narragansett Country   59
JOHN B. BROWN III AND PAUL A. ROBINSON

6. Ancient Burial Grounds on Monument Road
*Abenaki and Archaeologist Efforts to
Find a Solution in Vermont* 76
DEBORAH E. BLOM, JAMES B. PETERSEN, AND FREDERICK WISEMAN

7. Working with the Abenaki in New Hampshire
The Education of an Archaeologist 94
ROBERT G. GOODBY

8. Forging New Partnerships:
Archaeologists and the Native People of Maryland 112
RICHARD B. HUGHES AND DIXIE L. HENRY

Part Two: Collaboration and Regulatory Compliance
Sites and Places

9. Highway Archaeology in Western New York
*Archaeologists' Views of Cooperation between State and
Tribal Review Agencies* 131
ROBERT L. DEAN AND DOUGLAS J. PERRELLI

10. Green Mountain Stewardship
One Landscape, Multiple Histories 150
DAVID M. LACY AND DONNA ROBERTS MOODY

11. The Past Is Present
CRM *Archaeology on Martha's Vineyard* 165
HOLLY HERBSTER AND SUZANNE CHERAU

12. Tribal Consultation in Pennsylvania
*A Personal View from within the
Pennsylvania Department of Transportation* 183
IRA BECKERMAN

13. Working Together
*Developing Partnerships with American Indians
in New Jersey and Delaware* 197
CARA LEE BLUME

14. Native American Collaboration in the Delmarva
New Meanings and an Expanded Approach to
Delaware Archaeology 213
MICHAEL D. PETRAGLIA AND KEVIN CUNNINGHAM

Part Three: Voluntary Collaboration
Research and Education

15. Case Studies in Collaborative Archaeology
The Oneida Indian Nation of New York
and Colgate University 233
JORDAN E. KERBER

16. Research and Dialogue
New Vision Archaeology in the
Cayuga Heartland of Central New York 250
JACK ROSSEN

17. Indigenous Archaeology in Southern New England
Case Studies from the Mashantucket Pequot Reservation 265
BRIAN D. JONES AND KEVIN A. MCBRIDE

18. From the Ground Up
The Effects of Consultation on Archaeological Methods 281
ELIZABETH S. CHILTON

19. Constructing Alliances along the Northern Border
Consultations with Mi'kmaq and Maliseet Nations 295
BERNARD JEROME AND DAVID E. PUTNAM

20. Passamaquoddy Homeland and Language
The Importance of Place 314
DAVID SANGER, MICAH A. PAWLING, AND DONALD G. SOCTOMAH

References 329
About the Contributors 361
Index 365

Foreword

JOE WATKINS

American Indian issues have always been interwoven with politics, and even American holidays are not exempt. Think about your earliest memories of Thanksgiving. Remember the stories of how the Pilgrims, starving that very first winter, were saved by the Indians? Remember the story of Squanto, the Indian who taught the Pilgrims to plant corn kernels and fish in the same mound—the fish serving as fertilizer to help the corn grow better? If you remember those stories, you have probably come to realize how large a role American Indians played in helping the Pilgrims survive and flourish.

But there are other stories that are rarely told, stories about how some of the Pilgrim explorers, in search of the inhabitants of the land, happened across a grave. They dug into it and found the bones and skull of a man, and the bones and head of a little child along with some cultural material placed with the bodies. One of the discoverers wrote that they took some of the prettiest things away and covered the corpse up again. In November 1620, only days after the Pilgrims had anchored off Cape Cod, American Indian graves had already been plundered for their contents (Heath 1963 [1622]).

The Indians of the northeastern United States bore the brunt of the European colonial expansion. Even while the English settlers "treatied" with the Indians as separate nations, they continued to play one group against the other in the quest to dominate the environment and to establish a nation apart from England. With independence from England in 1776, the fledgling United States government continued to maintain formal relationships with American Indians through treaties. In the early days of the United States, when it was still a small country, the government entered into treaties with the tribes to gain land, friendship, and military allies against the French to the north and west and the English to the south and east.

While generally the relationships between the federal government and Indian tribes were good, there were often conflicts between local nonindigenous populations and tribal groups at the individual state and local level. With the continued movement of American citizens into westward lands, there came to be more conflicts over Indian rights and the need for more land for non-Indians. As both the population in the east and the need for arable land grew, the United States entered into more and more treaties with the tribes for land. Some tribes signed treaties whereby they agreed to give up tracts of land in exchange for promises of protection, for money, and for other lands to the west, while others continued to fight to maintain control over their homelands.

In the 1830s, Samuel J. Worcester, a missionary residing within the Cherokee country lands in Georgia, was placed in a Georgia jail for refusing to take an oath of allegiance to the state and for failing to obtain a permit to allow him to reside in Cherokee country. The case went all the way to the U.S. Supreme Court, and in 1832 the Court decided that the Cherokees (and all Indian tribes, by extension) were sovereign nations not under the jurisdiction of the states. The decision, written by Chief Justice John Marshall, is important in that it established the idea that American Indians were "domestic dependent nations"—separate nations that exist within the borders of the United States but that rely on the United States government for particular benefits.

This decision should have been enough to establish a firm relationship between the states and the Indian tribes, but the president of the United

States at the time, Andrew Jackson, supported the State of Georgia over the Supreme Court and refused to enforce Marshall's decision (Prucha 1962:245).

With the precedent set by the removal of the southeastern tribes, federal policy pushed many other tribes out of their homelands and to faraway places in Indian Territory. Many of the tribes that had once existed in the Northeast were forced farther and farther west. The Lenni-Lenape (also known as the Delaware), for example, moved from the East Coast to Ohio, then on to Missouri and Kansas. One band moved to the Brazos River in central Texas, where they stayed until being moved to western Oklahoma along with the Caddo, Wichita, and other affiliated bands of Indians in 1859. The remainder of the Lenape remained in Kansas until, following the Civil War and continuing encroachment onto tribal land by whites in Kansas, the tribe moved to Indian Territory, where it aligned itself with the Cherokee Tribe. They were subsumed under the Cherokee Nation in 1867 (Wright 1979).

During the remainder of the 1800s, Indian tribes continued to be pushed to the limits of American "civilization." Some coped with the demands for their land by agreeing to treaty stipulations, while others chose to withdraw from the public eye. Tribes signed treaty after treaty, each treaty promising to protect their new lands and their boundaries. By the end of the 1800s, as treaty after treaty was broken or as tribes moved farther and farther from encroaching populations, Indian tribes no longer had free access to the land that was once theirs.

As a result of the stream of treaties made between the U.S. government and Indian tribes, most Indians chose to move westward to newer lands. Since the treaties called for Indian people to give up their lands in their traditional homelands, it was easy for people in the East to believe that Indians no longer existed in the northeastern United States. And while some tribal people did remain in the East, their earlier withdrawal made it easier for state and local governments to ignore their continued presence.

Thus, throughout the nineteenth and the first half of the twentieth centuries, people in the northeastern United States grew complacent in the incorrect knowledge of the vanished Indian. Sure, everyone knew Indians still existed in places like Oklahoma, New Mexico, and Arizona, but no one believed there were still Indians where the Pilgrims had established their dominance over the land, since, by treaty, the Indians had supposedly moved from the area. While the bulk of the Lenni-Lenape, as described above, did journey west, many chose to stay on their traditional lands and "hide in plain sight," as Cara Blume put it to me (personal communication 2003). They publicly hid their "Indianness" but privately maintained their Indian way of life so that they could remain on the lands their families had owned and controlled rather than being forced westward with the others.

Other tribes throughout the United States have had to deal with governmental programs aimed at helping them disappear and "melt" into the so-called American melting pot. In the 1930s, the United States government tried to change the ways that American Indians' relationship with the U.S. government was structured. The Wheeler-Howard Act, better known as the Indian Reorganization Act of 1934, encouraged the creation of tribal councils and constitutions in an attempt to allow the Indians to govern themselves, to change the existing injustices on the reservations, and to point the Indians on the road to "progress." Some headway toward creating better tribal control of their affairs was made, but a new policy came into being that seemed to stop those gains.

In 1953, with the passage of House Current Resolution 108, Congress indicated its intent to "terminate" federal relations with tribes and to allow Indians to assimilate into the mainstream of the American public. This act, in effect, would simply have allowed the U.S. government to ignore all the treaties it had entered into with the Indian tribes. This proposed program was met with resistance by the tribes, although some (such as the Menominee) actually chose to "terminate" and divide their holdings among tribal members. Finally, however, in 1958 the government ceased trying to terminate Indian tribes and reinstated programs aimed at providing care and support to them.

The Mashantucket Pequot situation is another example of the "disappeared" Indian of the Northeast. While once a prosperous nation under the English, after the founding of the United States the tribe's fortunes grew thin. The move by the Connecticut General Assembly in 1855 to sell off all but 86 ha of tribal land was intended to provide the tribe with funds to help the tribe endure, but it seemed to produce the opposite result by furthering the erosion of the tribe's land base and forcing tribal members away from the reservation. According to a tribal Web site (http://www. pequotmuseum.org/TribalHistory/TribalHistoryOverview/Timelineof Events.htm), by 1935 only 42 people lived on the Pequot Reservation. In 1975, with the election of Richard "Skip" Hayward as tribal chairman, the Pequot began the lengthy process of regaining federal recognition, which was finally regained in 1983. While the Mashantucket never "disappeared," they were required to go through the lengthy recognition process in order to "reappear" within the federal Indian affairs process. This seems to be true for many Indians in the Northeast. They never disappeared, but no one seemed to see them as they "melted" into their surroundings.

There are other stories—of the Stockbridge or Housatonic, the Munsee, the Lumbee—stories of people recognized as different from the general population around them yet no longer recognized as "Indian" by that same population. They were people without a country, to a great extent, and people without standing within the Indian affairs that separated them from their ancestors and their ways of life.

Federal law has, in some regards, acted to place blinders on many archaeologists and anthropologists involved in cultural or heritage resource management by legislating the standing of Indian tribes within the historic preservation process. While federal law has decreed that projects undertaken with federal monies or requiring federal permits must involve a cultural resources inventory to document the impact of that action on historic properties, it has done so at the expense of those groups of Indians that are not federally recognized as Indians under federal law. The 1992 amendments to the National Historic Preservation Act of 1966 have allowed increased tribal participation in the federal historic preservation program, and the Native American Graves Protection and Repatriation Act (NAGPRA) of 1990 has given tribal groups standing to participate in the repatriation of human skeletal remains, funerary objects, sacred objects, and objects of cultural patrimony. These laws, however, do not grant equal standing to federally recognized and non-federally recognized tribes. Non-federally recognized tribes have no greater standing within the historic preservation process than that of an "interested party," equal to the standing of the Sierra Club, for example; under NAGPRA, museums and other parties can repatriate materials to non-federally recognized tribes *only if* federally recognized tribes do not protest the proposed repatriation.

Who speaks for the non-federally recognized groups of Indians that, by all accounts, are Indians, have suffered the fate of all Indians, but who stayed behind rather than migrate west? In the past, I have argued that staying behind and "hiding," rather than openly being "Indian" and moving, was "copping out." But who among us should judge people whose fear of removal coupled with their love for their land or their religious duty led them to tacitly deny their "Indianness" by not openly admitting to it?

Since federal law does not require consultation with these non-recognized Indians, many archaeologists do not feel it necessary to consult with them. While it may not be legally necessary to consult with them, is it not ethically necessary to do so? Shouldn't we involve these groups in the federal preservation process to the greatest extent possible rather than bury our heads in the sand and claim legal freedom *not* to do so?

I think it important that archaeologists in the Northeast—where colonial and later U.S. relationships with Indians were forged—work with all Indian people to gain a greater understanding of the culture history of their areas. I feel that the need for collaboration among all parties in the Northeast is greater than in other parts of the country where there is a strong and active Indian presence. Indian life and culture are experiencing a rebirth in the Northeast. Some local populations are afraid of that rebirth, while other groups, as represented by the chapters in this volume, recognize and embrace the opportunities that rebirth offers. Those of us who have been outsiders watching from a distance are far from neutral about the burgeoning growth of American Indian activities in the Northeast, and I do believe all of us will benefit from it.

Acknowledgments

I wish to acknowledge the indispensable contribution of several individuals for assisting me in the preparation and completion of this project. I extend my heartfelt gratitude to all the contributors to the volume for their commitment to this publication and for their rigor in completing and revising their manuscripts. Thanks are also due to Steven Cox, Michael Gregg, Dixie Henry, Giovanna Peebles, the late James Petersen, Brona Simon, and Nina Versaggi for suggesting names of and helping to recruit potential contributors to the book. Also worthy of recognition are Gary Dunham, director of University of Nebraska Press, for his support and advice; Charles Cobb, Larry Zimmerman, and an anonymous reviewer for their many helpful comments on the proposal and completed manuscript; Gosia Mahoney, acquisitions assistant, and Linnea Fredrickson, assistant managing editor at University of Nebraska Press, for their assistance; Ruth Melville for copyediting the manuscript; and Scott Smiley for his indexing skills. I acknowledge Colgate University for providing me with a supportive work environment in which to produce this volume and the Colgate University Research Council. Last, I am deeply grateful to my wife, Mary Moran, and to my children, Pearl and John, for having given me the much-needed time to complete this project, and to my parents, Sidney Kerber and the late Pauline Kerber, for being everlasting sources of inspiration and encouragement.

Introduction

JORDAN E. KERBER

The involvement of indigenous peoples in archaeology is on the rise, despite a stormy political past and, sometimes, present. Case studies are increasingly reported in the Americas, Australia, and elsewhere (see Davidson et al. 1995; Harrison and Williamson 2004; Smith and Wobst 2005). In North America, as argued by Watkins (2003:273), American Indians and First Nations of Canada have frequently opposed archaeologists over who should control research designs and research questions, the interpretation of the indigenous past, and the representation of past cultures in the present. Before 1990 in the United States, Native mistrust and scorn of archaeologists and archaeology were both deep and rampant, largely due to the excavation of Native American skeletal remains and burial objects, and the retention and display of these materials in museums (see Biolsi and Zimmerman 1997; Bray 2001; Fine-Dare 2002; Mihesuah 2000). During these years, "as a rule, American Indians tend[ed] to equate archaeologists with pot hunters, grave looters, or even worse, animals who feast off of the dead" (Watkins 2000a:21).

While this perception may still continue among some, Native Americans are increasingly collaborating with archaeologists and even doing archaeology themselves on (and off) tribal lands (see Stapp and Burney 2002), largely as a result of two seminal pieces of federal legislation: the Native American Graves Protection and Repatriation Act (NAGPRA) of 1990 and the 1992 amendments to the National Historic Preservation Act (NHPA) of 1966. Both laws represent a sea change in the way archaeology in this country is practiced today. Not only have these statutes begun to improve the often contentious relationship between archaeologists and many Native communities, but they have also broadened the role of Native Americans in archaeology. In her review of *Indigenous Archaeology: American Indian Values and Scientific Practice*, Mills (2003:473) states that "the relationship between American Indians and the discipline of archaeology is at an important turning point." The present volume examines that turning point in the northeastern United States, now that NAGPRA and the NHPA amendments have been operating for more than 10 years. Indeed, this is an opportune time to observe the state(s) of Native American involvement in and relationship to archaeology across the region, and to address the obstacles that remain.

Both NAGPRA (Public Law 101-601) and the 1992 amendments to the NHPA (Public Law 102-575) put into place formal consultation procedures between Native Americans and archaeologists, as mandated by the legislation. Briefly, NAGPRA pertains to the protection of Native American burials on land belonging to federally recognized tribes and to the federal government. This statute also established a framework for the returning of Native American skeletal remains, funerary objects, sacred objects, and objects of cultural patrimony kept in federally funded museums (see Adams 2001; American Indian Ritual Object Repatriation Foundation 1996; Fine-Dare 2002; McKeown 1995; http://www.cr.nps.gov/NAGPRA).[1] American Indian individuals and federally recognized tribes may receive these materials, upon request, if they can demonstrate cultural affiliation to such items.

The 1992 amendments to the NHPA authorized federally recognized tribes to take on more responsibility for the preservation of significant historic properties on their land and to create tribal historic preservation offices/officers (THPOs) (http://www.achp.gov/THPO.html). Further, for development projects on land owned by such tribes or by the federal government, or for projects involving federal funding or permits, archaeologists may be required to consult with THPOs and other Native Americans in advance of such undertakings. As stated by Watkins (2003:276): "Consultation (defined in the federal regulations that govern the NHPA as 'the process of seeking, discussing, and considering the views of other participants, and where feasible seeking agreement with them regarding matters' arising in the compliance process [King 1998:94, cited in Watkins]) is required at various stages in the historic-preservation compliance process."

Thus, for more than 10 years, in one way or another, NAGPRA and the NHPA have brought Native Americans face-to-face with archaeologists and have produced active dialogues. This interaction in and of itself does not ensure positive results, but it has often led to the building of mutual respect and trust. In this book, collaborative archaeology refers to the practice of archaeologists and members of Native communities working closely together to understand the history and to protect the artifactual and human remains of these communities. Although such an approach usually involves consultation and repatriation associated with the NHPA and NAGPRA, cross-cultural collaboration in archaeology has also occurred voluntarily, increasingly so in the past decade, beyond the narrow scope of regulatory requirements established by the two laws. Watkins (2003:283) asserts that such instances of voluntary collaboration need to continue so that Native populations may become more fully involved as equal partners in archaeological research.

Collaboration is not new to cultural anthropology, either. Collaborative programs in indigenous communities have been ongoing in North America and elsewhere for many years (see Clifford 2004; Harrison 2001). Lassiter (2004:2–3) discusses how collaborative ethnography began in the early 1840s in the northeastern United States when Lewis Henry Morgan met Ely Parker, a Seneca Indian, which led to the two working together on writing a cultural description of the Iroquois: "In the final version, *League of the Ho-de-no-sau-nee, or Iroquois* (published in 1851), Morgan dedicated the book to his friend: 'To Ha-sa-no-an'-da (Ely S. Parker), A Seneca Indian, This Work, The Materials of Which Are the Fruit of our Joint Researches, is Inscribed: In Acknowledgment of the Obligations, and in Testimony of the Friendship of the Author' " (cited in Lassiter 2004:3).

According to Ferguson et al. (1997:240–241) and Nicholas (1997:93), archaeology benefits American Indians and First Peoples of Canada, respectively, by contributing important historical information; assisting in land claims; managing cultural resources and burials for protection from current and future impacts; promoting sovereignty; offering employment opportunities through fieldwork, interpretive centers, and tourism; educating the young; aiding nation (re-)building and self-discovery; demonstrating innovative responses of past groups to changing environmental and social circumstances; and providing populations themselves with skills and experience in doing archaeology. Clearly, collaborative archaeology is not a panacea for the difficulties facing indigenous groups, but in certain situations, as elaborated above and in this volume, it can be a powerful tool.

This book is about Native American involvement in archaeology primarily in the Northeast and how the relationship is changing between archaeologists and many federally and state-recognized, as well as non-recognized, tribes in the region. In addition to consultation mandated by legislation, the volume also explores diverse ways in which both groups work together outside the regulatory compliance process. There has been much written recently on cooperation between indigenous populations and archaeologists in the United States and Canada (e.g., Adams 2001; Dongoske et al. 2000; Ferguson 1996; Klesert and Downer 1990; Nicholas and Andrews 1997; Swidler et al. 1997; Watkins 2000a, 2003). These publications feature a host of outstanding examples among such nations as the Secwepemc (Shuswap) in British Columbia and the Navajo, Zuni, and Hopi, and others in the American West and Midwest who have combined their efforts with archaeologists to achieve mutually beneficial goals. This book, however, is the first to concentrate on collaborative archaeology in the northeastern United States (specifically, the six New England states, New York, Pennsylvania, New Jersey, Delaware, and Maryland). Some readers unfamiliar with the Northeast may be surprised that, as this volume and the foreword emphasize, numerous Native people and nations, including federally and state-recognized (and nonrecognized) tribes, still reside in the region, and that various archaeologists and American Indian communities here collaborate successfully.

In addition to the foreword and introduction, the volume includes 20 chapters prepared by 33 authors (26 archaeologists and 9 Native Americans), covering material largely from 11 northeastern states, as well as portions of the Maritimes in southeastern Canada. The chapters highlight the process and details of collaborative case studies in archaeology, ranging from consultation in compliance with federal, state, and local laws and regulations to voluntary cooperation involving educational, research, and museum-related projects. The fact that several Native Americans, a few of whom are archaeologists, including the author of the foreword, have contributed to the volume is a positive sign of collaboration in its own right. The chapters examine such key questions as: Why is collaboration between American Indians and archaeologists important (ethically, theoretically, and practically)? What are some of the benefits and pitfalls? How can the process be improved? Are there steps to achieve effective collaboration? The book is relevant to other geographic areas, since it offers a comparative framework for addressing and evaluating a growing number of collaborative case studies elsewhere.

Part 1 consists of eight chapters, written by twelve people, including four American Indians, that investigate collaboration and regulatory compliance surrounding Native American burials and repatriation. The first chapter, by Richard Hill Sr., a member of the Tuscarora Nation at Six Nations in Ontario and Chairperson of the Haudenosaunee (Six Nations Iroquois Confederacy) Standing Committee on Burial Rules and Regulations, discusses the repatriation experiences of the committee and its consultations with museums in the Northeast and elsewhere. In addition to summarizing ongoing issues that have been stumbling blocks to positive interaction with New York State officials and agencies, he provides an overview of the committee's policy and thinking about the protection of cultural resources, the treatment of human remains, and the Haudenosaunee view of cultural affiliation and of archaeologists. In her chapter, Nina Versaggi, Director of the Public Archaeology Facility and NAGPRA Coordinator at Binghamton University, reflects on some of the difficulties involved in the repatriation consultation process with the Six Nations Iroquois Confederacy, especially over assigning cultural affiliation. She explains that, instead of occupying a neutral position in consultation, archaeologists are in the middle of a more wide-reaching debate that involves Native American sovereignty, traditional cultural practices, and struggles for recognition. Versaggi points to the need for consultation on a more regular basis rather than as a sporadic event to satisfy federal requirements. Chapter 3 is written by Ramona Peters, Repatriation Coordinator of the Wampanoag Confederation and a member of the Mashpee Wampanoag Tribe in Massachusetts. She articulates a personal reflection on her consultation experiences in attempts to repatriate and to protect her ancestors' remains. Peters admits that she still feels some bitterness and distrust in the consultation process toward the "bone keepers."

The remaining five chapters in Part 1, prepared by eight archaeologists and two Native Americans, explore cases involving burial protection and repatriation in compliance with state and federal legislation. In her chapter, Brona Simon, Massachusetts State Archaeologist and Deputy State Historic Preservation Officer, presents a 20-year retrospective on the growth of the productive collaboration that has resulted from the Massachusetts Unmarked Burial Law. The bill was drafted to respect both American Indian spirituality and archaeologists' research interests, giving strong preference to site preservation, not excavation, and allowing for the reburial of any Native remains that cannot be preserved in place. Simon insists not only that a strong Native American constituency has emerged in the state in support of site preservation and collaboration with archaeologists, but that archaeologists have also been enriched through their interactions with Native people and have developed a greater understanding of Native perspectives. In Chapter 5, John Brown, THPO and member of the Narragansett Indian Tribe in Rhode Island, and Paul Robinson, Rhode Island Principal State Archaeologist, trace the relationship between archaeologists at the Rhode Island Historical Preservation and Heritage Commission and the Narragansett Indian Tribe. They also discuss the historical context of this relationship and the contemporary political environment, both of which facilitate and limit the ways in which Brown and Robinson have collaborated for more than 20 years. Early cooperation in the excavation of an endangered Narragansett Indian cemetery led to the formation of the Narragansett Indian Anthropological-Archaeological Committee, the passage of state legislation to protect unmarked cemeteries, and the establishment of the Narragansett Indian THPO. Their working relationship has been a complex and intriguing one that at times intentionally sought to blur the edges between what some consider the separate domains of scholarly research and political action.

The next piece by Deborah Blom, an archaeologist at the Univerity of Vermont, the late James Petersen, formerly an archaeologist at the University of Vermont, and Frederick Wiseman, a member of the Abenaki Nation and Director of the Abenaki Tribal Museum and Cultural Center, examines the complicated interactions between Vermont Abenakis, state officials, and archaeologists surrounding the excavation, analysis, and repatriation of Native American human remains from two sites. The authors maintain that the nature of scholarship has changed in Vermont, owing to the recently increasing voice of Native Americans in the archaeological process, despite an absence of state and federally recognized tribes. They also make the political connection between tribal recognition and site protection and repatriation efforts in Vermont. Similarly, in Chapter 7, Robert Goodby, an archaeologist at Franklin Pierce College, offers four case studies tracing the development of his 10-year working relationship with the Abenaki Nation in New Hampshire vis-à-vis the discovery and repatriation of Native burials. According to Goodby, the evolution of this relationship has been shaped in part by the difficulties the Abenaki have in representing their interests, and by an archaeological history that includes neglect and mistreatment of Abenaki remains. Each situation raises substantive and distinct issues for ongoing cooperation between the archaeological community and the Abenaki in the state. The last chapter in this part, by Richard Hughes and Dixie Henry, both archaeologists at the Maryland Historical Trust, elucidates the process of collaboration that has evolved in the state, and the many benefits, pitfalls, and new ideas discovered along the way. Hughes and Henry illustrate ways in which archaeologists at the trust and at other state organizations have forged new alliances with Maryland's Native people and have crafted the field of archaeology into a discipline that is both acceptable and relevant to multiple constituencies. Despite an absence of federally and state-recognized tribes in Maryland, these agencies and Native communities joined forces to draft legislation allowing the repatriation of human remains and funerary objects to culturally affiliated indigenous groups. Following the passage of this legislation and subsequent regulations, American Indians and archaeologists in the state have continued to seek an expanded cooperative relationship by creating a foundation of mutual trust, by exchanging information, and by working together to address common interests, ranging from education to site protection.

The six chapters in Part 2, prepared by ten contributors, including two Native Americans, focus on sites and places within the context of collaboration and regulatory compliance. In the chapter by Robert Dean, a member of the Seneca Nation of New York and an archaeologist in the Seneca Nation's THPO, and Douglas Perrelli, an archaeologist at the University at Buffalo, the State University of New York, the authors provide insights into the process of historic preservation compliance for highway archaeology projects in western New York State. In particular, they propose possible solutions for some of the difficulties involved in archaeological consultation between the Seneca Nation THPO and numerous state agencies. Chapter 10 is cowritten by David Lacy, an archaeologist at Green Mountain National Forest in Vermont, and Donna Roberts Moody, Repatriation and Site Protection Coordinator of the Abenaki Nation. Although many landscape values are shared by Abenaki and Forest Service personnel, Lacy and Moody stress that other values are embedded in different worldviews and histories. Actively managing the Green Mountain National Forest while protecting places integral to the Abenaki people requires an appreciation of these cultural differences. Using two separate voices for half of the chapter, the contributors not only describe collaborative efforts, ongoing for more than 15 years, to share understandings and to identify and evaluate archaeological sites but also reveal the challenges, successes, and prospects for continued collaboration from tribal and Forest Service perspectives. Drawing on archaeological work on Martha's Vineyard in Massachusetts, Holly Herbster and Suzanne Cherau of the Public Archaeology Laboratory, Inc., discuss their relationship with the Aquinnah Wampanoag Tribe on the island. The dynamic interaction with the tribe has resulted in the recording and often preserving of important Native resource areas that in previous years would likely have been destroyed. The coauthors elaborate critical shifts in the practice of contract archaeology and in the interpretations of excavated sites on Martha's Vineyard that resulted from increased tribal participation in archaeology on the island. They also direct our attention to the distinct benefits of collaboration for the tribe, archaeologists, and private developers and landowners alike.

Chapter 12, by Ira Beckerman, an archaeologist with the Pennsylvania Department of Transportation, explores the example of a large multistate highway improvement project in which the state of Pennsylvania and federal agencies had to adjust approaches to consultation with 15 tribes. While Beckerman admits this "trial by fire" was exceedingly difficult and "mistakes were made," the postproject relationship with the tribes is vastly improved. Reflecting on lessons learned from this experience, he offers eight guiding principles for productive tribal consultation in the state. In the next piece, Cara Lee Blume, an archaeologist with the Delaware Division of Parks and Recreation, highlights two projects illustrating an open model of interaction that she has developed in working with the Nanticoke Lenni-Lenape Tribe of New Jersey and the Lenape and Nanticoke tribes of Delaware. In distinguishing between collaboration (i.e., working together) and consultation (i.e., seeking advice or information), she makes the perceptive point that collaboration involves more than cooperation—it implies sharing of power so that each partner brings to and receives from the process something of value. Blume concludes that a truly collaborative approach must accept Native communities into equal partnership with archaeologists, as owners of their own past and as active participants in the full archaeological process. In the last chapter in Part 2, Michael Petraglia and Kevin Cunningham, archaeologists at the University of Cambridge and the Delaware Department of Transportation, respectively, also describe their work with the Nanticoke and Lenape tribes of Delaware. They write about the intensity of dialogue and the performance of several ceremonies by the tribes at the site of the authors' large-scale excavation project in the state. The positive effects of their interaction with both Native groups have had substantial personal, public, and research benefits.

The final section of the book, containing six chapters prepared by ten people, including two American Indians, explores a range of collaborative efforts largely outside the constraints of the regulatory compliance process. These chapters underscore the importance, and assorted challenges and benefits, of archaeologists and Native Americans voluntarily working together on diverse educational, research, and museum-related projects. In Chapter 15, I present two case studies in collaborative archaeology involving the Oneida Indian Nation of New York and Colgate University, where I am an archaeologist. The first centers on an archaeological workshop, at nonsacred sites, offered by Colgate to over 100 Native teenagers for nine years. During the past few summers, the project has been located on Oneida territory in central New York State and has been funded almost entirely by the Oneida Indian Nation. The other example is of ongoing collaboration between the Oneidas and the university over the repatriation, exhibition, and curation of certain Oneida archaeological remains in Colgate's Longyear Museum of Anthropology. This cooperation stems from the experiences of both groups in working together in compliance with NAGPRA and in voluntarily reaching agreements on other issues. Similarly, Jack Rossen, an archaeologist at Ithaca College, articulates his sensitive and meaningful research with the Cayuga Nation of New York. Situated in the heart of the Cayuga homeland in the state, Rossen's project involves Native American participation, stresses site protection, investigates nonsacred sites, and illuminates research issues relevant to the Cayuga people and their present-day concerns. Further, it serves as a focal point for community outreach and discussion of the Cayuga Nation's continuing land claim, it counters local efforts at historical revision, and it shows how archaeology can be a powerful force in improving Native–non-Native relations.

In their chapter, Brian Jones and Kevin McBride, archaeologists at the Public Archaeology Survey Team, and the Mashantucket Pequot Museum and Research Center, respectively, outline the historical and contemporary factors that have led to the development of the archaeology program at Mashantucket and the tribe's ongoing support of archaeological and historical research. They also describe the Mashantucket Pequot Ethnohistory Project. Since the project's inception over 20 years ago, tribal members, tribal archaeologists, and historians at Mashantucket have joined forces with University of Connecticut faculty and students on several initiatives, including archaeological training programs for tribal youth; NAGPRA grants; excavation, study, and reburial of remains recovered from an endangered Mashantucket Pequot cemetery; and survey and excavation of dozens of prehistoric and historic sites. As Jones and McBride emphasize, this close working relationship has fostered an atmosphere of mutual respect and trust, solid anthropological research, and unique perspectives on the past. Chapter 18, by Elizabeth Chilton, an archaeologist at the University of Massachusetts Amherst, reports on a topic that is not widely covered in the published literature: how recent consultations with Native groups in the United States have affected archaeological methods of excavation, sampling, analysis, and curation. Chilton delineates her experiences collaborating with the Aquinnah Wampanoag of Martha's Vineyard on an archaeological field school that she directed for two summers. Her field school excavation and her close interaction with the Aquinnah have had a great impact on the way she practices archaeology and on her approach to archaeological resource management.

The remaining two contributions to Part 3 also present examples of voluntary collaboration, specifically in the Maine-Maritimes area of the northeastern United States and southeastern Canada. In Chapter 19, Bernard Jerome, a member of the Aroostook Band of Micmacs of Maine and the band's Director of Cultural Programs, and David Putnam, an archaeologist at the University of Maine at Presque Isle, describe their informal partnership. They discuss, in separate voices, a case study involving archaeological consultation with Mi'kmaq and Maliseet nations in Maine and New Brunswick, Canada, concerning a field school excavation in northern Maine that raised a variety of contentious issues. The problems were resolved through a series of traditional councils in which tribal elders and archaeologists reached consensus on a procedural outline for the project. In the last contribution to the volume, David Sanger, an archaeologist and emeritus professor at the University of Maine at Orono, Micah Pawling, a graduate student in history at the university, and Donald Soctomah, a member of the Passamaquoddy Nation, introduce their research on Passamaquoddy place-names, part of the larger Passamaquoddy-Maliseet Dictionary Project. Soctomah recruited Pawling and Sanger to participate by providing place-names derived from early historical documents and archaeological sites in the Passamaquoddy homeland on both sides of the U.S.-Canadian border. These place-names are restructured, translated, entered into the dictionary, and, after consultation with tribal elders, placed on digitized maps of nation territory before the reservation period. The authors maintain that this collaborative work adds new words, place-names, and oral traditions to the dictionary project, while also contributing invaluable data for language and culture retention programs currently underway. They conclude that their research reveals how Natives and non-Natives can collaborate in ways that are mutually reinforcing and beneficial, and that scholarship does not have to split into Native and non-Native ways of knowing.

In conclusion, this volume demonstrates, as others have similarly argued, that collaboration between Native Americans and archaeologists is valuable to both groups, and that there is no one way or formula to ensure successful collaboration. Improving communication, sharing power and control as equal partners, and maintaining mutual respect are key ingredients. While this has not always been an easy road to follow—indeed there are multiple roads that may lead to collaboration—and some resistance lingers in the two camps, the prospects have never been greater for Native involvement in archaeology and archaeologist involvement in Native American concerns about the past. The case studies explored here provide concrete models for moving forward in the Northeast and elsewhere. They are also evidence that cross-cultural collaboration in archaeology is well worth the effort.

Note

1. NAGPRA also pertains to the protection and repatriation of Native Alaskan and Native Hawaiian skeletal remains and objects in certain circumstances.

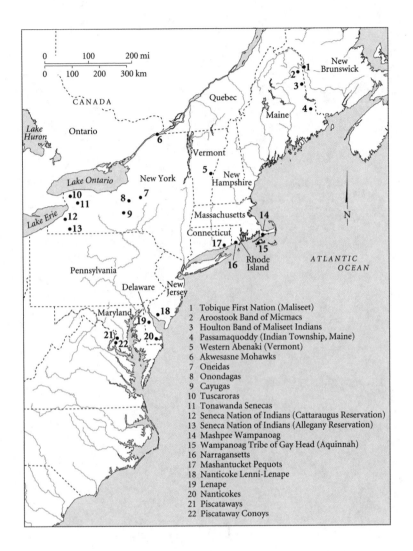

1 Tobique First Nation (Maliseet)
2 Aroostook Band of Micmacs
3 Houlton Band of Maliseet Indians
4 Passamaquoddy (Indian Township, Maine)
5 Western Abenaki (Vermont)
6 Akwesasne Mohawks
7 Oneidas
8 Onondagas
9 Cayugas
10 Tuscaroras
11 Tonawanda Senecas
12 Seneca Nation of Indians (Cattaraugus Reservation)
13 Seneca Nation of Indians (Allegany Reservation)
14 Mashpee Wampanoag
15 Wampanoag Tribe of Gay Head (Aquinnah)
16 Narragansetts
17 Mashantucket Pequots
18 Nanticoke Lenni-Lenape
19 Lenape
20 Nanticokes
21 Piscataways
22 Piscataway Conoys

1

Collaboration and Regulatory Compliance
Burials and Repatriation

1. Making a Final Resting Place Final
A History of the
Repatriation Experience of the Haudenosaunee

RICHARD W. HILL SR.

Introduction

It was a cloudy day on June 30, 1988, as horse-drawn caissons made a slow march across the Peace Bridge from Fort Erie, Ontario, to Buffalo, New York. In each of the 28 flag-draped caskets were the remains of an American soldier who had been killed in action in the War of 1812. Their bodies were uncovered earlier that year during construction at the bridge. No one knew their names, but they were being treated to a full military funeral as they made their way for reburial at a national cemetery in Bath, New York.

"No matter how long ago this happened, it's all history . . . whether it happened 200 or 2,000 years ago," said Michael Perez as he witnessed the procession. "We all fit in as a piece of the puzzle of history," he told reporters from the *Buffalo News* (Warner and O'Brien 1988). Tears flowed as these unknown soldiers made their way to their final resting place, being repatriated by the United States at great expense and even greater ritual.

Found next to those American soldiers were several Native American allies who were also killed in action. Their remains were not handled with the same care and respect. Instead of being repatriated to any Indian nation, they were unceremoniously carted off to a museum, where they remain to this very day. This double standard goes to the heart of why we have a federal law that requires museums, historical agencies, archaeologists, and collectors to respect the Native right to a final resting place. The museum shelf is not the kind of resting place that the law had in mind.

The Haudenosaunee, like many other Native nations, have been forced to use federal law to get curators and archaeologists to the bargaining table to resolve this long-standing dilemma.[1] It has not been a rewarding experience for us, since we find it very strange that we have to negotiate for the proper handling of our ancestors' remains in the first place. The convoluted legal definitions, questionable archaeological practices, convenient museum myopia, and governmental "white" tape have often gotten in the way of fruitful discussions. Yet our efforts have not all been without success. In many cases, museums and archaeologists have gotten the message and are working cooperatively with us.

Love it or hate it, the Native American Graves Protection and Repatriation Act (NAGPRA) has provided us with unparalleled access to our ancestors' remains, burial objects, sacred objects, and objects of cultural patrimony. Once the playground for a small circle of scholars whose work did not have an impact on our communities, museum collections are now having a powerful effect on contemporary Native societies. NAGPRA and cooperative curators have allowed us to rethink our relationship with our ancestors, to reaffirm our shared values, to learn more about the archaeological record, and basically to ask ourselves, What are the most important spiritual traditions that we need to keep alive? This essay is our first summary of what we have learned from this experience and how it has changed the course of our collective, cultural lives.

The Haudenosaunee Standing Committee

Our nations operate their repatriation programs under the auspices of the Haudenosaunee. The Grand Council of the Haudenosaunee, in accordance with the Great Law of Peace and based on Haudenosaunee protocols and cultural beliefs, established the Haudenosaunee Standing Committee on Burial Rules and Regulations (HSCBRR) to deal with the fact that New York State did not have an effective law to protect the final resting places of our ancestors. Unfortunately, after nearly two decades of work, the situation has not changed.

The HSCBRR works with the Six Nations of the Haudenosaunee to develop protocols and procedures for a coordinated approach related to protection of burial remains and, since NAGPRA was passed, to deal with related matters of repatriation. These traditional nations are governed by the Council of Chiefs and Clan Mothers. There are other governments that are not part of the Haudenosaunee but are recognized as having rights under NAGPRA. We cooperate with the governments of the Seneca Nation of Indians, the Seneca-Cayuga Tribe of Oklahoma, the Oneida Nation of Wisconsin, the St. Regis Mohawk Tribal Council, and the Council of Chiefs at the Grand River Territory in Ontario. We try to maintain the position that we are one people and that the Canada-U.S. border does not sever our rights or concerns.

Through our own internal governance, we decide what our priorities are, what collections to pursue, and where repatriated objects will be assigned. I have been the chairperson of the HSCBRR for five years. Previously, Peter Jemison (Allegany Seneca) was the chairperson, from the inception of the committee in 1989.

The first issue that the Standing Committee dealt with was to propose a law to replace New York State Indian Law 12A. Onondaga Chief Irving Powless Jr. and Peter Jemison worked on that legislation through several successive administrations and several lawyers from the New York State Office of Parks, Recreation, and Historic Preservation. I am sad to report that we have still not been able to have a successful burial site protection law approved. New York State is the last of the states to deal with this issue, just as it is the last of the original thirteen states to settle longstanding land claims. The lack of such a law has been a great source of conflict between the Haudenosaunee and the New York State Office of Parks, Recreation, and Historic Preservation. Ironically, we share much with the archaeologists of this state, and many of them have told us horror stories of their own frustration in trying to work with that office. The lack of an enforceable law has also caused conflict with archaeologists, local governments, and land developers.

The first on-site consultation trip of the Standing Committee was to the Field Museum in Chicago shortly after the passage of NAGPRA. Representatives from each of our communities visited with the museum staff and viewed appropriate collections. Some medicine masks were returned; however, we have still not been able to recover the human remains in the museum's collection. The museum has refused to recognize the Haudenosaunee as a government entity and insists on dealing with individual governments. This is a problem created by the U.S. Department of the Interior, since they also refuse to list on their Web site the oldest surviving government of North America. Our pleas to the department have gone unaddressed.

The key people on the first Standing Committee were Geraldine Green (Cattaraugus Seneca), Chief Leo Henry (Tuscarora), Chief Bernie Parker (Tonawanda Seneca), Chief Emerson Webster (Tonawanda Seneca), Chief Irving Powless Jr. (Onondaga), Clayton Logan (Seneca), Ron LaFrance (Akwesasne Mohawk), Ken Poodry (Tonawanda Seneca), Richard Johnny John (Seneca), Darwin John (Seneca), Sharon Leroy (Cayuga), Judy Green (Seneca), Clint Halftown (Cayuga), Doug George (Akwesasne Mohawk), and Ray Henry (Tuscarora). I would like to express my gratitude to these folks and to others who attended the early meetings, since they set in motion principles that still drive our repatriation efforts.

The HSCBRR had intensive discussions and fostered community dialogues on the issues we faced. How should the burial sites be protected? What do we do when human remains are uncovered? Will we rebury our ancestors? Where will we rebury them? What words will we speak? What protocols must be followed?

The HSCBRR also discussed the handling of burial objects and finally reached a consensus that we will request the return of all Native American remains found within the territory of the Haudenosaunee and that all burial objects will be returned to the Earth as they were intended. Many of our people were very hurt and angered by the desecration of the graves of our ancestors, and often our discussions became heated. There is a lot of resentment toward archaeologists and museums that look at the dead as objects of study and label our ancestors as if they were specimens. From the beginning, the HSCBRR considered this to be an issue of the denial of our basic human rights—the right to a final resting place. It was also a denial of our spiritual rights, and we were determined to see all of the remains eventually returned to the Earth.

Internally, we had to deal with a lot of complicated cultural and spiritual ideas for which we did not have a working model. We had to ask ourselves some deep questions about the conduct of our ancestors and relatives, those who cooperated with the desecration of the graves or sold sacred objects to curators. We had to face some harsh truths. Ultimately, we decided that many of the social ills we suffer today are a result of such losses. The consequences of our relatives' actions are being felt by our young people today.

The return of our ancestors to their graves was the first order of business. We did not see how we could have a respectful future if we were disrespectful to our ancestors. We had to restore the balance. Our thinking was that the ancestors would lead the way. Once they are brought back home and have received a final resting place, they will bring along the rest of the objects we are concerned about. So our priority has been to recover the human remains and burial objects first, then to seek the sacred wampum and finally the medicine faces that are part of our ongoing cultural expression. That has been our general plan, but we have had to make some adjustments on a case-by-case basis.

Since I have become chairperson of the Standing Committee, we have repatriated human remains and funerary objects from the Peabody Museum of Archaeology and Ethnology at Harvard University, the Rochester Museum and Science Center in New York, the Hood Museum at Dartmouth College, the Geneva Historical Society in New York, and several private collectors. We have worked with the American Indian Ritual Object Repatriation Foundation to recover several items held in private collections. In addition, we are currently negotiating with several museums to identify objects for repatriation, including the National Museum of the American Indian, the New York State Museum, the University Museum at the University of Pennsylvania, and Binghamton University in New York (see Versaggi, this volume).

Problems with Defining Connections

One of the most difficult issues that we face is the need to prove our cultural and spiritual connection to ancient ancestral remains. There are four things that have complicated this:

1. Archaeological theory has created unrealistic notions about cultural eras which have been used in an attempt to disassociate the current generation of Haudenosaunee from any Native Americans who walked this land before A.D. 950, the date most professional archaeologists consider to be the formative era of historic Haudenosaunee culture. They argue that we are not culturally affiliated with any of the folks who lived before that time. It is frustrating to try to explain that we did not fall out of the sky in A.D. 950 and that we are related to the first human who walked this Turtle Island. This is why we call ourselves Ongwe'o:we, "the Original, Real People." *Ongwe'* means "person"; *o:we* means "original" or "real." They were the original, real people, living as humans were intended to do. They are the real people, just as there are real animals, real trees, and real tobacco.

2. NAGPRA is not clear on what constitutes an acceptable level of evidence of cultural affiliation. While several categories are loosely defined in the law, the further back we go the more difficult it is to provide evidence of those connections, and archaeological evidence becomes the primary proof. Most museums, when determining cultural affiliation, focus largely on the archaeological evidence and discount our oral traditions and ongoing beliefs. There is no clear policy on how to weigh the evidence, and there is confusion about how much detail we need to provide to make our claim. The lack of clarity on dealing with "culturally unaffiliated" has been an ongoing problem across the country. Saying that remains and objects are "culturally unaffiliated" places the burden of proof on us, and we do not have the resources to do the necessary museum research required to make those affiliations clearer.

3. Our own hesitation to document and share our oral traditions and sacred history has made it difficult for us to make our case. We have learned that once things are put in writing, they are often used against us, and that just because something is written does not make it true. We are reluctant to commit our beliefs to writing because such writing then becomes part of the public record and is subjected to a validating process that we feel is pejorative. Why should our beliefs be subject to academic and legalistic debate? Who is to judge the validity of our beliefs? This issue has racial undertones that make us very nervous.

4. Overlapping federal laws have created confusion about which law applies to any given situation. There are some problems in understanding how Section 106 of the National Historic Preservation Act and other requirements under other federal laws come into play. We have had to consult with various federal agencies and have conducted our own training in these areas, but I must admit it is still confusing.

On a related matter, we have felt that there is a serious conflict of interest in these matters. The National Advisory Council on Historic Preservation was given some authority over the implementation of Section 106 requiring Native American consultation. However, the chairperson of that council was none other than the director of the New York State Office of Parks, Recreation, and Historic Preservation, the very agency with which we have had so much trouble. We have lost hope in working with the state agencies, especially in the politically charged atmosphere in the state. State agencies were instructed by the governor's office not to say anything to us. In a memo to all departments, instructions were given not to respond to any request from Native Americans until clearance was given by the governor's staff. Since the State of New York refuses to recognize the Haudenosaunee and has tied all of our discussions to casinos and sales taxation, we have not made any progress with the state. We might just have to wait them out. A new governor will come along someday. When it comes to New York State, we have learned how to wait.

Our View of Cultural Affiliation

The Haudenosaunee believe that we are connected biologically, socially, artistically, and culturally to the most ancient of ancestors who lived within our aboriginal territories, as well as to those who once lived within the expanded territorial range of the Confederacy of the Seneca, Cayuga, Onondaga, Oneida, Mohawk, and Tuscarora nations. Those affiliated nations who came under the protection of the Haudenosaunee were considered culturally and politically affiliated with the Haudenosaunee. Cultural affiliation can be seen in the relationships we had, and in many cases continue to have, with each other. There is also cultural affiliation because of our shared spiritual beliefs.

Because of our common Iroquoian languages, there is a cultural affiliation with all other Iroquoian-speaking peoples: Seneca, Cayuga, Onondaga, Oneida, Mohawk, Tuscarora, Huron, Neutral, Susquehannock, Cherokee, Nottoway, Wenro, Erie, Petun (Wyandot), and St. Lawrence Iroquoians. Since the Iroquoian languages were in place at the time of Contact, it is impossible to determine the origin of the languages.

Linguist Floyd Lounsbury (1978:336) suggests that the centrality of the Iroquoian languages in New York "should be seen as favoring a long occupation of the area of central New York State and north-central Pennsylvania, extending back in time for perhaps as much as four millennia, with expansions or migrations first to the south and then to the north and immediate west." This would mean that we have a cultural relationship with the Native people who walked this land over the last 4,000 years. Lounsbury's linguistic theory coincides with the geographic relationship between the Haudenosaunee and their neighbors. The lands to the immediate west of lands of the Haudenosaunee are the location of the Erie, Neutral, Wenro, and Shawnee. The lands to the south include the Delaware and Susquehannock. Lands to the north include the Huron, Algonquian, and St. Lawrence Iroquoians. Together, the original territory of these nations makes up the larger realm of the Haudenosaunee at the height of our political sphere of influence in the seventeenth to eighteenth centuries.

The lands of the other nations that joined, or were a protectorate of, the Confederacy were considered Haudenosaunee land. The people on that land abided by Haudenosaunee cultural protocols. They did not abandon their own traditional ways but added a cultural affiliation with the Haudenosaunee, especially in the case of the condolence ritual that was incorporated into nearly every council meeting. This ritual was a way of restoring the minds of those assembled at the council by paying respect to the recently deceased. It was conducted to ritually cleanse the visitors, delegates, chiefs, and people attending the council. The mind, eyes, ears, and throat were made "clear." In addition, the Covenant Chain of Peace, while largely a political tool, also created a culturally based relationship with many other Native nations. By extending the "rafters" of our metaphysical longhouse, we extended our family ties as well. It is this mutually agreed cultural protocol that has connected the Haudenosaunee to many Native nations in the Northeast in spiritual and political ways.

On a deeper level, we share the concept that the Earth is our mother and is a living entity that provides for the health and welfare of the people. The soil of the Mother Earth is thought to be composed of the decayed flesh and bones of the ancestors, replenishing the Mother Earth. In this way, our physical bodies are connected to the Earth as well. In death, all the Native people become one. This is a difficult reality for scholars to accept, but it is in our worldview that by being Ongwe'o:we we are connected to the ancient ones who walked and are buried in the same lands from which future generations spring forth.

Ever since humans were first created on this land, they have been learning by keen observation, dreams, visions, and messages delivered by the animals and spirit beings of the universe. Each generation experienced new understandings of the working of the universe, and those lessons have been translated through story, song, dance, ritual, collective action, and the arts. The subsequent stories help to explain the physical, intellectual, spiritual, and emotional aspects of the universe. Together, this knowledge is referred as the *Ongwe'o:weheka*, "The Way of Life of the Original, Real People." It includes everything that makes up the unique identity of the Original, Real People—language, customs, traditions, beliefs, and patterns of behavior. This Way of Life, as an inheritance from the many generations of the past, creates a seamless connection, even though we know that the people of the past went through many transformations. Each transformation added additional ways to express the core worldview of the Ongwe'o:we.

We believe that our ancient ancestors were given basic instructions about how to live on this Mother Earth in a simple but sacred way. We call these the "Original Instructions." The Ongwe'o:we were given seasonal and human life cycles that create the rhythms of life that we still acknowledge. Ecological time is marked by an annual cycle of rituals of giving thanks for natural and agricultural phenomena. Natural events include the flow of maple sap, the ripening of the wild strawberry, the appearance of thunder and rains, and the ripening of corn, beans, and squash. By connecting to these cycles, we are connected to those countless generations who preceded us, as they manifested those original instructions as best they could. We have inherited their experiences on the land in the way of life we have been given.

It is important to remember that these Original, Real People, from whom we are descendant, were not known by the nationalities that came into play later. These ancestors, while they provided the basic blueprint of our current cultural worldview, were not known as Haudenosaunee, nor by the tribal names common in the historic literature. We acknowledge that their ways of life continued to grow and change. Yet, no matter how much we have added to our forms of cultural expression, the root of our identity is tied to the ancient ones and the way of life that was laid out before them.

Haudenosaunee View of Archaeology

The Haudenosaunee do not subscribe to the idea of a cultural sequence that separates us spiritually from the first humans to walk on this land. We believe that we are biologically, culturally, and spiritually related to the Original, Real People. Through time, these ancestors invented new tools, techniques, and ideas; however, they are still our ancestors. The way in which cultural sequencing is used by archaeologists today has created an illogical gap in our cultural affiliation with any ancestors that date prior to A.D. 950.

We reject the anthropological notion that ancient peoples are "prehistoric" in that we believe our history begins with the Creation of the

Turtle Island and runs through today. By using the term "prehistoric," non-Haudenosaunee scholars make an artificial break in the cultural and biological connection between the first people to walk this land and our current generation. Many anthropologists have tried to define Native culture on the basis of physical evidence of the internal development of social systems in adaptation to their natural environment. That definition of culture is based on technological changes, and we feel it does not provide enough evidence of spiritually or culturally based thinking.

The most commonly agreed aspects of the traditional anthropological approach look at subsistence, technology, settlement, social organization, and political structures. Seldom are spiritual beliefs factored in, mostly because such beliefs are not usually reflected in the archaeological record. Subsequent historical periods defined without such spiritual considerations represent non-Haudenosaunee archaeologists' definition of culture, but such preconceived ideas about cultural continuity do not reflect an insider's point of view. Thus we have an "Archaic" Indian or "Paleoindian" defined by technological invention, not by spiritual, political, or shared values that unify a people's sense of place and identity through time. We believe that this sets up the false notion that we are disconnected from our ancestors because they made their pottery, arrowheads, or houses in a style different from that seen at the time of European Contact. Our stories of the connections to the ancient ones are an essential part of our identity. Our identity is founded on our belief in these connections.

We agree that the style of life in the past was different from that at the time of Contact. Our oral history explains that after the world was created, the people went through a series of experiences that revealed the mysteries of their universe. With each such event, the people added to or altered their conduct to reflect the lessons learned from those experiences. They had to learn how to live on the land, how to harvest the resources, how to hunt properly, and how to plant properly. They had to learn how to relate to the animals, and often received sacred instructions from them that resulted in new dances, songs, or rituals. There was also contact with spiritual beings that changed the course of life among the original people. The oral traditions reflect those epitomizing events and experiences that accumulated through time to define the world and culture of the Haudenosaunee.

There can be no denying that we descended from the people who archaeologists call "Paleoindians." They lived from approximately 12,500 to 10,000 years ago within the aboriginal territory of the Haudenosaunee nations. These are the most ancient of the ancestors and are the Ongwe'o:we whom we refer to as "the Original (Real) People." These were the first people to live on the land. There are also ancestors referred to as "Archaic," from the Greek *archaios*, meaning "ancient." These ancient people are also our ancestors. By the same token, we are culturally related to all the people described by scholars as Laurentian, Susquehanna, Adena, Hopewell, Point Peninsula, and Owasco.

It is important to remember that these are arbitrary names given to real humans. The fact is that the people had beliefs that were influenced by, and deeply reflective of, their environment. Knowledge that was gained in one period was passed on to the next generations through story, song, art, and ritual. It is unrealistic to think that those culturally defined systems would come to an end, and that an entirely new set of beliefs and traditions would start with each of the cultural eras described above. As an example, the so-called Owasco people inherited ideas, beliefs, and ways of life from the so-called Point Peninsula people. In turn, the Owasco people passed on their ideas and beliefs to the people who came to call themselves "Haudenosaunee." The changes noted by scholars, in architecture, toolmaking, or agricultural practices, do not destroy the underlying belief systems, which may not be evident in the uncovered artifacts.

Haudenosaunee Policy on Human Remains
Haudenosaunee Beliefs

We have been taught that we bury our dead relatives in the ground so that their bodies can become part of the sacred Earth. We believe that we come from the Mother Earth and that the human remains that rest within the Earth are an important spiritual connection to the spirit of the Earth. The Earth is enriched by the dead as our flesh becomes part of the soil. The souls of the dead have a path of destiny that they must follow. We refer to this as their journey after life. In this way, we feel that the dead are around us and hover over us as we hold our ceremonies or dances. We believe that the dead have power, and it is dangerous to neglect the spiritual needs of the dead. The protection of the human remains and associated graves, sacred burial sites, and related objects from the graves of the Haudenosaunee are the responsibility of each generation of chiefs, clan mothers, and faith keepers. We believe that the remains, the associated burial objects, and the actual soil in which they rest is sacred. There is no acceptable excuse to justify the desecration of this sacred burial.

Violation of Our Spiritual Rights

Removing the remains from their eternal resting place is a great desecration of both the dead and the living. The disturbance, destruction, and theft of the dead are violations of the religious and spiritual welfare of the Haudenosaunee. As long as the human remains are disturbed, there will be spiritual consequences to our people. The desecration of the graves of our ancestors, no matter how long ago the burial, is a violation of our religious freedom. Permits issued by the State of New York or any other local government to allow anyone to violate the sanctity of the graves of our ancestors can no longer be tolerated. In the past, our ancestors buried many objects along with the body with the belief that in the afterlife one would need all the things that one needs in this life. All types of objects have been associated with burials, including decorated clothing, glass beads, shell beads, silver combs, tools and weapons, ceramic and metal cooking pots, wampum belts, strings of wampum, and a variety of personal items. The removal of these objects from the grave is a theft from the dead.

Violation of Our Human Rights

The remains of our dead relatives are not "archaeological resources" that are subjects of study. They are human beings who once lived on this land. They had real lives and feelings. They had spiritual expectations about their final resting places. To look at Native peoples as objects rather than as human beings is a gross violation of our human rights. All graves and burial sites, Native or not, deserve respect. Our dead relatives deserve the basic human right to a dignified burial. We do not believe in the use of permanent headstones to mark the graves of our ancestors, but state law makes a distinction between cemeteries and unmarked burials. Our burial sites deserve to be considered hallowed ground whether they are marked or not. There has been a double standard in dealing with our people and non-Native remains. Non-Native grave sites are often afforded more protection than Native burials. Despite the efforts of state agencies to identify Native grave locations, construction permits are issued nonetheless. Our dead relatives deserve the same right to an eternal resting place as do all other races and religions.

Violation of Our Treaty Rights

The unearthing of the remains of our ancestors from their eternal resting place is also a violation of the promises made to the Haudenosaunee under the terms of the Canandaigua Treaty of 1794. By that treaty, the United States, including the State of New York, promised not to "disturb" the Haudenosaunee in the free use and enjoyment of their lands. We have been on record as protesting the desecration of our graves. The continual destruction of Native graves, the stealing of the Native remains, and the looting of burial objects cause us serious mental, emotional, and spiritual harm. Our people are continually upset by these events, and we have been forced to adjust our spiritual traditions to accommodate outside developments. The desecration of our dead violates the mutual respect promised by the United States when it pledged a firm and permanent friendship between our peoples. The treaty also promised to remove this cause of complaint that upsets our peace. We therefore make it clear that the desecration of the graves of our ancestors causes great harm to our people and that the United States and the State of New York have an obligation to protect the general welfare of our people as promised in the legally binding treaties.

What We Have Learned from the NAGPRA Process

There is no doubt that we have learned much about the daily experiences of our ancestors from the archaeological record, about our more recent ancestors from the museum archives, and about ourselves through community discussion and the meetings of the Standing Committee.

The archaeological record in many ways confirmed our oral history and gave a deeper sense of history to the cultural patterns that we still see in our communities. Through NAGPRA consultations, we have had nearly unlimited access to museum records, archaeological reports, and artifact collections. In our consultations with museum and professional staff at various venues, we have been able to gain more insight into the lives and times of our ancestors. Much of the work of archaeologists has been helpful in that regard. The difficulty comes when we have to review burial desecration reports, see photos of exposed human bones, and actually handle the human remains and burial objects. We still view such work as a theft from the dead in that we feel that no person has the right to take from the grave that which was intended to be buried forever.

Note

1. Haudenosaunee means "the People of the Longhouse" and comprises the traditional people and governance of the following Iroquois Nations in New York State: Tonawanda Seneca Nation, Cayuga Nation, Onondaga Nation, Oneida Nation, Mohawk Nation Council of Chiefs, and the Tuscarora Nation. These people maintain the way of life of their ancestors and operate under the Great Law of Peace.

2. Tradition, Sovereignty, Recognition
NAGPRA *Consultations with the*
Iroquois Confederacy of Sovereign Nations of New York

NINA M. VERSAGGI

The Native American Graves Protection and Repatriation Act (NAG-PRA) has been described as a statute that halts the unethical acquisition of Native American human remains and sacred objects, and as a course of action to "reverse the historic pattern of one-way property transfers" (Echo-Hawk 1996:1; Hill 1996:93). The law has been characterized as human rights legislation that corrects historical wrongs (Hutt 1994:2) and as a process that centers on the "humanization of Native Peoples" (Harjo 1996:3). An important aspect of NAGPRA is the federal directive that archaeologists and curators of collections collaborate with Native Americans to reach decisions leading to the repatriation of human remains and objects covered by the law. While phrased as a mandate or requirement, the instructions to consult offer a unique opportunity for archaeologists and Native peoples to share information, to have a meaningful dialogue, and to repair a past of mutual mistrust. When applied in a good faith, "the law and regulations encourage a spirit of cooperative engagement" (Echo-Hawk 2002:17).

However, it is often tempting to lapse into a compliance mode in which consultation is treated as a task to be checked on the to-do list rather than as ongoing dialogue. As King (1998:116) notes, "when people get too focused on the *process* of consultation . . . what gets lost is the recognition that consultation has a *purpose*." There is no cookbook approach to consultation, and archaeologists are beginning to realize that the process is often complex and the purpose multifaceted (Stapp and Burney 2002:119). Within this context, King (1998:114) discusses two forms of consultation, the formal, regulated process (Consultation with a capital "C"), and the less formal, everyday conversations (consultation with a small "c") that often serve as the prelude to formal decisions. In my experiences with compliance with NAGPRA and with Section 106 of the National Historic Preservation Act, it is the noncompliance interactions that are the most fruitful, paving the way to building mutual respect and trust and thus facilitating the negotiation of formal decisions. Native Americans also have stressed that "frequent communication can lead to effective communication" and that ongoing communication is critical for reaching consensus decisions (White Deer 2000:13).

This paper focuses on Binghamton University's NAGPRA consultations with the Six Nations of the Iroquois Confederacy as an example of collaboration between Native Americans and archaeologists in the federal compliance arena. Some of the principles I have found to be of importance include tradition, sovereignty, and recognition. I see these as major factors in the successful completion of consultation under NAGPRA, but I also view these as sources of tension that can make the whole process difficult to navigate.

Binghamton University and NAGPRA

After NAGPRA was signed into law in 1990, I notified our university of its responsibilities regarding collections and repatriation. The Public Archaeology Facility (PAF), a research center at Binghamton University (BU), had been working with Native Americans on issues pertaining to burials and sacred places before NAGPRA was enacted. BU, part of the State University of New York, has always been very supportive of our archaeological initiatives as well as our work with the Six Nations of the Iroquois Confederacy. As noted by Hill (this volume), the Iroquois Confederacy, known as Haudenosaunee, consists of the Seneca, Cayuga, Onondaga, Oneida, Mohawk, and Tuscarora nations. When the administration asked me to be the NAGPRA coordinator for our campus, I readily agreed and enrolled in a University of Nevada course on NAGPRA compliance (Hutt 1994). The course offered step-by-step instructions for compliance, including in-depth discussions of the very important step of consultation. Since about half the class identified themselves as Native peoples, including federally recognized tribal representatives, these discussions were lively, and they enhanced the sometimes dry facts of the statute. My notes from that class include a direct quotation from one of the presenters: "Do not get involved in tribal politics!" I recall that many Native American participants vehemently agreed and stated that they did not want or need interference from non-Indians when there were disagreements. That made a distinct impression on me, and I vowed to remain neutral in all matters that involved inter- or intra-nation politics.

However, as the realities of consultation unfolded, I soon realized that "tribal" politics at some scale are inherently part of consultations. This is not a negative observation, merely a statement of fact. The politics of Native peoples are important in the consultation process, particularly during discussions of cultural affiliation. As I found out, archaeologists should not expect to be neutral consultation facilitators; active participation requires an understanding of Indian issues in order to negotiate meaningful results. My role in NAGPRA involves a more wide-reaching debate centered on the issues of Native American sovereignty, traditional cultural practices, and struggles for recognition by individuals and groups who for decades had been denied a voice in the decision making that affects their indigenous groups. My experiences with the Six Nations may not be unique, but they certainly raise questions about the federal consultation process: What constitutes a successful consultation? Does the process encourage inter- and intra-nation conflicts to surface? What are the best ways to resolve these conflicts? I do not presume to have the answers to these questions, but I have learned from my experiences and have benefited from the guidance of others, especially the Native Americans with whom I consult.

The advice of one of the Six Nations' chiefs in particular has served me well: "You need to listen with a good mind, learn, and respect who we are." At his funeral in 2002, a clan mother took me aside and told me, "You know, it is all about mutual respect." As Williams (2000:35) so eloquently stated, "The clear mind, the Good Mind, is the beginning of peace. That is one of the most important lessons of the Kaianerekowa, the Great Law of Peace." For me, consultation (with a small "c") is first and foremost about the process of building mutual respect. In order to navigate through the process, we all need to listen, to learn, and to understand what is important to the people with whom we work. Along the way, I have started to understand that "importance" is often based on tradition and spiritual beliefs (see Hill, this volume), and I have tried to use this information during various new and ongoing Consultations (with a capital "C"). However, it is necessary to recognize that "it is extremely difficult to offer a single 'Native American perspective' on anything" (Watkins 2000b:91), and that is true within as well as between nations. Often it is tradition that forms a common base among related groups, and therefore this is a critical concept during collaborations.

Tradition

In my many conversations with one of the Six Nations' chiefs, he shared with me some of the oral traditions he felt I needed to know in order to understand and to respect "who we are." Native Americans and others have recorded many of these traditions in publications, and these serve as an important component in the process.

Iroquois oral tradition, passed down through generations, presents the history of the formation of the Iroquois Confederacy and the development of the Five Nations Constitution. Arthur C. Parker, Seneca ethnologist and archaeologist, spent the early part of the twentieth century interviewing chiefs and faith keepers of the Iroquois and collecting early manuscripts in order to record the most accurate version of the constitution of the then Five Nations (Fenton 1968:38). This compilation showed that the constitution resulted from years of negotiation among the nations which culminated in the formation of a confederacy of all Iroquoian peoples. The Iroquois Constitution and the formation of the Iroquois Confederacy are important to this discussion of consultation in that they provide the context for understanding a political system that today is relatively intact for some groups, and greatly modified for others. The differences between "traditional" and "nontraditional" forms of government are a source of some tension during consultation when trying to reconcile the rights to make claims and negotiate repatriation among traditional and nontraditional groups. This is best explained by a discussion of the principle of sovereignty and the absolute importance of this principle in the Iroquois Confederacy.

Sovereignty

Iroquois oral tradition chronicles the lives of two key individuals: Hiawatha of the Onondaga, and a Huron, known as the Peacemaker, who lived among the Mohawk (Parker 1968:14–15). These two people traveled from group to group, securing agreements of peace and membership in a Confederacy of Nations (Powless 2000:16). The Great Immutable Law of Peace resulted, and through time the dispersed nations of the Iroquois agreed to abide by this law. As part of the agreement, the Onondaga Nation was assigned the role of Keepers of the Grand Council fire. The sovereignty of each nation to govern themselves was assured, but major decisions of importance to the whole Confederacy were to be discussed at Onondaga in the Grand Council, which was accepted as the "imperial regency" of the Iroquois (Parker 1968:9). All decisions required consensus: "You must compromise your differences until you become of one mind" (Powless 2000:25). To that end, they selected a "Chief of Chiefs," the Tadodaho of the Iroquois, who resides at Onondaga. For centuries, this was accepted as the traditional form of government of the Six Nations, a system that valued sovereignty within the Confederacy, and consensus over majority rule. This Confederacy is recorded in a wampum belt, known as the Hiawatha belt. Here the original Five Nations are shown linked to the right and left of the Great Tree of Peace, which is viewed as the heart of the Confederacy, planted at Onondaga (Parker 1968:11–12).

With the coming of the Dutch to the Hudson Valley of New York, the Iroquois began negotiating a series of treaties, some of which are still invoked today. The earliest treaty was recorded in the Two Row Wampum belt, or *Guswenta* (Powless 2000:22–23; Jemison 2000:149). This belt shows two parallel rows of purple shell beads, separated by three rows of white shell. One purple row symbolizes a boat in which the Dutch, and all Europeans who followed them, travel. The other row is a canoe, which carries all the Iroquois. The three white rows represent peace, friendship, eternity (forever). The agreement made in this treaty is one of sovereignty and independence: it means that we will not try to steer your boat, and you will not try to steer ours. This agreement has implications for the consultation process and is frequently invoked when NAGPRA is involved. For instance, many Iroquois view federal legislation, specifically NAGPRA, as a "crossing of the lines" and an attempt to "steer our boat."

Through time, some of the nations have moved away from a traditional form of government whereby hereditary clan mothers select chiefs who rule for life or until the clan mothers remove them. In some cases, the arrival of missionaries and their attempts to convert the Iroquois to Christianity changed the traditional system and resulted in the migration of nonconverts out of nation territories, some into Canada and the Midwest and some into other nations. However, the Grand Council still sits at Onondaga, the Tadodaho still presides, and all nations with traditional forms of government participate. These issues of sovereignty, traditional values, and the *Guswenta* treaty are important factors in negotiating assignments of cultural affiliation and repatriations. Understanding the importance of these issues to Native Americans is a critical step in NAGPRA consultations.

Recognition Today

The U.S. federal government recognizes each nation as a sovereign entity with its own tribal representatives, including groups living outside New York's borders, such as the Oneida Tribe of Indians of Wisconsin and the Cayuga Seneca Tribe of Oklahoma. However, the U.S. government does not at this time recognize the Iroquois Confederacy as a decision-making body for the Six Nations, even though this is the traditional decision-making group of the Iroquois. Where NAGPRA is concerned, each nation's sovereignty takes precedence over whether they follow a traditional or nontraditional form of government. Many Iroquois demand federal recognition for the Confederacy and to that end have established the Haudenosaunee Standing Committee on Burial Rules and Regulations (see Hill, this volume). They cite the *Guswenta* treaty and the 1794 Treaty of Canandaigua as giving them the sovereign power to govern themselves in whatever way they see fit (Jemison 2000:149). The Standing Committee is composed of a representative of each of the Six Nations; all representatives have signed letters agreeing to have the committee speak for them on NAGPRA issues and in consultations. In fact, the committee has started making written claims for collections subject to NAGPRA. However, not all Standing Committee representatives are federally recognized. As a result, some nations do not recognize the Standing Committee as a voice for their group, and not all accept the Grand Council as the main governing body. This is especially true with nontraditional groups, who do not have representation on the council.

Therefore, during the consultation process, issues of tribal representation and recognition for individual Native groups can produce tensions. Conflicts within nations, and a federal regulatory system that is sometimes at odds with the goals of individual nations, provide challenges to the successful completion of consultation and subsequent repatriations. For instance, the Oneida Indian Nation of New York has asserted their complete sovereignty in the NAGPRA process and other issues and does not recognize the Grand Council and the Standing Committee as representing their nation. Their position weakens the claim that the committee acts on behalf of the entire Confederacy and should be federally recognized. At one time, there was dissension even within some participating nations about the role and authority of the Standing Committee. Soon after the enactment of NAGPRA, the Tadodaho of the Iroquois designated an Onondaga chief to act as his representative on matters regarding repatriation of human remains. This representative did not sit on the committee but operated as a negotiator for nonfederal repatriations both within and outside New York State. When some of these negotiations occurred within the aboriginal territories of nations other than Onondaga, a breach of sovereignty was said to have occurred.

There are other internal conflicts as well. For instance, some traditional governments do not recognize the existence of some nontraditional groups. Also, there are multiple branches of some nations, all of which are federally recognized but not all of which follow traditional forms of government. For non-Native NAGPRA facilitators, there is sometimes confusion over representation, and conflict about who has the right to make claims for a particular nation under NAGPRA. The potential for disputes and counterclaims increases when there is no consensus in representation.

Thus there are serious concerns within and among nations that have little to do with NAGPRA and a lot to do with issues of sovereignty and tradition within the Confederacy, while other issues are NAGPRA related, having to do with federal recognition of individual nations and nonrecognition of the Confederacy. Into this mix enters the archaeologist, usually a non-Native American who is charged with coordinating the federal process of consultation and attempting to finalize the assignment of cultural affiliation to NAGPRA-related remains for their eventual repatriation. In cases like these, the federal process fosters a climate in which non-NAGPRA-related conflicts surface, increasing the chances that the consultation process will result in challenges needing resolution. It is difficult for the archaeologist to stay neutral in these situations, especially if she or he has been fostering relationships with all the nations involved. An archaeologist fully involved in the process of consultation cannot stand on the side and merely observe. Native Americans and archaeologists are both important contributors to the negotiation, and sometimes that means involvement in the politics of Native peoples. I will illustrate this with a case study from the BU NAGPRA Consultation Project.

BU NAGPRA Consultation Project

The Department of Anthropology at BU has extensive collections of artifacts from prehistoric and historic sites. Some of these were excavated before 1974, the date when professional archaeologists on the New York Archaeological Council voluntarily agreed to a moratorium on excavating human remains from Native American sites. Our initial collections summary showed that a small number of the sites previously excavated contained human remains, and one of these sites produced over 125 human burials. Hardly any of the other categories of objects covered by NAGPRA are part of the BU collections. A detailed collections inventory was completed in 1996 and sent to all federally recognized tribal representatives of the Six Nations of the Iroquois Confederacy and to the Haudenosaunee Standing Committee on Burials.

Figure 2.1. Location of the approximate territories of the Six Nations Iroquois Confederacy and other Native tribal groups in New York (After Grand Council of the Haudenosaunee 2002: Figure 1; prepared by Mary Lou Supa).

The consultation process started with an invitation from BU to all the federally recognized tribal representatives to visit the campus in order to discuss our collections and give us their thoughts on cultural affiliation. We also notified the chairman of the Haudenosaunee Standing Committee. A National Park Service NAGPRA grant (36-95-GP-071) provided funding to assist tribal representatives with travel and lodging during their visits, and all tribal representatives pledged their commitment to participating in the consultation process.

We started with a model of the geographic territories of the Six Nations as recorded by Lewis Henry Morgan (1969 [1851]), which is generally accepted by Native Americans, ethnologists, and archaeologists. The Haudenosaunee Standing Committee has used a similar geographic model (Figure 2.1).

We assumed that these geographic boundaries were approximations and not the only means of determining the cultural affiliation of the sites in our collections. We expected that the consultations would fine-tune this model and allow consensus in assigning cultural affiliation. Consensus is both a key goal of successful NAGPRA consultations and a central part of all decision making in the Confederacy. However, after repeated invitations, no tribal group responded to our request to consult with them. In 1998, three years after we completed and circulated our detailed inventory, two groups responded to our invitation and visited the campus: the Oneida Indian Nation of New York and the Oneida Tribe of Indians of Wisconsin. We realized that most groups were swamped with requests for consultation and did not have the infrastructure to respond to all of them. Some groups contacted us and explained their priorities. We were told that our collections were so small in comparison to major museums that we were not in the first rounds of consultation visits. Many of the groups also knew that our university had an established record of non-federal repatriations and an ongoing relationship, not related to compliance mandates, with individuals in some nations. It is my belief that this less-formal dialogue contributed to a general sense of trust in our good faith efforts regarding repatriation.

But although these nonfederal repatriations had a positive impact on building mutual trust and respect, they may also have had a negative impact on the actual NAGPRA consultation process. As mentioned previously, one chief at Onondaga had assumed the role of primary negotiator for burial issues as a representative of the Tadodaho. We had been working with him on several nonfederal repatriations throughout the state and had built a relationship of trust well before NAGPRA was enacted. Conflicts arose when the Tadodaho died, and it was no longer clear whether his appointed chief had the authority to continue acting as a tribal representative for burial issues. As the formal NAGPRA process began to unfold, it was apparent that we had inadvertently set a precedent for a process that was not consistent with federal regulations or Native American policy. For a while, there was no federally recognized NAGPRA representative with whom to negotiate at Onondaga, nor was the Six Nations Standing Committee federally recognized. The chief with whom we had a long-standing relationship, though not a federally recognized representative, expected to be our contact during the formal consultation process. In other words, consultation with a small "c" had become entangled with consultation with a capital "C" (King 1998). All of a sudden, personal relationships cultivated over the years became a negative rather than a plus.

Because of our past record of negotiating nonfederal repatriations with the chief at Onondaga, he did not understand our reluctance to give him the same recognition under NAGPRA. Federal versus nonfederal situations did not have any meaning to him, but recognition did. He started to be more assertive in stating the rights of his nation to claim human remains throughout New York and beyond, thereby infringing on the sovereign territories and rights of other recognized nations. This was viewed by many as a violation of inter-nation independence, but it was also consistent with the role of the Tadodaho and the Onondaga Nation as the seat of the Confederacy. Before discussions could advance and a consensus be reached, the chief died. At about the same time, the leadership of the Standing Committee changed. These two events affected the course of the NAGPRA process. The new chair of the committee contacted archaeologists across the state and federal agencies (see Hill, this volume). He became very active in asserting the role of the committee as the seat of NAGPRA discussions yet acknowledged the sovereignty of each individual nation. There is now a sense that consensus building will again be paramount and that communication with archaeologists will be fostered.

In March of 2003, members of the Haudenosaunee Standing Committee came to BU, and we discussed the sites in our collection and potential cultural affiliations. The university's vice president for research welcomed the group, and a chief of the Cayuga Nation gave the Thanksgiving Address. He encouraged us to discuss with a Good Mind and to reach a point where our minds are one. This was a welcome first step in the formal consultation. I expect that the next step will be communication from the members of the Standing Committee identifying which nations will claim affiliation with which sites. Verbal, written, or even electronic relays of this information are possible and acceptable. However, NAGPRA requires that the consultation process be completed with written claims that include justifications for affiliation. These claims must be from federally recognized tribal representatives—the Standing Committee to date does not have this status. Although this is a possible source of conflict, it is hoped that while decisions on cultural affiliation will be made in committee, it is the individual nations that will make claims. It is also understood that the Oneida Indian Nation of New York will operate independently from the Standing Committee, and that they will communicate with the Oneida Tribe of Indians of Wisconsin in determining how claims will be made. It is possible, of course, that agreement between some groups may not be reached, thus moving the consultation process into conflict resolution involving the NAGPRA Review Committee.

Although so far there have been no final determinations of cultural affiliation or claims, the process has started. Some members of the Standing Committee have even expressed an interest in the further analysis of one of our collections, which may prove useful in clarifying the assignment of cultural affiliation. There is no pressure to rush the process, and there is no doubt of our commitment to complete the process. For now, it will unfold gradually, and we will continue to maintain our relationships.

Conclusions

I have found from personal experience that consultations today are all about tribal politics. That is not necessarily a bad thing—it is part of our responsibility to understand what is important to the people with whom we work, and why it is important. However, NAGPRA is fraught with the potential for conflicts. Multiple Native voices lobby for recognition and are asked to "claim" the remains of their ancestors. As King (2002:104) notes, making claims suggests that human remains are someone's property, a repugnant thought to Native Americans and most archaeologists. The principles of sovereignty and tradition also present the potential for challenges during consultation, especially when groups with nontraditional governments exert their sovereignty rights outside the Confederacy.

There are other pitfalls and obstacles inherent in the federal process itself. I have conducted successful nonfederal consultations, and I have been asked to participate in repatriation and reburial ceremonies. However, consultations and the repatriation process under NAGPRA are different. First, the rules and regulations require a uniform process for all groups. There is also the requirement for written documents—for example, in making a claim and justifying the legitimacy of a claim. I understand the need for uniformity and for creating a paper trail, but I have been told on numerous occasions that this is not "the Haudenosaunee way." In a traditional society where a clan mother decides who is a legitimate chief, and a string of wampum beads gives that chief the authority to represent his clan and to speak on their behalf in council, there is anger when I ask for these documents. I am told that federal rules violate the spirit of the Confederacy and the *Guswenta* treaty. The successful consultations and repatriations in which I have been involved have been those where I "stayed in my own canoe," as the Two-Rowed Wampum states, and allowed friendship to guide the process. I do not presume to have solutions that will resolve these potential problems. However, in the spirit of consensus, each group must give a little to achieve the end result. For NAGPRA, the end result is repatriation.

When the chief with whom I worked died in 2002, I was concerned about how this would affect the NAGPRA process. I am pleased that the Standing Committee has emerged as a strong yet flexible negotiating entity, exercising an openness for input from archaeologists. I will continue a relationship of friendship and respect with those nations who do not seek representation by the committee. This will require that we represent fairly each group's views and encourage a direct dialogue when necessary. The fostering of mutual respect continues and is key to the success of the process. For now, the Haudenosaunee have allowed the university to care for their ancestors' remains while they discuss cultural affiliations and plan for the next steps in the NAGPRA process.

The consultation process has highlighted some important points that I think are crucial to successful negotiations. First, compliance is not the goal—meaningful consultation and eventual repatriation is. Second, schedules for compliance are not important—allowing the process to take the time it needs is what matters. Finally, consultation is not an event, it is a process that should be conducted on a regular basis, not just within the regulatory compliance context (Stapp and Burney 2002:119–120). It is even possible that archaeological research can be important to the dialogue, especially in achieving the goals of repatriation. Consultation affords all parties the opportunity to listen with a good mind, to learn from each other, and to build mutual respect. However, consultation does not guarantee consensus or success every time. The true test of the process will be in how conflicts are mediated and by whom. Will violations of the principles of sovereignty, tradition, and recognition derail the process? This is a real possibility. However, if all parties strive to make NAGPRA a true collaboration between Native Americans and archaeologists, then the process has a greater chance to succeed and will not become just a step in a regulatory mandate.

Acknowledgments

This chapter is a revised version of a paper presented in the 2001 Society for American Archaeology symposium "Managing the Cultural Landscape through Consultation" (Kurt E. Dongoske and Cindy K. Dongoske, organizers). I appreciate the support of Binghamton University, the Public Archaeology Facility, and the National Park Service, all of whom provided funding to assemble NAGPRA inventories and to conduct consultations. I would like to thank Jordan Kerber for organizing this volume and inviting me to participate. Timothy Knapp and Janice McDonald read versions of this chapter and offered insightful comments. Mary Lou Supa drafted the base map for Figure 2.1, and I thank her for graciously assisting me with this task. I continue to appreciate the advice of members of the Haudenosaunee Standing Committee, particularly Rick Hill, the chair, during the consultation process. Anthony Wonderley and Brian Patterson, NAGPRA representatives of the Oneida Indian Nation of New York, also offered much-needed assistance with consultation issues, both within the NAGPRA process and beyond it. Finally, I am grateful to the late Paul Waterman, chief of the Turtle Clan, Onondaga Nation, for sharing his time, advice, and beliefs with me. I learned a great deal from our discussions. Any errors or omissions in this paper rest solely with the author.

3. Consulting with the Bone Keepers
NAGPRA *Consultations and Archaeological Monitoring in the Wampanoag Territory*

RAMONA L. PETERS

I have been actively involved with both the Wampanoag Confederation Repatriation Project and tribal historic preservation officer (THPO) activities for the past six years. During this time, I believe that I have consulted with every leading archaeologist, museum staff member complying with the Native American Graves Protection and Repatriation Act (NAGPRA), and all federal agency representatives in archaeology in New England. This experience has been both rewarding and disappointing. Coming from the Mashpee Wampanoag Tribe, whose homeland was colonized nearly four hundred years ago, I have found it challenging to enter into the consultation process without some feelings of bitterness and distrust. Since I took on the role of repatriation coordinator of the Wampanoag Confederation, I have learned a great deal about the people and philosophies behind the institutions that collect and trade Native American cultural resources. This chapter is about some of my consultation experiences attempting to repatriate and protect my ancestors' remains.

The needs of the living are the priority for most tribal nations; however, I believe it is of the utmost importance that we honor the ancestors who made it possible for us to be here. In our traditional culture, the ancestors are as much a part of our daily lives as anyone else in the family.

Mashpee Wampanoag people regularly call on the ancestors to guide us through hard decisions, reflections on the past, and assessment of tribal needs, among other things. Repatriation and reinterment demonstrate our thanksgiving to them. Our tribe joined the Wampanoag Confederation to relieve the spiritual tension that exists due to the desecration of our ancestors' graves.

The Wampanoag are among the first indigenous people in New England who encountered European colonists. The story is hard, the assaults and insults are many—and all of this is reviewed constantly while we consult. Wampanoag leaders instructed me by saying that we must always represent our people and ancestors in a way in which they can be proud. I have approached consultation being mindful of this obligation to my people and have relied on it to shape the way.

The Wampanoag Confederation Repatriation Project

Through a combination of disease, warfare, and colonial encroachment, most Wampanoag tribes were dispersed and villages destroyed. The tribal communities of Mashpee, Aquinnah, and Herring Pond are still living on their original village sites. Currently, only one of the three is a federally recognized tribe (Wampanoag Tribe of Gay Head [Aquinnah] recognized in 1987; see Herbster and Cherau, and Chilton, this volume). The Mashpee Tribe has had a petition for federal recognition pending since 1980. Other surviving Wampanoag descendants live among American communities in New England and throughout the world.[1] Some Wampanoag descendants serve our nation as volunteer monitors of reinterment sites.

The formation of the Confederation made the most sense for Wampanoag territory because the only Wampanoag federally recognized tribe in Massachusetts lives on the island of Martha's Vineyard, leaving a vast area of our nation's homeland to cover. The Aquinnah Tribe is part of the Wampanoag Nation politically within the domain of a Massasoit.[2] Geographic constraints made it necessary to employ the assistance of off-island Wampanoag to fulfill our national interest in repatriation. The three Wampanoag groups of Mashpee, Aquinnah, and the Assonet Band joined the Wampanoag Confederation through formal resolutions passed during council meetings.

The Wampanoag Confederation was formed specifically to provide a way for the Wampanoag Nation to participate in NAGPRA. Gatherings of other Wampanoag clans, bands, and tribal representatives were convened to define the appropriate territorial boundaries and to address cultural, spiritual, and political concerns. Spiritual and political leaders from each group participated in the development of the Confederation's repatriation policies. Repatriation officers were selected to engage in the process by representing their tribal people.

The three repatriation officers of the Confederation are Edith Andrews of the Aquinnah, John Peters Jr. of the Mashpee Wampanoag Tribe, and Kenneth Alves of the Assonet Band of the Wampanoag Nation. We travel together as a consulting team to the museums that have Wampanoag material in their collections. The Confederation requires consensus for any action to be taken. With their combined talents, the current Confederation repatriation officers make a fine consultation team. Their presence makes each consultation interesting, thorough, and respectful. Part of my job as repatriation coordinator is to set the tone for our team consultation. These individuals deserve the highest regard for their diligence and dedication.

Edith Andrews is the elder of the group. She has represented the Aquinnah Wampanoag as a cultural liaison for over fifty years in a variety of important capacities. Edith is elegant and poised, which seems to help Westerners relax during consultations. She has an intuitive ability to sense when tensions need to be broken with gentle humor or with news of the performing arts. This talent helps reel us in when we have lost patience with the process or the personalities at the consultation table.

John Peters Jr. is probably the most politically active Native American in the state of Massachusetts. He is the executive director of the Massachusetts Commission on Indian Affairs, which involves extensive outreach and networking with statewide tribal groups, including transient Natives working in the area (see Simon, this volume). John received degrees from Boston College and MIT. As a statesman, he is well versed in negotiating techniques and legislation, and he is a stickler for process. He keeps us on task when the process becomes drawn out or stuck.

Kenneth Alves is a traditionalist and an excellent researcher. He is a very humble man with deep convictions about the sacred nature of our ancestors' remains. He is the keeper of our blessed items, which protect us during viewing visits to museum bone rooms and the storage areas of many tribes' sacred objects.

The Wampanoag Confederation incorporated as a nonprofit organization [501(c)(3)] in May 1999. Incorporating enables us to legally hold state preservation covenants that enforce restrictions over land containing ceremonial grounds, burial sites, and other sites of significance to the Wampanoag Nation. We also developed computer software to help tribal repatriation officers track museum inventories and repatriation status in an electronic database. Thanks to dozens of tribes across the country and private donors, our project has continued without an additional National Park Service grant.[3]

Setting a Precedent: Non-federally Recognized NAGPRA Tribal Repatriation

Although most Americans have forgotten who the Eastern Woodland tribes are, we know each other well and have relied on the strength of surviving New England tribal groups since early colonization. The Wampanoag Confederation is proud to have helped the Nipmuc and Abenaki nations to repatriate their ancestral remains by sending letters of support and appearing before the NAGPRA Review Committee on their behalf. The unique situation of the northeastern tribes and their varying federal recognition statuses make it necessary for us to unite when possible to protect indigenous rights.

In 1983 my late father, John Peters Sr. (Slow Turtle), and Massachusetts State Archaeologist Brona Simon crafted amendments to the Massachusetts Unmarked Burial Law, which thereafter included protection for Indian burials (see Simon, this volume). This legislation precedes NAGPRA by seven years and provides an enforceable protection process with the full cooperation of the Massachusetts Commission on Indian Affairs, the state archaeologist, and the medical examiner. Regardless of tribal federal recognition status, the Massachusetts Unmarked Burial Law protects our family grave sites and is more efficient at repatriating them than NAGPRA is.

NAGPRA excludes the Mashpee Wampanoag from first-level entry into the repatriation process because they are not a federally recognized tribe.[4] Non-federally recognized tribes are allowed to participate as repatriation claimants through a NAGPRA Review Committee hearing. Upon receiving the NAGPRA inventory from the Robert S. Peabody Museum at Phillips Academy in Andover, Massachusetts, the Mashpee Tribe began efforts to repatriate Wampanoag ancestral human remains. As the nearest federally recognized tribe, the Aquinnah sent a letter of support for the repatriation. In 1994 Mashpee tribal representatives went before the first Review Committee meeting, held in Albany, New York, to request the return of ancestors removed from the Titicut site in Bridgewater, Massachusetts. The Review Committee ruled in favor of repatriating to the Mashpee Wampanoag. This successful NAGPRA repatriation by the Mashpee Tribe set the precedent for other non-federally recognized tribes across the United States.

Graves and Grave Robbery

The past has everything to do with who we are in this present moment, both individually and collectively. Personal and collective histories shape our dominant thought patterns—what we value, what we desire, and what we miss.

The first recorded grave robbery on this continent happened in Wampanoag territory in November 1620. *Mourt's Relation* conveys important information about the thought processes of the Pilgrims, the first Europeans in our territory to unearth a Wampanoag grave. Initially, they left the graves alone: "We supposed there were many other things, but because we deemed them graves, we put in the bow again and made it up as it was, and left the rest untouched, because we thought it would be odious unto them to ransack their sepulchers" (Heath 1963 [1622]:21).

Thus at first these early English colonists acknowledged that Natives would not appreciate the desecration of their graves. But only three days later, the Pilgrim resistance to digging up Indian graves fell by the wayside:

> When we had marched five or six miles into the woods and could find no signs of any people, we returned again another

way, and as we came into the plain ground we found a place like a grave, but it was much bigger and longer than any we had yet seen. It was also covered with boards, so as we mused what it should be, and resolved to dig it up, where we found, first a mat, and under that a fair bow, and there another mat, and under that a board about three quarters long, finely carved and painted, with three tines, or broaches, on top, like a crown. Also between the mats we found bowls, trays, dishes, and such like trinkets. At length we came to a fair new mat, and under that two bundles, the one bigger, the other less. We opened the greater and found in it a great quantity of fine and perfect red powder, and in it the bones and skull of a man. The skull had fine yellow hair on it, and some flesh unconsumed; there was bound up with it a knife, a packneedle, and two or three old iron things. It was bound up in a sailor's canvas cassock, and a pair of cloth breeches. The red powder was a kind of embalmment, and yielded a strong, but no offensive smell; it was fine as any flour. We opened the less bundle likewise, and found of the same powder in it, and the bones and head of a little child. About the legs and other parts of it was bound strings and bracelets of fine white beads; there was also by it a little bow, about three quarters longs, and some other odd knacks. We brought sundry of the prettiest things away with us, and covered the corpse up again. After this, we digged in sundry like places, but found no more corn, nor any thing else but graves [Heath 1963 (1622):27–28].

The Pilgrims took the "pretties" (white wampum and other funerary objects) from the Native corpses and went on about their business. The Wampanoag Confederation is in the process of repatriating the "pretties" taken from that very grave.

Indeed, the Wampanoag, both before Europeans arrived and today, view grave robbery as a horrible crime. As Thomas Morton wrote in 1637,

They [Wampanoag people] hold it impious and inhumane to deface the monuments of the dead. They themselves esteem

of it as piaculum [an offense requiring atonement] and have
a custom amongst them to keep annals; and come certain
times to lament and bewail the loss of their friend; and use to
black their faces. Which they wear instead of a mourning or-
nament for a longer or shorter time, according to the dignity
of the person [Dempsey 1999 (1637):44].

We indigenous people are sometimes offered the rationale that Native
American grave sites should be excavated because eventual or planned development will have an adverse impact on them. Desecrating Native American grave sites has adverse effects on Native American spiritual well-being. It does not feel better when archaeologists dig up our ancestors in the
path of construction. The destruction of the land itself is hard to bear. We
are often called on to monitor both archaeology and the destruction of
our ancestral homeland at the same time.

Lucy Vincent Beach

There is a memory that will be imprinted on my mind as long as I live.
In 1998 I was visiting our sister tribe the Aquinnah on Martha's Vineyard
when Tobias Vanderhoop, an Aquinnah tribal member, asked me to accompany him to Lucy Vincent Beach, in Chilmark. We were not going for
a swim but to check on the activities of Harvard University's archaeological field school (see Chilton, this volume). Tobias informed me that his
tribal council had agreed to allow the field school to remove burials from
an eroding sand bluff above the beach. He explained that remains were fall-
ing out of the bottom of the bluff onto the beach below. I asked why tribal
members themselves were not moving their ancestors instead of a group of
college students. He seemed perplexed and frustrated by the entire event,
so I did not press him further about his tribe's decision. He asked me to
help him conduct a ceremony for the ancestors when we arrived at the site.
The area was sectioned off with yellow tape, and the ocean was choppy
with whitecaps in the distance. There were about six open 1-x-1-m pits,
with smiling college kids covered with soil, some kneeling around with
trowels, others handling plastic bags, clipboards, and shovels. My heart
sank as I watched the students try to clean up by smearing the biological

material of my ancestors across their faces. I was shaken. It was a ghoulish sight. They were innocent, young, and covered from head to toe with the same soil that hugged the bodies of departed Wampanoag people.

We invited them to join us in ceremony. The students formed a circle and listened to our prayers. Spiritual and psychological precautions are not part of the field school curriculum. I can only hope that they were not harmed by their ignorance.

The soil matrix found in burials is as important as skeletal material and should be repatriated whenever it has been collected. Soil matrix is often collected from Native graves, but there is no NAGPRA category for this material to be repatriated. The Wampanoag Confederation considers this matrix to be biological material and repatriates it with ancestral human remains.

Emotional and Cultural Costs of Consultation

During the early stages of NAGPRA consultations, it seemed that museum staff were not culturally sensitive and did not grasp the magnitude of the spiritual and emotional impacts of the repatriation processes on tribal representatives. One heard statements like, "It is disturbing to see skeletal collections such as the Crow Creek Massacre material reburied. From the viewpoint of a skeletal biologist this is similar to burning the books in our libraries" (William Bass, quoted in Echo-Hawk and Echo-Hawk 1994:34). It is shocking for me to hear anyone oppose the reinterment of human remains. Allowing my body and bones to melt back into Mother Earth after I have died provides a spiritual offering to the physical world. I would naturally choose to be buried within the homeland of my tribe on the lands of my nation. I believe that as long as my bones are still present on this planet, I may return to this world in spirit to respond to the prayers of my grandchildren and those open to my assistance. My bones are both a compass and plummet for my spirit to find its way back to the homeland. If my bones are molested and removed from my ancestral homeland, I will probably not be able to return to my loved ones. Reinterment assures the possibility of return.

During a consultation with NAGPRA staff members at Harvard University's Peabody Museum of Archaeology and Ethnology in the fall of 1998, the Wampanoag Confederation was given a curious excuse for classifying ancestral human remains as "unidentifiables." Museum staff members said that no present-day Indian tribe could be considered related to human remains more than a thousand years old. This idea seems destructive to the spirit of the law. I fail to see any mention of the thousand-year criterion in NAGPRA. Indigenous people who maintain a relationship with their ancestors live in a state of timelessness with no clear dividing line between past and present. There truly is no difference between the way we regard our recently departed and our ancient ones.

I also feel a sense of responsibility to protect the intellectual property rights of our people during consultations. We know that if we record certain information we are in violation of tribal law and perhaps that of the medicine societies. Who knows what consequences may befall the tribe if we divulge too much to the uninitiated. It is likely that other tribal NAGPRA and THPO representatives feel the same resistance or internal conflict, which prevents them from offering more-accurate information about the objects. This is just another dilemma that Native consultants face during the course of repatriation and while attempting to protect a ceremonial site. Further, there are times when we are asked to make the choice of another golf course or a housing development on a site that is now private property but was once tribal land. This is not consultation; this is extortion.

Now that I know more about the people with whom we consult, I have no problem protecting my tribe's intellectual property rights. I have learned that archaeologists tend not to consult with cultural anthropologists, which makes me wonder about the validity of any purported scientific approach toward understanding my people. I have also learned that museums compete over collections, which causes me to think of archaeology as the glorified hobby of materialists. The manner in which my ancestors are stored in underbudgeted places is often appalling. We have even seen skulls stored in cigar boxes on a museum shelf with melted wax on their crowns.

Archaeological Monitoring in Contaminated Homelands

Archaeological monitoring in contaminated areas of the homelands has been an exasperating experience. Several years ago I was asked to explain our tribal names. The following statement was later published:

We name ourselves after the land we live with. Because not
only are we breathing in, we are also drinking from the water that is flavored by that very land. Whatever is deposited
in the soil is in the water, in us. So we are all one thing, and
we name ourselves after the place that is our nurturing, that
sustains our life [quoted in Vaughan 2002:58].

On April 27, 2003, Bouchard Tank Barge 120 released nearly 371,000 li-
ters of oil into Buzzards Bay. The area affected comprised 85 km of shoreline primarily along the western side of Buzzards Bay, which is part of the
coastal Wampanoag Nation ancestral homeland. Roque Monterio and
I were assigned the duty of monitoring the cleanup activities for three
months. I attended daily briefings at the Coast Guard Command Center
and consulted with division managers on sensitive areas to be protected
from heavy equipment being used to remove oil-covered rocks. We were
able to protect an ancient fishing weir, which is a fantastic achievement
considering all the events and personnel working on the cleanup.

Monitoring the archaeologists conducting surveys in contaminated
areas of our homeland has a double emotional impact. There are two
Environmental Protection Agency (EPA) Superfund sites in Wampanoag
territory. The Acushnet River emptying into New Bedford harbor is contaminated with high levels of hazardous polychlorinated biphenyls (PCBs),
heavy metals, and hydrocarbons. These contaminates leached into the
Acushnet River between the late 1940s and 1977. There are 16 identified
archaeological sites within the project area. Through excellent consultation with Jim Brown and David Peterson of the EPA, Marcos Paiva of the
Army Corp of Engineers, Eric Johnson of the Massachusetts Historical
Commission, Joel Klein and William Chadwick of John Milner and Associates, and Helen Douglas of Foster Wheeler, the 16 sites were minimally
harmed during the cleanup. A 40-hour HAZMAT training course was required for people monitoring this site. The Wampanoag Nation can thank
Roque Monterio and Ken Alves for their willingness to risk their personal
health to protect sites of cultural significance.

The other EPA Superfund site in Wampanoag territory is the Massachusetts Military Reserve, which has become a national model. The reserve

borders the town of Mashpee and has a variety of contaminates flowing through 12 separate groundwater plumes. Over 20 million kg of contaminated soils were excavated last year. The military reserve also has an unknown number of unexploded ordinances that are being removed by hand. The task of monitoring this cleanup fell mainly on my shoulders; however, as the federally recognized tribe, the Aquinnah have the final word. I was introduced to military humor by being intentionally led into the center of a field of shallowly buried unexploded ordinances, only to be consulted on the preservation of low-bush blueberries. No further Wampanoag tribal monitoring is being conducted in artillery-impact zones. In the words of Paul Hawken, "Business is destroying the Earth including all cultures and living systems, and never before has there been a system so ubiquitous, so destructive, and so well managed. It is our creation" (quoted in van Gelder 1999:40).

Closing Remarks

Early English writers describing Wampanoag culture often used scant information that they concocted into elaborate stories. Most of these stories lacked insight into Wampanoag cosmology, and some of them seem to have been written simply to fascinate seventeenth-century readers in London. Nevertheless, some valuable information can be gleaned from Morton's observations and (assumed) interviews: "These people, that have by tradition some touch of the immortality of the soul, have likewise a custom to make monuments over the place where the corpse is interred" (Dempsey 1999 [1637]:43). Because of the constant grave robbing of the English colonists, Wampanoag people began the practice of disguising grave locations (especially those of leaders) (Axtell 1981:119). Where is there a safe place to reinter the ancestors we have repatriated?

The answer to that question has yet to be determined, since there has already been looting at our reinterment sites. An early recorded instance of looting was observed by Abram Quary, who is said to have been the last Nantucket Wampanoag (he died in 1854).

> At one point he [Quary] was hauled off to court for threatening to shoot some trinket gathers who were digging in a nearby Indian burial ground. When the judge (who ultimately

dismissed the case) asked if he would have shot the people if they had continued to dig, he replied without hesitation, "Yes I would" [Philbrick 1998:3].

This is a hard situation for Native Americans to be placed in. Yes, Abram was arrested, and so would I be if I threatened to use a gun to oppose an amateur or professional archaeological dig in Wampanoag burials.

In the contexts of real-life cultural circumstances, it is difficult to live in a society that seems to be spiritually bereft and so terribly removed from the earth. There are plenty of religious denominations but no collective agreement regarding the sanctity of the grave. I would like to say something more positive about my experiences consulting with the bone keepers, but at this point in the consultation process, I think it is still time for them to listen to Native American people earnestly without looking for rewards or seeking more treasures.

I will end this chapter with another quote from Thomas Morton, whose seventeenth-century interviews lacked cultural sensitivity yet reveal a peculiar sort of inquisitiveness: "It was a thing very offensive to them, at our first coming into those parts, to ask of them for any one that had been dead . . ." (quoted in Axtell 1981:127).

Notes

1. A majority of nineteenth-century Wampanoag men from Mashpee and Aquinnah participated in the whaling industry. Wampanoag relatives are found in the Hawaiian Islands and among the Northwest Coast tribes.

2. "Massasoit" is a title for the leader of greatest esteem among the Wampanoag Nation. It is not a person's name, as commonly believed.

3. The Wampanoag Tribe of Gay Head sponsored and administered a National Park Service grant for the Confederation to conduct consultations during the years 1996 to 1998.

4. First-level entry into the repatriation process includes, for example, receiving museum inventories or being invited for a viewing visit as an official tribal delegation.

4. Collaboration between Archaeologists and Native Americans in Massachusetts
Preservation, Archaeology, and Native American Concerns in Balance

BRONA G. SIMON

Prologue

John Peters Sr. (Slow Turtle) was one of the architects of the Massachusetts Unmarked Burial Law. As the executive director of the Massachusetts Commission on Indian Affairs, he oversaw its implementation from 1983 until his death in 1997. I had the pleasure of collaborating with him during those years. He taught me so many things. At every burial site discovery, he would always meet me with a reassuring look. "I'm looking out for you, girl," he would say. "I'm taking care of you, protecting you while you are working on this site." As supreme medicine man of the Wampanoag Nation, he knew of potential dangers. He once said: "We don't believe that the spirit ever dies. The spirit always lives. . . . But sometimes our spirits are confined to particular graves if they are negative spirits. Sometimes if negative spirits are dug up, they are released—but shouldn't be. We've seen this often. It's happened many times" (Currier 1989:10).

I remember the first time he conducted a smudging ceremony at a burial site as added protection for himself, me and my staff archaeologists, and the spirits. It was at the Abrams Point II Burial Ground on Nantucket in the summer of 1992. The landowner wanted to build a house within this Nantucket Indian cemetery, and only one grave needed to be removed; the rest would be preserved. We were just about to begin this delicate recovery. I had learned that this land had been named after Abram Quary, the alleged "last" Nantucket Indian, who had died in 1854, and that he had lived somewhere in the vicinity of the site (Little 1994). Quary had been arrested in the early 1800s for having threatened some "relic hunters" with a gun at a cemetery near his house. During the court proceedings, he told the judge he did it "because they were disturbing the graves of my ancestors" (Folger 1910). The court granted him leniency. I was thinking of Abram Quary and wondering whether this cemetery was the same cemetery he had defended from "relic hunters" nearly two centuries earlier. I was wondering whether that was the reason why John Peters had smudged us and the site that day, as a way of assuring the spirits that we were working on their behalf. After the smudging, we began and finished our recovery efforts without incident. A year later, the remains from that site were respectfully reburied by John Peters at a protected Native American burial ground on Nantucket, not far from the original site.

Introduction

The Massachusetts Unmarked Burial Law was enacted in 1983, at a time when Native Americans and archaeologists had conflicting agendas concerning the care and treatment of Native human remains. Although some conflicts may persist today between these two groups, the overall result of the legislation has been to provide opportunities for productive collaboration between archaeologists and Native Americans. The state burial law is an effective tool for the protection and preservation of burial sites located on both public and private property. The law was drafted to respect both Native American spirituality and archaeologists' research interests, giving strong preference to site preservation, not excavation, and allowing for the reburial of any Native remains that could not be preserved in place. The law requires careful archaeological investigation of burial sites in consultation with Native Americans, and has resulted in private support of archaeological surveys and the systematic physical analysis of skeletal remains. A strong Native American constituency has emerged in support of archaeological site preservation and collaboration with archaeologists. Archaeologists have been enriched through their interactions with Native people and have developed a stronger understanding of Native perspectives. Cooperation between archaeologists and Native people has succeeded in preserving many burial sites and understanding more about the past and each other. This chapter offers a 20-year retrospective on the growth of collaborative relationships between archaeologists and Native Americans in Massachusetts and highlights a number of case examples.

Background

In the late 1970s, Native Americans in Massachusetts expressed a growing desire for more sensitive treatment of Native burials and skeletal remains by archaeologists, developers, and landowners. Native Americans were so incensed by the destruction of Native burial sites by developers and by the excavation, study, and curation of human remains by archaeologists that in 1977 they filed a bill that would place a five-year moratorium on any construction or archaeological activities likely to disturb burials (Talmage 1982a).

The Massachusetts Historical Commission (MHC), Office of the State Archaeologist and State Historic Preservation Officer (SHPO), was also concerned with the issue and with balancing the interests of the archaeological and Native communities. The MHC solicited a study of the then existing state statutes by a student at the John F. Kennedy School of Government at Harvard University. The study examined the body of laws dealing with burials and treatment of the dead from a public policy point of view (Mattfeld 1980).

The moratorium bill died in committee. The state archaeologist at the time, Valerie Talmage, collaborated with John Peters Sr., executive director of the Massachusetts Commission on Indian Affairs (MCIA), in establishing an administrative solution to the problem of the destruction of burial sites (Talmage 1982a, 1982b). These administrative procedures involved the close cooperation of the medical examiner, state archaeologist, and MCIA in investigating unexpected discoveries of human skeletal remains. The state archaeologist's archaeological permit regulations (950 CMR 70.00), promulgated in 1979, include a special provision for the excavation of human skeletal remains only if they are imminently threatened by nonarchaeological activities, with a strong preference for in situ preservation.

The study of Massachusetts legislation revealed that the preservation of marked graves and known cemeteries is well established under state law (Mattfeld 1980). In fact, the excavation or removal of dead bodies or disturbance of graves is a criminal felony (Massachusetts General Laws [M.G.L.] Chapter 272, Sections 71 and 72). However, state law did not provide for the protection of unmarked graves, and therefore it did not protect the vast majority of burials of Natives and those of other ethnic, religious, or socioeconomic groups that did not mark their graves with stones or place them within easily recognizable cemeteries (Mattfeld 1980). In addition, the MCIA had asked the state's attorney general about the legality of the cemetery statutes. The attorney general's office found that the state cemetery laws were indeed unfair and discriminatory under the equal protection clause of the Massachusetts State Constitution.

In 1982 the MCIA was successful in piquing the interest of several key legislators and their staff. In 1983 John Peters Sr. and Valerie Talmage collaborated with legislative staff to establish the balanced wording of the Massachusetts Unmarked Burial Bill. The bill was passed by a simple voice vote in both the house and the senate and went into law in late 1983.

Description of the Unmarked Burial Law

The Unmarked Burial Law formalized into law the administrative procedures that had previously been put into effect (Talmage 1982a, 1982b, 1984). The principal state officials involved in the treatment of human skeletal remains were given clear responsibilities and duties, and unmarked burials of any cultural affiliation were given protection under the law.

The state medical examiner's (ME) office initially investigates discoveries of human remains and determines whether they are recent or more than 100 years old. Any person who discovers human skeletal remains must immediately notify the police and the ME (M.G.L. Chapter 38, Section 6). The forensic anthropologist at the ME's office determines whether the remains are more than 100 years old and, if so, then notifies the state archaeologist, who immediately conducts an investigation of the site (M.G.L. Chapter 9, Sections 26A and 27C). The law requires that all ground-disturbance activities cease until the site is investigated and the treatment of the site is decided. The burial law applies to everyone in the state, including archaeologists. Even archaeologists who discover a burial during any archaeological investigations must cease work and immediately notify the state archaeologist.

If the remains are known or expected to be Native American, the state archaeologist notifies and consults with the MCIA (M.G.L. Chapter 9, Section 26A, and Chapter 7, Section 38A). The MCIA is the state agency that oversees matters concerning Native Americans in Massachusetts. MCIA's members include representatives of the indigenous Native groups of Massachusetts, such as the Wampanoag peoples of Aquinnah, Mashpee, Assonet, Herring Pond, Seekonk, and Pocassset, and both the Nipmuc and the Nipmuck groups. The MCIA also acknowledges the Abenaki (as descendants of the Pocumtucks), the Chappaquiddicks, and the Stockbridge-Munsees.

The MCIA may, and almost always does, send a representative to monitor the archaeological site investigation in order to ensure that it is being conducted in a respectful manner. The archaeological investigation of burial sites is conducted with somber respect. There is no joking around, no radio or music, and no publicity. With the assistance of the police, we do not allow the press on the site. In deference to the concerns of Native peoples, we do not allow photographs of the graves to be taken for magazines, newspapers, or television but only for archaeological research purposes.

The state archaeologist and the MCIA consult with landowners to determine whether burials can be protected in place. In this aspect we act as a team, advocating for site preservation where it is feasible. In cases where it is not feasible to protect burials from development or natural threats such as erosion, the MCIA must approve the archaeological recovery of the burials (M.G.L. Chapter 7, Section 38a). The state archaeologist, or an archaeologist with a special permit from the state archaeologist, carefully excavates and removes the remains.

The analysis of the remains must be completed within one year of excavation, unless further consultation allows for a longer period. Skeletal remains are analyzed by a physical anthropologist in accordance with standardized *Guidelines for the Analysis of Human Skeletal Remains* (MHC n.d.). In response to the MCIA's concerns about damaging human remains, these guidelines emphasize nondestructive techniques. A complete set of osteometric measurements are taken for all remains, morphological characteristics and pathologies are described, and photographs are taken. Through our consultation with the MCIA, it has also agreed in a few specific cases that radiocarbon dating and isotope analysis could be performed (e.g., Medaglia et al. 1990; Little and Schoeninger 1995), and a few small samples of hair, bone, or teeth could be retained for future study.

After the analysis of the remains is complete, the state archaeologist transfers them to the MCIA. There is no requirement in the state's Unmarked Burial Law that the remains be "affiliated" with a federally recognized tribe, as is the case with the Native American Graves Protection and Repatriation Act (NAGPRA). Stated simply, all Native remains discovered in Massachusetts since 1983 are repatriated to the MCIA. The policy of the MCIA is to rebury the remains (M.G.L. Chapter 7, Section 38A), preferably in a protected location as near to the original burial site as possible. The reburial is conducted by the Native community specifically identified by the MCIA for each case. The MCIA keeps a record of all the reburials and their locations.

There is no "grandfather clause" in the law, and the issue of repatriation of skeletal remains uncovered before 1983 is not addressed. The law deals only with skeletal remains and does not explicitly mention artifacts or grave goods. However, there is no prohibition against reburial of associated grave goods or mortuary artifacts, so these objects can be reburied as appropriate.

NAGPRA applies only to federal land, federally recognized tribal land, and existing collections in institutions that receive federal funding. In Massachusetts, as in most states in the Northeast, there is very little federal land and federally recognized tribal land, so NAGPRA has not been as effective in protecting burial sites here as it has in the western states, where there is more federally owned land and federally recognized tribal land. State burial laws apply to all nonfederal land (Price 1991; see Chilton, and Herbster and Cherau, this volume). Thus, it is the states' burial laws that are put into effect most frequently for Native American burial sites in the Northeast (Simon and Talmage 1989).

Results

The implementation of the Massachusetts Unmarked Burial Law has had several beneficial results, including more frequent reporting of the discoveries of burials and threatened burial sites, greater opportunities for archaeological site protection, more archaeological surveys and investigations, systematic and consistent physical analysis of skeletal remains, opportunities for archaeologists to work cooperatively with Native people, and the emergence of the Native community as a strong constituency in support of historic and archaeological site preservation activities.

Before the passage of the Unmarked Burial Law, the state archaeologist was notified very infrequently (perhaps only about once a year) when human skeletal remains were uncovered. Since its passage in 1983, we have been notified of endangered burial sites on an average of six times a year.

The Unmarked Burial Law has provided a new tool to protect sites on private land. The majority of burial sites reported to our office end up being preserved in situ. Between 1983 and 1994, we were notified of threats to 72 sites containing unmarked Native burials. Of these sites, 30 required excavation, and the remaining 42 were preserved in situ. Thus we were able to negotiate with property owners to preserve burial sites in more than half (59 percent) of the cases. In only 41 percent of the cases were burials unavoidably threatened by development, construction, or erosion, necessitating their excavation and recovery. Over the past 10 years, we have had similar results.

In Massachusetts, there are basically two types of Native burial sites: single, isolated graves; and cemeteries (or burial grounds) of multiple graves. Both types of burial site often occur on elevated locations consisting of sandy soils near, or within sight of, a source of water such as the ocean, lakes, ponds, rivers, or wetlands.

When a single, isolated burial is accidentally discovered, it is usually during construction activities when workers observe remains in the excavated soil. In these cases, when the MCIA and we arrive at the site, it is often too late to preserve the burial in its original location. The MCIA asks us to recover as much of the person's remains as possible from the disturbed context and the backdirt, so that the remains can be reburied at another location.

The Native practice of establishing burial grounds or cemeteries occurred at various times in the pre-Contact and historic periods. Depending on the size and extent of the burial ground, we have a better chance of preserving the cemetery by negotiating with the landowner for project redesign, written agreements, or preservation restrictions placed on the deed.

The Unmarked Burial Law has also given us the opportunity to convince landowners of suspected burial sites that it is to their benefit to hire a team of archaeologists to conduct a survey well in advance of construction, and to plan proactively for burial site protection.

Our ability to analyze the remains for a year after their discovery has resulted in much new knowledge about Native people in the past. The initial disdain of the living Native community for any analysis of remains began to dissipate during the 1980s as we shared the information with the MCIA and the descendant Native communities. In a newspaper interview in 1989, John Peters Sr. said, "Sometimes the study is as important to us as it is to the archaeologist. Before [the Unmarked Burial Law was passed], the archaeologist would do the study and we would never see their work" (Currier 1989:10). Through analysis, we are able to identify the age, sex, and physical characteristics of each individual. This information is used by the MCIA in choosing the practices and prayers for the reburial ceremony.

One of the most important results of the implementation of the Unmarked Burial Law, in my opinion, has been the change in the sentiment and attitude of the Massachusetts Native American community toward archaeology, toward the state archaeologist, and toward historic preservation in general. This change has emerged from our office's close working relationship with the MCIA. From 1983 to 1994, the MCIA reburied the remains of over 100 individuals from 34 sites. Of these individuals, 43 were from one site, the Wellfleet Ossuary, which was excavated in 1979 (McManamon et al. 1986). The practice of repatriating Native remains nurtured the growth of a strong sense of trust between the Native community and the state archaeologist's office. The Native Americans with whom we have worked are also a strong and vocal constituency that supports the MHC and the state archaeologist. The most dramatic instance of this support occurred in the mid-1980s when a bill was filed that would have eliminated the office of the MHC and state archaeologist. A sizable contingent of Native people came to the hearing at the State House and opposed the bill. The bill failed. The implementation of the Unmarked Burial Law has been a catalyst for the emergence of the Native community in Massachusetts as a strong supporter of historic preservation.

Since NAGPRA was passed in 1990, our office has become involved in assisting private museums in their efforts to repatriate Native remains (Simon 1995). Many small museums and historical societies in Massachusetts chose to comply with NAGPRA immediately after it was enacted and before the publication of its implementing regulations in 1995. During the critical first four years after NAGPRA was enacted (1990-1994), the remains of over 30 Native individuals were repatriated by various small museums and historical societies to the MCIA for reburial. Most prominently, in 1992 the Massachusetts Archaeological Society voted to repatriate Native remains from the Robbins Museum to the MCIA (Warfield 1995). Museums that have contacted our office for direction on how to comply with NAGPRA invariably hear us tell them to contact the MCIA. Whenever John Peters Sr. was given remains by well-meaning people who wanted to "do the right thing," he would transfer the remains to me temporarily (for one year) for study.

Case Examples

The island of Nantucket, located off Cape Cod, is well known for its pre-Contact and historic period Indian sites. In 1988 a workman on a construction site accidentally encountered a skull inside the building foundation of a new home in the Miacomet section of the island. We discovered it was one of several graves in an unmarked eighteenth-century cemetery of the Miacomet "Praying Indians." We quickly negotiated with the property owner, the Nantucket Housing Authority, who agreed to stop construction on the three buildings that had been started within the area of the cemetery and to relocate these buildings elsewhere on the parcel (Simon 1988; Carlson et al. 1992). The housing authority set aside the cemetery for permanent preservation. The cemetery was fenced, and a stone marker was placed to recognize the site. A moving ceremony led by John Peters Sr. demonstrated the importance of the preservation of this burial ground to living Native people, to the residents of Nantucket, and to the archaeologists in attendance (Bell and Simon 1993).

A few years after our investigation and preservation of the Abrams Point II Burial Ground (see Prologue, above), there was a second burial ground, Shawkemo II, discovered not far from Abrams Point during construction excavation. Our archaeological investigation revealed an extensive cemetery containing at least 27 graves, probably dating to the seventeenth or eighteenth century. After our consultation with the landowner hit a bumpy period, John asked me to approach the attorney general's office with him for help in the negotiations. As a result of the involvement of an assistant attorney general, the entire Shawkemo II Burial Ground was protected and preserved through a written agreement with the landowner. This agreement has been passed on to subsequent owners.

In contrast to Nantucket, Martha's Vineyard still boasts a living, vibrant Native community known as the Wampanoag Tribe of Gay Head (Aquinnah), a federally recognized tribe. In practice, whenever burial sites are discovered on the Vineyard, the MCIA notifies the Aquinnah, who send a representative to site. This has given MHC and other archaeologists a wonderful opportunity to collaborate with the descendants of the people whose sites are being investigated (see Herbster and Cherau, this volume; Chilton, this volume). Under the Unmarked Burial Law, any remains that have been found on the Vineyard since 1983 have been transferred to the MCIA, who then transfers them to the Aquinnah for reburial. Members of the Aquinnah also keep a watchful eye on new construction activities throughout Martha's Vineyard and notify us of any suspicion of disturbance to a burial site. We will then conduct a site visit and enter into negotiations with the landowner to explore ways of preserving the burial sites.

MHC archaeologists have had the privilege of working collaboratively with John Peters Sr. and a number of other Native Americans he would send to the sites. Other archaeologists also have had this opportunity, in cases where the scope of the archaeological investigation exceeded MHC's budget and staffing level, or investigations were undertaken in compliance with Section 106 of the National Historic Preservation Act. These investigations were funded by the private landowner or a state or federal agency.

The Massachusetts Highway Department experienced its first consultation with the MCIA under the Unmarked Burial Law in 1985 with the discovery of a partially marked and partially unmarked poor farm cemetery in the Route 146 project area in Uxbridge (Elia and Wesolowsky 1989, 1991). A number of Nipmuck Indians, John Peters Sr., and I met on-site with representatives of the highway department (then known as the Massachusetts Department of Public Works). Since there was no prudent or feasible way to realign the highway layout, it was agreed that an archaeological data recovery would be conducted.

Boston University conducted the archaeological investigation. In their report, Elia and Wesolowsky (1991:xiii) stated:

> Much of the success of the excavation was the result of the friendliness and cooperation displayed by the Nipmuck Indians who were our constant observers at the site, and ultimately, became our friends. Chief Wise Owl, White Bear, and Star were at the site each day; although they began as observers, and keeping mind that they feared that the graves contained the remains of their ancestors, doubtless harboring some suspicions about the "scientists" who were coming to exhume the graves, they soon became our friends and allies in the project.

The analysis of the remains of the Uxbridge Almshouse Cemetery indicated that the majority of people buried there were Caucasian, but there was also one Native American man and an African American woman. The highway department not only supported the archaeological investigation but also set aside land for the reburial of all the remains except those of the Native man, which were transferred to the MCIA for reburial at the Nipmuck burial ground, at the Nipmucks' request.

The second consultation with the Massachusetts Highway Department occurred in 1992, after the discovery of a Middle Archaic (ca. 8,000 years ago) burial by the Public Archaeology Laboratory, Inc., during archaeological data recovery for the Route 44 project in Carver (Doucette and Cross

1997; Doucette 1997; Doucette 2003). John Peters Sr. agreed that the site could continue to be excavated but asked the highway department to hire a Native monitor for the site. Since the site had been subjected to some looting (thankfully not near the grave site, but troubling nonetheless), the highway department was able to hire Paul Iron Turtle Gagne under a security contract (John Rempelakis, personal communication 2004). Cindy Shining Star Ryan-Elderkin and Lee White Wolf Maddox also participated. Doucette and Cross (1997:8) stated, "The participation of the Native American community awakened the team's sense of purpose and helped bring the material past back to life." Their collaboration helped Doucette (1997) visualize and describe in her popular report a story of what might have happened on the site.

The Millbury III site was a Susquehanna cremation cemetery complex, dating to between 3,000 and 4,000 years ago, that was investigated by the Public Archaeological Laboratory, Inc., in 1990–1992 (Leveillee 1998, 2002a). Chief Paul Pollard was the Native monitor during the site's archaeological excavation. Leveillee (2002a:Appendix A) transcribed his and his crew's conversations with Chief Paul Pollard in a diary format, which gives others a unique opportunity to share the archaeologists' experience on a day-to-day basis. The Native involvement helped shape the archaeologists' view of the site. "Working with a Native American consultant afforded us an opportunity to reaffirm the validity of Native perspectives and interpretations as an important element of our research" (Leveillee 2002a:119). "It is an old place, safe and quiet," John Peters Sr. told Leveillee (2002a:133), as a summary of his impression of the site and its archaeology.

The current director of the MCIA is John Peters Jr. (Jim), who continues his father's commitment to burial site protection. A recent success involving Jim and his sister Ramona Peters (see Peters, this volume), repatriation coordinator of the Wampanoag Confederation, was the preservation of the Mashpee Indian Burial Ground in New Seabury from being developed for a large residence and swimming pool. The site was accidentally discovered by workmen in 1999. MHC's investigation and research revealed that this historic-period cemetery contained the graves of at least 17 individuals, most likely the relatives of Rosanna Jonas, a Mashpee Indian who owned the land in the nineteenth century. The MHC, the MCIA, the

Mashpee Tribe, and several descendants of Rosanna Jonas entered into consultation with the landowner under the Unmarked Burial Law. The landowner was willing to sell the parcel to a third party for its permanent preservation. I contacted the Trust for Public Land (TPL), a national land conservation organization that conserves land for the protection of natural and historic resources. TPL's Tribal Lands Program specifically helps tribal communities with efforts to save land important for Native American cultural heritage preservation. TPL negotiated with the landowner and obtained an option to buy the site. It raised enough funds from the MHC's Massachusetts Preservation Projects Fund, the Division of Conservation Services, the Department of Environmental Management (now the Department of Conservation and Recreation), and TPL itself and purchased the site in 2002. TPL placed preservation and conservation restrictions on the deed and immediately donated the site to the Mashpee Tribe (Gonsalves 2002; Rowland 2003; Trust for Public Land 2002).

Mortuary studies can reveal information about the physical characteristics of a people and their customs and beliefs (e.g., Beck 1995; Bell 1994; Binford 1971; O'Shea 1984). A number of historic-period cemeteries associated with "Praying Indians" have been investigated by MHC under the Unmarked Burial Law. These include the Miacomet, Abrams Point II, and Shawkemo II burial grounds on Nantucket, the Chapman Street Ponkapoag Praying Indian Cemetery in Canton, and the Mashpee Indian Burial Ground in New Seabury. Each case has given us new evidence that the conversion to Christianity was not as complete as the missionary Reverend John Eliot and his successors reported. Instead, many of the traditional spiritual and religious practices of the Native peoples continued well into the eighteenth and possibly nineteenth centuries (e.g., Simon 1990). This information has been well received and appreciated by the Native communities who are reconstructing their culture histories.

John Peters Sr. encouraged us to share knowledge from archaeological investigations with the Native community. He also encouraged our efforts to educate the general public about the deep history of the Native presence in Massachusetts. Originally our state's celebration of Archaeology Week took place in June. John asked me to change it to October, to coincide with Columbus Day and history classes in the schools. He said,

"That way you can teach them Columbus didn't discover America. We always knew it was here." Owing to the increased interest among residents of Massachusetts, we expanded the program to Archaeology Month, beginning in October 2004.

The success of the state's Unmarked Burial Law is the institutionalized cooperation between the state archaeologist and the MCIA. The funneling of responsibilities to both of us in our respective arenas can help to mediate any conflicts that might arise within our respective constituencies. I hope that this success will continue as both Jim and I continue our ongoing work with the next generation of archaeologists and Native Americans. For example, when an archaeologist or a Native American has his or her first experience with a burial site, there is a need for us to educate them about the Unmarked Burial Law, and also to counsel them, since it can be a very emotional situation. The few cases of conflicts that have occurred over the past few years have invariably involved individuals new to the scene. It is important that we conduct outreach and introduce newcomers, both Native Americans and archaeologists, to the procedures and benefits of the Unmarked Burial Law.

In summary, the benefits of the Massachusetts Unmarked Burial Law are numerous, and many of these benefits are archaeological. More than ever, we are being informed about sites containing burials and are able to obtain more archaeological information about the undocumented past. Unmarked burial sites are now being researched, and systematic physical analysis of the skeletal remains is being conducted. More burial sites are being preserved in situ. Through consultation with developers, the majority of cases have resulted in negotiated plans to avoid impact on burial sites. We have been able to protect burial sites on private property, an area over which our office has no other jurisdiction. The Native community has become part of our grassroots information network. When Native Americans living in any part of the state learn of a threatened site, whether it includes burials or not, they will call us, giving us an opportunity to try to protect the site.

Collaboration between archaeologists and Native Americans has occurred in a variety of beneficial and productive ways. First, as a team, the state archaeologist and the MCIA work together in negotiating for site preservation and protection. Second, in cases where there is no prudent or feasible alternative to disturbing the burial, the archaeological recovery is done with the approval, and under the watchful eye, of the MCIA. Third, the archaeological information we have gathered is shared with Native communities as they continue to restore their own histories. Although largely ignored for the last three centuries by the mainstream population, the Native peoples of Massachusetts did not all disappear, as Watkins observes in the foreword to this book. On the contrary, they are actively seeking to reconstruct their own culture histories and to engage in the preservation and investigation of their ancestral sites.

Acknowledgments

This article is an expansion of several papers I have given at archaeological meetings. I would like to thank all the Native people whom I have met and whose conversations and interactions have benefited me: John Peters Sr. (Slow Turtle), Jim Peters, Ramona Peters, Maurice Foxx, Windsong, Kenny Alves, Mark Harding, Matthew Vanderhoop, Beverly Wright, Helen Manning, June Manning, Donald Widdess, Gladys Widdess, Edith Andrews, Cheryl Andrews-Maltais, Randy Jardin, Linda Coombs, Chief Malonson, Loving One, Chief Wise Owl, Rae Gould, Walter Vickers, Nanepashemet, Russell Gardner, Helen Oakley, Sherry White, Steve Comer, Marge Bruchac, Lee White Wolf Maddox, Frank James, Chief Paul Pollard, Gil Solomon, and many, many others. I would also like to acknowledge the invaluable contributions made by MHC staff archaeologists Ed Bell, Leonard Loparto, Eric Johnson, Margo Muhl Davis, Liz Kinery, and Ann-Eliza Lewis, and by physical anthropologists Michael Gibbons, Harley Erickson, and Ann Marie Mires. I continue to be grateful to Valerie Talmage and John Peters Sr. for establishing a groundbreaking cooperative program for us to follow. This article is dedicated to John Peters Sr., who continues to live on in our memories.

5. "The 368 Years' War"
The Conditions of Discourse in Narragansett Country

JOHN B. BROWN III AND PAUL A. ROBINSON

It is about politics. The dispute is about control and power, not philosophy. Who gets to control ancient American history—governmental agencies, the academic community, or modern Indian people?

David Hurst Thomas

Introduction

When a large earth-moving machine struck an unmarked seventeenth-century Narragansett Indian cemetery in 1982, the Rhode Island Historical Preservation and Heritage Commission (RIHPHC) and the Narragansett Indian Tribe decided to work together to excavate, study, and plan for the reburial of the 56 individuals interred there. This cooperative project was undertaken well before passage of the Native American Graves Protection and Repatriation Act in 1990; moreover, there was no state legislation that required the state and tribe to work together or that provided any protection for the cemetery. The site, known in the archaeological literature by its state inventory number, RI 1000, has been the source of many scholarly publications and in large part was the beginning of the relationship between the state and the tribe in the study and protection of archaeological sites. It was one of the first Native American cemetery projects in the United States that began with the assumption that most, and perhaps all, of what was taken from the earth would be reburied. Archaeologists and tribal leaders sought a way to share control of the project, although that notion was contested, argued, and sometimes ignored by those working on the project; and while following standard archaeological field practice, the archaeologists almost always deferred to the tribe regarding the individual treatment of burials, the removal of some artifacts, and decisions about letting the public visit the site and keeping the media informed. Overall, the relationship was appreciated by both archaeologists and tribal participants. John Brown, who represented the tribe at the site on a daily basis, commented to a newspaper reporter on the good relations with the archaeologists and noted how rare such a relationship with non-Indians was in general: "Our past experiences have shown us that there are very few people who have the sensitivity to understand the connection between the contemporary and ancient Indians and realize that we are one and the same" (Murphy 1986).

Nearly 20 years later, the RIHPHC published a book titled *Native American Archaeology in Rhode Island* (Robinson et al. 2002). Written for a lay audience, the book synthesized some of the previous three decades of archaeological research in Rhode Island, nearly all of which had been done with public funds by federal and state agencies in compliance with the National Historic Preservation Act. The RIHPHC acknowledged the contributions of those who conducted the research and helped review the text before publication. It also acknowledged the Narragansett Indian Tribe and its Historic Preservation Office for reviewing the draft text: "In particular we thank Chief Sachem Matthew Thomas, and John Brown and Doug Harris from the Tribal Historic Preservation Office. These three offered many comments, and we recognize that we sometimes differ on our interpretations of Narragansett history offered in this book. We appreciate that the Chief Sachem agreed to our use of his photograph on the book's cover" (Robinson et al. 2002:iii).

While the book presented the findings of many archaeological projects, it included little of the long-standing and complex relationship between the state archaeologists and the Narragansett Indian Tribe and not much about the tribe's involvement on many of the projects. A letter from the Narragansett Indian Tribal Historic Preservation Office (NITHPO) to the RIHPHC commented on the draft text:

> Aside from the numerous places in the document where Narragansett Indians and Native Americans are erroneously re-

ferred to, the discrepancies in historical content have the
potential to affect the treatment of cultural properties and historic properties within the state of Rhode Island. As crafted,
the content will adversely impact properties in the National
Register of Historic Places, as well as properties that are eligible for listing in the National Register of Historic Places.
In its current form, we oppose the publishing of this document [Brown 2001].

With this letter, Narragansett tribal officials formally objected to the
state-published synthesis of the past 30 years of archaeological research
in Rhode Island. After working so well together at the RI 1000 cemetery
site, how had the RIHPHC, which is Rhode Island's State Historic Preservation Office (SHPO), and the Narragansett tribal office come to such a fundamental disagreement? The RIHPHC had sent a draft of the book to the
NITHPO in January 2000 and had met with them in May of that year, but
it had made only several minor changes to the text based on comments
at that meeting. With an acknowledgment that "we sometimes differ on
our interpretations," the RIHPHC published the book. The disagreement
masked beneficial aspects of the relationship that had contributed to some
of the research presented in the book, particularly the work involving RI
1000; it also disregarded the many small but consequential matters of daily
routine that often go well—that is, the many phone calls, letters, site visits, and discussions about projects between the THPO and SHPO staff that
more often than not are conducted in a friendly and respectful manner. In
other ways, however, the disagreement over the book's content obscured
even stronger and broader areas of disagreement between the tribe and
the state involving jurisdictional issues of artifact ownership and the regulatory supervision of archaeologists working within the state.

In this essay, we trace the relationship between archaeologists in the
SHPO and the Narragansett Indian Tribe since the late 1970s, but primarily since 1982 when the RI 1000 burial ground project began. In describing our relationship, we also discuss its historical context as well as the
contemporary political environment, both of which contribute to, and
limit the possibilities of, what we do. John Brown has been the Narra-

gansett Indian Tribe's primary liaison to the archaeological community since 1982, has chaired the Narragansett Indian Archaeological-Anthropological Committee (NIAAC) since its inception in 1985, is Understudy to the Tribal Medicine Man, and is the Tribal Historic Preservation Officer (THPO). Paul Robinson has been the Principal State Archaeologist at the RIHPHC since 1982 and has worked in this office since 1979.

Although the book in which this essay appears takes as its theme collaborative efforts between archaeologists and Native Americans, we cannot characterize the 25-year relationship between Rhode Island state archaeologists and the Narragansett Indian Tribe as collaborative, although in specific instances we may work together to achieve a common goal, such as the protection of a significant archaeological site. We often disagree: we may, for example, have opposite opinions on whether a particular site is eligible for listing in the National Register of Historic Places. More fundamentally, on the issue of who controls the practice of archaeology in Rhode Island, the SHPO and the NITHPO sharply disagree with each other.

Webster's New Collegiate Dictionary provides a double-edged definition of "collaboration" that points both to the possibility of specific opportunities and to the historical and political circumstances that make working together very difficult: "1. to work jointly with others, especially in an intellectual endeavor; 2. to cooperate with or willingly assist an enemy of one's country and especially an occupying force" (see also Dean and Perrelli, this volume). Sometimes we do work jointly together in the first and preferred meaning of the word. Underlying and coloring those joint efforts, however, and contributing to much of the disagreement over jurisdictional issues is the harsh historical fact that, since the founding of the Rhode Island Colony in 1636 to the present day, representatives of both the state and the tribe have disagreed, argued, and physically fought over many matters, large and small. Webster's second definition of "collaboration" quite often applies literally, since many in the tribe view the state as the governing entity of an enemy that has occupied the core of Narragansett country for 368 years. Under these circumstances, tribal representatives sometimes decide that they cannot work with state archaeologists, since it would be harmful to tribal interests; it would be collaboration with the enemy as expressed by Webster's second, pejorative meaning.

Archaeology and the "368 Years' War" (and Still Counting)

It is not overstating the difficulties of working together to say that each specific instance or possibility of cooperation between archaeologists and Narragansetts takes place within the broader context of a war that began in the seventeenth century and in some ways continues today. Narragansett Chief Sachem Matthew Thomas said as much in an essay in the editorial pages of the state's most prominent newspaper:

> [In 1675] the Narragansetts were forced to fight in King Philip's War—a particularly bloody conflict against the English which resulted in the loss of thousands of Narragansetts at the Great Swamp Massacre. . . . In a sense we are still fighting [the war] . . . the tribe is continually stripped of its rights and dignity in the executive, judicial and legislative branches— as evidenced by the excessive use of force in the smoke-shop raid, and the loss in federal court [Thomas 2004].

The smoke-shop raid was the most recent battle in the long war. On July 14, 2003, Rhode Island state troopers shut down a smoke shop on the Narragansett Reservation: a daylight raid that became a violent brawl as Narragansett leaders and tribal police officers attempted to repel what they viewed as an illegal invasion. As reported in the *Providence Sunday Journal* on the day of the raid, "The seventeenth century crashed into the twenty-first" (Davis and Mulvaney 2003:A1). Bella Noka was one of the tribal members forcibly restrained by the state troopers: "I always wondered how my ancestors felt," she said of the July 14 raid. "On that day I knew" (Davis and Mulvaney 2003:A1). A federal district court judge in Providence, Rhode Island, upheld the state's right to go on tribal land. On appeal, that decision was reversed, in part, as tribal sovereignty was upheld and the tribe was granted an en banc reconsideration regarding state enforcement which is scheduled for December 2005.

In discussing the problems between the state and the tribe, the chief sachem remarked that the Narragansetts were looking for a way to "coexist" with the non-Indian population, that is, according to Webster's, to live in peace with one another, *especially as a matter of policy*. The Narragansett Indian Tribe's policy of coexistence does not exclude the possibility of working together; rather, it deliberately distances the tribe from others in the hope that non-Indians will refrain from interfering in tribal programs and ambitions. In doing this, the policy attempts to preserve tribal autonomy and sovereignty while holding open the possibility of collaboration when beneficial. Often, however, Narragansett attempts to achieve their aims—whether opening a casino or smoke shop, or protecting an archaeological site—clash with state, and sometimes local, claims of jurisdiction. The possibility of beneficial collaboration, coexistence, or conflict is decided at the juncture of tribal and state assertions of jurisdiction and sovereignty.

The modern policy of coexistence is a fundamental change from the first years of the relationship in the seventeenth century when the Narragansetts sought to make the newcomers part of the circle of mutually beneficial and obligatory relationships that characterized Indian society. Most English people, however, were not merely not interested in this relationship but hostile to it. Within a few years of the first English settlement in Narragansett country in 1636, few colonists were trusted by the Indians. According to colonial records, commissioners of the United Colonies of New England arranged to have their Mohegan allies, led by Uncas, assassinate Miantonomo, one of the chief sachems of the Narragansetts, since in 1642 he had attempted to persuade Indian communities around Long Island Sound to rise up against the English. Miantonomo had complained that the colonists and their livestock had ruined the land, spoiled shellfish areas, and driven away the deer, turkeys, and other wild fowl. After the English and Mohegans conspired to kill Miantonomo, the historical documents suggest that these same colonial officials, with the help of some in Rhode Island, thwarted Narragansett attempts to avenge his death, leveled large fines against the Narragansetts for raiding Mohegan villages, and threatened war if they persisted in their efforts to settle with the Mohegans for the murder (Robinson 1990; Salisbury 1982).

Mohegan and Narragansett oral traditions provide a different account of the events surrounding Miantonomo's death and the relationship between the Mohegan and Narragansett Indian tribes. Discussions between Melissa Zobel, Tribal Historian of the Mohegan Tribe, and John Brown reveal that there was no hatred and angst between the tribes as indicated in the colonial records. Today, the Narragansetts understand that the killing of Miantonomo was necessary for the protection of the Mohegan Tribe against English threats. "It was," as John Brown (personal communication to Paul Robinson 2004) says, "as if someone held a gun to your head or your family's heads and said, 'kill that guy or else.' " So too had the English threatened the survival of the Mohegan Tribe. It was important, however, that if Miantonomo was to die for conspiring against the English, that an Indian person carry out the deed. In Narragansett culture of the time, continuance of a person's spirit was guaranteed if he or she was killed by a worthy adversary or friend. If Miantonomo had been killed by a European, then at some place and time, according to prevailing tribal beliefs, he could not return in the future.

By the 1650s the dislike and contempt were deeply felt, and many Rhode Island colonists and Narragansett people became exasperated with what each considered the bad behavior of the other. Scutop, a Narragansett leader who lived near the RI 1000 cemetery, expressed the Narragansett view of the problem. His immediate frustration was directed at a group of colonists who sought to remove Indians from Conanicut, an island midway between Newport and Wickford in Narragansett Bay. The colonists insisted they had bought the land a generation earlier with Miantonomo's approval, and were upset over what they considered harassment by some "barbarous . . . and drunken" Indians (Lafantasie 1988:488–499). Scutop reminded the colonists that Miantonomo had not sold the land outright; rather, he had granted certain use rights, and in exchange for these he expected the English to provide regular and specific favors to the Narragansets. Now that Miantonomo had been killed by the Mohegans at the direction of English assassins, Scutop wanted the Rhode Islanders using Conanicut Island to help the Narragansetts settle the score with the Mohegans by providing poison and soldiers. The English not only refused but blocked and penalized Scutop's attempts to settle with Uncas (Robinson 1990).

Thus began a relationship of mutual mistrust, disrespect, and contempt, one that led to the destruction of many villages and towns and the killing of hundreds of English and thousands of Indians in King Philip's War in

1675–1676. The enforced servitude of Indian people by the colonists followed the war's end. In 1709 the colony established a large reservation encompassing much of the modern town of Charlestown, but as the years passed, much of that land was either sold by corrupt Indian leaders or appropriated by Rhode Island colonists. In 1880 the state declared the Narragansett Indian Tribe extinct, and through an act of the General Assembly, the Narragansetts were "detribalized" and their public lands sold at auction (Simmons 1989).

Some Narragansetts objected to the detribalization and brought a series of land claims against the state during the early 1900s. These "shore claims" were unsuccessful (Lafantasie and Campbell 1978). A later claim, however, which based its argument on the idea that the state's detribalization and land sale had violated federal law, was successful. In 1975 the tribe filed a land claim against the state and 32 private landowners for 1,296 ha, arguing that detribalization in 1880 had violated the federal Non-Intercourse Act of 1790. The suit was settled out of court by an act of Congress; as requested by the State of Rhode Island, the U.S. government provided funds to a state-chartered land management corporation made up of tribal, state, and local officials for the purchase of 729 ha from the defendants in the case. The Narragansett Land Claims Settlement Act was tantamount to federal acknowledgment of the tribe's continued existence (pursuant to 25 CFR Part 83) and the legitimacy of its land claims; it provided a means to establish a land base for the tribe, and it instructed the Narragansetts to petition the U.S. government for formal acknowledgment. Over state opposition, the petition was filed, and on April 11, 1983, less than two months from the beginning of the first full summer of fieldwork at RI 1000, federal acknowledgment was granted.

The RI 1000 Project: A Brief Reprieve from a Long War?

When a sharp-toothed, diesel-powered front loader "discovered" RI 1000 by tearing into several unmarked graves in June of 1982, scattering human skeletal remains and burial artifacts in its track, many Narragansett people viewed that disturbance as part of, and consistent with, the previous several hundred years of mistreatment, ill will, and disregard for the wishes and human rights of the tribe. Although the initial disturbance of the cemetery took place within the historical context of foreign occupation, oppression, and abuse, with archaeology there was reason for the Narragansetts to think things might be different. In 1972 William Simmons had approached certain persons in the tribe and asked if they wanted to rebury the skeletal remains from a Narragansett cemetery he had excavated the previous decade. They readily agreed to the request, and in what was one of the first examples of reburial in the country, the people were returned to the earth that summer (Simmons 1989:80). It was significant that the discovery of RI 1000, during the period between the land claims settlement in 1978 and federal tribal acknowledgment in 1983, provided a rare opportunity for the state and tribe to work together, and for the tribe to demonstrate to outsiders its continuing and ongoing knowledge of its history and cultural traditions.

In 1982 Rhode Island lacked legislation for protecting unmarked cemeteries during construction projects or for protecting small historic cemeteries in the path of development. State law required only that several cities and towns notify next of kin when graves were moved, although this requirement was generally followed throughout the state. To find interested relatives, a property owner or developer was required to place a notice in the local newspaper announcing the intent to move the graves. After a three-week period, the graves could be moved to an established cemetery under the supervision of a mortician. There was little that descendants could do to prevent graves from being moved or to protect an unmarked cemetery after it had been unearthed by excavators, apart from attempting to persuade the developer to preserve the cemetery. State law made no mention of involving archaeologists or tribal people.

It was within this limited and unhelpful legal framework that a relationship between the state and the tribe in regard to burials and archaeology began in the late 1970s. The Narragansetts understood that they would be notified when burials were discovered on state-sanctioned archaeological projects or when the state was notified that unmarked Indian graves had been discovered during construction projects. In 1982, when RI 1000 was unearthed, there had been only one previous instance of this—a single burial at Greenwich Cove in 1979. The site was being studied prior to house construction when the burial of a seven-year-old child was found in a large shell deposit. Pierre Morenon, the project archaeologist, notified the tribe of the discovery. After ceremony, the child was removed for study and ultimately returned to the Narragansetts for reburial in 1993 (Bernstein 1993; Morenon 2003:111–112).

With that limited experience, and with no legal framework other than the state's very weak and unhelpful "notify and move" requirement, discussions over RI 1000 began among the landowner, tribe, and state. There was much to do. Ribs and cranial fragments were scattered on the ground; a large pile of soil, roughly 40 m³, had been excavated and piled up. We had to secure the site, persuade the landowner to postpone further excavation, determine the limits of the cemetery, and estimate how many individuals had been unearthed and redeposited in the pile, and how many graves remained intact. Once we had ascertained what had been disturbed and what, if anything, remained undisturbed, we could determine whether a plan to protect the area was necessary. The landowner, Paul Lischio, was quite cooperative in working through these issues. In response to our request, he placed barriers at the dirt road leading to the site from the state highway and agreed to postpone further excavation. We screened through the excavated pile, recovered the full and partial remains of 11 individuals and their grave artifacts, determined that most of the cemetery was intact, and estimated that between 30 and 50 graves remained.

We needed to decide how best to protect the cemetery against the threats of vandalism and possible development. Mr. Lischio wanted the cemetery removed so he could proceed with developing the land, but he was willing to delay his project until after the following summer, which would allow time to plan and carry out an excavation. The research potential of the cemetery was clear to the archaeologists: the region lacked a comprehensive study of a Narragansett cemetery that included an examination of morbidity, mortality, and material culture. The archaeologists thought the cemetery offered an excellent opportunity to examine firsthand the effects of European colonization on the daily lives of Narragansett people. Given the threats to the cemetery and the lack of any legislation protecting burial sites, it seemed to the archaeologists that the best way to protect the cemetery was through excavation and study. The Narragansett Tribal Council was less interested in the site's "research potential" and more interested in preserving the cemetery in place. Without any legislation protecting the cemetery, however, the Tribal Council reluctantly agreed in the spring of 1983 to allow archaeological study, but was clear about why they approved the project: it would provide tangible evidence to state officials and the academic community of the tribe's direct and sustained connection to the past.

In the summer of 1983 the RIHPHC secured a historic preservation fund matching grant from the National Park Service for excavation. This grant was awarded to Patricia Rubertone at Brown University. Although unable to participate in that summer's excavation, she agreed to codirect the overall project with Paul Robinson and to join the project full-time in September. John Brown was appointed by the Tribal Council to work with the archaeologists. Marc Kelley, at the University of Rhode Island, was the project's physical anthropologist. William Turnbaugh, at the University of Rhode Island, joined the project as historical archaeologist; he would provide identification and interpretation of the site's material culture (Turnbaugh 1984). Gail Brown, an archaeologist at the RIHPHC, directed the laboratory and, with Dennis Piechota, worked on artifact conservation; Michael Nassaney, then a graduate student at the University of Massachusetts Amherst, directed the fieldwork. We prepared a calendar for the excavation and analysis so that all participants could measure the project's progress and agree on what kinds of analysis would be done.

Robinson and Rubertone sought a close working relationship with the tribe on all aspects of the project, from determining the need to excavate, discussing various interpretations of what we recovered, and planning for the ultimate reburial of all or some of the cemetery. This relationship was based on the moral premise that the Narragansetts owned the skeletal remains and artifacts in the cemetery (Robinson 1990:22). At the time, this was an uncertain legal premise and a controversial archaeological proposition. In Rhode Island, the accepted legal principle was that artifacts belonged to the landowner; it was not until 1986 that the Louisiana Supreme Court would find otherwise: in the case of cemeteries, the ownership of artifacts can never be given up. Ruling for the Tunica-Biloxi Tribe against an artifact collector who claimed ownership of a burial collection, the Louisiana court found that "the intent of interring objects with the deceased is that they will remain there perpetually, and not that they are available for someone to recover and possess as owner" (*Charrier v. Bell* 1986:605). Although the decision was limited to Louisiana, it raised the possibility that courts elsewhere might rule similarly and thus gave support to those in other states who argued that Indian tribes should have some control over their burial sites.

Control was the central issue for the Narragansetts: it was important to control the dissemination of information, whether in press releases, television appearances, or published articles; it was important to control the excavation itself, that is, the removal of some artifacts had to be done with special care; it was important to assert and to attain legal ownership of the entire "collection," that is, the skeletal remains of the dead and their artifacts. The state's position, that the state and the tribe should share responsibilities, was stated by SHPO Frederick Williamson (personal communication, 1983): "The state supervises the scientific aspect of the project; the tribe supervises the religious." That optimistic, perhaps idealistic, division of supervisory responsibilities soon blurred in the everyday practicalities of the project. It was, however, a well-intended misstatement. State archaeologists had based the project, above all else, on the premise that the Narragansetts had moral, if not legal, primacy with respect to the excavation. It was one thing to state the premise, however, and quite another to carry it out. Some on the project worried that the position might lead to censorship, the selective release of information by the Narragansetts or a prohibition on publishing positions contrary to their own.

Nonetheless, the premise stood, and as it was put into practice—in press briefings, in joint presentations to public groups, and in publications—it became, in most instances, a negotiated sharing of power and control rather than an absolute set of dictums from the Tribal Council and Medicineman and Medicinewoman. Public presentations and published manuscripts (e.g., Robinson et al. 1985; Kelley et al. 1987) were generally reviewed by the tribe. The closeness of the project archaeologists and the tribe may also explain, in part, the emphasis placed in conference and published papers from that period on the idea of persistence. We were impressed with those aspects of the burial ground that symbolized and represented the persistence of Narragansett beliefs about the afterlife and the care that people extended to the dead, even while their world in many ways was collapsing around them. Some objected to this emphasis (Nassaney 1989). As one anonymous reviewer of a manuscript prepared by Kelley and Robinson put it, we had been "led down the garden path by the Narragansetts" in our stressing the persistent aspects of their culture. The Narragansetts, however, were pleased at the clear evidence of continuance.

Accomplishments and Arguments: The Struggle to Control Archaeology after RI 1000

The official "completion" of the RI 1000 project came in 1985 with the filing of a brief report with the National Park Service. Regular and formal tribal review ended, although close communication was maintained between the state and tribal offices. The two principal archaeologists, however, completed lengthy works that made extensive use of the information from the RI 1000 project without review by the tribe prior to publication (Robinson 1990; Rubertone 2001). The first of these, Paul Robinson's (1990) doctoral dissertation, took apart the idea of persistence by examining its ideological aspects and the way this idea was used by the Narragansett leaders in the seventeenth century to deny the rights of other Indian groups and communities to pursue their autonomous goals, a conclusion with which John Brown and others in the tribe strongly disagree.

And what of the guiding moral premise that gave de facto control of the RI 1000 project and collection to the Narragansett Indian Tribe? With the ending of that project, it was difficult for the state and tribe to extend the premise to other situations. For one thing, the SHPO was unwilling to surrender its control of nonburial collections, even as the tribe pushed strongly to achieve such control. Moreover, the SHPO was opposed to, nor did regulation enable, the granting of supervisory control over archaeologists and archaeological projects to the Narragansetts. These disagreements were discussed at length. The SHPO issued *Guidelines for Indian Participation on Archaeological Surveys* (RIHPHC 1988). This document was based on the Advisory Council on Historic Preservation's (ACHP) *Fact Sheet: Section 106 Participation by Indian Tribes and Other Native Americans* (ACHP 1986). The RIHPHC's guidelines recognized the NIAAC as a knowledgeable tribal body and set forth a procedure for the state to notify the tribe about archaeological projects and to provide it with information. The guidelines instructed project archaeologists to contact the tribe and to discuss the proposed study with them. It also included a section titled "Indian Consultants" that encouraged, but did not require, adding "knowledgeable Indian consultants to projects when it appears that the information to be contributed will increase understanding of a particular site, place or research topic" (RIHPHC 1988:3).

The NIAAC objected to the guidelines, since they (and the ACHP's *Fact Sheet*, on which they were based) granted only "interested party" status to the tribe on projects outside Indian lands. This status required only that tribes be notified about projects and that the SHPO and federal agencies "be sensitive to the special concerns of Indian tribes . . . which often extend beyond Indian lands to other historic properties" (ACHP 1986:3). The NIAAC wanted "consulting party" status on all projects, whether on or off Narragansett land. Such a status might give the tribe equal standing with the SHPO on all projects in the state. At the time, federal regulations did not require, nor was the SHPO willing to grant, this status. Tribes did not attain the regulatory right of meaningful consultation on projects outside tribal lands, but within their ancestral lands, until passage of the 1992 amendments to the National Historic Preservation Act; and it was not until 1998 that the ACHP passed regulations implementing this change.

But although disagreements over who controlled archaeology later became a major problem and a source of friction between the state and the tribe, there were immediate benefits to both groups that flowed directly from the beneficial collaboration at RI 1000. For the tribe, the project was a catalyst for the formation in 1985 of the NIAAC. Established to work with archaeologists, the NIAAC included tribal members and elders as well as academic archaeologists and the state archaeologist. And for a time, the NIAAC helped to foster cooperative efforts, the most noteworthy being the passage in 1992 of state legislation protecting all historic cemeteries, marked and unmarked, Indian and non-Indian (Robinson and Taylor 2000:115). The NIAAC was also influential in helping to ensure that federal agencies adequately protected and studied archaeological sites (Robinson 1994). In one instance, they argued that the 25 percent data recovery sample that the Federal Highway Administration and the SHPO had agreed on as the major part of a data recovery plan was inadequate. The NIAAC objected to this plan and was successful in persuading the highway administration to study the entire site (Kingsley and Roulette 1990; Leveillee 1999).

In 1996 the tribe established the NITHPO within the NIAAC pursuant to tribal resolution 90.35. This action was affirmed by the National Park Service and enabled the tribe to assume historic preservation duties on tribal land. The tribe named John Brown as the THPO, and he soon pushed aggressively for a stronger role in all aspects of the historic preservation program, most particularly for consulting party status on projects off Indian lands, as required in the 1992 amendments to the National Historic Preservation Act. These amendments enabled tribes to establish historic preservation offices and to function as the historic preservation office in consulting with federal agencies on projects on tribal lands. Most important for tribal-state relations, the amendments required federal agencies to consult with tribes on projects within their ancestral lands, and the Narragansetts defined these as including all of Rhode Island and parts of Connecticut and Massachusetts.

This requirement was not codified in regulation until 1998, and the Narragansetts were one of the few tribes in the country that began asserting its right to consultation before any federal agencies or state offices had considered it. The SHPO strenuously disagreed with the NITHPO's assertion until the ACHP's regulations were issued, and federal agencies, accustomed to consulting only with the SHPO, found it difficult to accommodate both the state and the tribe. On some projects, the SHPO's advice was taken; on others, the federal agency might agree with the NITHPO. In many cases, the NITHPO's opinions and requests were quite different from the SHPO's. These differences ranged from project details to basic principles. On one project, for example, a shell deposit that the SHPO considered a refuse pit was named a cremation burial by the NITHPO. On other projects, the two preservation offices disagreed on determinations of the effect and the efficacy of data recovery as a method for protecting sites. These disagreements delayed projects, much to the dismay of all, while the federal agencies determined how best to consult with the tribe and its newly formed historic preservation office (Robinson and Taylor 2000; Waller et al. 2001).

The new ACHP regulations, issued in 1998, clarified the new role of THPOS. With these regulations in place, some federal agencies (most notably the Federal Highway Administration and the Army Corps of Engineers) began to treat the NITHPO as a consulting party with equal status to the SHPO, and federal officials began to take seriously their regulatory role in sorting through the sometimes conflicting opinions of the SHPO and NITHPO.

Conclusion

With the promulgation of the new ACHP regulations, the state lost some of the control it had over archaeology, while the Narragansett Indian Tribe gained power through its ability to consult with federal decision makers and thereby influence the conduct of archaeology. The ACHP regulations, by requiring that the state and the tribe negotiate and share control, have been helpful in clarifying the relationship between the two offices. As John Brown sees it, the regulations have established parallel roads, one for the NITHPO and the other for the SHPO. Each road leads to the same goal: the protection of the archaeological resources within Narragansett country.

In the summer of 1983, with fieldwork at RI 1000 underway, John Brown asked Paul Robinson, "Whose bones do you think these are?" Knowing that many archaeologists would disagree, and unaware of how the issue would play out in ensuing years or that the Narragansett Indian Tribe would seek control of nonburial sites, Robinson answered, "They're yours, of course." When the RIHPHC published *Native American Archaeology in Rhode Island* in 2002 (Robinson et al. 2002), its silence on the state's relationship with the tribe seemed to deny that the state had lost any power to control the state's archaeology—but it certainly had. As we write this chapter, the Federal Highway Administration is building two artifact repositories: one for the tribe at the Narragansett Longhouse; another for the state in an old railroad station in Woonsocket. The tribe has asked, and the state has declined, to repatriate artifacts from some state-owned, nonburial collections to the new repository on Indian land. The issue of who controls archaeology within the state and within Narragansett country, an issue that was readily and narrowly resolved at the RI 1000 burial site, remains an issue of contention, and perhaps it will remain so, until peace is made and the long "368 Years' War" ends. The very existence of this jointly authored essay, however, suggests that cooperative ventures are both welcome and possible.

Acknowledgments

The authors thank the Narragansett Indian Tribe and the Rhode Island Historical Preservation and Heritage Commission for their work in protecting historical and archaeological resources. We are also grateful for the opportunity provided by Jordan Kerber to contribute to this volume. We deeply appreciate his encouragement, patience, and hard work in seeing the effort through to completion.

6. Ancient Burial Grounds on Monument Road
Abenaki and Archaeologist Efforts
to Find a Solution in Vermont

DEBORAH E. BLOM, JAMES B. PETERSEN,

AND FREDERICK WISEMAN

Although the state of Vermont currently has no federally recognized Native American tribes, local Native Americans actively participate in archaeological site protection and repatriation in the state. This chapter presents one history regarding Native human remains found along Monument Road in Swanton-Highgate, Vermont, and the changing nature of scholarship in the state with the increasing role of Native Americans in the archaeological process.

We highlight interactions between Vermont Abenakis,[1] Vermont state officials, and University of Vermont (UVM) archaeologists,[2] and outline how including Native Americans in all aspects of the archaeological process has led to better relations between Native people and archaeologists in the state. Finally, we discuss how bids for federal and state tribal recognition have been linked to repatriation efforts. As the Abenakis face growing struggles for sovereignty and self-determination, their role in protecting Native remains in the state has been affected, as has that of archaeologists. In the face of changing political environments, the importance of these issues has become more pronounced.

The authors of this chapter include two Euroamerican archaeologists and one Native American historian and archaeologist. Deborah Blom is an archaeologist and human osteologist who works with Aymara communities studying ancient Tiwanaku society in the Lake Titicaca Basin of Bolivia. Deborah was introduced to Vermont's Abenakis and the present situation in 1998 when she moved to Vermont to join the Department of Anthropology at UVM. She has since worked as a human osteologist with the Abenakis on various occasions. The late Jim Petersen, an archaeologist and former chair of the Department of Anthropology at UVM, was a student in Vermont in 1973 when some of the events described here took place. Jim first became involved in the analysis of artifacts from the Boucher site when he was a student and has been involved with this work ever since. Fred Wiseman is an Abenaki academic, educator, and tribal historian. He is currently chair of the Humanities Department at Johnson State College in Johnson, Vermont, and directs the Abenaki Tribal Museum and Cultural Center in Swanton, Vermont. The account presented here is a product of dialogue between these three individuals and others involved.

Contextualizing the Abenakis' Situation in the State

After 200 or more years of self-protective hiding—from hostilities ranging from European colonialism to a eugenics movement aimed at poor, "undesirable" Vermonters in the 1920s and 1930s (Gallagher 1999:122–126)—Vermont's Abenakis publicly reasserted their Native identity and rights in 1972. After research by the state into the Abenakis' declaration (Baker 1976), state recognition was granted by Governor Thomas Salmon on Thanksgiving Day 1976. However, newly elected governor Richard Snelling rescinded recognition only a few months later.

The Sovereign Abenaki Nation of Missisquoi–St. Francis/Sokoki Band initially applied for federal tribal recognition with the Bureau of Indian Affairs (BIA) in 1982. They withdrew their petition in the early 1990s when names on the accompanying tribal roll were being released to the State of Vermont for a pending court case involving aboriginal fishing rights (Carol Neptôn, personal communication 2004). In January 1996 the Abenakis resubmitted their bid for federal recognition (Carol Neptôn, personal communication 2004), but it has yet to be reviewed by the BIA.

Bills for state recognition have been proposed in the Vermont State Legislature several times since state recognition was rescinded, but all have remained "in committee," so no vote has taken place. Governor Howard Dean's administration (1991–2002) vocally opposed all legislation supporting Abenaki state recognition and, with the Vermont attorney general's office, used recognition bids as a way of inciting Vermonters' fears of gaming and land claims (e.g., *Switchboard*, Vermont Public Radio, April 9, 2002; see also Hemingway 2003). Accordingly, the wording of bills has changed over time so that state assistance in federal recognition is no longer mentioned, and the Abenakis are referred to as a "people" rather than a "tribe." Most important, in December 2002 the state attorney general's office released a lengthy report challenging the legitimacy of the Sovereign Abenaki Nation of Missisquoi–St. Francis/Sokoki Band as a group suitable for federal tribal recognition (Jacobs-Carnahan 2002). The administration's opposition was extended to any legislation or state-agency activity that might recognize or name the Abenakis as a tribe or a sovereign nation, and this included policy designed to protect Native American graves (see below).

Another piece of legislation indicative of local attitudes toward the Abenakis was proposed in 1999 by former state representative Fred Maslack of Poultney, Vermont. His bill (H.809) would require DNA testing "at the request and the expense of the individual" to provide "conclusive proof of Native American ancestry." The bill's problematic nature was discussed in a recent book by molecular anthropologist Jonathan Marks (2002), who rightly characterizes the proposition as "scientifically impossible." So far, no such legislation has been adopted. Nonetheless, the threat was very real to Vermont's Abenakis, who still remember the eugenics movement of the 1920s and 1930s.

In keeping with Vermont's generally liberal bent, the state government has a vested interest in keeping quiet any perceived attacks on Native American culture. State officials actively voice their support of the Abenakis in public forums. While opposing Abenaki state recognition, former governor Howard Dean supported the Abenakis in ways that clearly benefited the state. For example, in response to initiatives by the Governor's Commission on Native American Affairs, U.S. Senator Jim Jeffords made it possible for schools educating Abenakis to obtain funding through federal Native American education funds. Likewise, money was transferred to the Abenaki Tribal Center's museum and educational endeavors, and Abenaki festivals were supported to boost state tourism. Although he was not responsible for initiating these measures, Governor Dean approved them. Current Abenaki chief April St. Francis Merrill (personal communication 2002) describes these acts, which promote the presence of Abenakis in the state and bring funds into state education coffers, as "carrots" held out to appease the Abenakis and quiet their activist efforts.

Over almost 30 years, the late chief Homer St. Francis was a vocal activist who protested the Abenakis' need for state automotive and fishing licenses and spoke out on several issues affecting the tribe. Following in her father's tradition, albeit with her own style, Chief April St. Francis Merrill has taken on the role of defending tribal rights. Like her father, Chief Merrill has intensely engaged the state and others on issues of repatriation. Despite lacking the full benefits of federal recognition and, thus, of many applications of the Native American Graves Protection and Repatriation Act (NAGPRA), the Abenakis have been quite successful in their efforts to repatriate Native American remains held in institutions throughout the state and elsewhere, even before the passage of NAGPRA in 1990.

The Boucher Site

The most important event in shaping the early relationship between UVM anthropologists and the Abenakis involved a disturbed Native burial site located in northwestern Vermont near the Missisquoi River on Monument Road in Franklin County. Monument Road divides the towns of Swanton and Highgate and is so named for a stone monument erected at its western terminus in honor of the French Jesuit mission established during the 1740s among local Abenakis on the lower Missisquoi River (Haviland and Power 1981, 1994). Therefore, this location is within territory centrally related to many Vermont Abenakis.

The ancient Native American cemetery, called Boucher after the landowner at the time, was discovered in 1973 during house construction. In use at least between ca. 2,800 and 2,000 years ago, Boucher is one of the most important pre-Contact cemeteries discovered in North America, owing to highly unusual conditions of organic preservation caused by the presence of native copper. Along with the human remains in many of the 80 or more graves, burial offerings included plant-fiber textiles; hide clothing and containers, including several presumed "medicine bags"; worked and unworked animal bones; lithics; wood; and ceramic artifacts assigned to the so-called Middlesex complex of the Early Woodland period of northeastern prehistory (Heckenberger et al. 1990a, 1990b, 1996).

In 1973 Louise Basa, then a UVM anthropology faculty member, led an extensive project to salvage the Boucher site when the landowner insisted on developing the property. Louise officially left her position at UVM in 1974, but she remained integral to the laboratory work that followed at UVM and elsewhere for more than 15 years. Since it fell outside most direct faculty interests and few funds were available, no one else at UVM completed analyses of the Boucher remains for years. The exception was occasional analyses done by students supervised by anthropologists William Haviland and Marjory Power. The department felt that there was no rush to complete the analyses, given that UVM had secured "ownership" of the collection.

In 1986 a UVM student was working with the human remains from Boucher, and the university promoted his study to the *Burlington Free Press* (Schoch 1986a). The reporter writing the story also contacted the Abenakis and reported their opinion that the remains should be returned to Highgate for reburial (Schoch 1986b). Shortly after, in response to the articles and a *Free Press* editorial on June 8, 1986, Haviland (1986) agreed publicly that the Abenakis should eventually be given the remains. Troubled that the collection had not been adequately studied, Haviland, Power, and other anthropologists began to negotiate with the Abenakis for more time to complete nondestructive, scientific analyses (Allen 1986). Subsequent analyses over two to three years were completed with limited private funding and much gratis work at several institutions. Haviland and former student John Krigbaum oversaw the osteological studies, while Petersen and Michael Heckenberger carried out the artifact analyses. However, communication was somewhat poor between the Abenakis and UVM, and from 1986 to 1989 anthropologists interpreted the Abenakis' request for "the remains" as including only the human skeletal remains. But a written resolution from the tribe in May 1989 made it apparent that, for the Abenakis, "the remains" also included the grave offerings (Birchfield 1989).

The anthropologists working with the remains and their supporters asked the Abenakis to consider preserving the entire collection or, minimally, the artifacts for future study. They questioned when the Abenakis or archaeologists would ever again see, for example, 2,500-year-old hide medicine bags, textiles, or imported smoking pipes. Multiple meetings were held at UVM, on state property in Waterbury, at tribal headquarters in Swanton, and elsewhere to resolve what should ultimately be done with the remains. Through the Division for Historic Preservation (DHP) and the division's archaeologists Giovanna Peebles and David Skinas, the State of Vermont was involved and attempted to mediate a resolution in favor of the Abenakis. Progressively more incensed by the slow pace of the 1989 negotiations, Chief St. Francis threatened that if the remains were not returned immediately, he would "cremate them in place," referring to the Department of Anthropology at UVM (Jones 2000:6A, quoting April St. Francis Merrill). UVM administrators and lawyers suggested that the Department of Anthropology surrender the remains as soon as possible.

All Boucher remains that had been under study elsewhere were called back to Vermont in 1989.[3] By the winter of 1990 they had been sent to a state-owned storage facility in Berlin, Vermont. Negotiations to purchase the Boucher property then began, and the Abenakis prepared to take control of the remains. The Boucher property was purchased for $325,000 with state funds supplemented by an anonymous donation. The house, driveway, and all other disturbances were removed from the property in 1995 (Wiseman 2001:182–183). In spite of requests by some anthropologists that the remains be placed in an accessible subsurface mausoleum, the Abenakis remained resolute that the entire Boucher collection be reburied. From their perspective, religious, community health, and civil rights concerns made compromise or alternatives impossible.

The Abenakis decided that the remains would be brought back to Monument Road by premodern transport. A canoe flotilla was assembled to paddle the remains down the Winooski River from Montpelier to Colchester and then northward along the eastern shore of Lake Champlain, and up the Missisquoi River to tribal headquarters. Some archaeologists who had helped mediate for or otherwise worked with the Abenakis were also included in the portage (Douglas Frink, personal communication 2004).

During the transport, some of the remains were deposited in the water when one of the canoes capsized, indicating to the Abenakis that this was where those particular remains were meant to rest. The remainder of the Boucher collection was reburied in 1996, grave by grave, in roughly the same locations from which they had been excavated 23 years earlier, on land that is owned by the state of Vermont but overseen by the Abenakis.

In telling the story of the Boucher site, one encounters some deep-seated disagreements, and we have found it impossible today to arrive at a consensus. Overall, one sees problems of communication, which initially took place through the press or other mediators rather than face-to-face (Birchfield 1989). Although some disagreements are due to differing memories of the events, others are due to differing worldviews on the part of the people involved.

Some archaeologists we spoke to stated that neither the Abenakis nor any other Native Americans had asked for repatriation of the Boucher remains at the time of excavation in 1973 or for 13 years afterward. Certainly, the archaeologists felt that the best-case scenario would have been to have halted construction entirely, but that was not an option at the time (Birchfield 1989).

Basa told the press in 1973 that there was a question whether burial sites should be disturbed at all (Stetson 1973), and Haviland states that it was always assumed that the remains would be reburied after study (personal communication 2004). Nevertheless, an editorial published by an independent newsletter in the state, the *Vermont Freeman*, called the archaeologists "grave robbers" at the time of the excavations (Ignorant Savages 1973). In his response to the editorial, Haviland (1973) wrote "that burials of native Americans (i.e., American Indians) are as deserving of respect as are those of early white settlers, or those of the people who currently inhabit the State."

Abenakis say that they had always been aware of the desecration of the Boucher cemetery and understood that the remains would be returned as soon as possible. They argue that before 1986 they had been occupied with other battles and did not yet have the political power necessary to address the issue (Birchfield 1989). By 1986 they had waited too long and realized that direct action to fight for the rights of the Boucher dead was necessary.

Much of this debate seems to be a result of differing views about just what "the remains" constituted, as discussed previously. As can be seen in a video documenting the 1989 meeting at UVM and the reading of a resolution that the Tribal Council presented to the Department of Anthropology at that time (Birchfield 1989), when the Abenakis spoke of "the remains" they were referring to the skeletal remains and all grave offerings. Until this point, the archaeologists had interpreted "the remains" to mean only the skeletal remains.

Many conflicts also arose regarding the spiritual and physical consequences of the disinterment, largely because both sides had significantly different views about death and the dead. The Abenakis assert that the human remains were poorly treated while at UVM, mistreated to such an extent that bones were used "as doorstops and dust collectors!" (Jones 2000:6A, quoting April St. Francis Merrill). The archaeologists, on the other hand, contend that Haviland and Power were generally careful caretakers of the Boucher collection. Clearly, these two groups hold such widely differing views of what constitutes proper care of the dead that an agreement will likely never be reached on this matter.

Many Abenakis believe that there is a residual part of the deceased's spirit that remains in the bones and burial goods, and if they are disrespected, even unintentionally, unforeseen effects on the ancestors and the living may result. The Abenakis explain that they attempted, with varying success, to make the scholars aware that disinterring ancient burials has spiritual and physical consequences and can cause illnesses involving both mind and body (generally called "bone disease" by some Abenakis and their advocates). The Abenakis say at least 30 Native people in the community were directly affected as a result of the Boucher exhumation and archaeological study, suffering from ailments ranging from heart disease to suicide, minor illnesses, and misfortunes such as divorce. During this time, the archaeologists, too, experienced tragic personal events. These misfortunes of the scholars merely confirmed the Abenakis' worst fears, and the archaeologists were told that their actions were the cause of the problems.

Resentment grew on the part of the Abenakis as archaeologists publicly presented photographs and scholarly publications on Boucher and other Native American sites in Vermont. From an archaeological perspective, the Boucher site revealed rich information about ancient society in Vermont that could never have been imagined without the unusually fine preservation of the Boucher remains. Feeling the need to inform others about Native history in Vermont and to counter the 200-year-old myth that Vermont had never been home to Natives, archaeologists published books such as *The Original Vermonters*, by Haviland and Power (1981, 1994), as well as several articles on the Boucher site and related discoveries (Heckenberger et al. 1990a, 1990b, 1996). Haviland and Power recognized that while select people—mainly artifact collectors, a few academics, and Native people themselves—were aware of the former presence of Natives in Vermont before the Europeans arrived, relatively few members of the public recognized that Natives were living in Vermont during the colonial period and more recently. Their work was designed to counter this incomplete and often erroneous understanding of the Native presence in Vermont.

While the publications were well within the bounds of scholarly protocol at the time, most Abenakis believed that these publications, which showed burial goods and general locations of sacred areas, were desecrations. For many Abenakis it was dangerous and disrespectful even to look at the published illustrations, not to mention to read the publications. Nevertheless, Haviland, Petersen, and others were awarded certificates by the Abenaki Tribal Council thanking them for making the Boucher reburial possible.

In reading the experiences described here, one can see that most of the scholars and the Abenakis approached the Boucher situation from very different worldviews. Throughout, everyone was trying to do what he or she felt personally was "right," but the Boucher experience was extremely unpleasant for all involved. Collaboration was virtually absent, and the use of jargon and disagreements about the definition of words and phrases compounded the problems. The state, through DHP archaeologists, was instrumental in helping the Abenakis in their efforts to rebury the remains. Overall, empathy and greater understanding gained through the Boucher experience helped us to deal better with such matters in the future.

The Bushey Site

As has happened several times since the Boucher cemetery was disturbed, in 2000 human remains were found during construction on Monument Road, this time on the Bushey property, roughly 1 km from the Boucher site, on land beside the Missisquoi River, next to the monument and near where other burials had been discovered in the eroding riverbank in the 1990s. After hearing from the Abenakis that human remains had been disturbed at the Bushey site, Scott Dillon, a DHP archaeologist, called Petersen, Blom, and John Crock, the director of UVM's Consulting Archaeology Program.

They confirmed that the construction on the Bushey property had disturbed a mortuary area. Dozens of human bone fragments were visible in the backdirt from a cellar hole, along with in situ remains in one of the profiles. The state Agency for Community Affairs (in which the DHP resides) became involved and filed a motion in Vermont Superior Court to halt construction based on criminal (Title 13, Chapter 81, Section 3761) and health (Title 18, Chapter 107, Section 5212) laws that prohibit the intentional removal of remains without a permit.

Over the course of the summer and fall of 2000, under direction of the Abenakis, numerous volunteers and consulting archaeologists from Vermont and Maine spent 15½ weeks sifting through the construction backdirt to remove the human remains for proper reburial. Much of this work was done voluntarily in response to requests for help from the Abenakis, although the state contributed a small amount of funding to employ some of the archaeologists. The human bones recovered on Monument Road were carried to the tribal headquarters of the Sovereign Abenaki Nation of Missisquoi–St. Francis/Sokoki Band, and the state negotiated the purchase of land for the reburial. At this time, out of frustration over the state's inability to stop construction at nearby locations before they could be examined for evidence of further archaeological sites, Chief Merrill and Abenaki supporters blocked construction equipment from entering Monument Road for several weeks.

During the disturbance of the graves on Monument Road, some local people and government officials began questioning whether the remains were indeed Native American, and others even claimed that they were not human, or that they did not actually exist, or that the site had been "salted" with bones by the Abenakis or their allies. Anti-Native sentiments increased, and Natives at the roadblock were subjected to verbal and written forms of racism. Upon reflection and discussion, Chief Merrill allowed community members and government officials to view the remains, which covered six large tables in the tribal headquarters. The room was smudged through the ritual use of incense to spiritually cleanse the area and prepared for the temporary viewing.

Although visitors sometimes insensitively treated the remains as a museum display, the viewing in the tribal offices established to others in the community that there was a very serious problem to be addressed on Monument Road. After some rough starts, in 2002 a committee appointed by the local selectboards and the Abenakis began drafting proposed bills (H.600/S.258) to deal with Native American burials in the state, since existing laws allow only siblings, spouses, parents, or children to oppose permits for removal of remains from graves (Title 18, Chapter 107, Section 5212). However, members of Governor Dean's administration voiced their opposition to this legislation because it specifically named the Abenakis as an interested party, and the passage of the legislation might thus legitimize the Abenakis in some way. The bills stalled in committee.[4]

In 2001 Representative Maslack, undeterred by negative nationwide press toward his DNA bill on Native American ancestry, had proposed new legislation that would control the determination of Native American ancestors. Maslack's House Bill 678 proposed to require that "DNA/HLA [human lymphocyte antigen] Native American markers" be used to verify human remains as Native. The bill ultimately stalled in committee, and Maslack lost his bid for reelection in 2002. However, this was the political atmosphere in which the Abenakis and others sifted through buckets of backdirt to recover human remains from the Bushey site.

Once all possible remains were recovered, Dillon and Petersen asked that they be studied because of their archaeological importance. Although Vermont burial laws do not stipulate study of any kind, the Tribal Council agreed to let Blom examine the remains for six days in September 2000. Chief Merrill facilitated access to the remains throughout the duration of their study. She explained to Blom that during the screening of the fill, the bones, charcoal, and artifacts of stone, metal, wood, and ceramic that were found were placed in red cloth bundles, along with cedar, tobacco, sweet grass, sage, and corn.

Each of the approximately 70 bundles was unique in terms of the day the material was collected and, sometimes, the location where the remains were found around the construction site. This was done, in part, in the hope of preserving any information about which bodies and offerings were buried together, but also because, the Abenakis explained, it was an emerging local Native American archaeological methodology. The red cloth represents the ancient red ocher and acts to protect the living and to contain the spirit of the dead as well as the grave offerings that are meant to quiet the unease of the dead. Blom was asked to keep the remains from each bundle together, although bundles could be combined if they clearly contained bones of the same individual(s). This system—which we can only partially describe here—generally worked well for all involved.

The major objectives of the limited osteological study were to identify how many individuals were represented and to regroup the dispersed bones and fragments of each body. Chief Merrill made it clear that destructive or extensive analyses and measurements would not be tolerated. Analyses revealed information that was consistent with all the individuals being of Native American ancestry (see Blom 2002 for more details), an observation that was in line with the archaeological information.

Also not surprising, given the presence of complete burials in situ in the wall of the cellar cut, all staining and fragmentation patterns indicated that the mortuary area was disturbed by the construction. At least 21 people (3 male adults, 12 adult females, and 6 children) were buried in the space destroyed by the construction (and not, as some had suggested, simply placed in the construction fill by someone wishing to halt construction). Based on the fragmentary, poorly preserved nature of the remains and the presence of over 5,000 fragments of unidentifiable bone, an estimate of at least 30 individuals is more probable.

Wiseman's analysis of the material remains found with the burials provided additional information about the people interred in this cemetery. Hints of a relatively late date came from the associated artifacts, examples of which include a late eighteenth-century-style silver corpus from a rosary or crucifix, 1790s white seed beads, and an 1820s "Big cent" U.S. copper coin. Over 60 identifiable nails, many still embedded in remains of coffins, were also useful for dating the remains. Analyses indicated a burial ceremonialism separate from coeval "Anglo-French" cemeteries in Vermont (Kenny et al. 2003), documenting that the Missisquoi Abenakis maintained a separate sacred space locally from the late eighteenth to the mid-nineteenth century and establishing important evidence of cultural and political continuity needed for federal tribal recognition. Some Abenakis believe that these data becoming available just when needed indicate that the dead "came" precisely when the Abenakis needed them to help with modern political battles.

The experience of the Native peoples and the archaeologists during collaborations over the Bushey site was much different than that during the Boucher events described previously. In general, tensions were high and the atmosphere mournful during the many weeks of sifting to reclaim the remains from the construction backdirt. The amount of work to be done was monumental, and various archaeologists and others volunteered their time. During this process, the Abenakis and archaeologists explained the situation to the non-Native volunteers before they entered the area, and the volunteers were instructed on proper behavior.

The Abenakis and close friends also ensured the safety of the volunteers and the deceased, to the best of their abilities, by providing, for example, peppermint and tobacco, smudging, and instruction on the proper way to cleanse oneself at the end of each day. They also modeled the appropriate tone to be taken while the work was being done. It was very clear who had the authority, and the Abenakis were generally forgiving of the foibles of those who did not perfectly follow the proper customs, correcting where necessary.

In spite of care on the part of the Abenakis, archaeologists, and others, we still found ourselves with some misunderstandings. For example, Petersen, who was directing an archaeological field school at the time, brought his student volunteers to Monument Road to aid in the work. On their second day there, another volunteer at the site recognized a collector of Native American artifacts (including those from burial sites) among the field school students. When the Abenakis learned this, they felt that the burial ground had been further compromised. They argued that collectors have "bone disease" and suffer from an overwhelming desire to possess artifacts. Therefore, they must be spiritually and physically monitored and are not welcome on sacred Abenaki soil.

From Petersen's perspective, the field school was a way to educate this student and others about damage from development and looting, and since the student was enrolled in the field school, Petersen felt he had to include him. The collector was told by the Abenakis and others that he would be allowed to work at the site if he agreed to surrender all potential mortuary goods in his collection, but he refused. When Petersen realized that the presence of a collector was considered disrespectful and that neither party would compromise, he left the site with the students, and the land was smudged to cleanse it. This event continues to be a point of contention with some Abenakis.

During her analysis of the remains, Blom spent most of the six days at the tribal center to maximize her time. A typical point of conversation between Blom and some Abenakis was the problem of an obviously premenopausal woman interacting with the dead. Mostly, this was voiced kindly, with the concern that her activities would result in her infertility. Chief Merrill, who is the same age as Blom, had from the beginning explained the risks that both women were taking by doing this work, and smudging was done as often as possible. Thus the atmosphere was a more nurturing one than that experienced during the Boucher era.

Another problem involved the appropriate language to use in discussing the remains during osteological analysis and reporting. Blom was told that the Abenakis found certain statements made by archaeologists at the site quite macabre, for example, comments about features on individual's bones. Between these accounts and the overall mournful atmosphere at the tribal center, it was apparent that standard academic language would cause problems. In Bolivia Blom always works in a foreign language (Spanish or Aymara), and the vocabulary she uses to discuss the dead (e.g., *los abuelos*, or "the grandparents") comes from the Aymara with whom she works. When working with the Abenakis, however, she was working in English and with a vocabulary derived from university studies. Words such as "specimens," while sounding objective and scientific, were entirely inappropriate. In reality, these were the remains of children and elderly men and women. Not only were the remains seen as belonging to ancient individuals with histories (only some of which could be seen osteologically), they dynamically engaged the living.

The Abenakis, who had reburied the Boucher remains in solitude, decided to invite non-Native volunteers to attend the Bushey reburial ceremony, in November 2000. The volunteers had become emotionally invested in the project and were honored to be included in the ceremony. One archaeologist who had an especially intense experience with one particular set of remains was asked to place those remains for reburial. The inclusion of outsiders meant that certain events had to be explained to prevent errors. Although the reburial ceremony was a closure of sorts, a situation elsewhere in Vermont was causing further worries. A burial had been disturbed in Alburg, and the Abenakis were largely being denied access to the remains. Notably, this situation in Alburg has still not been resolved.

Conclusion

We present here only a small part of the daily struggle that the Abenakis face and some of the situations in which anthropologists have been involved. For the Abenakis, having the authority to determine who they are and the ability to guard Native American graves from desecration is paramount. The Vermont state government's fears that the Abenakis will be granted federal recognition have led to an erosion of these rights and have had a serious impact on Abenaki sovereignty in the protection of Native American burials. Proposed state legislation, while claiming to benefit the Abenakis, would result in a deeper control over Abenaki self-determination and the establishment of the Abenakis as essentially domestic dependents without sovereignty. Most threatening has been the proposed legislation designed to require DNA testing to establish Native American ancestry and ancestors. Throughout negotiations between the Abenakis and the state, the anthropological community has been intertwined in shifting roles as communication has increased, and we all feel the frustration in trying to reason with politicians.

Collaborations between anthropologists and the Sovereign Abenaki Nation of Missisquoi–St. Francis/Sokoki Band have been increasing, as indicated by this chapter and the chapters by Lacy and Moody, and Goodby (this volume). Because of their accepted role as educators, anthropologists can aid in productive collaborations. Over recent years, Vermont anthropologists have sponsored activities such as a three-day conference at UVM in 1999 to help educate scholars and the public about various Abenaki issues.

Additionally, in 2002 several anthropologists in the Northeast participated in an educational session held for legislators at the Vermont Statehouse. In 2003 professional meetings of the Northeastern Anthropological Association and the Vermont Academy of Arts and Sciences included sessions devoted to Abenaki issues. Lately, anthropologists have also appeared in the press and in meetings with the state attorney general, speaking out to protect Native burial remains and in support of tribal recognition based on archaeological and historical evidence, following the tradition started by Haviland and Power (1981, 1994) with their book *The Original Vermonters*, but now with more knowledge behind us.

Progress made over the 27 years between the Boucher and Bushey experiences suggests that we have learned more about collaboration, but there is still significant room for improvement. Tensions definitely exist between the Abenakis, who know their past through oral history and more spiritual means, and anthropologists, who often wish to preserve cultural material and human remains for scientific study and education.

Unlike some other tribes (see, e.g., Kerber, this volume), many of the Abenakis and some members of the Tribal Council state that not much could or should be learned about the past through archaeology. Others believe that it can be useful but should be used only in certain contexts. There may well be future cases like Boucher and Bushey, where ancient human remains are endangered by development. Let us hope that all relevant parties can learn to work cooperatively to resolve any problems without undue disturbance of sacred remains.

Efforts at repatriating the Boucher remains resulted in the forceful opening of lines of communication, and in many ways things have changed. We still confront epistemological conflict, as we did in simply writing this chapter. With dialogue, agreement is possible, even if the agreement is sometimes that we hold different views. In fact, we have learned that avoiding conflict can itself have many more repercussions. Only through facing conflict head-on and communicating can a solution be found.

The activities described in this chapter, especially the work on the Bushey remains by Blom, Merrill, and Wiseman to answer mutually interesting questions (such as the number of burials, postdeath trauma, and the dating of the remains), serve both the ideals of academe and the Abenaki Nation. In this way, everyone wins—the archaeologists can publish articles such as this one, and the Abenakis can respectfully garner information critical to current political aims, such as federal recognition. Lastly, new bonds of friendship were forged in this process, and that is what is needed. This chapter seems to present "the Abenakis," "the state officials," and "the anthropologists" as homogeneous masses, but thanks to the dialogue that we have experienced, we realize this is oversimplified. Amity is one way to fight the "us-versus-them" mentality seen occasionally in this essay, and move closer to an "us" mentality on shared issues.

Acknowledgments

Previous versions of this chapter were presented by Blom at the 2002 Annual Meeting of the American Anthropological Association (Blom and Merrill 2002) and the 2003 Annual Meeting of the Northeastern Anthropological Association (Blom 2003). The present version has been modified and expanded considerably. We would like to thank the individuals who helped with interviews, research, comments, and editing during the preparation of this chapter, who include (in no particular order) Chief April St. Francis Merrill, Scott Dillon, John Moody, Donna Roberts Moody, Carol Neptôn, Giovanna Peebles, David Skinas, Prudence Doherty, Doug Frink, Bill Haviland, Louise Basa, Michael Heckenberger, Sarah Ward, Jessica Dow, Adam Murray, Cindy Longwell, Jeff Clarke, Liz Guenard, Sara Block, and John Krigbaum. Because of the nature of this material, we were not able to incorporate all comments. As always, any errors are the responsibility of the authors, and the opinions expressed here are personal views of the authors rather than those of their employers.

Notes

1. Although other Abenaki groups exist (see Goodby, this volume), we use the term Abenakis to refer to the Sovereign Abenaki Nation of Missisquoi–St. Francis/Sokoki Band. We choose to use the plural, Abenakis, rather than Abenaki. The Sovereign Abenaki Nation of Missisquoi is closely related to the broader Western Abenakis, indigenous inhabitants of northern New England in the United States and adjacent Quebec in Canada. There are two Abenaki First Nations reserves in Quebec (Odanak and Wolinak) but no Abenaki reservations in the United States.

2. Although other archaeologists have worked in the state, we tend to focus more on those at UVM. These archaeologists were involved in the greatest conflicts with the Abenakis, and two of the authors of the present chapter are from that institution. This should in no way be read as an attempt to ignore other efforts in the state.

3. That same year, state burial laws (specifically Title 13, Chapter 81, Section 3761) were amended to add human remains and objects interred with remains to the language specifying that "a human body" could not be disinterred. The maximum fine was increased to $10,000 and the maximum sentence to 15 years.

4. As a result, a law was added (Title 18, Chapter 107, Section 5212b) to establish an "unmarked burial sites special fund" to which money could be transferred in the event of an emergency and to fund studies designed to prevent grave desecration. Ironically, this fund exists in the absence of an "unmarked burial law" in the state.

7. Working with the Abenaki in New Hampshire
The Education of an Archaeologist

ROBERT G. GOODBY

Prologue

This was the third week of our search. Room by room, drawer by drawer, box by box, we had looked for the fragmentary remains of two Abenaki children and an adult that had been excavated by archaeologists 20 years before. A battered, lidless cardboard box with the word "Seabrook" scrawled on the side sat on the table. Examining in turn each of the dirty plastic bags it contained, I came to an old bread bag, knotted at the top, that contained two unmarked, crumpled business envelopes. I opened the bag, opened the envelopes, and emptied the contents onto a tray. I stared at a few fragments of bone and two wooden Popsicle sticks, to which small teeth had been glued. My partner, a young Abenaki man, focused his stare on me. "There they are," he said, in quiet disbelief.

Introduction

My experience working with the Abenaki in New Hampshire closely mirrors an evolving relationship in the state that began in the early 1990s. Over the past decade, this relationship has grown from a period of considerable tension to an ongoing cooperative relationship based on mutual

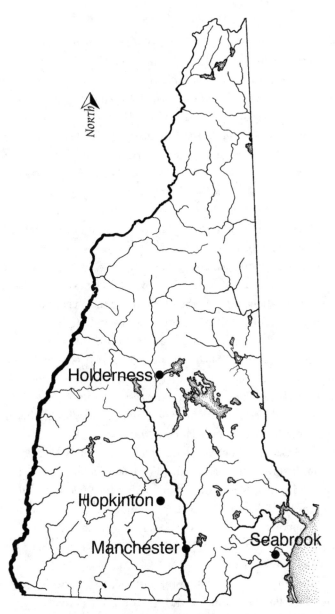

Figure 7.1. Locations in New Hampshire of the Davison Brook site (Holderness), Native American burial (Hopkinton), Smyth site (Manchester), and Rock's Road site (Seabrook) discussed in the text (Prepared by Amy McIntyre).

trust and clear, established procedures. The evolution of this relationship has been shaped by the peculiar difficulties the Abenaki, a non-federally recognized tribe (see Blom et al., and Lacy and Moody, this volume), have in representing their own interests, and by an archaeological history that includes the neglect and mistreatment of Abenaki remains. Examples of my collaboration with the Abenaki discussed in this chapter include the search for lost Native remains at the University of New Hampshire (UNH); the recovery and repatriation of Native remains from the Davison Brook site in Holderness, New Hampshire; the discovery and repatriation of Native remains from the Smyth site in Manchester, New Hampshire; and the discovery and reburial of a Native American burial in Hopkinton, New Hampshire (Figure 7.1).

My work with the Abenaki began in 1994 when I was teaching at UNH and had just been elected president of the New Hampshire Archeological Society. Relations between the Abenaki and the archaeological community were strained, following a summer of protests and demonstrations at a site in North Haverhill, New Hampshire, being tested by the New Hampshire Division of Historical Resources (NHDHR) State Conservation Rescue Archaeology Program (SCRAP). On a warm October day in 1994, the lead figure in the Haverhill protests, Donna Moody, an Abenaki woman affiliated with the Abenaki Nation of Missisquoi Abenaki in Swanton, Vermont (see Lacy and Moody, this volume), and ethnohistorian John Moody sat in front of me on the grass by the UNH Archaeology Lab. It was our first real conversation, filled with tension born, on my part, of a combination of distrust, fear, and unfamiliarity. While none of the artifacts in the lab had been excavated by me or under my supervision, I had mentally appointed myself their guardian. When John asked me if there were any Native remains in the building, I said "no," a reply that was both honest and erroneous.

That meeting began my relationship with Donna. A series of letters and phone calls followed, in which I laid out my earnest views of the main issues separating Native people and archaeologists. Sure, the archaeological treatment of Native remains had been less than perfect, but we needed to study these remains to illuminate Native history and (in what I thought a clever argument) to replace the racist notions of conventional history with the shining light of science that would reveal how sophisticated and well adapted Native people had been. Furthermore, while I acknowledged that sincerely held spiritual views led Donna and other Native people to oppose so much of archaeological research, I argued that my science could not yield to their religion—if I did so for them, I must for others, with the end result being the triumph of creationism in the name of religious tolerance. This exchange of views, taking place over many months, helped ease our mutual suspicions, and culminated in the spring of 1995 with an invitation to Donna and John to speak to my New England Prehistory class at UNH. Our tentative relationship became a friendship, developing further when Donna's son Chris became a student at UNH and enrolled in a number of my courses.

In the spring of 1996, Chris came into my office with a message from his mother. A few years before, a Native American skeleton from the Rock's Road site in Seabrook, New Hampshire, had been transferred from the university to the NHDHR in preparation for eventual repatriation, but the fragmentary remains of three other individuals from the site had been reported missing. The Rock's Road site was excavated in 1974 and 1975 as one of the first projects in New Hampshire performed in compliance with Section 106 of the National Historic Preservation Act. A record of continuous occupation from the Late Archaic through Contact periods (ca. 5,000–300 years ago) was uncovered (Goodby 1995; Robinson and Bolian 1987), including the remains of four individuals tentatively dating from the Late Woodland to Contact periods (ca. 800–300 years ago). One of these was the tightly flexed skeleton of a man in his 30s; the poorly preserved remains of another adult were found 5 m away, and in a burial some 35 m to the southwest were the teeth and a small fragment of mandible from two children between 5 and 10 years of age (Hecker 1981; Robinson and Bolian 1987:32–33).

Chris and I began a long, systematic search of the nine rooms, two closets, cabinets, hundreds of drawers, and attic of the UNH Archaeology Lab. As an archaeologist who had been so vigorously defending my discipline to both Chris and his mother, I was embarrassed that something as significant as human remains could be lost, and mortified at their condition when they were finally found. My personal transformation to an advocate and practitioner of repatriation began in 1996 on the day Chris and I discovered those remains. Following the discovery of the missing remains, all four individuals were brought together at the NHDHR in preparation for repatriation.

The process of repatriation under certain circumstances is clearly outlined by the Native American Graves Protection and Repatriation Act (NAGPRA). In Section 2, the act clearly privileges federally recognized Native American groups, defining them as "tribes" who alone are given standing in the law to present claims under NAGPRA. Despite this, the NAGPRA Review Committee has developed an ad hoc process by which non-federally recognized Native groups may petition for repatriation. In the case of the unrecognized Western Abenaki people of New Hampshire and Vermont, their representative has standing to appear before the committee. But before repatriation can occur, they must receive from two federally recognized groups, the Wampanoag of southeastern Massachusetts and the Wabanaki Tribes of Maine, formal concurring support for every individual repatriation. While this system has made repatriation possible, it has also made it more cumbersome and created extensive delays. The second-class status that results from a lack of recognition manifests itself in other ways: in the formal language of NAGPRA, and in all the inventories and notices submitted as part of the repatriation process, the remains of the Western Abenaki must be labeled as "culturally unidentifiable (Western Abenaki)," despite the clear understanding by the Abenaki of who they are and what their connection to these remains is.

Lacking federal recognition and a centrally organized political structure, the Western Abenaki comprise a number of local, autonomous groups who, to varying degrees, recognize long-standing ties to particular places or regions within N'dakinna, the Abenaki homeland. Prominent among these groups is the Abenaki Nation of Missisquoi, and for years their repatriation coordinator, Donna Moody, worked to assemble a broad coalition of Abenaki groups that she represented on matters of repatriation (see Lacy and Moody, this volume). These groups include the Abenaki Nation of Missisquoi; the Cowasuck Band of the Pennacook-Abenaki People; the Abenaki Nation of New Hampshire, led by Charlie True; and the First Nation of New Hampshire. Under this system, the Abenaki became the second non-federally recognized tribe to receive remains under NAGPRA (Donna Moody, personal communication 2004) and the first to receive ancient remains. Repatriations and subsequent reburials have proceeded slowly but steadily ever since. Notable among these was the repatriation by the NHDHR to the Abenaki Nation in 2002 of 17 individuals from 11 sites, including all 4 individuals from the Rock's Road site and 2 individuals from the Smyth site in Manchester.

In response to the growing advocacy and public profile of Native American groups in New Hampshire, the NHDHR initiated an ad hoc program of consultation with Native Americans in relation to archaeological projects completed in compliance with Section 106. The state archaeologist at the time, Gary Hume, determined on a case-by-case basis which of the Section 106 projects required consultation, and which Native American groups or individuals would be consulted. While the inclusion of Native American input in the review process was a significant step forward, Native Americans remained the only consultants in this process whose work was expected to be pro bono. No budget lines for Native consultation were included in Section 106 projects, and no hourly wage, stipend, or reimbursement for expenses was offered. If informed input required any time or travel (e.g., visits to sites, libraries, consultation with far-flung elders), those expenses would be borne by them. For Abenaki people with full-time jobs and typical family obligations, the growing number of requests for free consultation became increasingly difficult to meet. Many projects passed with no Abenaki input at all, even though on paper they were increasingly included in the review and compliance process.

Davison Brook Site

In the spring of 1999 the New Hampshire Department of Transportation (NHDOT), in coordination with the New Hampshire Fish and Game Department, requested that a Phase IA preliminary archaeological reconnaissance study be undertaken for alterations to existing roadways and proposed parking lots and a wetland mitigation area in the town of Holderness. The study area was on land owned both by the state of New Hampshire and by the Squam Lake Natural Science Center, a nonprofit educational and scientific institution whose campus is visited by thousands of students and tourists every year. Situated on a level terrace of well-drained outwash soils at the confluence of Davison Brook and the Squam River, in between Big Squam and Little Squam lakes, this area was determined to exhibit very high sensitivity for pre-Contact Native American sites (Goodby 1999), and a Phase IB study involving excavation of shovel test pits was recommended. At the direction of the state archaeologist, requests for input were sent to six Abenaki groups and individuals in New Hampshire and Vermont before the beginning of Phase IB fieldwork, but no responses were received before field testing began in June 1999.

Phase IB testing and a subsequent Phase II intensive archaeological survey resulted in the discovery of an extensive Native American site spread over an area of at least 16,000 m². Aside from a small cluster of Middle to Late Woodland ceramics (ca. 1,600–600 years ago), diagnostic artifacts from the Late Archaic period (ca. 5,000–3,000 years ago) dominated the assemblage from the site. Cultural material at the site was present in a well-developed plow zone stratum and in the upper 20 cm of the underlying subsoil strata. A number of hearth features truncated by plowing were identified during the Phase II study. The site was determined to be eligible for inclusion on the National Register of Historic Places, and a recommendation was made for Phase III data recovery before any construction (Goodby 2000:16). During this time, I worked closely with the science center, consulting with their director, giving public talks, and speaking to their docents and at the annual meeting of the board of trustees. At every opportunity, I emphasized the unique resource present in this location, and how preservation of the archaeological resources and the study of those artifacts already unearthed would complement the mission of the science center. Copies of the Phase IA and combined Phase IB/II reports were provided to the science center. The latter report emphasized specifically that the Davison Brook site was situated on areas of science center property on the southern and northern side of Davison Brook, that with a known area of over 16,000 m² it was one of the largest sites ever identified in the state, and that its ultimate extent was unknown, since its boundaries extended beyond the limits of the study area (Goodby 2000).

Phase III data recovery was conducted in the summer of 2000 and followed a detailed data recovery plan written by the NHDHR. This plan

called for the excavation of 40 m^2 excavation units and specified their locations within the overall site area. The recovery plan identified a "core
area" of the site (determined by the relative quantity of artifacts and features) where, following conventional excavation, the plow zone stratum
would be mechanically removed to expose any intact or partially intact
features in the relatively undisturbed subsoil. These features would then
be recorded and excavated. No provision was made for examining the
plow zone soils, which were stockpiled on the edge of the "core" area before being removed to an old gravel pit, the location of a proposed New
Hampshire Fish and Game Department shooting range in another part
of Holderness. The recovery plan stated that "burial features are not expected but may be present." If they were discovered, excavation of the feature would not be allowed without further authorization by the NHDHR
(Goodby 2001:157–165).

The Phase III study at the Davison Brook site resulted in the identification and excavation of 27 features and the identification of four spatially
and temporally distinct occupation loci, dating to the last portion of the
Late Archaic period, between 2,800 and 4,100 years ago. During the final
Late Archaic occupation of the site, the occupants constructed unusually
large hearths; unlike earlier hearth features, two of these lacked associated stone tools or faunal remains, suggesting some special sort of purpose or associated activity (Goodby 2001:31). The site was abandoned following the construction of these large hearths and, with the exception of
ephemeral visits by Woodland period people over 1,000 years later, was
never reoccupied by Native people (Goodby 2001:32, 2002a:4). No burial
features were identified during any phase of archaeological study at the
Davison Brook site, and no human remains were recovered.

Native American skeletal remains were first identified at the Davison
Brook site in April 2001 when contractors employed by the science center
were hand excavating a trench for an electrical conduit passing through
the southern portion of the site area. No Section 106 consultation was required for this excavation, and even though a significant site was known
to be in this location, neither the NHDHR nor the archaeological contractor, Victoria Bunker, Inc., was notified that this work would take place.
The discovery of an in situ flexed burial was brought to the attention of

the state archaeologist, who notified law enforcement officials and Donna Moody. At Donna's request, the remains, identified by the state archaeologist as belonging to a Native American female in her early teenage years, were preserved in place (Goodby 2001:86).

In June 2001 a second discovery, this time of a cranium fragment, was made as loam was being spread during construction of the Fish and Game Department parking lot. This loam was initially thought to have originated from the just-completed construction of an adjacent science center parking lot, part of a larger construction program that would include a new visitors' center. Concern over the uncertain provenience of the loam led to the discovery that soil from construction of the science center parking lot had been trucked to the same gravel pit where soil from the machine stripping of the archaeological site had been dumped a year earlier. When Donna and John Moody visited this location, they discovered over 40 dump-truck piles of soil, each covered with weeds, distributed across the bottom of a sun-baked, abandoned gravel pit (Figure 7.2). Additional human skeletal remains were recovered from the surface of some of these piles, some of which included pieces of flagging tape, indicating they were indeed from the Phase III machine stripping of plow zone soils from the southern side of Davison Brook.

A small group of Native people, including Donna Moody and Charlie True, began what seemed like the impossible task of recovering all the human remains from these dirt piles. At Donna's request, I visited the site and was stunned by the magnitude of the task. After a week or more of working alone, the NHDHR, at my encouragement, initiated what would be a months-long recovery effort at the gravel pit. At the direction of the state archaeologist, participants in SCRAP, under the direction of the then deputy state archaeologist Richard Boisvert, began the process of systematically screening each pile of loam. In addition to working as a volunteer at the site, I was retained as a consultant by the Fish and Game Department and spent a number of days at the site. Under an agreement worked out between the state archaeologist and Donna Moody, all artifacts and bone fragments recovered during the screening were turned over to the Abenaki representatives upon recovery. Potentially diagnostic artifacts such as bifaces were photographed and sketched in the field by SCRAP members before being given to the Abenaki.

Figure 7.2. Dirt piles from the Davison Brook site. Charles True, Speaker, Abenaki Nation of New Hampshire on right (Photo courtesy of Robert Goodby).

The work of recovering all artifacts and bone from the dirt piles stands out in the minds of everyone involved as an extremely difficult and trying experience. The working conditions were oppressive and included a lack of shade, relentless heat, and constant thick dust. Archaeologists were placed in the unusual position of having to consult with, and defer to, the requests of Native Americans in determining the methods employed and the interpretation of items recovered during screening. Richard Boisvert and his SCRAP team responded with grace and understanding, and as the days passed with Abenaki and archaeologists screening side by side, a camaraderie born of enduring common difficulties emerged. For the Abenaki, of course, this was a much more trying experience, for the scene in the gravel pit represented a grotesque desecration that had disturbed the spiritual journey of their ancestors and threatened the spiritual and physical well-being of the living.

While the difficult work of recovery continued in the gravel pit, a battle was raging over continued construction of the parking lot and visitors' center by the Squam Lake Natural Science Center. Given the documented presence of human remains at the Davison Brook site, and the possibility that some of the remains had come from the areas under construction by the science center, Donna Moody requested that all construction by the science center be halted. This request was rejected. On August 2, 2001, Gary Hume, Donna and John Moody, Charlie True, and I met with the director and the board of trustees of the science center. The archaeologists and the Abenaki argued strenuously that additional burials were likely present in the vicinity of the proposed visitors' center and that the ongoing construction should be halted and the proposed visitors' center either canceled or moved to another location. The board rejected our advice, claiming they were unconvinced that burials were present at the visitors' site location. They did agree to have an archaeologist present to monitor the site during removal of topsoil before construction. This monitoring, which was completed in 2001, did not result in the discovery of human remains at the visitors' center location (Goodby et al. 2001).

While the recovery efforts at the gravel pit continued, Abenaki political pressure also began to mount. Daily demonstrations were held at the entrance to the science center in August 2001, and advertisements were placed in local newspapers urging politicians and the public to halt the science center's construction (Figure 7.3). These efforts did not result in a cancellation of construction, and the visitors' center and expanded parking lot were eventually completed. The recovery efforts at the gravel pit concluded in the early autumn of 2001, with all the artifacts and human remains left in the custody of the Abenaki for ultimate reburial. Overall, what was an exceedingly difficult experience for all concerned provided a precedent for sustained cooperation between previously antagonistic parties and brought into being an alliance born of overlapping concerns for archaeological resources and sacred burial grounds.

Smyth Site

The Smyth site is located at Amoskeag Falls in Manchester, a focal point of intensive Native occupation for over 8,000 years and the location of deeply stratified archaeological sites (Dincauze 1976; Foster et al. 1980, 1981). Situated on the eastern bank of the Merrimack River, the site was excavated by separate teams from the New Hampshire Archeological Society (NHAS) and Franklin Pierce College in the late 1960s, before the construction of

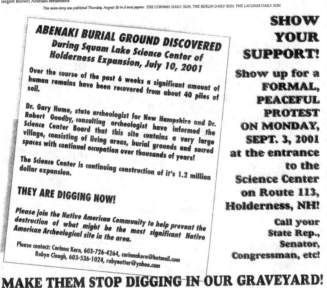

Figure 7.3. Newspaper advertisement protesting Holderness construction (*Conway Daily Sun*).

Amoskeag Bridge. A cremation burial was excavated in the NHAS portion of the site, and students from Franklin Pierce, directed by Howard Sargent, excavated the remains of at least eight other individuals (Foster et al. 1981:41). A report on the NHAS excavations was prepared for the NHDHR in 1980 (Foster et al. 1980). A condensed version of this report published in 1981 by the NHAS (Foster et al. 1981) had only a single paragraph devoted to a discussion of the burials, together with a photograph of a complete adult skeleton in a flexed position. Information from the Franklin Pierce portion of the excavation was not incorporated into these reports, and it remains unanalyzed and unreported at the time of this writing, 35 years after the excavations.

While most of the data from the Franklin Pierce excavations went unanalyzed and unreported, this was not the case with the skeletal remains. L. Cabot Briggs, a colleague of Howard Sargent's affiliated with the Peabody Museum of Archaeology and Ethnology at Harvard University, published a little-known article on them (Briggs 1971). A brief summary of his analysis was included in the 1980 report but was omitted from the 1981 report because "detailed analysis had not been completed" (Foster et al. 1981:41). No data were published on the provenience or nature of these burials, and no documentation on the excavation of these burials was known to exist in Sargent's papers (Wesley Stinson, personal communication 2001). A brief report on the cremation burial excavated by the NHAS was published more than 30 years after its excavation (Winter 1999).

Briggs's analysis provided some basic information on the number, age, and sex of the burials, which he reported to include four adult males, two adult females, "one doubtful," and one infant. In a report replete with antiquated and racist terminology, individual skeletons were described with terms like "eagle beaked," "Negroid," and "ape-like," and he described the group overall as representing "a rather more primitive physical type than I would expect" (Briggs 1971:51).

After Briggs's early and questionable analysis, at least some of the Smyth site remains resided at Franklin Pierce, where they were used as teaching specimens in undergraduate anthropology courses. The inventory of these remains required by NAGPRA, due by 1995, was never submitted. Two of the Smyth site skeletons were turned over to the then state archaeologist Gary Hume in 1997, and he coordinated their repatriation to the Abenaki coalition under NAGPRA. In a 1999 letter to the NAGPRA Review Committee chair at the time, Tesse Naranjo, Hume wrote, "It is our opinion that the human remains . . . are culturally affiliated with the Western Abenaki. We therefore respectfully request you recommend repatriation of the remains in question to a coalition of Western Abenaki groups, as represented by Donna Moody." This request was approved by the Review Committee, and a notice of inventory completion that included these remains was published in the Federal Register on July 9, 2002.

The remains of the other individuals from the site remained unaccounted for until I began a teaching appointment at Franklin Pierce in September 2000. Within 20 minutes of entering my new archaeology_lab, I discovered on the top shelf of a bookcase five large, green, metal open-topped army surplus ammunition boxes that contained remains from five of the burials from the Smyth site, covered with a thick layer of dust. One of the crania had, at some point in the past, been wrapped in synthetic foam padding, which had decayed and adhered to the bone in uneven, sticky patches. Almost all the bones were numbered according to burial, and it was evident that in being used as laboratory props they had become intermingled. Furthermore, the complete skeleton depicted in the photograph in the Foster et al. 1981 report was not included among these remains, nor was it one of the two sets of remains turned over to NHDHR in 1997.

Efforts to repatriate these remains began immediately. On the advice of Donna Moody and Gary Hume, I made a formal request to the NAGPRA Review Committee in September 2001 to have the remains at Franklin Pierce attached to those already submitted to the Review Committee by Gary Hume, so that repatriation to the Abenaki coalition represented by Donna Moody could take place. The request was placed on the agenda of the November 2001 meeting of the NAGPRA Review Committee at Harvard University, but unbeknownst to Donna and me there was a movement underway to thwart the repatriation of these specific remains. Two days before Donna's and my scheduled appearance, I received a call from Mary Downs, assistant to Review Committee chair Armand Minthorn, informing me that our request had been removed from the meeting's agenda. Donna Moody, who had already left for the meeting, received this news when she arrived in Cambridge and immediately began to lobby the Native American committee members for a reversal of the decision. Less than 24 hours after Mary Downs's phone call, she called again to say that our request had been put back on the agenda.

Donna Moody and I presented our request to the NAGPRA Review Committee on November 19, and the committee accepted our request, under four conditions: (1) that an osteological analysis of the remains be conducted and a detailed inventory be submitted to the Review Committee, (2) that copies of the inventory be provided to the Confederated Tribes of

Maine and the Wampanoag Confederation, (3) that both groups provide written concurrence with the proposed disposition, and (4) that a Notice of Inventory Completion be published in the Federal Register. The third condition was frustrating, since representatives of both groups had testified the previous day in support of our request. Waiting for formal letters ultimately delayed the repatriation of the remains by almost a year.

Our removal from the agenda had been the result of intensive lobbying by Wesley Stinson, director of the Sargent Museum of Archeology. As would be made public within a year, Stinson believed that the remains from Amoskeag belonged to Iroquoian peoples, and that analysis of the remains could determine this (Clark 2002a:A1). Stinson requested that the remains from the Smyth site be subjected to CAT scans and other procedures to "give them a face" (Clark 2002b:A16). When his request was denied by newly appointed state archaeologist Richard Boisvert and the Abenaki coalition, Stinson attributed the "tragic loss" of archaeological data to "zealots out there who hate archaeologists, hate everything we do . . . [and] quite frankly just act like terrorists" (Clark 2002b:A16).

All the conditions set forth by the NAGPRA Review Committee for the repatriation of the Smyth site remains were eventually met. A competent, professional osteological analysis was performed (Dhody and Erickson 2001), a summary of which was published in the newsletter of the New Hampshire Archeological Society (Goodby 2002b). When, after the passage of almost a year, the final letter of concurrence was received from the Confederated Tribes of Maine, a Notice of Inventory Completion was published in the Federal Register on April 4, 2003. No Native groups challenged the proposed repatriation, and the remains were subsequently reburied.

Working with the Abenaki: Present and Future

The process of repatriating the Smyth site remains highlights a number of recurrent themes in working with the Abenaki, including gross neglect and mistreatment of Abenaki remains by archaeologists and the questioning of Abenaki legitimacy, due in part to their marginalized status as a non-federally recognized tribe. This marginalization makes it easier for opponents to impede the repatriation process and imposes considerable delays not faced by federally recognized tribes. This marginalization also grants more power to archaeologists to act as either the advocates or the opponents of repatriation.

Despite not being federally recognized, the Abenaki themselves have been agents in reducing their marginalized status. A political and cultural renaissance has been going on among the Abenaki since the 1970s, and the various Abenaki communities have become increasingly visible and outspoken in both New Hampshire and Vermont (Calloway 1989:93–103; Haviland and Power 1994). In October 2002 the Monadnock Institute of Nature, Place, and Culture at Franklin Pierce College held a day-long symposium dedicated to exploring the deep presence of Abenaki people in the Monadnock region. Over 200 people, many of them Abenaki, attended the event, held under a huge tent on a lawn overlooking Pearly Pond. Speakers included Abenaki storyteller and historian Marge Bruchac, Donna and John Moody, Abenaki basket maker Judy Dow, and Don and Beverly Newell of the New Hampshire Intertribal Council. I gave a talk on my archaeological research in the Monadnock Region and my thoughts on the relationship between anthropologists and the Abenaki. Also, I took advantage of the opportunity afforded by the presence of so many Native people to request their help in interpreting some of the patterns I was seeing at archaeological sites.

The Monadnock Institute conference was intended to be a venue for the Abenaki to tell their own story to a large audience and, in so doing, to reverse the traditional pattern in which their history was left to white archaeologists to study and to interpret for the larger public. The presence of many educators from the Monadnock region meant that an Abenaki perspective, and consciousness of the continued presence of Abenaki people, would be taken to a larger audience. The conference set an example of how archaeologists and other academics could empower Native people, not by telling their stories for them as sympathetic outsiders, but by using their resources to create venues where Native people could speak directly to a larger public. The huge turnout for this conference reflected a substantial interest in Abenaki history and culture among the non-Native people of the Monadnock region, and helped put Abenaki perspectives and oral traditions on an equal footing with archaeology and anthropology in a traditional academic setting.

Despite their nonrecognized status, years of effort by the Abenaki have created an informal system of consultation and cooperation that can, in some cases, work very well, as seen with the discovery of Native American remains at a site in Hopkinton in the fall of 2002. While conducting an archaeological survey at a location on the Warner River, students from Franklin Pierce College under my direction discovered human skeletal remains eroding from the riverbank. Following the New Hampshire State law governing the treatment of unmarked burials (RSA 227C-8), the state archaeologist and law enforcement authorities were immediately notified. Once the remains were determined to be, in all likelihood, Native American, State Archaeologist Richard Boisvert took charge of the remains. Within a week, he had arranged for a basic osteological analysis and transferred the remains to Donna Moody, who promptly oversaw their reburial. The entire process was marked by amity, goodwill, and understanding of both the legal statutes and the cultural and spiritual significance of the remains to Abenaki people. This experience showed how the relationships that have developed between archaeologists and Native people, and the trust resulting from shared ordeals such as the recovery effort at Holderness, have become the keys to an emerging understanding of how the Abenaki people can represent themselves and speak for their ancestral remains despite the burdens imposed by a lack of federal recognition. In the end, it is these human relationships, and the goodwill (or lack thereof) among individuals in both the archaeological and Abenaki communities that will determine the future of Abenaki-archaeologist relations in New Hampshire.

Epilogue

On a cool, cloudy day in the summer of 2003, Donna's son Chris and I were part of a small group assembled in a wooded area by a salt marsh. The remains of the people from Seabrook had been carefully placed next to their newly dug graves. A variety of preparations were going on, with the mix of solemnity and informality that has marked all the Abenaki reburials I have attended. All morning, Chris and I had been thinking about our search for these people so many years ago, and thinking how this day marked the end of a sad chapter in Abenaki history, of which we had become a part. Donna looked at me and asked quietly if Chris and I would take the people for a walk. I looked quizzically, first at Chris and then at her, not understanding.

"Their spirits are here," she explained. "Walk with them to the edge of the woods, so they can see the marsh and know that they are home."

Ultimately, to me, that is what repatriation has come to mean.

Acknowledgments

I would like to thank Tracy Botting for her skilled editing and wonderful advice on the writing process, Victoria Bunker for her editorial guidance, Jordan Kerber for his editorial suggestions and patience, Amy McIntyre and James Van Campen for their technical support, Edna Feighner for helping me check my facts, John Moody for all his insights over the years, and my Abenaki friends for their friendship, and for all I have learned from them. I am particularly grateful to my friend Donna Moody for teaching me to see the things that were there all along.

8. Forging New Partnerships
Archaeologists and the Native People of Maryland

RICHARD B. HUGHES AND DIXIE L. HENRY

A s T. J. Ferguson (1996) asserted, archaeologists and American Indians are in the midst of restructuring their relationship with one another in ways that are exciting to some archaeologists and frustrating to others. Both the passage of the Native American Graves Protection and Repatriation Act (NAGPRA) in 1990 and criticism by Native people have led archaeologists to reexamine the epistemological basis of our discipline. This chapter examines the ways in which archaeologists at the Maryland State Historic Preservation Office (SHPO) and Maryland's Native people have joined in subsequent efforts to forge new partnerships and craft the field of archaeology into a discipline that is both acceptable and *relevant* to its multiple constituencies.

In 1987 the discovery of an American Indian burial on the state-owned property of Jefferson Patterson Park and Museum, followed by the discovery of a Late Woodland ossuary on the Eastern Shore of Maryland, prompted the Maryland SHPO and American Indian community members to initiate consultation with one another and to work toward resolving the sensitive issue of how the state should provide for the respectful and appropriate treatment of indigenous human remains that happened to be in the state's possession. As will be discussed below, the consultation process was predictably challenging, complex, and problematical owing to a variety of competing concerns and interests that were brought into the open as archaeologists and Native people struggled to acknowledge each other's beliefs and values. The process was further complicated by the fact that although the 2000 federal census recorded nearly 16,000 American Indians living in the state, there are no American Indian tribes currently residing in Maryland that are state or federally recognized. There are, however, numerous, and sometimes opposing, groups who claim an American Indian identity and maintain that they are, in fact, indigenous to the state. Duane Champagne (1999) has observed that today "native identity is neither homogenous nor taken for granted," and that "contemporary (Native) identity issues . . . are increasingly political and controversial." These observations certainly hold true in Maryland, where at least 12 groups currently assert an identity as "indigenous" Maryland Indian tribes, and some of these groups, such as the three distinct groups who claim Piscataway identity, assert competing claims to the same tribal affiliation.

Despite these often confounding factors of organization and identity, the tireless efforts of the Maryland SHPO, the Council for Maryland Archaeology (CfMA), the Archeological Society of Maryland, Inc. (ASM), the Maryland Commission on Indian Affairs (MCIA), and members of the various American Indian communities eventually led to the passage of legislation in 1992 (Article 83B, Section 5-627), enabling the state to return human remains and funerary objects to those Native groups who are culturally affiliated with the remains. Following the passage of this legislation and the subsequent regulations (Code of Maryland Regulations 05.08.07), American Indians and archaeologists throughout Maryland have continued to seek an ever-expanding cooperative relationship by creating a foundation of mutual (albeit cautious) trust, exchanging information, and working together to address common interests ranging from education to site protection. Our present purpose is to relate and to discuss how this process of collaboration has slowly developed and evolved in Maryland, pointing out the many benefits, pitfalls, and new ideas that have been discovered along the way.

A Rising Discourse

In 1987 the discovery of an American Indian burial within the state-owned Jefferson Patterson Park and Museum property would irrevocably alter the way archaeologists and American Indians in Maryland interact with each other. Before 1987, interaction in Maryland between the two groups could be characterized as infrequent and, with few exceptions, informal. An official state agency, the MCIA, had been established in 1976 by the Maryland General Assembly to represent and further the interests of American Indians in the state. The legislation creating the MCIA (Annotated Code of Maryland: Article 83B, Section 5-403) directed it to undertake activities that could be expected to lead to close interaction with archaeologists and historians, such as "further the understanding of Indian history and culture," "conduct a survey of historic buildings, sites, artifacts, archives and repositories," and "locate, preserve and disseminate information to the public about significant buildings and sites relating to Indian history and culture." Yet for most of the years before 1987, formal interaction between Maryland's professional archaeological community, the MCIA, and individual Indian groups remained infrequent, and when it did occur, it focused almost exclusively on issues surrounding the treatment of American Indian burials and human remains—an area that continues to serve as a nexus between the two groups.

State government archaeology programs, of which there were two before a merger within the Maryland SHPO in 1991, were under no statutory obligation to consult with the MCIA or the Indian community, and records indicate that very little official interaction took place. On the federal level, the Advisory Council on Historic Preservation (ACHP) placed special attention on ensuring that Indian tribes were full participants in reviews done under Section 106 of the National Historic Preservation Act when it revised its regulations in 1986 (ACHP 1986). However, federal actions such as these had little to no direct effect in Maryland, since consultation was only required with federally recognized tribes, none of which resided in Maryland. Nonetheless, the relationship between archaeologists and American Indians in Maryland would be significantly affected as American Indians nationwide reasserted their identity and successfully worked to ensure that their voices would be heard.

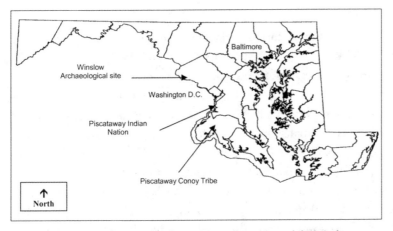

Figure 8.1. Location of Piscataway Indian communities and the Winslow
site in Maryland (Prepared by Richard Hughes).

As elsewhere in the nation, Indians in Maryland have increasingly de-
manded recognition of their Indian identity, not only by the public but
by the government as well. In 1979, for example, the Piscataway Indians
successfully lobbied for passage of a federal law allowing Turkey Tayac,
the first modern chief of the Piscataway Indians, to be buried within Piscataway National Park, where at least four large Piscataway ossuary burials were excavated in the 1930s (Curry 1999). Maryland Indians also increasingly asserted their right not only to be consulted but also to be the
decision makers on some issues, particularly when human remains were
involved.

Maryland archaeologists were well aware of this rising national discourse, and of the growing voice of the state's own Indian population,
and some efforts at opening a broader dialogue with the Indian community on issues of common interest were made. Among the most notable of
these efforts was Paul Cissna's (1986) dissertation research among the Piscataway Indian Nation of southern Maryland (Figure 8.1). Another effort
to broaden the dialogue occurred in November 1986. In response to an
MCIA inquiry regarding artifacts from an excavation on federal land, the
SHPO archaeologist, Richard Hughes, responded that the MCIA's inquiry
had implications beyond this particular site, and he invited the MCIA to
open a discussion on this and related issues with the SHPO and with the
broader archaeological community.

These tentative efforts at dialogue and collaboration were soon greatly expanded in July 1987 when an American Indian burial was discovered on state-owned property. Stimulated by this discovery, Maryland archaeologists and American Indians began meeting regularly for the first time to discuss an issue of common concern—the treatment of American Indian burials and human remains—and to collaborate on the development of a common policy dealing with this sensitive issue. Interaction became increasingly regularized and formal, as demonstrated by the creation of the Indian Burial Policy Committee, with membership drawn from both the archaeological and Indian communities. Efforts to create a common policy on the treatment of Indian burials, however, were not to be completed before a second inadvertent discovery of remains was made in April 1989 when a Late Woodland ossuary burial was revealed during construction of a private home on Maryland's Eastern Shore.

The discovery of this ossuary and its subsequent excavation by Maryland SHPO archaeologists provided a catalyst that would lead to an often confrontational expansion of archaeologist and American Indian interaction and place it on the pages of some of the nation's most prominent newspapers, the *Washington Post* and the *Baltimore Sun* (see Ehrlich 1989; Shen 1989). While certainly not the only factor at work, this inadvertent discovery directly contributed to the passage of the state's first repatriation law, and it also helped to clarify for both archaeologists and American Indians in Maryland that interaction and (whenever possible) collaboration on issues of vital common interest were no longer an option but a necessity.

In previous years, the SHPO's decision to excavate the threatened ossuary would most likely have been taken without involving or even informing the Indian community, but in the new atmosphere of collaboration, one of SHPO's first actions was to inform the MCIA of the discovery and to seek their input. Until this point, the archaeological and Indian communities had been in general agreement on how to proceed, but once these two burials were recovered, the two groups could no longer agree on a mutually acceptable course of action. Indians called for immediate reburial, while most archaeologists insisted that proper scientific examination and analysis be conducted. Many archaeologists also strongly opposed any notion of reburial.

As the debate escalated and was increasingly played out in the media, the SHPO and MCIA negotiated an agreement to allow for the study of the skeletal remains by a physical anthropologist, followed by reburial. The negotiation process was difficult and often acrimonious, and in the end neither group felt the outcome was satisfactory. The process did, however, serve to reinforce the ever-growing realization that the relationship between archaeologists and American Indians in Maryland had fundamentally changed. It also led each group to realize more than ever that issues of common interest—such as the need to establish a working process for state recognition of Maryland Indian tribes, the need for an agreed-upon repatriation process, and the definition of a process for determining when and how archaeology and other scientific studies could be undertaken— had to be addressed not only at the policy level but at the legislative and political levels. Political pressure from the Indian community for a state tribal recognition process had resulted in the passage of the Recognition of Maryland Indian Status Act in 1988 (Annotated Code of Maryland, Article 83B, Section 5-406). However, development of required regulations to implement the new law had languished and would not be put in place until 1992. In that same year, the SHPO introduced a bill in the state legislature to allow for the repatriation of American Indian human remains in state-held collections to "culturally affiliated" Indian groups, a concept and term borrowed from the federal NAGPRA. Although the legislation was controversial in its attempt to strike a balance between the Indian community's desire for reburial and most archaeologists' wish to preserve some ability to study human remains, the Transfer of Human Remains Act (Annotated Code of Maryland, Article 83B, Section 6-627 [b–d]) was enacted that year.

Some of the issues that have continued to figure prominently in the interactions of archaeologists and Indians in Maryland were clearly defined at this time. For American Indians, the greatest issue facing them in Maryland is the lack of official government recognition of their status as "Indians." This issue, in turn, leads to still further unanswered questions, such as who or what entities are legitimate representatives of Native people, could the MCIA be seen as fulfilling that role, and if there are no groups unequivocally recognized as "Indian," how can a group be determined to be "culturally affiliated" with remains and therefore an eligible claimant or recipient of repatriated remains? For archaeologists, the very legitimacy of their discipline was called into question, since they were often portrayed as uncaring despoilers bent on looting the bones and sacred objects of the ancestors from the graves of Native people. Even the way archaeologists defined themselves was publicly called into question when a leader of the Piscataway Indians stated in a public meeting that she saw archaeologists as nothing more than "pothunters with degrees."

Passage in November 1990 of NAGPRA, followed two years later by enactment of a Maryland repatriation law modeled closely on the federal statute, further spurred the growing, if often difficult, interaction between archaeologists and American Indians in Maryland. In an attempt to overcome the challenges outlined above, the SHPO and various archaeological organizations have increasingly relied on the MCIA as the principal point of contact with Maryland's Indian communities. Predictably, this practice has met with only partial success. The arrangement places a grueling burden on the MCIA by asking the commission to provide representation for an extremely diverse, fluid, and often fractious Indian population. In the midst of the competition between the various Indian groups, the MCIA itself, as a government agency, has frequently been accused of being too constrained by official state policies and not representing the full range of Indian interests or entities in Maryland.

In an attempt to avoid the pitfalls of working only with the MCIA, the SHPO and others in the archaeological profession have tried to interact directly with specific, known Indian groups, particularly when an archaeological project was located in the group's perceived home territory. The experience with this type of direct interaction has generally not been positive. Competing Indian groups resent archaeologists interacting with other groups that they view as interlopers, and groups that are not included in the consultation process often feel betrayed and marginalized and view archaeologists as favoring one group over another.

It has become evident that interaction must occur on multiple levels and within a structure that is clearly recognized by all parties. To broaden and regularize the dialogue between American Indians and archaeologists, both the MCIA and the CfMA have established standing liaison committees (the Archeological and Historical Liaison Committee and the Native American Liaison Committee, respectively) to deal with issues of common interest. These committees have been largely successful, although some difficulties have arisen, for example, when the two committees attempted to compile a list of regional Indian contacts and were presented with conflicting information and advice from the various competing Indian communities. While some of these problems could also occur in the case of recognized tribes, the lack of recognized entities undoubtedly makes consultation a more difficult process.

Ultimately, the lack of recognized tribes has had a clear, and mostly negative, effect in Maryland whenever archaeologists and Indian people attempt to address the recurring issue of the repatriation of human remains and cultural items. Implementation of NAGPRA has proved difficult owing to the current federal policy of defining an American Indian tribe as a group that is recognized by the federal government. While NAGPRA does not prohibit repatriation to nonrecognized groups, it does little to facilitate such actions (see Watkins's foreword, this volume). The central tenet of repatriation under NAGPRA is the demonstration of a group's "cultural affiliation" with claimed remains and objects. This is a difficult challenge for a group that has been unsuccessful in even gaining official recognition of its American Indian identity. In Maryland, some effort has recently been made to identify out-of-state federally recognized tribes that might present a valid repatriation claim by demonstrating cultural affiliation to remains from Maryland. This is conceivable, since portions of a number of tribes, such as the Piscataway and Nanticoke, left Maryland and eventually merged into Iroquoian groups now living in New York and Canada. Local Indian groups, however, tend to resent these overtures toward outside groups and see them as an attempt to denigrate or dismiss their own claims of American Indian identity. More research in this regard needs to be done—research that could potentially aid Maryland groups in obtaining the historical documentation needed to support their state and federal recognition petitions.

"This Is Not a One-Way Thing"

It is clear and undeniable that the processes of opening the lines of communication between the state's archaeologists and Native people and establishing the state repatriation law and regulations have often been difficult and fraught with painful misperceptions. These processes *have*, however, succeeded in laying a solid foundation for the ever-evolving relationship between archaeologists and Maryland's Indian people, and they have established an ongoing dialogue that has led to an increased level of cooperation and mutual respect, as well as the development of collaborative projects ranging from site protection to cosponsored powwows. Two years ago, for example, the director of the Piscataway Indian Museum, Natalie Proctor, contacted the MCIA and the SHPO to inquire about possible site visits that might be available to Piscataway youth and other community members. She discussed how for many years her people had been completely opposed to any and all archaeology, fearing that archaeologists were simply out to "dig up" the remains of their ancestors. She suggested that perhaps it would be beneficial at this time to learn more about the role and purpose of archaeology, to learn more about how archaeology is done, and to learn more about the past ways of life of her Piscataway ancestors as their story is told through the archaeological record.

State Terrestrial Archeologist Charlie Hall and Preservation Officer Dixie Henry (who was then serving as the administrator of the MCIA) accepted Natalie's invitation to come to the community's cultural center in Waldorf to talk about issues ranging from the importance of "context" to the variety of threats currently facing archaeological sites throughout the country. The ensuing discussion was extraordinary as community members of all ages asked the state archaeologists questions about basic archaeological field methods, the history of American archaeology, and ongoing research agendas, while also taking advantage of the opportunity to express their various concerns and perceptions regarding both the discipline and its practitioners. The discussion was fun, exciting, dynamic, and revealing, and plans are now being made to bring a group of Piscataway youth and their families to a site where they can observe and participate in archaeological investigations that are currently underway.

There are other signs, of course, that both archaeologists and Indian people in Maryland are in the process of building bridges to span the distance that has existed between them for far too long. The MCIA, for example, has begun to sponsor an annual American Indian Heritage Month symposium in November, bringing together Indian people, students, teachers, historians, and archaeologists to discuss topics ranging from the prehistory of western Maryland to the ever-increasing need for multicultural education. As mentioned earlier, the MCIA has also established the Archaeological and Historical Liaison Committee (AHLC), whose role, as it is laid out in the MCIA bylaws, is to coordinate projects that will further the understanding of Indian history and culture; develop solid relationships with the SHPO, CfMA, and ASM; and assist the SHPO in developing an effective policy for protecting American Indian human remains throughout the state. After being dormant for several years, the AHLC has been resurrected, and Gina Hamlin, the current chair of the MCIA, has stepped forward to chair this committee as well and to appoint new committee members. Already the AHLC has begun to work in concert with CfMA in revising the protocol for managing unanticipated discoveries of indigenous human remains, and in designing a brochure aimed at increasing public awareness of the need to protect archaeological sites (particularly those with a high potential of containing interred human remains) from vandalism and looting. During the summer of 2003, the AHLC also helped to coordinate the Common Ground Powwow in Charles County—an event that was designed in part to bring together archaeologists from across the state and people from all of Maryland's Indian communities.

Perhaps the most poignant example of how the ongoing dialogue between archaeologists and Maryland's Indian people has led to an increased level of cooperation can be glimpsed in the collaborative efforts and interactions that took place during the spring of 2003 when American Indian human remains were inadvertently discovered during the excavation of a prehistoric village site (the Winslow site) located along the Potomac River in southwestern Montgomery County. The Winslow site (18MO9) was discovered in 1934 by two local avocational archaeologists, Richard Slattery and Hugh Stabler (Dent 2003). Their early investigations, conducted during the 1940s and 1950s, resulted in the mapping of several features, including 15 human burials, four canine burials, a semicircular arrangement of refuse pits, and 168 post molds, as well as the recovery of a substantial collection of artifacts ranging from triangular quartz projectile points to Shepardware ceramics (Slattery and Woodward 1992). In the spring of 2002, archaeologists returned to the Winslow site to resume excavations in a cooperative effort between the Potomac River Archaeology Survey, the Maryland SHPO, and ASM. The site has in fact served as the location for ASM's annual summer field session in both 2002 and 2003, providing an opportunity to pursue questions regarding the physical features of the village, the subsistence practices of its occupants, and its relation to other nearby sites along the Potomac.

In May 2003 archaeologists suddenly came upon some human remains (two teeth and a long bone) while screening the plow zone level of a unit that had been opened in the hopes of revealing additional post molds associated with a circular structure. Principal Investigator Richard J. (Joe) Dent promptly contacted Charlie Hall at the SHPO, who indicated that excavation of the unit should cease immediately and the remains be covered. Hall also notified the SHPO's Office of Archeology chief Richard Hughes, who then contacted MCIA administrator Suzanne Almalel and MCIA chair Gina Hamlin, in an effort to determine how the MCIA would like the archaeological team to proceed with the treatment and protection of the remains. Hamlin, in turn, made contact with Piscataway Conoy chairwoman Mervin Savoy, since the remains had been uncovered in a part of Maryland that is believed by many Piscataway people to have once been occupied by their ancestors. Several key issues and questions were raised and addressed during these initial consultations. What, for example, should the next course of action be? Should the remains be moved to a more secure area or be left where they were found? Should any level of study be conducted to determine the age and nature of the interment and its relation (if any) to the nearby line of post molds? Could members of the Piscataway Indian community possibly be culturally affiliated with the remains, and would they want to visit the site before any decisions were made regarding the treatment of the remains?

Decisions had to be made fairly quickly, since the time during which we would have access to the Winslow site was rapidly coming to an end, and before long it was determined that representatives from the Office of Archeology, from the MCIA, and from the Piscataway Conoy community would go to the site together and discuss possible courses of action with the site's principal investigator, Joe Dent. SHPO staff members Hughes, Hall, and Dennis Curry, MCIA administrator Almalel, MCIA chair Hamlin (accompanied by her husband, Guy Wells), and Piscataway Conoy members Savoy and Rico Newman met Dent at the site, and he talked to the group about the age and possible size of the site, the different activities in which Indian people may have been engaged while living there, and the possible relationship between the site and other villages located along the Potomac. Dent then described how the excavation was being conducted and how the human remains had been discovered. While emphasizing that he and the SHPO archaeologists were prepared to adhere to whatever decision was made by the MCIA and the community members, Dent cautiously asked whether it would be acceptable and appropriate for a small team of professional archaeologists to spend just two days uncovering the interment (with minimal disturbance) in order to observe the remains in relation to the nearby post molds and to collect some basic data regarding the sex and age of the individual. The remains could then be left in place and reburied. Dent responded to some questions concerning the proposed methodology and reiterated that the archaeological team was committed to accepting whatever decision was made. The representatives from the MCIA and the Piscataway Conoy community were then left to talk among themselves and arrive at a decision.

It was not long before a decision was made, and it was agreed that limited research could be conducted with the understanding that (1) a limited number of qualified individuals would be involved in the process; (2) the study would be done in a sensitive and respectful manner, and the MCIA would be notified of the results; (3) a minimal number of photographs would be taken and would not be made available to the public; (4) no media would be involved; and (5) the remains would be carefully reburied to prevent further disturbance, and members of the Indian community would be given the opportunity to return to the site and conduct a ceremony in an effort to ensure that the remains were, once again, at rest. Later that day, Hall turned to Hamlin and said, "I'm really glad that we're talking," and Hamlin responded, "That's why we're here."

Once the remains were uncovered, physical anthropologists from the Smithsonian Institution came to the site to examine the interment and found that the remains were those of a petite young woman who had given birth shortly before she died and was buried in a flexed position with no accompanying burial goods. After the woman's remains were reburied, we spoke with Almalel and Hamlin to determine how the consultation process and the treatment of the remains had been perceived by the MCIA and by the Indian community. Almalel (personal communication 2003) stated that the commission saw the entire process as a positive step toward more-effective communication between archaeologists and Maryland's Native people and as an example of how more and more archaeologists were beginning to respect the wishes and values of Indian communities. She observed that many community members were cautiously becoming more comfortable with individual archaeologists and with the field of archaeology in general, and that recent demonstrations of growing respect and sensitivity on the part of some archaeologists have led some Native people to view archaeologists as potential allies in the struggle to protect the village sites and unmarked graves of their ancestors.

Similarly, Hamlin noted that she was "positively impressed" by the care that had been taken by archaeologists to be respectful of the remains found at the Winslow site, and that she and Savoy had been particularly pleased that Hughes had come to the MCIA and the community to ask (rather than to inform) the commissioners and community members about what course of action should be taken. While acknowledging that the relationship between archaeologists and Maryland's Native people has in the past been marked by distrust and a severe lack of communication, Hamlin feels that the various parties are beginning to listen to and learn from one another. "So much of our culture has been lost," says Hamlin (personal communication 2003), "that we have to depend to a certain degree on archaeology to help us preserve our past and our culture, and this is not a one-way thing. We have to talk to each other and learn from each other and *with* each other in a respectful way." In the case of the Winslow site, "everyone is pleased," says Hamlin.

The community appreciated the reverence and respect that was demonstrated by the archaeologists, and they are waiting almost breathlessly for the site report so that they may learn more about how these people lived—these people who may very well have been their ancestors. *Listening* is what made the difference here [Hamlin, personal communication 2003].

State Terrestrial Archeologist Charlie Hall is also pleased with how the consultation progressed once the remains were discovered:

We recognized that they (the Indian community) had a higher moral authority to determine how the remains should be treated, but at the same time, we learned that we don't have to be ashamed of our interests as archaeologists and that our interests are not always in conflict with those of American Indian people. The best we can do is present ourselves honestly and listen, and be willing to compromise and accept values and decisions that may run counter to our own [Hall, personal communication 2003].

A Common Endeavor

In many ways the discovery of the remains at the Winslow site and the ensuing consultation, brief study, and reburial illustrate several of the benefits *and* challenges being encountered throughout the country as archaeologists and Native people work toward more-collaborative relationships. On the one hand, both archaeologists and Indian people stand to benefit greatly and to learn much by working together more closely. Archaeological data, after all, offer yet another window into a people's past, particularly for those groups who are striving to reinvigorate their cultural identity but have lost significant portions of their cultural knowledge owing to a variety of historic processes, ranging from population decline to racial segregation. Indian people also stand to gain the support of strong and dedicated allies within the archaeological community who have the ability and desire to lend their support on a variety of issues that go beyond the protection of archaeological sites, such as state and federal recognition and multicultural education. In fact, while we were in the process of writing this chapter, Maryland governor Robert L. Ehrlich Jr. (2003) made a determination on the Piscataway Conoy Tribe's petition for recognition of Maryland Indian status, which had been submitted for review in 1995, stating that the petition did not "meet the criteria established for a tribe to be recognized under the Maryland recognition statute as a Native American group indigenous to Maryland." This decision was a severe disappointment to the Piscataway Conoy community and effectively prohibits the repatriation of any human remains or cultural materials to this particular community. Hamlin has suggested that it is now more important than ever for Maryland's archaeologists and Indian people to develop a cooperative relationship in an effort to retrieve more information about the past and to preserve that portion of the Piscataway Conoy's cultural heritage that is found in the archaeological record.

Maryland archaeologists, in turn, are beginning to recognize that archaeologists and Native people often view the past in fundamentally different and equally valid ways, and as a result, many are working to develop a more multitiered methodology that can incorporate the use of several approaches, including oral tradition. Coordinating with Indian communities often adds a much-needed humanistic dimension to archaeological research as well, compelling archaeologists to acknowledge that the sites they are excavating are frequently the cultural heritage of *living* Native communities, and that these communities often have strong connections not only to the interred remains of their ancestors but also to the sites themselves. Consequently, archaeologists are beginning to attain a more complete understanding of the various concerns and viewpoints of Indian people regarding the role of archaeology in the investigation and portrayal of their people's history, and many are finding themselves able to adopt a broader perspective and to consider alternative interpretations of the archaeological record.

As discussed above, a number of daunting challenges and dangerous pitfalls have been encountered by both Maryland's archaeologists and Native people as they have struggled to adopt these broader perspectives and to communicate with one another over the past several years. We have recounted how competing Indian groups often resent archaeologists interacting with other groups that they view as interlopers, and how groups that are not included in the consultation process may feel betrayed and marginalized. In Maryland, in fact, much of the direct consultation with nonrecognized groups has resulted in increased intergroup competition and the perpetuation of the view that archaeologists are favoring one group over another. This has been a particularly difficult obstacle for the SHPO, since interaction with one particular group can be (and has been) construed by other Indian communities as tacit state recognition. Other challenges include the risk of confrontational dialogue; the tendency not to separate the issues of repatriation and reburial from other issues (such as site protection and public education), which can obscure the common interests and goals shared by archaeologists and Indian groups; and the constant need to be willing to compromise, which can make either party feel like they are "selling out" and relinquishing control.

Despite these and other challenges, many feel that the relationship between Maryland's archaeologists and Indian communities is moving in a positive direction as lines of communication continue to be opened and maintained. There are several steps that can be taken to ensure that these lines remain open and that even more successful collaboration can occur in the future. As Nina Versaggi (this volume) has noted, there is no cookbook approach to consultation. Joe Watkins (2000a), however, has effectively summarized a number of strategies and approaches that can be used to facilitate more-effectual communication and collaboration.

First and foremost, of course, is the need for *education*. Archaeologists must be sure to educate affected cultural groups about a project so that "they can have an informed understanding of the reasons for the project, the types of information being sought, and the implications and utility of the study to the group studied and to archaeology" (Watkins 2000a:171). In turn, American Indian communities must also engage in educating archaeologists about their own wishes and values, clearly defining the ways in which they may want to be involved in the project, the types of information they themselves hope to obtain, and the types of information they feel should be protected and not released to the general public. This need for mutual education has also been acknowledged by Hamlin and Hall, who have urged both archaeologists and American Indian communities to communicate clearly with one another, to take the time to listen to one another, to engage in face-to-face dialogue, and not to make false assumptions about the goals or concerns of either party. In addition to working toward this goal of reciprocal education, Watkins (2000a) also recommends that archaeologists form partnerships with American Indian groups that go beyond archaeological projects, develop decision-making and conflict-resolving mechanisms in consultation with Indian communities, and strive to be aware of the diverse social, political, and economic issues currently affecting Indian people.

Our experiences in Maryland have shown that consistent attention to these recommendations can, indeed, lead to fewer conflicts and more-productive relations, pointing us toward one of the most clear and visible benefits of close collaboration—shared stewardship of cultural resources. We would like to refer once again to Ferguson (1996), who has pointed out that American Indians are stewards of the archaeological record because it is their ancestral legacy, while archaeologists are also stewards because they want to protect the archaeological record as a source of information. More and more archaeologists in Maryland are becoming aware that they are not the only source of protection for archaeological sites, and while the definitions of "protection" and "destruction" are often different because they are culturally defined, both archaeologists and Native people are recognizing a common desire to protect sites from "*unnecessary* or unwarranted destruction from all sources" (Watkins 2000a:172). It is this common endeavor of seeking to know and to protect the past that will enable archaeologists and American Indians in Maryland to continue to build a relationship based on mutual respect and trust. By establishing and building on these cooperative relationships, we can exchange valuable knowledge and act as powerful allies in efforts to preserve archaeological resources from looting and development. In Maryland and elsewhere, it is this shared stewardship that will serve as the foundation for future relations between archaeologists and indigenous people.

Collaboration and Regulatory Compliance
Sites and Places

9. Highway Archaeology in Western New York
Archaeologists' Views of Cooperation between State and Tribal Review Agencies

ROBERT L. DEAN AND DOUGLAS J. PERRELLI

Introduction

The practice of contract archaeology in western New York State has changed dramatically over the last 10 years. Changes are due to numerous factors, mainly the adoption of more rigorous statewide standards for conducting and reporting archaeological investigations, and the inclusion of Native American groups in this process. The formal adoption of the New York Archaeological Council (NYAC 1994) standards by the State Office of Parks, Recreation, and Historic Preservation (OPRHP) and the New York State Museum/State Education Department (NYSM/NYSED) has greatly improved the quality and consistency of work conducted across the state. In addition, the Native American Graves Protection and Repatriation Act (NAGPRA) and the subsequent creation and recognition of the Seneca Nation of Indians (SNI) Tribal Historic Preservation Office (THPO) in 2001 changed the complexion of cultural resource management (CRM) in western New York and elsewhere.[1]

The existence of NAGPRA and the SNI THPO adds an important (and sometimes uneasy) step in the local compliance process, because in cases where state or federally funded projects have an impact on tribal land,

NAGPRA and the THPO combine to add a review agency like the OPRHP and NYSM to the complex process of compliance. The footing can be uneasy because the agencies involved are unaccustomed to cooperative interaction in the rarefied atmosphere of state and tribal politics. Another factor is the different levels of experience of state and tribal compliance officers. These factors have pushed CRM archaeology to the forefront of cooperation and conflict between sovereign nations and state review agencies where archaeologists often act as mediators.

In recent years, the New York State Department of Transportation (NYSDOT) and NYSM have taken the lead in cooperating and consulting with the THPO—with the help of state university–based CRM firms in New York. The State University at Buffalo (UB) Archaeological Survey has been conducting CRM projects in western New York for over 30 years. Today, there is good cooperation in the implementing of highway archaeology projects in western New York. Still there are misunderstandings between bureaucracies. One group tends to be unsure of how another operates and what their respective roles are. Often there are uncertainties about who has the authority to make and to enforce decisions about projects, sites, and collections.

As archaeologists representing the SNI (Dean) and the UB Archaeological Survey (Perrelli), we act as facilitators of communication and consensus between the NYSM and NYSDOT. Robert Dean is an enrolled member of the SNI, a member of the Wolf Clan, and lives on the Allegany Reservation near Steamburg, New York. He is president of Heritage Preservation and Interpretation, Inc., a CRM firm, and serves as a consultant to the SNI THPO on all archaeological matters within the tribe's aboriginal territory. He has also acted as a principal representative and monitor on most projects that have been performed by the UB Archaeological Survey on and near the Allegany and Cattaraugus reservations in western New York (Figure 9.1). Douglas Perrelli is director of the UB Archaeological Survey. The survey performs most of the highway archaeology work for NYSDOT Region 5, along with numerous other projects throughout the region.

Together we are uniquely aware of perceptions held by different individuals and organizations and of the compliance process at the local and state levels. We are happy to collaborate and to provide insights into these

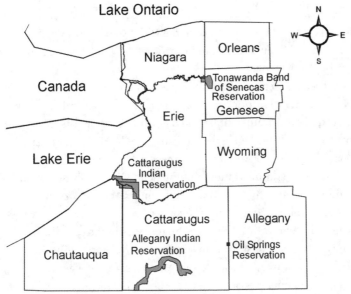

Lake Ontario

Canada

Niagara

Orleans

Tonawanda Band
of Senecas
Reservation

Erie

Genesee

Lake Erie

Cattaraugus
Indian
Reservation

Wyoming

Cattaraugus

Allegany

Chautauqua

Allegany Indian
Reservation

Oil Springs
Reservation

NYSDOT Region 5 includes Niagara, Erie, Chautauqua and Cattaraugus Counties

0 5 10   20 Miles

Figure 9.1. Map of western New York State counties and Seneca Nation reservations
(Prepared by Mary Perrelli).

issues. This chapter outlines the development of CRM and highway archaeology from a western New York perspective, and introduces the UB Archaeological Survey and SNI THPO. The case studies presented here serve to explain the process of collaboration between Seneca and UB archaeologists
during the implementation of highway archaeology projects.

Highway Archaeology in Western New York

The history of highway archaeology in western New York began in 1963
when, following the Federal Highway Act of 1956 and other authorizing
state legislation (1945, 1958), the New York State Education and Public
Works departments partnered to begin a highway salvage archaeology
program. The NYSM and Science Service, as part of the NYSED, implements
this program for state agencies such as the NYSDOT. Cooperation with state
universities was characteristic of the program since its inception (White
1970:1). Early in the program (1963–1968), the UB Archaeological Survey
performed the majority of highway archaeology projects in New York.

133

More recently, the workload is shared with two other universities—Binghamton and Stony Brook—and Binghamton's Public Archaeology Facility directs the program.

Subsequent legislation including NAGPRA (1966, Section 106) and the New York State Historic Preservation Act (1980) further directed the Federal Highway Administration and NYSDOT to consider the effects of roadwork on sites listed, or eligible for listing, in the National Register of Historic Places. Compliance requires the NYSDOT to provide information to the highway administration and the State Historic Preservation Office (SHPO) for federally funded projects, and to the SHPO/OPRHP for state-funded projects. To do this, the NYSDOT hires the NYSM to oversee the statewide Highway Archaeology Program. As in the past, the NYSM hires university-based CRM firms to share the work. Starting in 1990, NAGPRA legislated consultation with Native American groups when highway projects locate human remains, funerary and other sacred objects, or objects of cultural patrimony on federal or tribal lands. Compliance with this law has also been shown to apply to research conducted on nonfederal or nontribal lands as well, if the work has some level of federal funding.

The UB Archaeological Survey

The UB Archaeological Survey is a not-for-profit research, contracting, and applied archaeology division of the Department of Anthropology at UB. The program was created in 1963 by Marian White, who was a staunch proponent of historic preservation and CRM archaeology. The publication series Reports of the Archaeological Survey was established in her memory in 1976 by then survey director Neal Trubowitz. The series presents the results of the survey's research and contract projects. In addition to publishing numerous CRM reports every year, the survey staff present findings to local community organizations and at professional meetings, reaching other audiences through public outreach and community access programs. The primary function of the survey is to implement the Highway Archaeology Program for NYSDOT Region 5 in western New York.

The SNI THPO

The members of the SNI have maintained an interest in regional history and prehistory that predates the establishment of modern archaeology.

Until recent years, it was common for elder members of several communities to return to former village sites and other habitations to remember the people who had lived at these places and who were buried there. There have also been many instances of archaeological investigation, professional and avocational, conducted on and near reservation lands, and many Seneca people have contributed their knowledge and assistance to these projects. In other cases, proposed or active archaeological research has been opposed by the Seneca people, but their concerns were not always taken into consideration.

It was not until 1986 that the SNI Tribal Council formally established procedures for allowing archaeologists and other researchers to conduct projects on reservation land. That document (Seneca Nation of Indians 1986; see Appendix 1 below) recognized that the SNI could not impose regulations in areas outside the boundaries of the existing reservations, but suggested that researchers take the wishes of the SNI into consideration and outlined basic procedures for research. The document also recognized that when projects were conducted on federal and state lands, some protection was afforded to cultural resources through existing legislation. Before the establishment of the THPO, all archaeological research projects were reviewed by the Seneca Iroquois National Museum and forwarded to the SNI Tribal Council, whose members voted whether to approve the proposal. A resolution was then adopted to allow the research to proceed. The archaeological research policy document has recently been amended to incorporate changes resulting from the establishment of the THPO. Most of the changes to the text simply indicate that the THPO has responsibility for issues pertaining to cultural resources and traditional cultural properties.

The SNI THPO was established in September 2001, and Kathleen Mitchell was appointed tribal historic preservation officer. The THPO has assumed responsibility for all matters relating to cultural resources and traditional cultural properties within the aboriginal territory of the Seneca Nation. This includes all of western New York west of the lands between Seneca and Cayuga lakes, many of the counties of northwestern and western Pennsylvania, and several counties in West Virginia and eastern Ohio. Interaction between the THPO and the UB Archaeological Survey have been limited to archaeological surveys conducted for road and bridge renovations on the Cattaraugus and Allegany reservations (Figure 9.1).

A Tale of Two Archaeologists

Through a mutual acquaintance, Perrelli met Dean and began working part-time as an archaeological field assistant around 1985. The authors began working together more regularly in 1987 after Perrelli graduated from the State University of New York at Geneseo. Robert Dean was directing cultural resource surveys mainly in the Allegheny National Forest, in Pennsylvania, and in western New York as co-principal investigator of a private CRM company. Dean continued to work under contract in the Allegheny National Forest through 1989. When the forest contract lapsed, Perrelli sought work at the UB Archaeological Survey, directing his first small project in April 1989. He began graduate school at UB in 1992, obtaining advanced degrees in 1994 and 2001.

Years earlier, Dean too had worked for the UB Archaeological Survey and attended graduate school at UB. He worked with Marian White in the 1970s and obtained his M.A. degree from UB in 1978. Between 1973 and 1983, he was involved with the department's archaeological field school (1973–1975) and the Highway Archaeology Program, and was a research assistant assigned to the archaeology lab and collections.

Over the course of a few years, interactions between Dean and Perrelli led to considerable understanding between the two, and the sharing of many professional goals and interests.

Case Studies in Cooperation

The first large-scale, formal interactions between the UB Archaeological Survey and the SNI in terms of highway archaeology began in 1997, before the creation of the THPO. A series of bridge replacement projects located on and adjacent to the Allegany Reservation in Cattaraugus County was proposed by the NYSDOT. Cultural resource surveys for these projects were implemented, on behalf of the NYSM and NYSDOT, by the Archaeological Survey with permission from the SNI, achieved through communication and cooperation between archaeological representatives Dean and Perrelli.

The process began when the NYSDOT and NYSM/NYSED provided the survey and SNI with preliminary information about the projects. After conversations with Dean and Perrelli regarding project details, archaeological potential, fieldwork strategies, and scheduling, the survey director contacted the sni transportation manager to request permission to perform the work on reservation land. Having agreed to several stipulations, the survey director received written permission to perform the work, as granted by an sni Tribal Council vote at a monthly meeting. Typically, the sni requests that a Seneca archaeological monitor be present for all fieldwork. Further, the sni has the right to keep artifacts and information obtained from reservation projects. In some cases, the thpo requests artifacts and information from nontribal land. Finally, project reports are requested so that the sni has the opportunity to review and comment on reports.

The sni typically allowed a limited amount of time for projects conducted on reservation land. Tribal Council approval was generally granted for one year on a project-by-project basis. This could be a problem, since projects have a way of taking longer than expected, particularly when new sites are located and additional phases of investigation are needed. Fortunately, requests for extensions of project deadlines were routinely granted, thanks to open lines of communication about schedules and findings. This cooperative interaction naturally served as a model for future interaction.

More-recent collaborations between the sni and the Archaeological Survey are more formalized owing to the existence of the thpo, but are still based on the trust and cooperation that stems from interaction between archaeologists. Two case studies serve as examples of the collaboration process involving ub and the thpo in the context of highway archaeology.

Vandalia Bridge Project

The Vandalia Bridge project was initiated shortly after the first series of bridge replacements associated with the Allegany Reservation (Perrelli et al. 1998). The project was particularly interesting for a number of reasons. First, prehistoric sites were located, which necessitated additional investigation phases. The project was also going on when the sni was creating the thpo. Further, it was a special case in that half the project area was located on the Allegany Reservation, and half in the town of Allegany, Cattaraugus County, New York.

The limits of the project area were defined in 1998 in consultation with NYSDOT Region 5. Permission for the initial reconnaissance survey was obtained through formal request and SNI Tribal Council approval. As part of the Highway Archaeology Program administered through the NYSM, all aspects of the investigation were to conform to the NYSED *Work Scope Specifications for Cultural Resource Investigations*, formally adopted in 1998. An initial conflict arose during the planning for the project when Dean, on behalf of the SNI, pointed out that the standards required for archaeological field investigations done on reservation lands were slightly different from those for off-reservation areas. Work done on Seneca Nation lands must generally conform to the 1994 NYAC standards. The exceptions relate specifically to shovel testing, where the SNI standards mirror those used in Pennsylvania: shovel tests must be 50-cm square and must be excavated at no greater than 10-m intervals. Compared to NYSED regulations, this standard provided more intensive coverage, at correspondingly greater expense to the highway program. The potential costs and benefits of the proposed changes were debated. The location of the project on reservation land added considerable weight to the THPO request, and the revised methods were used.

The Vandalia Bridge reconnaissance survey resulted in the identification of several prehistoric archaeological sites. One of these was a stratified site, a rarity in western New York, located on the southern bank of the Allegheny River. The value of investigating such sites has increased substantially since the construction of the Kinzua Dam in the 1960s. The river valley, including a vast acreage of the Allegany Reservation, was flooded to form the Allegheny Reservoir. The river valley was one of the most densely occupied locales throughout the prehistoric period, and creation of the reservoir removed many areas from further investigation. Yearly fluctuations in the water level have destroyed many cultural resources and effectively eliminated the possibility of fully assessing cultural developments along much of the river valley. The extent of the damage incurred over the last 40 years has only recently begun to be assessed.

Requests for site examinations were submitted and implemented over the course of the next few years. The process was slow owing to the involvement of the SNI and the nature of their interactions with the NYSDOT and

NYSM. No one entity was to blame for the tentative nature of interagency communication during this time, when the THPO was being formed. A lack of familiarity with procedures, protocols, and personnel led to hesitations in sending and receiving material and information. It was unclear whether the SNI would review reports and comment before reports were finalized by the NYSM for NYSDOT.

The issue of artifact and information ownership is an important part of the Vandalia Bridge project story. Only about half of the project area is actually situated on Allegany Reservation land and under the purview of the SNI. The other half is under the jurisdiction of New York State. A large, multicomponent prehistoric site is artificially bounded within NYSDOT project limits and bisected by the reservation boundary. Both the SNI and NYSM have asserted their authority over materials obtained on their respective sides of the line. As it stands now, the collection is to be split according to provenience, with portions of the collection curated separately by each agency. Despite consistent cooperation by the archaeologists doing the work, the agencies overseeing the project seem unwilling to employ "Solomon's wisdom" and to cooperate in this matter of authority and ownership.

This appears to be an example of state and tribal political history creating a problem for archaeology. On the one hand, the SNI is asserting its right to control cultural material found on sovereign territory. Conversely, state agencies feel that they have clear authority over artifacts collected off-reservation. However, the state can claim ownership of cultural materials from off the reservation only when the subject lands have already been placed in state ownership. In some circumstances, it is entirely possible that such acquisition might not occur until after a portion of the archaeology has been completed. It has generally been held that until the lands in question have been acquired by the state, artifacts recovered through fieldwork would be the property of the current landowner. The NYSM, as a justification for seeking control of artifacts recovered by the Vandalia Bridge project, has cited its "mandate" to enhance its collections. This argument seems to run counter to other mandates of the museum. It also seems contrary to conditions experienced by similar institutions across the country which have reached the limits of their ability to curate archaeological collections. As the archaeologists directly involved with this project, we are opposed to the splitting of archaeological collections. It also seems more appropriate to house the materials at a location near where they were collected.

Irving Bridge Project

In 2000 a cultural resource survey for proposed road improvements to State Route 5 and US Route 20 and a potential bridge replacement was conducted at the western end of the Cattaraugus Reservation in the town of Brant, Erie County, New York. This project, too, involved roadways in an area that straddled reservation and nonreservation lands, and it also was undertaken before the formation of the THPO. Experience gained during the Vandalia Bridge project, however, allowed UB to quickly prepare a work plan utilizing the same testing standards. This plan, in part owing to the familiarity of the format, was promptly reviewed and submitted for approval to the SNI Tribal Council.

The Stage 1 survey identified within the project area a single prehistoric site, designated the Washburn site (Perrelli et al. 2001). The site lay entirely within the Cattaraugus Reservation, and thus there were no questions about the disposition of the archaeological collection. UB would be allowed to maintain any collections taken from the site until analyses were completed and samples processed. All artifacts would ultimately be turned over to the Seneca Iroquois National Museum.

During Stage 1, cultural material was discovered in significant enough quantities and distributed over a broad enough area to warrant Stage 2 investigations. Although much of the material used to prepare a Stage 2 proposal is standardized, there was a period of review by the SNI during which comments and suggestions could be made and clarification obtained on specific details of the work plan, analyses, and report format. Again, the trust between the UB and SNI archaeologists involved with the project was a factor in streamlining the approval of the proposal.

Stage 2 investigations were conducted by UB during July and August 2002. The Washburn site contained no ceramics, and the several fragmented projectile points/bifaces were not diagnostic of a specific archaeological culture. A single cultural feature in the form of a cooking pit filled with fire-cracked rock was identified and excavated. A segment of a charred butternut shell (*Juglans cinerea*) was recovered, and a corrected AMS date of 470±40 B.P. (years before present) or A.D. 1440–1520 was obtained (Beta-181731). The presence of one buried cultural feature was sufficient to recommend that Stage 3 data recovery excavations be conducted. Again, the cooperation between the archaeologists on this project will allow for a reasonably rapid review of the UB data recovery plan and authorization for the project to proceed.

In the case of both the Vandalia Bridge and the Irving Bridge archaeological projects, the establishment of the THPO has allowed for a more efficient method of scheduling the work. As has been noted, under the former system—under which the Tribal Council passed a resolution authorizing research—fixed time limits would have been imposed. The direct oversight of these matters by the SNI THPO allows for much more flexibility, and it is much easier to obtain extensions of arbitrary time limits for the completion of projects. The Stage 3 investigations scheduled for these two projects have not yet been completed. However, the necessary clearances and approvals required from the SNI have been obtained, and delays in the completion of the fieldwork have been the result of other scheduling difficulties.

Conclusion

Collaboration and cooperation between the UB Archaeological Survey and the SNI are important on a number of levels. Such an approach facilitates a portion of the larger Highway Archaeology Program in New York and allows lead agencies to work within existing regulations and legislation, while at the same time it recognizes the rights and interests of the SNI. The interaction also brings about a better understanding between disparate groups of people who could easily be, and sometimes are, antagonistic toward each other.

Friction is to be expected between Native Americans who want to preserve and protect their cultural heritage and archaeologists who want to learn more about local prehistory through destructive excavation techniques, intrusive analysis, and public reporting of findings. Collaboration and cooperation help to break down barriers between these two seemingly mutually exclusive goals. Each side learns something from the other. In the long run, Native peoples may better understand the interest and motivations of archaeologists, who rely on material culture, archaeological evidence, and science. Similarly, archaeologists and bureaucrats can learn about the Seneca worldview, ways of life, and belief systems, which shape their interactions with others. Together, these advances in understanding should lead to archaeologists practicing a more respectful and appropriate methodology, on the one hand, and Native Americans participating in the excavation and interpretation of the archaeological record, on the other.

It is generally possible for the THPO to make most of the decisions necessary for the successful completion of research projects within the aboriginal territory of the Seneca Nation. The projects discussed above have been rather ordinary in that no special circumstances, such as the discovery of human remains, have occurred. We must always be mindful that this is a possibility. If such a case should arise, the THPO will ultimately decide on the disposition of any remains. However, the THPO has the ability and the responsibility to seek the input of the local community regarding the treatment of such discoveries. This has been done for projects located off the reservation and introduces an entirely different set of challenges.

Collaborations between the Archaeological Survey and the SNI THPO improve the quality of the archaeology conducted in western New York by upholding exceptionally high standards. In many cases, because the THPO is well informed about archaeological standards and practice, projects conducted on reservation land are actually held to a higher standard of testing, excavation, and reporting than projects conducted elsewhere. This fact reveals the depth of interest in archaeology held by Seneca Nation administrators.

The unique aspect of our situation in western New York with respect to nation and state agency interactions is the relationship between the SNI and the survey archaeologists. As graduates of the same academic institution and as longtime CRM practitioners and collaborators, we share an awareness of both academic and Seneca Nation values and procedures. We understand how these potentially antagonistic value systems work, and we strive to integrate them for the benefit of archaeological practice. This is achieved through a mix of professional conduct and a personal friendship that transcends politics.

Strong personal relationships greatly affect professional interaction. In order for a complex process like a statewide Highway Archaeology Program to work, people have to establish trusting relationships at some level. This is perhaps best achieved at a local level, with most of the interaction occurring between local representatives of a larger program subdivided by regions, as in western New York. Otherwise, the process may not run smoothly, since suspicion may promote checks and balances, reviews, and grievances. In New York State, communication and interaction are legislated so that the NYSM, NYSDOT, and SNI THPO must deal with each other in certain cases. But while this creates the potential for cooperation, it also creates the potential for conflict and confrontation. Cooperation cannot be legislated. It occurs when people trust each other, and usually after a program has a record of working well.

Real trust can be formed only between people, not institutions. Although we may come to believe that a particular institution is more likely than another to abide by its written principles, we come to that point only through interaction with individuals who have shown a willingness to cooperate, to speak freely and honestly, and to follow through on ideas and issues.

Ira Beckerman (this volume) has identified many of the fundamental requirements for successful cooperation between people, institutions, or nations. These are all subsumed under the necessity for individuals to be willing to discuss their fundamental differences fully and frankly. One item mentioned is the somewhat nebulous concept of respect. An important point is that respect must be earned, which can be a difficult task when the reasons for initiating interaction are adversarial.

In recent years, the THPO has provided constructive, insightful comments during the report review phase of the process. While these comments could result in improved reports, unfortunately they are often received after reports have already been approved by the NYSM and OPRHP. The result is that the THPO's suggestions are seldom incorporated into the final product. One perception is that the SNI's review is a courtesy rather than an important step in a process that necessitates a response. Therefore, it seems that the THPO, OPRHP, and NYSM are not on the same footing. In some cases, the OPRHP is the leading authority on compliance, while in other cases, it is the NYSM that determines whether a report is acceptable. Rarely does a THPO review and comment occur at a step in the process where they can elicit a reaction on the part of compliance archaeologists.

If cooperation is to take place at a level beyond appearances, the institutions involved must modify the process of report review as we know it, or make the different oversight roles more explicit. One course of action would be to establish areas of authority where different entities have sole jurisdiction, or are at the top of the review pyramid, for specific projects. This seems to be the situation today; however, the SNI THPO's authority is usually limited, and the authority of the NYSM and of the OPRHP often seem to overlap. The THPO could have the final say over all activities on reservation land, including final reports. The OPRHP could maintain authority over those projects that require federal and state permits, and those where a local municipality is willing to take on the role of lead agency, outside the confines of the Highway Archaeology Program. The NYSM could have authority over all state and federally funded NYSDOT projects that occur in the various subregions of New York.

One way to improve the processes addressed here is for people from the OPRHP, NYSM, and THPO to meet face-to-face and to discuss issues, problems, and solutions on a regular basis. We propose an annual meeting of these different groups to discuss the statewide Highway Archaeology Program in terms of progress, problems, and potential changes. There is no substitute for trust built on personal interaction, communication, and following through with statements, agreements, and action. Once a track record of successful interaction and performance is established, people can begin to trust that someone's words will correspond with their actions.

A final, and very important, point to address is touched on by Jack Rossen (this volume). From his perspective, the idea of involving Native peoples in the process and incorporating their views as well as their knowledge is a "new vision." But remember that this attempt at collaboration and cooperation is something new only from the perspective of the dominant culture. American Indian people have been cooperating and collaborating with their neighbors and visitors for hundreds of years. In part, this has been due to necessity. At other times, it has simply been a manifestation of the basic principles of most Native cultures, which seek to attain a balance or some degree of harmony in their lives and interactions with others. The greatest difficulty in obtaining cooperation between cultures has simply been the lack of effort. There has been a shift away from the view of Native peoples as objects of study and toward a view of them as other people. The process has been painfully slow. There are still misconceptions, and probably some fear, about visiting and interacting with Native communities. The only way to change that is to foster interaction through cooperation on all levels. The people with knowledge and interest have been here throughout the years. To obtain their help and assistance, one only needs to ask.

Postscript by Robert Dean

One of the first thoughts that occurred to me after hearing about this proposed volume was the choice of the word "collaborate." I had dropped this short digression from the major topic until I read the concluding remarks in Cara Lee Blume's chapter in this volume. Blume sees the negative definition of collaboration as related to the relinquishing of some level of power. That particular use had not occurred to me, but I believe it is an important point.

The real reasons for my sensitivity to this specific word may be so deep that I truly do not understand them. Whatever the reasons, I would rather be considered a person who cooperates with anyone who asks for assistance rather than as a collaborator. To assess whether or not my aversion to the word was warranted, at least in some measure, I consulted my trusty 1966 edition of Funk & Wagnalls *Standard College Dictionary*. The word "cooperate" had two principal definitions: "1. To work together for a common objective; act in combination. 2. To practice economic cooperation." There are two associated entries, "cooperation" and "cooperative," both of which can be seen as positive words that stress the initial meaning of "cooperate."

Turning to the word "collaborate," one again finds two definitions in the dictionary. The first is "to work or cooperate with another, especially in literary or scientific pursuits." The second is the one germane to my hesitation to use the word: "2. To cooperate traitorously, be a collaborationist." There is only one related word that follows in this dictionary, and it is "collaborationist," which is defined as "a citizen of a country invaded or occupied by foreign troops who cooperates with the enemy." Hardly the most positive word choice considering the ultimate aims of the present volume (see Brown and Robinson, this volume). Anyone who was alive in the late 1960s and early 1970s may remember just how contentious those years were on all levels. To those practicing archaeology at that time, the feelings of the Native American communities were presented loudly. Anyone who has been involved in a controversial CRM project understands the difficulties—regular condemnation becomes a part of the job.

It is worth noting that when I voiced these thoughts to my writing partner, although he seemed to understand some of the reasons for my reluctance to use the word, he was reasonably comfortable continuing with it. This difference, by its very subtlety, may point out a basic problem that we confront daily and that marks a fundamental difference in our views of the world.

Note

1. The Seneca Nation is one of the six tribes of the Iroquois Confederacy (Haudenosaunee). The SNI, organized in 1848, follows a constitutional form of government and has three primary reservations: Allegany, Cattaraugus, and Oil Spring (see Figure 9.1). Two other tracts have recently been added to the nation's land holdings as a result of casino operations, one in Niagara Falls and one in the town of Cheektowaga, near Buffalo, New York. The Tonawanda Band of Senecas, residing on the Tonawanda Reservation near Akron, New York, have maintained a traditional form of government and formal ties to the Iroquois Confederacy. The SNI and the Tonawanda Seneca consult and cooperate on issues involving cultural resources that arise across their aboriginal territory and in nearby localities. Issues specific to individual reservations are handled by the respective political entity. Both Seneca political divisions are represented on NAGPRA issues through the Haudenosaunee Standing Committee on Burial Rules and Regulations (see Hill, this volume).

Appendix 1: Seneca Nation of Indians Archaeological Policy
(Seneca Nation of Indians 1986)

The Seneca Nation of Indians (hereafter SNI), recognizing the need to exert their control over archaeological work done both on the reservations and on Seneca or Seneca-related sites off the reservation, wishes to establish official tribal policy on how such work should proceed.

On Reservation:

First, as with any research project which is planned for the reservations, official permission to do research on the reservations must initially be granted by the SNI Council. This permission may be granted on the basis of the submission of a written description of the proposed work and expected outcomes of the research. It is recognized that at any time in archaeological research, results may vary from the expected; but it is felt that most professional researchers can generally anticipate major results in most instances. The written proposal should include a résumé of the principal investigator and explain funding sources and staffing for the project. Copies of proposals submitted to funding agencies should be submitted to the SNI Office of the President for review. The researcher may be asked to appear before a meeting of the Council and Longhouse people in order to answer any questions which may arise.

If Council grants permission for the research to proceed, certain stipulations must be included:

1) If any osteological material, particularly human bone, is encountered, the principal investigator must stop immediately and report such a find to the Seneca-Iroquois National Museum (hereafter SINM), the tribal museum and an Authority of the SNI. If, indeed, the bone is found to be human, this material will be reburied with attendant grave goods in due time. It should be pointed out that non-human animal bone may also accompany human ritual burials, and that animal burials may also be the result of ceremonialism of a former time. The Longhouse people shall be in charge of the reburial of any human remains. Exact policy to be followed in case of osteological finds is available through the SINM.

Upon presentation of a work plan for the study of bone material, agreements may be made for limited off-site study of bone material, but permission will depend on the purpose of the study and the need for off-site study. Permission should be sought by submission to the SNI of a written proposal specifying the need and benefits of such a study to the SNI. The proposal will be presented to a meeting of the SNI Council and Longhouse people.

2) Wherever possible, preference in hiring should be for Seneca or other Iroquois people to work on reservation sites.

3) Artifacts gathered in the process of the research study will belong to the SNI. Permission can be granted for limited study of artifacts off reservation, but a time limit will be agreed upon for such study.

4) Copies of all documents, reports, photographs, etc., developed as a result of the project will be placed with the SNI where they will be available for all interested people.

It must be clearly understood that all work done on the reservations must be cleared in advance by the SNI Council. No work may be done prior to receiving permission.

Off Reservation:

Off reservation sites are clearly different from on reservation sites in terms of how they should be handled. First, it will be noted that any sites located on Federal, State or Reservation lands are covered by legislation protecting such sites. Researchers are urged to investigate the requirements on Federal and State lands, since variable ordinances apply. In all cases, off reservation sites which contain Seneca material or Seneca-related material should follow these procedures:

1) Prior to beginning research, the principal investigator or researcher should file a copy of the plan of work and expected results of the field work with the SINM who will disburse the information to the appropriate SNI offices. It is recognized that, on occasion, Seneca or Seneca-related material may be found in the normal course of an excavation with no prior knowledge of such a component on the site. Should this occur, the researcher should immediately file an amended plan of work and expected results document with the SINM.

2) For the purposes of work covered by this document, Seneca-related material or sites shall also be inclusive of those materials or sites which are directly related to populations no longer extant, but ancestral to the Seneca. In the areas of New York, Pennsylvania, Ohio, and the Province of Ontario, these would include, for example, the Erie, the Delaware (especially along the Allegheny River), the Susquehannock, the Huron, the Wenro, and any prehistoric peoples and cultures found within original Seneca territory. It is recognized that it is occasionally difficult to determine actual tribal identification of cultural remains beyond a generalized Northeastern Woodlands or Iroquoian designation, in which case the researcher should file the above material with the SINM for distribution to other possibly related tribes.

3) If osteological material should be encountered within any site being investigated, particularly if the bone is suspected or known to be human, the project director should stop immediately and notify the SINM. The policy here should be the same as for on-reservation sites, with the general practice being reburial of all human remains with attendant grave goods. It should be stressed that by cultural definition, burials constitute both the osteological material and all of the associated grave goods.

4) Where practical, preference should be given to Seneca or other Iroquois people for hiring to work on the project. A list of experienced and qualified Seneca people is available through the SINM.

5) Copies of all final reports dealing with Seneca or Seneca related sites should be filed with the SINM where they will be made available to all interested peo-

ple. While there is no law which requires that the above be observed on private land, it is hoped that all responsible individuals, institutions, and organizations will abide by the intent of these directives. There is no attempt on the part of the Seneca Nation of Indians, either on or off reservation, to restrain all of the work done on Seneca or Seneca-related sites by responsible individuals, but rather this is the expression of a genuine interest in knowing what research is being done, what the results of such work are, and to insure that proper dignity and respect is afforded to the dead.

Approved by the Council of the Seneca Nation of Indians, August 1986.

10. Green Mountain Stewardship
One Landscape, Multiple Histories

DAVID M. LACY AND DONNA ROBERTS MOODY

The traditional Western Abenaki homeland encompasses a large geographical area consisting of what is now the entire state of New Hampshire, all of Vermont (excepting a portion of Bennington County), north-central Massachusetts, west-central Maine, and parts of Quebec Province in Canada. Within this area, both historically and contemporarily, exist a number of bands of Abenaki people. The Connecticut River is the geographic center of this homeland, lying between the White Mountains to the east and the Green Mountains to the west. In south-central Vermont, the Green Mountain National Forest (GMNF) has domain over a significant portion of this mountainous landscape.

While many values are shared by Abenaki and GMNF personnel, others are not, since such values are embedded in different histories and worldviews. Issues of repatriation and site protection have been a matter of consensus among all Abenaki groups, including one common representative, until recently when the Missisquoi Abenaki elected to have a separate voice in these areas. The rest of the Abenaki Nation in the United States remains in consensus. In order to protect sites and places within the GMNF that are significant to Abenaki people, while actively managing these federal lands for the larger public good, there needs to be an appreciation and accommodation of these cultural differences by both parties.

This chapter reflects on the collaborative work of the GMNF and the Missisquoi Abenaki, the only Abenaki band seeking federal recognition at this time. Efforts to identify, evaluate, and protect sites and to share cross-cultural understandings have been ongoing since the late 1980s. The authors—David Lacy, the GMNF archaeologist since 1986, and Donna Roberts Moody, the Abenaki Repatriation Coordinator since 1995—address the challenges, successes, and prospects for continued collaboration. The first half of the chapter takes the form of a dialogue in which the tribal voice and the GMNF voice are differentiated by italicized and regular typeface, respectively.

Our Dialogue
In the Beginning

We are the Abenaki. Our ancient stories, especially our Creation stories, define us as a people in this land. They connect us to the past and provide us with a sense of place. They connect us to our Ancestors and provide an identity as to who we are.

And so we are told that in the beginning Creator made beings of stone. These beings were large, clumsy—destroying everything in their path—and cold-hearted. In disappointment, Creator cast aside these ones. Creator then took his huge bow and, nocking an arrow, shot that arrow into an Ash tree. That Ash tree split open and from the heart of the Ash walked the first Abenaki man and woman, side by side.

The Green Mountains in Vermont are one arm of the Appalachian Mountains, testament to millions of years of mountain building and the crumpling effect of tectonic processes. Eons of weathering and four geologically recent glacial epochs have resulted in a relatively low, rolling topography, with mineralogically complex bedrock underpinnings overlain by a blanket of glacial till. Today's forest—northern hardwoods, giving way to spruce-fir at higher elevations—is the most recent in a long line of vegetative mosaics that have found this landscape hospitable over the last 11,000 years or so.

Once upon a Time

We are told by our ancient stories that we, the Abenaki people, have been here in this place we call N'dakinna, "our land," since the beginning of time.

We have stories that speak of the great ice covering the land and the great flood that followed.

Archaeologists tell us we have been in this land for 10,000 to 12,000 years. This time line has evolved from their excavations and explorations of our ancient villages, sacred sites, and the graves of our Ancestors. They talk about a land bridge thousands of miles away. They are wrong, but they never asked us where we came from, and how or when we arrived here.

Vermont was once alleged to be largely unoccupied until European colonization—an idea promoted in public school textbooks and town and state histories until the second half of the twentieth century (Calloway 1990; Day 1965; Haviland and Power 1994). Archaeological work over the last generation, however, has indeed established that there is a continuous Native American presence for the last 11,000 years (Haviland and Power 1994; Thomas 1994), with a thin but clear postglacial Paleoindian veneer, and a subsequent cultural historical trajectory comparable to the rest of northern New England. "Land bridge" stories are still told in schools, but other credible explanations about the movement of peoples via the Pacific Rim or other routes provide exciting new possible scenarios for the timing, frequency, and diversity of the occupation of the Americas in general, and New England more specifically.

Archaeological and historical evidence from the Woodland and Contact periods (ca. 3,000-350 years ago) establishes the extensive and permanent presence of Native people in Vermont. Estimates of the temporal depth of ethnically "Abenaki" (and, in southwestern Vermont, "Mohican") links to the landscape vary, but there is broad agreement among researchers that this tie definitely predates European contact (Calloway 1990; Haviland and Power 1994).

The Land Offered Us

N'dakinna is the traditional homeland of the Abenaki people. The Kwanitewk, or Connecticut River, is the geographical center of that homeland. There are many beautiful places in N'dakinna, including the Askaskadenak (Green Mountains) in the west, which are mirrored by the Wobiadenak (White Mountains) to the east.

Our original instructions, passed down to us for millennia, have taught us how to live with the land. We are taught how to walk in balance with the Nigawes Akik (Earth Mother) and with all of Creation. We are taught how to worship and to pray. We are taught how to heal ourselves of illness.

This land, N'dakinna, which Creator gave to us to care for, provides us with medicine plants for healing; Tall Ones (trees) to use for our basket making, canoes, snowshoes, toboggans, and shelter; Four-Leggeds (animals) and Fishes to feed our families and, in the past, clothe our bodies.

Much of what we need to sustain our lives we find in the mountains. As children we learned how to hunt, gather medicines and foods, harvest trees and the bark, and tap the Maples for syrup. We have ceremonies for all of these activities to honor what we take. And we have teachings in stewardship to ensure that there will be enough for the next seven generations.

The mountains have also provided us with materials for toolmaking— the beautiful flint and quartzite, the granite, and marble. We have used, for thousands of years, the mountains as a path of travel, the deep trails of which we can see today.

The Green Mountain National Forest (GMNF) is a nearly 162,000-ha swath of uplands and mountains in south-central Vermont. Historically, Euroamericans occupied most of these uplands later than the lowlands (i.e., mid-nineteenth century versus late eighteenth century) owing to difficult access and shorter growing seasons. But attractive mineral and ore deposits, rich forest stands, good lands for grazing and orchard production, and areas suitable for the hardscrabble subsistence farming common to Vermont before the Civil War were enticements to early exploitation and eventual settlement.

Abandonment of many upland properties between the Civil War and the early twentieth century was driven by a combination of poor land-management practices (particularly logging), improved agricultural technologies (designed for floodplain environments), changing transportation infrastructure (i.e., introduction of the railroads in the valleys), and economically driven population shifts (especially to the west). The legacy of environmental damage from unregulated logging and, to a lesser extent, broad-scale grazing was noted and documented relatively early—most notably by George Perkins Marsh (1998 [1864]) in his seminal appeal for thoughtful and responsible watershed management (Lowenthal 2000).

Although the primary purpose of late nineteenth-century legislation establishing eastern national forests (promoted by Marsh and like-minded colleagues) was the protection of watersheds, the actual creation of a national forest in Vermont did not receive popular support until after the great flood of 1927, which provided traumatically tangible demonstration of the need to better manage the headwaters and associated lands. The proclamation establishing the GMNF was signed in 1932.

It would be another 46 years before a formal historical overview was compiled (Casjens 1978) and more than a decade before the GMNF recognized that the inherited wisdom alleging that there were few pre-Contact Native American sites of significance in the mountains was an illusion (Lacy 1994). Native people, too, valued the mountainous landscape and its diversity of resources. In essence, the distribution of pre-Contact archaeological sites created by Native peoples in Vermont was perceived through a warped lens, ground to its particular shape by applying Western cultural values and insufficiently rigorous landscape-level archaeological analyses (Dincauze et al. 1980; Lacy 1999a).

The Mountains

Native people do not assign levels of sanctity to places; it is all sacred. However, there are times of heightened sanctity, times of ceremony, visioning, and places, and ceremonies for healing and the seeking of direction. Many of these activities and ceremonies have always been present in the mountains. Anyone who has traveled through them can feel the specialness of their quiet and a sense of awareness of all of creation.

The mountains have historically been viewed as an environment "apart," inhospitable to long-term residential settlement and development but offering an abundance of natural resources (e.g., timber and charcoal, gravel and marble, iron ore, clean water and water power, collectible plants, fish, and wildlife) and recreational opportunities (e.g., hiking, camping, skiing, fishing, hunting, experiencing wilderness, and the aesthetic context for these activities). The Forest Service is charged with protecting and conserving these resources and values. Our mission to conserve such resources is not inherently in conflict with the values held by many Abenaki people.

Who Are These People?

Many Native people have a sense of amazement at the way Euroamericans view the earth and the land. It is difficult for us to understand people who think they can possess what was given by Creator for the survival of all living beings. There is always a sense of sadness to see the great stands of Tall Ones brought down to satisfy people's need to accumulate and expand personal wealth. One-tenth of the world's population consumes one-third of the world's resources. Here in N'dakinna it has been this way since the first European set foot on our land. We view that land as something given to us to nurture and caretake, not to exploit and profit from. Farther and farther we have been driven from those places that Creator gave us for survival. Why do White people think that they have the right to take whatever they see, just because they want it?

The Forest Service mission is to "care for the land and serve people." This relatively modern phrase is consistent with the "conservationist" ethic of Gifford Pinchot, the turn-of-the-century father of North American forestry and the Forest Service itself. Even back in the 1890s, Pinchot believed that public lands should serve the public good while being managed in ways that perpetuate the natural resources on those lands. Over the last 100 years, the Forest Service has evolved from a small cadre of multi-skilled ranger-foresters to a large, modern, diverse workforce of specialists, administrators, and technicians working in concert to sustain healthy ecosystems. Despite changes in staffing and the scale of the organization, Pinchot's vision continues to be embraced today. Establishing good tribal relations clearly falls within this general mission, although the details vary from locale to locale.

When the GMNF first initiated contact with the Abenaki in the 1980s, the breadth of perceptions held by GMNF personnel about the Abenaki community reflected that of Vermont citizenry in general; that is, they ranged widely across apathy, ignorance, antipathy, curiosity, cynicism, and sympathetic support. The biases inherent in standard histories and educational institutions (particularly the perpetuation of the myth that the

Abenaki in particular, and Native people in general, did not have a permanent and continuous presence in Vermont), the lack of federal or state recognition, and the politicized nature of media images of tribal activities led GMNF employees to have doubts about both the possibility of significant sites occurring within the forest and the credibility of the tribe in commenting on them.

It was important, therefore, for the GMNF to hear from its own archaeologist (i.e., Lacy) that despite the lack of federal recognition for the tribe and the politically charged atmosphere of the times, it was nevertheless true that Native Americans were "here" for millennia; that a permanent Abenaki presence predated French and English settlement; that these indigenous peoples' legacy was reflected in part by known and yet-to-be-discovered sites managed by the GMNF; and that many people still living nearby were, or claimed to be, of Abenaki descent.

How Will the Outsiders Affect Our Landscape?

Historically, Euroamerican management of land has followed a doctrine of rape, pillage, and burn. There is no sense of management but rather a sense of colonized imperialism. Western society is one of "use it up, throw it away" with no thought to the future of the Earth. Conservation groups are now attempting to salvage and repair 500 years of egocentrism. There are so many places in the Green and White Mountains that would be irreparably destroyed if not for the conservation measures of the Forest Service. These measures can be based on the ever-changing priorities of federal government administrations. Some administrations lean toward more-aggressive exploitation of National Forest resources.

Creation is a circle of life. Imagine all of Creation standing in a circle, the Four-Leggeds, the Tall Ones, the Plant people, the Wingeds, the Insect people, the Fishes, the Waters, and the Two-Leggeds (humans). Now imagine the Two-Leggeds being removed from the circle. All that remained of Creation could survive without humans; however, if any of the other Beings were removed, humans could not survive. Our prophecies tell us there is a time when this scene will be possible.

Public input is a critical component of the management of all national forests. With the emergence of federal planning and environmental protection laws and regulations over the last 25 years, it is not only a valuable outreach activity but also a legal mandate. Processes for soliciting and accommodating public input (largely under the guidance of the National Environmental Policy Act [NEPA]) have been developed that establish appropriate time frames and means of communicating at programmatic and project-specific levels.

When the GMNF began soliciting input from the Abenaki, forest employees' questions about the tribe's historic right to comment on our management were compounded by concerns about what effect such comments might have on the forest's multiple-use management ethic and mission. There was also widespread sentiment that, however admirable Native culture and values were or are, they may not be realistic when applied to professional forestry in our current social and economic environment. Finally, there was some doubt expressed whether all comments received would be focused on the issue(s) at hand or whether they were going to be politically strategic public statements designed to enhance tribal recognition efforts or land claim suits against the federal government.

It would be less than forthcoming to say that these issues have disappeared or been resolved to everyone's satisfaction. Some GMNF personnel have been unable to let go of them, and new people are integrated into the organization all the time, so we revisit these concerns from time to time. But by keeping discussion alive, we also reaffirm the baseline values that have brought us together.

How to Cross the Cultural Divide

Cross-cultural collaboration is an exercise in learning and one of mutual respect. For there to be any collaboration, it is important for non-Native people to understand and to accept that there are lessons to be learned from the Original People of each area of the world. Here in N'dakinna there are those who still remember the original instructions given to us by Creator; some who still know and use the medicine plants, who still use the trees for purposes other than firewood, building houses, making matches, or, worse yet, making toothpicks.

Caring for the plant and animal life in the forest and mountains is a sacred task, for it ensures the continuation of life for generations to follow. The sa-

cred sites, which have seen thousands of years of ceremony, must, in the Native mind, be protected from destruction and looting. These are places that Native people honor, just as Europeans revere their churches and cemeteries.

All life comes from this planet we all share. If people could only understand that when they place their feet on the land, they are walking on the faces of their grandchildren yet to be born.

The GMNF's commitment to serving all of its publics is strong but not always as flexible as we might wish, trapped as it is in its own bureaucracy. However, individuals can make a difference by operating creatively within the system. Before passage of the Native American Graves Protection and Repatriation Act in 1990, guidance from presidential executive orders, or the Forest Service's national emphasis on tribal relations (USDA Forest Service 2003), the need and opportunity to work with the Native community were already apparent—but we lacked a channel of communication to address Native concerns and to increase our own awareness. It was in this context that the GMNF archaeologist began writing to the tribe.

A History of Crossing the Divide

Initial contacts (1986–1988) between the GMNF and the Abenaki Tribe consisted of an occasional letter from the forest archaeologist to Chief Homer St. Francis explaining the nature, intent, and results of survey work being conducted. This turned out to have been a source of unintentional, but substantial, amusement in the tribal offices inasmuch as the archaeologist was essentially informing the tribe of "great discoveries" (e.g., Indians used the mountains!) that were embedded in their oral history, thus patently obvious (to them), and in any case still an integral part of many tribal members' lifestyles. Nevertheless, the long-term value of this mostly one-way correspondence was to establish that someone at the GMNF was making an honest, if naive, attempt to open a channel of respectful communication that did not obligate the tribe to provide anything in return (e.g., information or labor).

The opening of this channel facilitated the beginning of a more meaningful and interactive relationship when the formulation of Forest Service (and other agencies') policies regarding the treatment of human remains gained momentum in 1988–1989 (Lacy 1989). Subsequent correspondence, conversations, and meetings helped establish stronger personal relationships and formal linkages between the GMNF and the tribe.

As an outgrowth of the policy discussions on human remains and a separate initiative to solicit Abenaki input for an interpretive poster about Indian use of the mountains, our relationship became more formalized—and the channel of communication became both busier and with more of a two-way flow. Since 1989 the Abenaki Nation of Missisquoi, through the Abenaki Research Project (ARP), and the GMNF, through its forest archaeologist, have worked together to manage Abenaki cultural resources in the forest (Lacy and Bluto-Delvental 1995; Lacy 1999b). ARP representatives to the GMNF have changed over the years, resulting in some false starts and transitions, but the basic goals (discussed below) and relationship have remained largely the same.

Initial meetings in the early 1990s revealed the need for immediate cooperation in four major areas. First, there were a number of ancient Native sites already found within the forest that required evaluation by the ARP. There were physical, sacred, and traditional considerations to be reviewed. Second, some of these sites were in forest use areas—on trails, in camping or timber sale areas—and buffering or further protection of the sites was an issue. Third, there were larger projects—like the relocation of a significant stretch of the Appalachian Trail/Long Trail corridor around Pico and Killington mountains—requiring very large areas to be studied for Native sites, and traditional and sacred uses, then reconsidered in terms of the course of the overall project. The fourth area of concern had to do with possible areas of ongoing subsistence, collection, or other traditional use of forest resources.

During one- or two-day planning meetings in the late fall or winter, ARP and the GMNF would plan the coming year's activities. Because neither group really knew much about the key beliefs and operating principles of the other, another basic objective of each of our meetings was to achieve a better understanding of one another's values and perspectives. Mutual goodwill, patience, and the use of questions, rather than assumptions, allowed both groups to learn a great deal.

Much of the time in the first three or four years was spent getting various Abenaki family and community leaders out to Native sites to begin full-scale research on Abenaki oral traditions and hopes for these sites. We also established, then expanded, a formal cost-sharing agreement to minimally fund the effort.

By the mid-1990s, the Appalachian Trail/Long Trail study (Lacy et al. 1992) and related work to sort out the massive erosion problems at the Deer Leap site reflected movement from study to policy change in ARP-GMNF cooperative efforts. By the late 1990s through 2003, several other sites, including an area where considerable looting was an issue and three proposed timber sale areas, were being evaluated.

Sites where damage and looting were the central concern have become test cases for a variety of cooperative protection methods ranging from signage and public education to trail or site closure. While working together, we have learned that education—of both the public and each other—takes, and lasts, much longer than just eliminating an activity completely. One-on-one efforts to raise the public's awareness and sensitivity (e.g., conversations with visitors to the forest at trail heads near sensitive sites) have shown that people are generally and genuinely sympathetic once they are informed, but this is clearly not an effective way to reach large numbers of people. We have also used signs at trail heads to divert foot traffic to alternate routes (i.e., away from sites), but striking a balance between providing too much specificity about the nature and location of a site, and simply asking people to "stay out," has resulted in good, but not total, success.

At a general level, we are still struggling to find consensus on how (or even whether) to use print, computer, or broadcast media to raise awareness about sensitive sites on a larger scale without revealing too much locational information, or betraying the trust of informants about confidential aspects of places or family histories. We do recognize that in the long run it will be education—not official closure orders—that will result in broad protection.

Problems

Our relationship has been good, right, and productive—but imperfect. Areas that pose hurdles or that could be improved on can be lumped into six broad (and overlapping) categories: people, knowledge claims, money, scale of analysis, legal status, and rules.

People

The lack of continuity of membership in ARP has been a challenge, but times change, people move on, and the transition to working with new partners can bring its own rewards. On the forest side, there is a concern that the relationship is dependent on a single actor; efforts are being made to include more forest personnel in both the administrative and field portions of the partnership.

Knowledge Claims

There has been some tension on the part of forest project managers regarding the source and nature of knowledge claims about places and landscapes within the GMNF. They are generally trained to be "science-based" decision makers, but are being asked to alter proposed land-management activities based on conclusions derived from oral histories or interviews, backed up with little or no empirical corroboration or documentation. This is at least partly attributable to the reluctance of many Abenaki families to come forward or to be identified, either out of distrust of the government or merely from a sense of privacy. On the other hand, some ARP members are loathe to put anything of significance in writing for fear that the GMNF will print it in a public document for all to see (as they have done occasionally in the past), thus potentially contributing to the looting of significant areas. In a roughly parallel vein, on-site identification of significant spiritual components of a site or place are met with skepticism by some forest employees. We would all benefit from a greater appreciation for the range of credible sources of knowledge, more diligence in editing sensitive content out of published reports, and an acknowledgment that more-substantial documentation, when possible, is always helpful.

Money

ARP does not have access to significant financial resources, and until the Abenaki are recognized by the Bureau of Indian Affairs they are ineligible for many grants that might otherwise subsidize their work. The GMNF does have some monies available for inventory and monitoring work, but not at the scale that would provide for a comprehensive overview of the traditional use and sacred sites located within the forest.

Scale of Analysis

While we have been successful in identifying and protecting specific sites and small areas of significance, we have yet to really address large-scale analyses. In at least two cases, Abenaki oral tradition has suggested that any development on a particular mountain should initially be curtailed and ultimately removed. We also have found that larger sections of some proposed timber sales or other larger activities in the forest may conflict with Abenaki or Native site protection, or traditional and sacred use. There is a need for large-scale, long-term watershed-by-watershed studies of ancient and continuing Native presence and use of the forest. The potential for landscape-level assessments that could dramatically alter management plans looms in front of us.

Legal Status

The Missisquoi Abenaki petition for federal recognition has been pending at the Bureau of Indian Affairs for several years, and there is little reason to think that that logjam will clear up in the near future. The lack of federal recognition has all sorts of implications. As far as our relationship is concerned, it affects access to money, the nature of the formal consulting relationship with the GMNF (i.e., legally obligated consultation versus a "not prohibited" relationship), and the relative influence of Abenaki comments in the NEPA process. In fact, all federal agencies operating in Vermont have been struggling with the best way to meet their consultation obligations while doing the "right thing" by the Abenaki. As of this writing, most federal agencies appear to have an informal consulting arrangement and provide opportunities for input through the NEPA process.

Rules

Finally, NEPA is the legal process that provides the best opportunity to comment on GMNF initiatives. It comes with rules that specify how, when, and where to send comments. Unfortunately, real-world constraints placed on many potential Abenaki commentators—for example, the availability of time and money to collect, analyze, and convey relevant data; access to appropriate technology; experience and education in these protocols; and trust that the information will be kept confidential—can result in well-intentioned but late, vague, and therefore difficult-to-accommodate input.

Lessons

Such problems notwithstanding, a signally important lesson to remember from the GMNF perspective is that an open channel of communication may be as significant in the long run as what is passing along it at any given moment. There have been extended periods when little of factual import has actually been exchanged between us. Nevertheless, the fact that a simple phone call can connect familiar and friendly voices to pass on information, to pose questions, or to provide support in a time of need is an indispensable key to our relationship.

As researchers and managers, we recognize that the synergy of bringing more than one perspective and source of knowledge to bear on a site or issue can be powerful. From an archaeological point of view, involving the descendants of the people who lived on, used, and are perhaps buried in the lands and sites we manage can only enhance our knowledge.

The collaborative efforts of forest employees and tribal representatives have been an exercise in proving that diverse cultures can collide without clashing. There is room within the GMNF to honor both traditional concerns and contemporary needs. Our collaboration should be used as a beginning model for governmental and tribal interactions.

A View to the Future

Building on past work between the GMNF and the tribe, we need to continue this collaborative work, ideally on an expanded basis. A renewed cost-sharing agreement, an expanded role for Native people in identifying sacred sites and landscapes, traditional input to identify unearthed artifacts and to determine their disposition, and an expanded role under the NEPA guidelines are the logical next steps. As always, an expanded program of education should be considered—both for the public and for representatives from each culture in order to foster a balanced understanding and respect.

At the time of this writing (January 2004), intratribal politics have put our relationship into a "transitional" mode (once again). The GMNF and the Abenaki remain committed to protecting significant sites and places on forest lands and maintaining our relationship. However, the Missisquoi Abenaki have elected to replace the Donna Roberts Moody as repatriation coordinator and liaison to the GMNF. A dispassionate observer should consider this to be just another point on the historical trajectory of our collaboration—and note that the channel is still open between the GMNF and the Abenaki.

Abenaki history over the last 350 years has been a story of resisting, or adapting to, dramatic forces of change, and Abenaki people and culture have persisted through time. We are proud to say that their archaeological legacy in the GMNF will be cared for today and in the future through our combined efforts.

Acknowledgments

The authors thank the members of the Abenaki Research Project who have worked with the Green Mountain National Forest and maintained the open channel between us over the years, most prominently John Moody, Carol Neptôn, Jeanne Brink, Cheryl Bluto-Delvental, Hilda and Bernard Robtoy, and Christopher Roy. We also acknowledge our debt to the late Chief Homer St. Francis for his vision and support of this relationship.

11. The Past Is Present
CRM *Archaeology on Martha's Vineyard*

HOLLY HERBSTER AND SUZANNE CHERAU

Introduction

For many New England archaeologists, the island of Martha's Vineyard has a historical connection to the excavation and interpretation of Native American sites. Beginning at the turn of the twentieth century, some of the region's most prominent scholars came to investigate complex habitation and ceremonial sites on the pristine shores of the island's coastal ponds. The work of Samuel Guernsey (1916), Douglas Byers and Frederick Johnson (1940), and especially William Ritchie (1969) served as the framework by which southern New England prehistory was (and in many cases still is) interpreted.

Martha's Vineyard is also home to the Wampanoag Tribe of Gay Head/ Aquinnah (WTGH/A), a federally recognized Native American tribe whose ancestors were the first to populate the island. Wampanoag ancestors have lived on Noepe, the island's Algonquian name, for the last 10,000 years, and this group is one of a few in southern New England that has been recorded as continuous residents of the land from the first European contact to the present day. The physical isolation of Martha's Vineyard and the unique patterns of settlement on the island have contributed to the

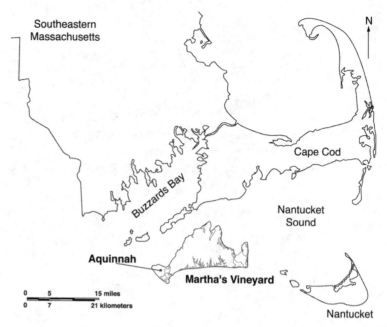

Figure 11.1. Location of Martha's Vineyard and the town of Aquinnah in southeastern
Massachusetts (Prepared by Jennifer Macpherson).

preservation of the town of Aquinnah (formerly known as Gay Head) as
a primarily Native American community that has been well documented
through oral traditions and non-Native historical studies.

Today, at the turn of a new century, the archaeological connection to
the Vineyard's Native people continues to evolve. Since 1990 more than 50
cultural resource management (CRM) projects have been completed on the
island. Archaeological survey and excavation have been triggered by rapid
islandwide development and subsequent state and local permiting requirements. In addition, local groups (Native and non-Native) have looked to
archaeological site identification as a mechanism to slow the construction
of golf courses and houses threatening the Vineyard's distinctive environmental and cultural setting. In addition, the emergence of the Aquinnah Wampanoag as a recognized regulatory voice in the community has
brought issues of heritage to the larger island population.

The growing power of Native peoples to control access to, and interpretation of, cultural sites is helping to shape archaeological research to-

day, and Martha's Vineyard is proving to be one of the most successful examples of Native American oversight and involvement in the region. This chapter discusses the significant changes that the tribe has brought about in both the practice of archaeology and the interpretations of excavated sites on the Vineyard.

Environmental and Cultural Context

Located seven miles off the southwestern tip of Cape Cod, Martha's Vineyard covers 310 km^2 and is the largest island in the region (Figure 11.1). It supports a year-round population of about 15,000 people and more than 100,000 during the summer. Academic archaeologists were drawn to the island, in part, because of its remote and relatively undisturbed setting. In particular, the up-island towns of Chilmark and Aquinnah were slow to develop as modern residential communities (electricity and telephone service arrived in Aquinnah only in the 1950s), and large areas of scrub forest, open pasture, and sand dunes characterize the area today.

The Aquinnah Wampanoag Tribe was federally acknowledged in 1987 and is currently the only federally recognized Native American tribe in Massachusetts. In trust with the Bureau of Indian Affairs, the tribe owns 196 ha on the Vineyard, much of it clustered around the nineteenth-century Wampanoag settlement area in Aquinnah. The WTGH/A is the most visible Native presence on Martha's Vineyard, although several other Wampanoag groups, such as the Chappaquiddick Tribe, hold annual gatherings on the island.

CRM on the Vineyard

The temporal range of Native occupation on the Vineyard was only partially identified by earlier professional and avocational archaeologists, who focused on large coastal shell midden sites that often contained ceremonial or burial sites. Few of these excavations included consultation with the Aquinnah community. Even as late as the 1960s, Ritchie's (1969) interpretations of Woodland period (ca. 3,000–500 B.P. [years before present]) habitation sites on the island were nearly devoid of any connection to the present-day Wampanoag living within view of his excavations.

CRM archaeology really began on the Vineyard in the early 1990s, and it is interesting to note that the tribe funded some of the earliest projects on their own lands, as discussed below. Although a few small CRM surveys had been completed in the late 1980s, most of the more than 50 completed projects on the Vineyard began after 1995. This "explosion" in CRM work was triggered primarily by regional and local review, rather than by federal projects requiring consultation under Section 106 of the National Historic Preservation Act (NHPA) (tribal lands projects excluded). The Public Archaeology Laboratory (PAL), Inc., and other CRM contractors on the island have rarely consulted under the scope of the Native American Graves Protection and Repatriation Act (NAGPRA); human burials identified during CRM projects are usually reviewed under the Massachusetts Unmarked Burial Law (see Simon, this volume).

The rapid increase in CRM projects is clearly linked to the development pressures most islanders feel are threatening the character of the Vineyard. As large open tracts of land are subjected to patchworks of new construction, Native and non-Native residents have viewed archaeological site identification and protection as one step to help preserve the landscape.

The majority of the island's larger survey projects are conducted as part of the local approval process for Developments of Regional Impact (DRIS), projects that have the potential to affect the character of the entire island or that physically span more than one community. Recent examples include public and privately funded clustered subdivisions, golf courses, and cell towers. DRIS are subject to approval by the Martha's Vineyard Commission (MVC), a body of island residents elected from each of the six towns to oversee the future growth of the island. The MVC reviews projects much as other agencies do, and potential impacts on cultural resources are usually considered as part of the review process. The Massachusetts Historical Commission (MHC), which houses the state archaeologist's office, is routinely asked to comment on projects under review by the MVC. MVC approvals are generally contingent on the project proponent meeting the MHC's requests for archaeological investigations. The tribe has also been asked to comment on projects under MVC jurisdiction and has in the past brought cultural resource issues before the group.

CRM for the Tribe

The WTGH/A trust lands are located in the southwestern portion of the island in the town of Aquinnah. In accordance with the 1987 Settlement Act with the federal government, there are approximately 196 ha of the tribe's lands in trust: 65 ha private lands (parcels I, IIA, IIB, and III) and 131 ha common lands (Gay Head Cliffs, Herring Creek, and Lobsterville). The private lands are clustered around the nineteenth-century Aquinnah Wampanoag residential and civic community center on Old South Road. In February 1991 the Tribal Council recognized the need to compile an inventory of cultural resources on the private trust lands as part of a master planning process that included future land acquisitions. The tribe knew that the 65 ha of woodland and wetlands contained long-forgotten Wampanoag house sites that once dotted the Old South Road landscape in the heart of the Gay Head peninsula. They also knew that the cultural resources investigations would need to be conducted by archaeologists who met the qualifications set by the secretary of the interior (36 CFR Part 61) and the MHC for the direction of archaeological projects, in accordance with Section 106 of the (NHPA) of 1966, as amended (36 CFR 800).

PAL, a private not-for-profit cultural resources firm based in Pawtucket, Rhode Island, quickly assembled a multifaceted research and field team to respond to the Aquinnah Tribe's request for survey proposals. The team included an experienced group of archaeologists who specialize in southern New England prehistory and history: Suzanne (Glover) Cherau, project co-principal investigator, PAL; Kevin McBride, project co-principal investigator, University of Connecticut at Storrs; Stephen Mrozowski, project historian, University of Massachusetts Boston; and Kathleen Bragdon, project ethnohistorian, College of William and Mary. Bragdon had previously assisted the tribe in their petition for federal recognition in the 1980s.

The PAL team was hired by the tribe in April 1991 to complete the first survey of the private trust lands—a small eight-acre parcel targeted for the tribe's administration complex (Glover and McBride 1991). While no culturally significant resources were identified during the survey, it was the start of a close working partnership between PAL and the tribe that would culminate in the development of a historic preservation plan, appointment of a tribal historic preservation officer (THPO), and assumption of Massachusetts State Historic Preservation Office (SHPO) responsibilities over the Wampanoag Nation ancestral lands in Massachusetts. The initial survey was followed by a comprehensive inventory of all cultural resources on the private 65 ha of trust lands that surrounded the new administration complex.

The survey was successful in identifying pre-Contact sites, documented and underdocumented eighteenth- and nineteenth-century home sites and farmsteads, remnant landscapes, and sacred or ceremonial sites (Glover and McBride 1992). It was quickly followed by additional inventory surveys of about 57 ha of abutting lands as part of the tribe's master plan for future land acquisitions. Again, the survey identified additional pre-Contact and historic period Wampanoag sites throughout these adjacent lands, all part of the eighteenth- and nineteenth-century Old South Road community. These inventory surveys were some of the first professional CRM investigations to be undertaken on the island, although site protection laws had been in effect in Massachusetts for more than two decades. It is ironic to note and important to stress that the Wampanoag Tribe in Aquinnah was the first such island sponsor of archaeological survey work in accordance with Section 106 of the NHPA. The tribe's master plan, including a cultural resources component, for the 65 ha of private trust lands was developed in 1993 following several years of investigative cultural and natural resource efforts.

The 1991–1993 PAL surveys were carried out as collaborations between the archaeologists and the tribal community. The survey methodologies followed all state and federal regulations for archaeological investigations, including the stringent MHC archaeological permitting guidelines (Massachusetts General Laws [M.G.L.], Chapter 9, Section 27c, 950 CMR 70). All work was funded and approved by the Tribal Council. The PAL field and research team lived in Aquinnah (in housing provided by local tribal members) during the many months of survey work and became quite familiar with the day-to-day workings and politics of the tribe. The PAL archaeologists met continually with the Tribal Council, tribal administrator, and tribal planner, who served as the primary point of contact, along with the tribe's Land Use Committee, Natural Resources Department, and land surveyors. The relationship expanded as word of the archaeologists' findings and sensitivity to the tribe's cultural heritage spread throughout the town, the tribe, and the whole island. Many tribal members, including Chief Donald Malonson and his wife, came to participate in the surveys by sharing knowledge about known prehistoric and historic-period site locations, passing on invaluable oral traditions and family histories, and interpreting identified archaeological deposits. The collegial exchange of information created a positive work environment for the archaeologists and regional exposure for the tribe. None of this would have been possible without what Hughes and Henry (this volume) term "the mutual education" of the archaeologists and tribal members: we respected each other's cultural backgrounds and worked together as one entity sharing the common goal of recording and preserving the Wampanoag heritage on the island.

To that end, the PAL archaeologists encouraged the participation of tribal members in the actual survey work. Several of the younger Aquinnah Wampanoag picked up shovels and screens and trekked across the woodland and wetland landscape to dig test pits, to record and collect artifacts, and to map their ancestors' home sites. They worked for many weeks alongside the seasoned PAL field crew and learned not only about our methods and techniques but also about our common goals to understand, to protect, and to preserve the ancient past. Of course, the tribal members also experienced firsthand the downside of archaeological fieldwork in coastal New England in the spring and early summer—dense greenbrier and bramble, deer ticks, poison ivy, and blistering insect bites. Throughout it all, however, lasting work and personal relationships were formed between the PAL archaeologists and the tribe. The years of collaborative surveys helped the archaeological team interpret historic Wampanoag social and settlement patterns, material cultural assemblages, and unique building styles within the Aquinnah community (McBride and Cherau 1996; Cherau 2001). The surveys also provided some of the earliest provenienced Archaic and Woodland period (ca. 10,000–3,000 B.P.) artifacts for interior locations at the southwestern end of the island. PAL produced several technical reports and a popular report of the survey results; the popular report is still offered to visitors at the tribe's Administrative Center in Aquinnah (Glover and McBride 1994).

In 1998 the Tribal Council, under the guidance of their natural resources director and designated THPO, hired PAL to conduct an archaeological survey of the Herring Creek parcel near the Aquinnah-Chilmark town line. This parcel, located on the southern shore of Menemsha Pond, was targeted by the tribe for its new, state-of-the-art shellfish hatchery. Previous PAL research of historic land use patterns had alerted the tribe to probable eighteenth- and nineteenth-century Wampanoag settlement on the parcel, not to mention the strong likelihood of pre-Contact habitation along the pond shoreline. The planning and survey process entailed close collaboration between the two PAL archaeologists (the coauthors of this chapter) and the tribal representatives overseeing the construction project.

The 1998 survey was successful in identifying a continuous Wampanoag occupation of the Herring Creek lands from the Archaic period through late historic and modern times. That was the easy part. The consultation process that ensued was much more problematic in that it required all involved to navigate through the island's complex system of intratribal politics and administrative bureaucracy to effectively manage these cultural resources in relation to the needs of the tribe's hatchery project. It was not until Chief Malonson and several other elders intervened on behalf of the cultural resources, which in this case included several ceremonial sites, that the tribe's own planners, surveyors, and engineers agreed to a major redesign of the hatchery project. With the redesign much more sensitive to the possible impact on cultural resources, PAL's original survey contract was expanded to include an archaeological data recovery program for the scaled-down project impact areas. At the chief's and acting THPO's insistence, the tribe also decided that rather than just sample the site through the data recovery, 100 percent of all features within the impact areas were to be excavated by the PAL archaeologists.

As for the remaining portions of the site on the Herring Creek parcel, after more lengthy discussions among the tribe's administrators, planners, THPO, and other tribal cultural representatives, a long-term preservation strategy was agreed on and implemented with PAL's technical assistance. All the preservation planning and archaeological investigations were done under the watchful eye of the SHPO, but the THPO and staff took responsibility for the really difficult consultation and coordination among the various tribal interests, land surveyors, and project engineers. The result of the nearly yearlong process was a precedent-setting, multidisciplinary effort to balance the tribe's past heritage with its future economic needs. It was also a serious wake-up call for the tribe's administrators that, just as for their counterparts in the non-Native island community, the balancing act between preserving the past and building for the future would be more challenging than they could have realized.

It so happened that two years earlier, in 1996, the tribal planner had approached PAL about the WTGH/A's desire to develop a historic preservation plan (HPP) as part of the tribe's ongoing master planning process. The preparation of the plan was funded by a grant from the National Park Service, obtained by the tribe with PAL's technical assistance. The HPP was intended to provide a comprehensive planning tool to assist in the long-term protection or treatment of significant archaeological resources and traditional ceremonial places, including burial sites and gathering places. The HPP was also designed to provide a basis from which the tribe could assume SHPO functions and develop a programmatic agreement for the future management of historic properties identified within tribal trust lands.

The plan was finalized by PAL and the tribe's planning director in October 1998 (Cherau 1998), after nearly two years of drafts, reviews, and redrafts by the tribal chair, Tribal Council, and other members at-large in the Aquinnah community. The Massachusetts state archaeologist/deputy SHPO was also consulted for input and approval of the plan. HPP recommendations included nominating to the National Register of Historic Places the Old South Road District and Herring Creek Archaeological District, both located in Aquinnah and surveyed and excavated by PAL, and establishing a tribal register of properties that are culturally significant to the Aquinnah Wampanoag.

Shortly after the HPP was finalized, the tribe formally applied to the National Park Service to assume the functions of the SHPO, pursuant to Section 101(b)(3) of the NHPA. The tribal planner, again with PAL's technical assistance, put together a program plan that included the HPP, a Tribal

Council resolution requesting the assumption of SHPO functions by the tribe, and the appointment by the Tribal Council of Matthew Vanderhoop as the THPO. In 1999 an agreement was executed between the park service and the WTGH/A for the assumption by the tribe of certain responsibilities pursuant to the NHPA.

Since that time, the Wampanoag THPO has assumed the role of SHPO on all tribal lands and consultation responsibilities concerning federal actions under Section 106 of the NHPA for the Wampanoag Nation ancestral lands (both on- and off-island) in Massachusetts. A Cultural Resource Commission (CRC) was also formed in October 1999 to provide advice to the THPO and the tribal repatriation officer in

> difficult decision-making situations regarding cultural resource protection (i.e., unmarked graves protection, archaeological surveys, repatriation and reinternment of human remains and associated funerary objects). The commission is composed of the THPO, the Tribal Repatriation Officer, the Chief of the Aquinnah Wampanoag, and one representative each from the Massachusetts Commission on Indian Affairs and the Aquinnah Cultural Center. A Cultural Resource Protection Ordinance is currently being drafted to define the roles and responsibilities of the Historic Preservation Program, its staff and the CRC [www.wampanoagtribe.net/protection/com miss.htm, January 17, 2004].

Several tribal members have completed cultural resource training, and one member is an archaeologist who works regularly with PAL on projects affecting Wampanoag Nation ancestral lands throughout the Commonwealth of Massachusetts.

CRM with the Tribe

The WTGH/A has also been an active participant in other CRM projects on the island involving archaeological survey and excavations of ancient Wampanoag sites. The most notable of these projects concerns a private development in the Squibnocket Ridge section of Chilmark. In 1992 PAL was hired by the Vineyard Open Land Foundation to survey a large 202-

ha residential subdivision that was once part of the summer estate of a wealthy Boston family. The property had been maintained throughout the historic and modern periods as open pasture, with sweeping views across Squibnocket Pond to the ocean and the lighthouse at the Aquinnah clay cliffs. The family members worked with the Vineyard Open Land Foundation to set off large lots for sale, with strict conservation restrictions on most of the property and with development areas limited to predefined building envelopes. The large-scale development was classified as a DRI by the MVC, which in turn asked the MHC to comment on cultural resource issues. The state archaeologist requested that an archaeological survey be completed before development in the proposed impact areas.

The initial survey resulted in the identification of pre-Contact Native sites in several of the proposed building envelopes and roadways (Herbster and Glover 1993). In the years that followed, PAL was hired to develop and to execute data recovery programs for two of the lots targeted for private house construction. Fieldwork began in the fall of 1997. By the time the data recovery programs were initiated, however, house construction was well underway at one of the sites, and delivery trucks and carpenters had to pass over the archaeological project area to get to work each day.

Human burials were exposed at this site in the first week of the excavations, and in accordance with the Massachusetts Unmarked Burial Law (M.G.L. Chapter 7, Section 38A), the state archaeologist, the Massachusetts Commission on Indian Affairs, and the tribe were immediately notified. Excavation was halted until representatives from the state archaeologist's office and the tribe could meet on-site to discuss the situation and to make decisions regarding the human remains. Tribal administrators were aware that the data recovery project was underway, but this meeting marked the first time members had visited the site area.

The exposure of two in-situ burial features in different portions of the project area concerned everyone. One of the burials was located less than 30 m from the house site, and it was easy to see that a tremendous amount of earth had been removed around the foundation. The two burial features were located in areas planned for a swimming pool and a driveway. It was clear from the outset that the ongoing construction within the restrictive two-acre building envelope limited options for both preservation and development. After the meeting, the burials were carefully backfilled together with the materials collected from them and their vicinity fenced off. The remaining data recovery units were excavated and filled, their contents returned to the PAL facility in Pawtucket, Rhode Island, for processing. Construction workers and materials continued to pass through the archaeological site area, although the property owner and site foreman had been notified that the fenced-off areas were to be avoided.

Since the site was located entirely on private property, the project did not fall under the scope of NAGPRA. No federal or state agencies were involved in funding or permitting the development, and thus there were no regulatory requirements under Section 106. The MVC's jurisdiction over the initial subdivision project was the only reason the project had come under MHC review in the early phases of the process. Cultural resource review of the current project was essentially confined to the state archaeologist's office and to the provisions of the Massachusetts Unmarked Burial Law. Fortunately, this comprehensive legislation ensures that when Native American human remains are identified, descendant communities are consulted prior to any excavation (see Simon, this volume).

All parties involved in the project agreed that the extent of the burial features and any related site components needed to be determined in order to make decisions regarding the site. In December 1997 PAL returned to the site and completed machine-assisted stripping across the intact portion of the building envelope. The topsoil removal across a 1,400-m² area resulted in the exposure of more than 200 features. The shape, size, and orientation of 110 features suggested that they could be burials, although no excavation into the features was completed as part of the delineation project.

With the mapping underway, a second on-site consultation meeting was scheduled to discuss the ongoing construction project and the identified archaeological deposits. The landowner and state archaeologist were present along with representatives of the WTGH/A Tribal Council and Cultural Committee, including several tribal elders. The landowner saw no real options other than excavation, since his house was nearly done, the pool and cabana had been started, and even the landscaping was underway around the house and driveway. The tribe felt strongly that the site was a sacred area and that the excavation of so many burials was unacceptable. The consultation meeting ended with no real resolution, although the landowner's architect agreed to look at redesign options that would minimize disturbance within the delineated site area around the house and garage/guest house.

The options of either avoidance of the entire site area or preservation in place were ultimately eliminated. The property owner had no other way to access the house (the site was located between the house and the driveway/garage area linking the property to the main access road), and the conservation covenants on the surrounding portions of the lot prevented the relocation of the driveway and utilities (all of which were required to be underground) outside the designated building envelope. Consultation with the state and the tribe, with PAL acting as the "good-faith" archaeologists for the landowner, ultimately led to a quasi redesign to avoid the portion of the site that contained one of the two burials identified during the data recovery. The size of the work area around the house was reduced so that 53 of the 110 potential burial features would not be affected by construction and landscaping.

Although the tribe's desire to see a preservation easement established around the entire site was not fully realized, the cultural importance of the site was carefully considered as the mitigation phase progressed. The PAL archaeologists, who had a strong commitment to respecting the Wampanoag heritage on the island, met privately with tribal members at their offices to discuss protocols for excavating and handling any human remains and associated cultural objects.

Ultimately, the tribe requested that all cultural materials and soils from the excavations remain on-site for the duration of the fieldwork and be reburied within the preserved portion of the site following completion of the project. The handling of artifacts was limited to basic recording tasks. Human remains were to be identified and recorded through noninvasive physical analysis. Screened soils from burials were to be kept separate from one another and from other features so that materials and soils could be reinterred together. Radiocarbon samples were collected from only a few features, and no destructive analyses were performed on any possible sacred features. Access to project data and especially photographs of burials was to be strictly limited following the archaeological work. The landowner also deeded to the tribe a preservation restriction on the unexcavated portion of the site, with full access rights to the burial ground area. It was clear to all involved that this site was not to be treated strictly as a research project. As stated in PAL's technical proposal, one of the primary goals of the investigation was "to insure that all archaeological tasks were completed in a careful, respectful manner and that the sacred/ceremonial nature of the burial ground be considered at all times." These protocols were included in a memorandum of agreement signed by the landowner, state archaeologist, and WTGH/A for this phase of the project.

Tribal representatives were on-site regularly to oversee and advise the PAL archaeological team. They provided round-the-clock security at the site while the archaeologists were not working. Randy Jardin, a tribal member who had worked unofficially with PAL on previous Vineyard projects, joined the field team for the duration of the project. In order to meet the tribe's requirements for field and lab work on an active construction site, the computer cataloging and photography were completed in an on-site trailer. The landowner's contractor built a temporary secure storage area in the house basement where all artifacts were stored during the fieldwork and where physical anthropologists Thomas Crist and Arthur Washburn completed their analysis. Opaque movable shelters were placed over the excavation areas to ensure that features were not exposed to construction workers or the elements. All site visitors were recorded in a daily log, and the tribe was notified before any nontribal visitors were allowed on-site.

The special circumstances of the site excavation meant that few archaeologists (outside the PAL team) were able to contribute to the analysis and interpretation of this unique cultural area. Tribal members who visited were generally reluctant to share their thoughts about the site with the archaeologists, other than to make it clear that this was a sacred area. Their displeasure with the outcome of the consultation process was constantly evident and affected the morale of the field team, many of whom felt that the excavation of this site was somehow disrespectful. Everyone seemed truly relieved when the months of fieldwork were finally over and the daily trips to the site stopped.

Following PAL's completion of the archaeological tasks and reporting to the MHC, the objects collected on-site were moved into temporary storage at the Tribal Administrative Complex. The private home was eventually completed, and the protected site area replanted with native grasses and plant species. The tribe reinterred the excavated human remains in a private ceremony and continues to watch over the site today.

The result of the project was a careful documentation of the archaeological site, but more questions about its creation and use were raised than were answered. The tremendous cost of the archaeological work, due in part to the special conditions imposed by the tribe and agreed to by all parties, did not contribute to any educational outcome for either the tribal membership or the professional archaeological community. In fact, most tribal members living on the island probably know only what the local newspapers reported: wildly inaccurate stories about a massive number of graves discovered by construction workers digging a pool foundation. The extremely sensitive nature of the site probably prevented some of the more open conversations that normally characterized PAL's relationship with the tribe. Although treating this sacred place as a "research project" was clearly not the right thing to do, it seems that some form of educational program could have been developed with the tribe following the completion of the project. This would have allowed PAL an opportunity to present the archaeological information to the tribe (or at least some portion of the membership), and it would have given tribal members an opportunity to ask questions, to share opinions, and to help both groups understand the importance of this site.

CRM in the Island Community

The most recent opportunities for CRM collaboration have occurred in what is literally the tribe's backyard—the town of Aquinnah. Tribal members make up a majority of the 201 year-round residents and are active participants in town government. Rapid development elsewhere on the Vineyard has now moved into Aquinnah, and in 2000 the residents reacted to these pressures by enacting a unique bylaw that requires every new building permit application to be assessed for the construction area's potential to contain archaeological deposits. If new construction is planned in an area deemed to be culturally significant by state *or* tribal authorities, an archaeological survey is requested, at the landowner's expense. This aggressive bylaw is the only one of its kind in the region and has led to the identification of 16 previously unidentified archaeological sites through 20 surveys. In cases where a survey is not required, or where site preparation activities (e.g., perc testing) are proposed, the Aquinnah Planning Board has the discretion to request tribal archaeologist Randy Jardin to be on site during construction to ensure that sacred sites, including human burials, are not inadvertently disturbed.

The bylaw surveys have located prehistoric sites in environmental zones previously considered to be unlikely to contain deposits, and have documented many small, short-term hunting and collecting sites that were missing from the earlier avocational and academic archaeological records. But perhaps more important, these surveys have provided an opportunity for archaeologists and tribal members to connect with individual members of the island community, to explain the need for site identification and protection, and to help nontribal members understand the historic connection the Aquinnah people have to the land. PAL has been fortunate to have completed all the Aquinnah surveys to date, and the knowledge gained from personal and professional relationships with the tribe over more than a decade has proved to be an invaluable advantage in such a small community. The PAL archaeologists communicate, often in person and on-site, with members of the planning board and regularly stop at the tribal offices for project updates. Camille Rose, the planning board chair, consults with Randy Jardin regarding upcoming permit applications and archaeological sensitivity at various building sites. The process has a decidedly informal feel at the town level but is backed up by the regulatory and reporting requirements of the MHC.

Although many new construction projects elsewhere on the island fall through the permiting cracks, the tribe has been successful in identifying and protecting many ancestral sites on Martha's Vineyard. Working together with the PAL archaeologists, the tribe has been able to use site excavation as a tool to educate the island community about the long history of the Aquinnah. Their efforts have greatly influenced the way PAL conducts archaeological work on Martha's Vineyard and surrounding mainland communities included in the Wampanoag Tribe's ancestral lands. The scope and methodology for each project are crafted not only to adhere to state and federal guidelines and standards but also to respect the sovereignty of the tribe and its active role in preserving the region's cultural heritage. This approach has been the greatest source of our success with the tribe, and we encourage other archaeologists to adopt similar strategies when establishing cross-cultural relationships with Native groups.

Conclusions

As demonstrated in the numerous examples provided in this chapter, allowing for innovative approaches to methodology and site interpretations is imperative to building partnerships in which both archaeologists and Native people are invested in the CRM process. This history of successful consultation with the tribe was challenged when Matthew Vanderhoop resigned from the THPO position in 2002. For several years, the WTGH/A was without a full-time tribal staff member to respond to CRM projects, including those being conducted under Section 106 of the NHPA. The absence of a THPO did not greatly affect the number or quality of archaeological surveys in Aquinnah, owing in large part to the adherence to the cultural resources bylaw and the vigilance of Randy Jardin, Camille Rose, and others. Unfortunately, many other off-island projects went through the consultation process without input from the tribe. On one visit to the tribal administrator's office, stacks of environmental impact statements, CRM reports, and federal agency letters were grouped into piles, and administrator Laurie Perry expressed frustration at the lack of time and resources to address each one.

Cheryl Andrews-Maltais has recently been selected as the new THPO and is working to get through the backlog of projects while trying to provide a strong tribal voice in future consultation projects. She has renewed the tribe's partnership with PAL through open and regular communication, and recently invited PAL to lead a training workshop for a group of Native cultural resource monitors who will assist her in the field.

These opportunities to exchange information, to talk and to listen, are critical in our current sociopolitical climate, where cultural resource protection is often a low priority. As archaeologists working in the tribe's ancestral territory, we must be willing to make the extra effort required to ensure that the relationship begun more than a decade ago continues to grow. Many challenges lie ahead, but only by working together can we expect to preserve the past for the future.

Acknowledgments

The authors would like to thank Jordan Kerber and Deborah Cox for reviewing the draft manuscript and for providing editorial suggestions that have improved the text. While this chapter highlights a few of the larger cultural resource projects that have been completed by PAL over the past decade, collaboration with the Wampanoag Tribe of Gay Head/Aquinnah and its membership occurs on a regular basis on Martha's Vineyard. The authors have benefited professionally and personally from the relationships developed with cultural and natural resources staff and Tribal Council members Matthew Vanderhoop, Mark Harding, Mark Andrews, Laurie Perry, Cheryl Andrews-Maltais, Berta Welch, Helen Manning, Beverly Wright, Bret Stearns, and Jeff Day. Randy Jardin has worked closely with the PAL staff both on and off the Vineyard, and his status as a tribal member and archaeologist provides a constant reminder of the need to balance the past and present.

12. Tribal Consultation in Pennsylvania
A Personal View from within the
Pennsylvania Department of Transportation

IRA BECKERMAN

Since 2001 federal regulations require agencies to consult with federally recognized Indian tribes when projects have an impact on historic properties that hold religious or cultural significance to the tribes. Both the Pennsylvania Division of the Federal Highway Administration (FHWA) and the Pennsylvania Department of Transportation (PennDOT) have been struggling to interpret and fulfill their regulatory requirements in an honest and efficient manner. This paper explores a specific case example on a large multistate highway improvement project where both the FHWA and PennDOT have had to adjust approaches to consultation. This trial by fire was exceedingly difficult and "mistakes were made." Nevertheless, the postproject relationship with the involved tribes is significantly healthier.

Legislative Changes

Five hundred years ago, a survey of the landscape that was to become Pennsylvania would find no archaeologists inhabiting the land. Nor would it find Pennsylvania, for that matter, or the National Park Service, the National Historic Preservation Act, FHWA, or PennDOT. Roads would be trails, and the people would be repairing pots instead of potholes. What one would find here would be Native Americans, organized into tribes and peacefully and not so peacefully tending their land.[1] In their activities, they created archaeological sites for future generations of archaeologists, although I doubt that was their main goal in life.

Today, a survey of the regulatory landscape in Pennsylvania would find the National Park Service, the Commonwealth of Pennsylvania, the Pennsylvania Historical and Museum Commission (within which the State Historic Preservation Office resides), PennDOT, and the FHWA. Roads would be paved, in between the potholes. There would be archaeologists and archaeological sites. One would find no Native American tribes, despite significant changes to the National Historic Preservation Act in 1992.

Those changes strengthened the role Native American tribes play in the regulatory process surrounding Section 106 of the National Historic Preservation Act. With the implementation in 2001 of revised federal regulations (36 CFR 800), the changes formally brought tribes to the table as consulting parties when those tribes attached religious or cultural significance to historic properties that might be affected by federally funded projects. The regulations apply to properties on and off tribal lands. That latter point is key, since Pennsylvania has not had tribal lands for almost 50 years.

Between 1992 and 2000, neither the FHWA nor PennDOT made any proactive effort to implement these changes in the regulations, although individuals within PennDOT, notably Jamie McIntyre (PennDOT Archaeologist, District 4-0), did raise concerns that ignoring these changes would lead to unpleasant consequences. Contacts with representatives from the Seneca Nation and Onondaga Nation, both federally recognized tribes located in New York State, were seen by PennDOT largely as an expedient to make the non-federally recognized groups go away.

Oops!

All this changed a few years ago, at the convergence of seemingly independent events. Early in 2001, when the final implementing regulations for revisions to the National Historic Preservation Act (36 CFR 800) were published, consultation with federally recognized tribes that attached significance to properties became directed, not optional. Such tribes were to

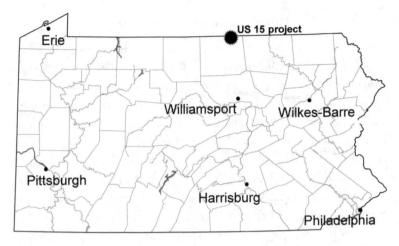

Figure 12.1. Map of Pennsylvania, indicating the location of the US 15 project in Tioga County (Prepared by Ira Beckerman).

be treated as sovereign nations, placing the FHWA in the role of U.S. governmental representative in government-to-government relations. Tribes appeared to have coequal authority with the State Historic Preservation Office(r) (SHPO) on projects in matters concerning identification of historic sites, eligibility of sites for listing in the National Register of Historic Places, potential effects of the project, and the resolution of any adverse effects.

The FHWA began to take its charge seriously, appointing a national tribal coordinator at the end of 2000. The FHWA also began working on policy through selected FHWA state divisions and state departments of transportation—an early summit in Iowa being one notable success. In Pennsylvania, Cathy Glidden, on rotation from FHWA Headquarters, provided support for the state division office during 2002. Concurrent with the FHWA's actions, the Advisory Council on Historic Preservation (Advisory Council) undertook a major training initiative on tribal consultation, offering on-site courses for tribes, SHPOs, and agencies. In 2001 one such course was offered to the Haudenosaunee (Six Nations, also known colloquially as the Iroquois Confederacy) in New York. Tribes were informed of their rights under the revised federal regulations.

The catalyzing event was the preliminary design for a major PennDOT project on US 15, in Tioga County, Pennsylvania, and in Steuben County,

New York (Figure 12.1). In addition to the usual environmental issues, this project required coordination between two states, New York and Pennsylvania, with two FHWA divisions (Pennsylvania ultimately took the lead), two DOTs, and two SHPOs. The project was the initiative of then Pennsylvania governor Tom Ridge and was on an accelerated schedule. Excavation of a major Late Woodland village (Site 36Ti28) (ca. A.D. 1000–1600) that was threatened by this project was undertaken during the spring of 2002, based on a work plan agreed to by (only) the SHPO. A programmatic memorandum of agreement for this project had been drafted and was being routed for signature. A month later, the Seneca Nation asked why they or other tribes had not been consulted on the project. Archaeological work stopped.

For PennDOT and the Pennsylvania Division of the FHWA, this was one of those moments of truth. This was the first time a federally recognized tribe had come forward to assert its rights to consultation, and the tribe did not even have lands in Pennsylvania. In other states when a similar situation occurred, the DOT would invariably react by experiencing denial, followed by anger, resistance, and failure, leading ultimately, after a number of years, to some level of understanding and cooperation.

Over the course of several tense weeks, key representatives from the Advisory Council (Valerie Hauser), PennDOT (Susan McDonald), the FHWA (Karyn Vandervoort and Deborah Suciu Smith), the SHPO (Jean Cutler), and the Pennsylvania State Museum (Anita Blackaby) worked with Kathy Mitchell of the Seneca Nation and other tribal representatives to try something different. The FHWA and PennDOT would follow not only the letter but also the spirit of the law. The specifics of the agreement for the project included *full* sharing of information and full consultation with the Seneca Nation, Cayuga Nation, and Delaware Nation. A Web site was established to provide accurate and rapid information, on-site meetings were planned for every five or six weeks or as requested, documents were to be submitted to all groups simultaneously, and e-mail and phone calls would fill in as warranted. Other elements of the agreement included creation of a scale model of the excavated longhouse for the Seneca-Iroquois National Museum, production of an interpretive video, and a willingness to loan artifacts recovered from the excavations to the Seneca Nation for an extended period. The final agreement was executed late that summer, and these elements have been and continue to be implemented. Following execution of the agreement, genuine consultation has not added unacceptable delays to the project. The Advisory Council ultimately sent a written commendation to PennDOT for its actions on this particular project.

Shortly after the agreement on US 15 was executed, PennDOT staff went to Onondaga, New York, in September 2002 for special Section 106 training in tribal consultation sponsored by the Haudenosaunee and the Advisory Council. More PennDOT professionals attended the training than from any other New York or Pennsylvania governmental office. The opportunity to break bread together and meet and talk outside the formal training was as valuable as the training itself. The ideas shared at Onondaga only reinforced the path we had begun to take with the US 15 consultation.

In late spring 2003, human remains in burial features, probably dating to the thirteenth century (based on associated artifacts) or sixteenth century (based on recent radiocarbon dates from remains of two structures known regionally as "key-hole" for their distinctive shape) were discovered on site 36Ti28 on the US 15 project. As specified in the agreement, work at the site in the immediate vicinity of the burials ceased, and the FHWA initiated consultation with the tribes that were signatories to the agreement, the SHPO, and the Advisory Council.

The goals the FHWA set out for the consultation were as defined in Section 106, regulations 36 CFR 800: "Consultation means the process of seeking, discussing, and considering the views of other participants, and, where feasible, seeking agreement with them regarding matters arising in the section 106 process." Because the FHWA considered presence of human remains a fundamentally new characteristic of site 36Ti28, notices of the remains were sent to all 15 tribes (see n. 1), not just the ones that were consulting parties to the agreement. Initially and informally, the Seneca Nation and other tribes that responded preferred that the project avoid the area of the burials. If that were not possible, the tribes favored leaving the remains in place, even though that portion of the project area was scheduled for the placement of an on-ramp to US 15, which would require some 6 m of fill directly over the burials. The Senecas also requested that further archaeological work cease, with the exception of the excavation of one "key-hole" structure feature that was of scientific and historic interest to both the archaeologists involved in the project and tribal historians. The SHPO's position, on the other hand, favored further archaeological investigations on the site, "scientific" analysis of the features containing human remains, and intrusive analysis of the human remains themselves. The SHPO also questioned whose Indians these were and suggested that ancestry be determined.

The Senecas' request to halt further archaeological work was based on the realistic expectation that a village the size of 36Ti28 would contain other burials and that the pattern of burial in and around longhouses, instead of in a cemetery, meant that those burials would not be predictable. Fortunately from PennDOT's standpoint, the request to cease further archaeological work did not compromise the data recovery from the site, since site fieldwork was projected for completion within two weeks. Tribal, consultant, and PennDOT archaeologists agreed that the information recovered to date could appropriately and adequately answer the research questions that had originally made the site eligible for listing in the National Register of Historic Places. In response to the SHPO's concerns over ancestry, the agreement that had been signed by all parties, including the SHPO, did not require the FHWA to determine ancestry of human remains, only to consult with the signatory tribes. Plans were made to bury the portion of the site containing human remains under geotextile fabric and fill, in a sensitive manner.

On June 12, 2003, the Seneca Faith Keepers' School brought its students to the site. There, the students asked why their ancestors were being buried under fill, with a road to be placed on top. The question resonated strongly among the Seneca Nation—who, along with other tribes, place a high value on not disturbing ancestral remains—and after much internal debate they reaffirmed their original preference that the burials be avoided, including any burials that might be found in the unexcavated portion of the site proposed for construction activities.

The FHWA and PennDOT traveled to Seneca, New York, to facilitate a meeting with the tribe to try to reach consensus, and on July 21, 2003, the FHWA and PennDOT facilitated another tour of the site by the Seneca Faith Keepers. PennDOT first offered to move the estimated six burials under tribal supervision to land adjoining a current Christian cemetery adjacent to site 36Ti28. Archaeologists would physically remove the burials for transport, but no studies would be conducted. The FHWA again informed the remaining tribes and sought their input, as well as that of the Advisory Council and the SHPO. None of the tribes found this option suitable.

At a November 2003 videoconference, the Senecas restated their position that the burials be avoided, pointing out that they had not requested the road improvement. The Senecas' (and other tribes') feeling was one of frustration. PennDOT and the FHWA seemed intent on building the road in their preferred path, regardless of tribal views. If avoiding the burial areas was out of the question because of costs, that meant that money was more important than respect for their ancestors. All of this continued the tradition of the dominant society dictating terms to the tribes. However, movement of the project footprint off the site would also affect other known and expected archaeological deposits along the Cowanesque Creek and Tioga Creek floodplains. And the relocation would have a large environmental impact on nearby wetlands, and socioeconomic impact on the local community. At an estimated additional cost of $28 million (out of a project cost of $118 million), the FHWA dismissed the possibility of spanning the site with a structure. Besides being too expensive, such a structure would also require additional excavation at the location of the piers, which could identify further burials. Considering these factors, the FHWA again restated the inadvisability of relocation. The SHPO clarified its position, requesting additional archaeological excavation on the site, but it did not expressly request further intrusive analysis of the burials. While the meeting could be characterized as civil and contained, it was by no means cordial.

After the meeting, and after additional consultation, the FHWA decided to leave the burials in place. The FHWA interpreted the tribes' position to be that leaving the burials in place was less harmful than removal. Plans were made after the meeting to cover the site immediately with geotextile and clean fill, to protect the site from further exposure to the elements and desecration. The tribes requested that the SHPO specify in writing its request for further work and archaeological analysis.

The Light Bulb Goes On

What was learned from the US 15 project? First and foremost, any successful relationship has to be built on mutual honesty, trust, and respect. Easy words to say, but hard and sometimes painful to put into practice. As PennDOT staff, we had to be honest with ourselves. We had to acknowledge that we did not do the right thing, even though we were trying to support the governor's initiative. We had to respect the concerns of the Seneca, Cayuga, and Delaware tribes as legitimate concerns, even though they were being raised to us for the first time. We had to trust the tribes, and we had to trust the process, even though we were feeling tremendous pressure to move the project forward and trust meant an immediate delay of unknown length. We had to trust people we did not know in a situation we had never experienced. It was not easy for the tribes to trust us, either. They also had to trust people they did not know in a new situation. Furthermore, they had to trust a DOT and FHWA division that had not been following the regulations.

Nonetheless, it appears that the FHWA and PennDOT reached a point with the tribes that allowed communication to occur. Given the complexity of the issues involved, communication was imperfect, but I believe the FHWA, members of the Seneca Nation, and the other consulting tribes made an extra effort to hear and be heard. Not surprisingly, the burial issue sparked internal debate within the Seneca Nation, proving again that tribes are not monolithic political or social entities. At this time, it appears that none of the feasible options available to the FHWA will be fully embraced by all tribal members, but there may be at least one option that is acceptable.

Building a Relationship and Navigating the Behemoth to Starboard

One project does not a relationship or policy make. In order to build on what we may have learned from the US 15 project, PennDOT and the FHWA had to take meaningful steps to integrate tribal consultation into its design process. If PennDOT was to make a significant shift in its policies, we all had to remember that getting an organization with $1.4 billion in annual construction on 1,000 projects to shift is akin to turning an ocean liner at full throttle on the high sea.

In February 2003 PennDOT issued a formal, internal memo to all district engineers and the district administrator providing interim guidance on tribal consultation.[2] The main purpose of memo was to explain the philosophy and regulatory basis behind tribal consultation, and who should be contacted, how they should be contacted, and when. A pair of notification forms—one for initial notification and one for subsequent notification—was provided. A list of rules was presented both for entering into appropriate tribal consultation when a project had been started previously and for beginning consultation on new projects. Contact information for each recognized tribe was included in an appendix to the letter.

PennDOT's memo deals primarily with federally recognized tribes. These are not, however, the only Native Americans or Native American groups out there. There are other individuals and groups in Pennsylvania that claim Native American ancestry and legitimacy as Native Americans. PennDOT is faced with certain choices in this matter. One choice could be to sort out who is Native American and who is not, and which groups are legitimate and which are not. After all, not every individual of Native American ancestry belongs to a federally recognized tribe. Not every tribe has sought federal recognition or, in the process of seeking recognition, has achieved that goal.

Fortunately, the decision of who is Native American, and who decides, is not one that PennDOT and the FHWA have to make. Special status for consultation under Section 106 of the National Historic Preservation Act belongs only to federally recognized tribes, not to individuals and not to other groups. However, other individuals and groups should not be ignored (see Watkins, this volume). Consulting party status should be given to groups or individuals who have a demonstrated interest. The standard for consulting party status is not whether the individuals or groups are Native American but whether they have a demonstrated interest, a much easier question to answer.[3]

Archaeological investigations generate collections, and these need to be curated. The Native American Graves Protection and Repatriation Act (NAGPRA) does not apply to PennDOT because the FHWA owns no lands, and in any case, there are no current tribal lands in Pennsylvania. Under the State History Code, the Pennsylvania Historical and Museum Commission (PHMC) has the right of first refusal for artifacts recovered from state lands. In situations where PennDOT (and hence the Commonwealth) has not secured title to the land, the artifacts belong to the landowner (which is consistent with federal regulation 36 CFR 79). Through a deed of gift, collections can be given to the Commonwealth for the PHMC to manage.

It is permissible for the FHWA to enter into an agreement with a tribe to loan artifacts to the tribe, but that loan is premised on the agreement of the SHPO (and thereby the PHMC). In the US 15 project, as mentioned previously, collections from the 36Ti28 site will be loaned to the Seneca Nation. An outright gift would be much more complicated insofar as disposition of state property is regulated by the Pennsylvania Department of General Services. For the present, long-term loans appear to be a reasonable solution to the goal of getting artifacts to those tribes that wish to exhibit and to study the objects.

Eight Simple Rules

Beyond simply meeting legal requirements, why should the FHWA and PennDOT consult with tribes, especially since there are no reserved tribal lands within the Commonwealth? Section 106 is a consultation process. Taken fully, it is about bringing interested parties to the table, getting their views, and coming to good decisions. This is also a goal of the National Environmental Policy Act. At one time PennDOT consulted only with the SHPO, and later occasionally with the FHWA. More recently, PennDOT has realized the need to identify other consulting parties and has taken measures to ensure they are identified and have their views heard.

If the standard for being considered a consulting party on a project is a having a compelling interest in the outcome of historic preservation, how is a tribe's interest in an archaeological site any less valid than the interest of any other consulting party, including the SHPO's? Why should we have less respect for the interests of a tribe than of a historical society or local municipality? The changes to the law and regulations extend to off-tribal lands precisely because removal of Indians from the land did not remove their heritage or their interest. Without the force of law, it is unlikely that PennDOT or any other agency would fulfill its obligation to bring an interested party into consultation on a project, especially if that party is 200 years and 1,000 miles removed from the project. Are distance and passage of time justifications for excluding tribes? One need only look to the Middle East or the Balkans to see the durability of a people's unflagging interest in their heritage.

These appear to be the guiding principles for tribal consultation:

1. Each tribe is a sovereign nation within the borders of the United States. Consequently, tribes deserve the respect afforded to sovereign nations. This does not mean that only the FHWA (or any other federal agency) can work with or talk to tribes. States routinely undertake trade missions to foreign countries without the direct intervention of the federal government. What it does mean is that there is a specialization of roles both within the tribe and within the DOT. Creating initial contacts, establishing major policy, and resolving major problems all need to occur between tribal leaders and the FHWA. Routine consultation on projects, exchange of information, and discussion of technical issues should occur at the staff level, where that expertise resides.

2. Currently, there are 15 federally recognized tribes that at one time lived in Pennsylvania. Each tribal government is organized differently, and some tribes (naturally) have long-standing relationships with other tribes. Consequently, PennDOT cannot and should not assume a one-size-fits-all policy on tribal consultation.

3. Developing a tribal consultation policy is an ongoing process, not a once-and-done effort. PennDOT's interim policy offers initial guidance, but it is unlikely that a fully detailed policy will ever be completed. This is a natural outcome of the fact that as PennDOT works on its relationship with the tribes, that relationship will evolve. The Haudenosaunee have a term for this, "burnishing the silver chain."

4. PennDOT's understanding of the history, political organization, and culture of each tribe is woefully inadequate, as is the tribes' understanding of PennDOT's corporate culture and its project development process. Effective communication is dependent on understanding each other. Language is culturally conditioned, so our ability to hold a meaningful conversation is premised on our ability to understand each other's culture. The only remedy is ongoing cross-training, and a willingness to ask questions and not to assume answers.

5. It is no longer satisfactory for PennDOT to sit down unilaterally with the SHPO to make decisions on those projects where there are historic properties of religious or cultural significance to any of the 15 tribes that are in consultation with PennDOT. Tribes may have desires and needs separate from the SHPO that the FHWA and PennDOT must address. Resolving the potential adverse effects of projects may take more time than in the past, but it will lead to better overall decisions.

6. Streamlining consultation is desirable for both tribes and transportation. However, the means for streamlining need to be culturally sensitive. From the perspective of each tribe, the Pennsylvania Division of the FHWA is one agency in one state. Pennsylvania's transportation program may or may not be a priority for a tribe that has other, more local issues and needs. Consequently, PennDOT can easily overload a tribe's office with data and diminish, rather than improve, communication and consultation. One small measure to address the need for concise and accurate information is using a form for tribal consultation that contains the basic information in a consistent format.

7. The mandate contained within regulations 36 CFR 800 is broadly drawn and would seem to require the FHWA and PennDOT to be mind readers. Consultation on historic properties to which tribes attach significance begins early in the project before any properties are identified. PennDOT is in-

volved in over 1,000 projects a year. As they get more familiar with each other's needs, PennDOT and the tribes will continually find and refine criteria for sifting through this mass
of projects.

8. Tribal consultation is an activity that takes place among human beings and is therefore necessarily intricate, nuanced,
and prone to messiness. The best "tools" an agency can use in
consultations are truthfulness, patience, understanding, and
trust. Even these qualities will not guarantee an outcome that
everyone can enthusiastically support, but they should allow
a working relationship to endure and grow.

Peering at the Crystal Ball

In the fall of 2002, the Haudenosaunee hosted a gathering of federal and
state officials at Onondaga. A year later, the FHWA and PennDOT returned
the favor in the form of a tribal summit, inviting to Harrisburg all tribes
with an interest in Pennsylvania. The goals were to continue to work on
relationships, to educate each other on our respective cultures, and to explore improving the quality and efficiency of consultation on projects. The
annual gatherings will likely occur for the near future.

As PennDOT and the PHMC extend the Cultural Resources Geographic
Information System (GIS) to the Internet, there is an additional opportunity to enhance consultation with tribes. Individual tribes will be able to
query active projects to identify which archaeological sites might be affected, in the same way that the SHPO and PennDOT staff do currently.
The underlying GIS database can also be used as a tool to automate notices
to tribes, and the Web environment can be used to elicit responses. Not
only does this powerful communication tool benefit PennDOT, but it has
the potential to allow each tribe to manage its relationship with PennDOT
with a minimum of paperwork and physical effort in return for rapid and
useful information. Most tribes seem to be enthusiastic about the GIS concept, although not all currently have the technological means to use the
system. PennDOT and the FHWA are exploring novel ways to place such
technology at the disposal of all the tribes.

Acknowledgments

A version of this chapter was originally presented at the Society for Pennsylvania Archaeology Meetings, State College, Pennsylvania (Beckerman 2003). A number of individuals have influenced my thinking on tribal consultation and on this particular project. They include Kevin Cunningham (Delaware Department of Transportation), Cathy Glidden (FHWA), Valerie Hauser (Advisory Council), Christine Kula (PennDOT), Jamie McIntyre (PennDOT), Kathy Mitchell (Seneca Nation), Scott Shaffer (PennDOT), Deborah Suciu Smith (FHWA), and Karyn Vandervoort (FHWA). I would like to thank PennDOT for institutional and moral support. The views presented in this paper are the mine and do not necessarily represent the views of PennDOT or the FHWA.

Notes

1. The word "tribes" is used in a specific way, following the definition in the National Historic Preservation Act, as a federally recognized Indian tribe, of which 15 formerly lived in Pennsylvania. It does not refer to a level of cultural evolution as known by anthropologists. Most of the federally recognized tribes that were in Pennsylvania refer to themselves as nations. Naming the peoples that were here in A.D. 1500 is increasingly problematic and issue-laden. Instead of such terms as "First American," "First Peoples," "American Indian," or "the People," I am staying with the regulatory term, primarily because that term carries specific meaning and regulatory force for the FHWA. The 15 federally recognized tribes that were formerly in Pennsylvania are Absentee-Shawnee Tribe of Oklahoma; Cayuga Nation; Delaware Nation, Oklahoma; Delaware Tribe of Indians, Oklahoma; Eastern Shawnee Tribe of Oklahoma; Oneida Indian Nation of New York; Oneida Tribe of Indians of Wisconsin; Onondaga Indian Nation; Seneca Nation of Indians; Seneca-Cayuga Tribe of Oklahoma; Shawnee Tribe of Oklahoma; St. Regis Mohawk Tribe; Stockbridge-Munsee Community of Mohican Indians of Wisconsin; Tonawanda Seneca Nation; and Tuscarora Nation.

2. This memo is strike-off letter 438-03-03 (revised March 5, 2003), available from the cultural resources Web site (via the portal at www.penndotcrm.org) under "Publications."

3. Individuals' demonstrated interest in an undertaking would stem from the nature of their legal or economic relation to the undertaking or affected properties or from their concern with the undertaking's effects on historic properties (36 CFR 800.2).

13. Working Together
Developing Partnerships with American
Indians in New Jersey and Delaware

CARA LEE BLUME

Over the last several years, there has been sporadic discussion throughout the Middle Atlantic archaeological community about the interaction between archaeologists and American Indians. Much of this discussion, at least in Delaware, has focused on the role of Indians as informants—as potential providers of new and interesting ways of analyzing or interpreting the data archaeologists recover through excavation. And to some extent, there seems to be a perception that this is the main reason why archaeologists would be interested in working with Indian people. As the discussion has unfolded, I have come to the conclusion that the archaeologist–informant relationship is essentially exploitive and patronizing because it takes place on the archaeologist's terms—the informant must address issues that the archaeological community is interested in pursuing in terms that archaeologists understand—and it excludes participation by Indians who are unable or unwilling to participate on those terms. Furthermore, focusing on the role of the Indian as informant allows the archaeologist to avoid dealing with Indian communities as the direct or indirect ancestors of the people we study. By avoiding dealing with Indians in communities, we archaeologists can ignore the ethical questions raised by our assumption that only *we* can make responsible decisions about *their* past.

At the same time that this discussion was taking place, I became intensively involved with the three genealogically related Lenape and Nanticoke
communities in Delaware and southern New Jersey through a variety of
projects encountered in my various roles as agency archaeologist with the
Delaware Division of Parks and Recreation, as senior archaeologist for an
archaeological consulting firm, and as a pro bono archaeological consultant to the Nanticoke Lenni-Lenape Indians of New Jersey and the Lenape
Indian Tribe of Delaware. Through these experiences, I have become increasingly convinced that the only responsible interaction between archaeologists and Indians is a comprehensive one that includes American Indian *communities*, regardless of state or federal recognition status, in the
entire archaeological process, from site identification through excavation
and analysis, often through various forms of public outreach specifically
designed for the Indian audience. In other words, I have become convinced
that it is ethically necessary for archaeologists to work *with* Indian people
to create partnerships that include them in various ways in both the study
of Indian archaeological sites and the preservation of those sites. Implicit
in the notion of partnership is the sharing of power, so that Indian people become part of the decision-making process.

The Indian People of Delaware and Southern New Jersey

The genealogically intertwined Nanticoke, Lenape, and Nanticoke Lenni-
Lenape tribes of Delaware and southern New Jersey live in similar flat low
coastal plain environments of sandy soils cut by slow-moving streams affected in their lower reaches by tidal movement and bordered by extensive
tidal marshes. Until after World War II, they made their living as farmers,
watermen, and craftsmen, interacting with the local economy but keeping
themselves socially apart. I use the term "tribe" in discussing these communities not only because this is the term they use for themselves but also
because they fit the definition of tribes outlined by Vine Deloria Jr. in his
testimony in support of a Massachusetts tribal designation for the Mashpee Wampanoag of Cape Cod as people who know who their relatives are
and where they come from (Bordewich 1996:68). In other words, in using
the term "tribe," I mean that each of the communities discussed here has
occupied a more or less definable space for at least the last 250 years, and

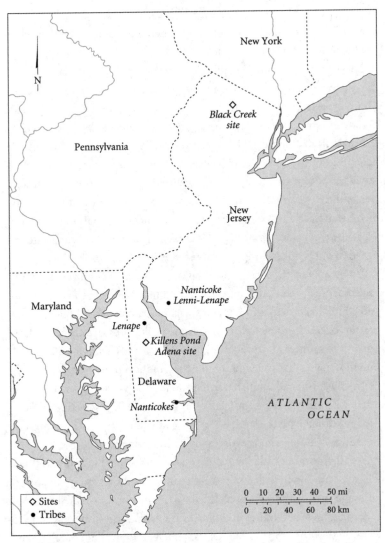

Figure 13.1. Location of tribal communities and sites discussed in the text.

the members of each community are all related to each other. The Nanticoke Tribe is located in southern Sussex County, Delaware, in and around the town of Millsboro and nearby Oak Orchard. The Lenape Tribe in Delaware is centered on the small town of Cheswold in Kent County. Almost directly across the Delaware Bay from Cheswold is the Nanticoke Lenni-

Lenape Tribe, located primarily in Cumberland County, New Jersey, in the Bridgeton area (Figure 13.1).

The Nanticoke Lenni-Lenape Tribe is recognized as an Indian community by resolution of the New Jersey legislature. There is no formal recognition process in place in Delaware, although the Nanticokes are treated as state recognized because there have been a number of legislative actions that specifically identify the Nanticoke Tribe. Both the Nanticoke Lenni-Lenape and the Nanticoke tribes are seeking federal recognition. An attempt by the Lenape Tribe of Delaware to gain state recognition by resolution of the Delaware legislature in 1993 was tabled when a politically active member of the Nanticoke Indian Association voiced vociferous opposition. The tribe is considering strategies for renewing its efforts to gain state recognition but is not seeking federal recognition at this time.

The people in these tribes are the descendants of Indian people who stayed behind when their relatives moved into New York, Pennsylvania, and Ohio, then north into Canada and southwest to Oklahoma. This migration began in the early to mid-1700s under pressure from the large number of immigrants, predominantly British and German, who flooded into the tribes' ancestral lands on the heels of the initial settlements by the Dutch, Swedish, and English trading companies (Weslager 1972). According to Canadian Lenape (or Delaware) tradition, they stayed to preserve the connection with the land, while those who left moved away to preserve the culture (Blume and Fragoso 2003; Crimmins 2002).

For the most part, all three tribes have survived by keeping to themselves, becoming invisible to the government and the dominant society, although one faction of the Nanticokes became more vocal about their Indian heritage beginning in the 1880s. The Lenape community in Delaware, on the other hand, remained extremely reticent about publicly identifying as Indian until the 1980s. The mixed Lenape/Nanticoke community in southern New Jersey also remained reticent about their heritage through most of the twentieth century, but began to speak publicly nearly two decades earlier than the Lenape in Delaware.

Much of the Nanticoke activism can be attributed to the leadership of one member of the community, William Russel Clark, and his descendants. Clark became the primary informant for a series of anthropological studies (Babcock 1899:279; Speck 1942; Tantaquidgeon 1942:52; Weslager 1943a:88–89), as well as a leader in political action, facilitated by his position as a messenger in the Delaware legislature (Weslager 1943a:93) and as the first chief of the Nanticoke Indian Association. Clark's political activism, extending over most of his life, coupled with his close relationship with several anthropologists, most notably Frank Speck, placed the Nanticokes at the center of academic and governmental interest in the Indian communities of Delaware. This position was maintained by the activities of his sons and a grandson who succeeded him as chief of the Nanticoke Indian Association, and a great-grandson who until recently served as assistant chief.

Each of the anthropologists who wrote about the Nanticokes reported that there was a second Indian community in Delaware—in and around the Kent County town of Cheswold—and most identified that community as having Delaware (Lenape) tribal roots (Babcock 1899:277; Porter 1987:67; Speck 1915:2, 8; Tantaquidgeon 1942:53). Nonetheless, no anthropological studies were conducted in the Cheswold community until the late 1930s and early 1940s, when C. A. Weslager made a number of visits. Of these researchers, only Weslager (1943a:142) mentions the Nanticoke Lenni-Lenape community around Bridgeton, New Jersey. During the 1980s and 1990s, however, a series of historical studies were conducted in and around the Lenape community as part of cultural resources management studies conducted by Heite Consulting for the Delaware Department of Transportation (Heite 1993; Heite and Blume n.d.; Heite and Blume 1992; Heite and Heite 1985). Most of the research in the Nanticoke Lenni-Lenape community has been conducted by a tribal member, anthropologist Tina Pierce Fragoso (2003), and is as yet unpublished.

Indians as Informants: Problems and Concerns

For more than a century, anthropologists have studied American Indian cultures through Native informants—often individuals who are willing to serve as guides and interpreters, but not necessarily those who are most knowledgeable or most representative of the community. The goal of the anthropologist has been to collect pieces of information that can be tied together to create a coherent verbal picture of the culture as a whole or of some aspect of that culture. In the all-too-rare instances where archaeologists have had the interest to interact with Indians, the goal has been to collect specific pieces of information that can be applied to questions that the archaeologist wants to answer. Because the anthropologist or archaeologist determines not only the questions that are asked but also the manner in which the answers are used, this process is inherently one-sided, no matter how cordial the interaction. This is not to say that this approach cannot be pursued respectfully. However, it is important that we understand the pitfalls of such studies.

In Delaware, the current interest in working with Indians in an informant–archaeologist relationship derives in part from two recent studies in which archaeologists have interacted with one particular Indian, Charles Clark IV, formerly assistant chief of the Nanticoke Indian Association, and a few of his closest associates (Clark and Custer 2003; Petraglia et al. 2002; Petraglia and Cunningham, this volume). Both of these studies have resulted in interesting new approaches to the analysis of pre-Contact American Indian archaeological deposits that will undoubtedly stimulate similar studies in the future—and will at the very least influence the analyses that are conducted for more conventional archaeological studies that do not involve collaboration with Indian people. But both were conducted in an atmosphere of antagonistic and divisive intertribal and governmental politics that effectively excluded the Lenape community from participation in the archaeological process, even though the sites in question are located only a few miles from their core area and within the area that is generally accepted as pre-Contact Lenape territory (Custer 1989:334; Goddard 1978a:214–215; Prewitt 2001:6; Speck 1915:8; Weslager 1943b, 1949).

An informant is often a single individual who can present information in a manner that is readily acceptable to anthropologists or archaeologists, or who is able to develop a rapport with a particular anthropologist or archaeologist. It is important to understand, however, that no one Indian or faction within an Indian community possesses all the traditional knowledge within the community, nor does one Indian or faction represent the full range of opinion within the community. Focusing on that one individual who can communicate comfortably the information the archaeologist is interested in receiving limits interaction with other members of the community. This not only limits the range of opinions and information available to the archaeologist but also denies access to archaeological information to other members of the community who might be interested in learning something about this arcane activity. Most important, it prevents the archaeologist from understanding the dynamics of Indian society and the place of her informant within that society—a place that may not be adequately defined by formal tribal structures.

Other kinds of problems can arise when the archaeologist bases her expectations for interaction with Indians on an informant model. Being asked, sometimes unexpectedly, to offer an opinion on a collection of artifacts or a site feature could be intimidating for anyone, Indian or not, who is not trained or experienced in archaeology or in any kind of academic dialogue. For many Indians, particularly for members of tribes that are not federally recognized, there can be the feeling that their Indian identity is being judged and found wanting. And if they never hear from the archaeologist again, this perception is confirmed. If the archaeologist has not taken the time to get to know the community and its history, there is the feeling that the tribe has, once again, been unfairly judged.

The informant relationship may also place the archaeologist (or anthropologist) in the position of taking sides in internal tribal or intertribal politics—sometimes without understanding the issues or social dynamics involved. In Delaware, William Babcock, Speck, and Weslager were all aware of an attitude of animosity on the part of their Nanticoke informants toward the Cheswold Lenape community despite a pattern of intermarriage between the two tribes. And this does seem to have influenced the research of Speck and his students (Weslager 1943a:128), most noticeably in the case of Gladys Tantaquidgeon, who included observations on Nanticoke practices in her study of Delaware (Lenape) folk medicine (Tantaquidgeon 1942) but did not look at folk practices in a community that her Nanticoke informant identified as Delaware.

If the informant relationship is not the right model for Indian–archaeologist interaction, what model should we use? Perhaps the first thing we should do is to ask ourselves whether we have the right to decide the one "correct" way to interact. Instead, shouldn't we allow each Indian community (as well as individuals within each community) to decide the nature and intensity of their involvement in archaeology by providing multiple opportunities for interaction on a number of different levels? Developing a relationship with any Indian tribe is a dynamic process. Attempting to constrain or manipulate the process through a single model or fixed set of procedures only exacerbates the tensions that already exist between archaeologists and Indian communities. Below I offer two examples from my own experience that illustrate how a more open model of interaction might operate. In the first, I describe my experiences working as a pro bono archaeological consultant for the Nanticoke Lenni-Lenape Indians of New Jersey in their efforts to protect the Black Creek site in northern New Jersey. We developed a set of standards for archaeological research at the site that emphasized the role of the tribe in managing the site. In the second, as an agency archaeologist, I sought the participation of all three tribes in deciding how to handle a remnant of the Killens Pond site, in Delaware, that was threatened by erosion.

The Preservation of the Black Creek Site

The Black Creek site is located in the Vernon Valley of northern New Jersey, at the point where Black Creek and Waywayanda Creek come together to form Pochuk Creek, a tributary of the Walkill River. The site preserves evidence of American Indian occupations dating from the Early Archaic period (ca. 8,000–9,000 years ago) to the end of the seventeenth century, when the Lenape people were forced to leave the Vernon Valley, in contexts that range from stratified floodplain deposits at the northern end of the site to the plow zone in fields at the southern end (Patterson 2001; Santone et al. 1997). The recovery of an effigy stone from a Late Woodland context (ca. 1,000–400 years ago) at the southern end of the site marks the site as a place of particular spiritual power for the Lenape people (Kraft 2001:325–330; Patterson 2001). It is this spiritual aspect of the Black Creek site, coupled with the long history of American Indian settlement, that led the Nanticoke Lenni-Lenape Indians of New Jersey to become involved in the site's preservation.

The campaign to preserve the Black Creek site began in April 2000 as a local land use planning controversy but became a collaboration between local residents concerned about the site and about the local governmental process, American Indians who had come to regard the site as an important cultural property, and archaeologists committed to historic preservation and collaboration with the descendants of the people we study. The process of preserving the site, which involved not only litigation but also intensive public relations and even political action, has been documented in hundreds of newspaper articles, letters to the editor, e-mails to discussion lists, and papers presented at regional archaeological conferences. I will not attempt to summarize it all here.

One of the avenues we explored in the effort to preserve the Black Creek site was the possibility that the Archaeological Conservancy would purchase the site from the local government. Because the mission of the conservancy is to preserve sites for future research, and because the Nanticoke Lenni-Lenape Tribe would likely be included in any management team if the conservancy did purchase the site, it was important to understand the tribe's views on archaeological research. After some discussion, we arrived at ten principles, paraphrased below, that the tribe felt should govern any future archaeological work at the Black Creek site if it came under Archaeological Conservancy ownership (Blume 2001):

1. Indian representation on the management team for the site must be more than token—it must be strong enough to ensure that Indian concerns will be affirmatively addressed.
2. Enough time should be allowed for the consideration of archaeological proposals, to permit the development of consensus within the leadership of the community. That is to say, there must be enough time for proposals to be taken back to the Tribal Council and discussed until consensus is reached. Arbitrary deadlines should not be set.
3. No excavation of burials for any reason.
4. Excavations could be considered if the researcher had a specific research question that could be answered at the Black Creek site. The question would have to address issues beyond "Let's see what's there."
5. The research question should be one that cannot be addressed by more-detailed examination of the data already collected by previous researchers.

6. The research question should be one that has meaning for American Indians.

7. Procedures should be developed to identify and deal with ritual contexts. This means the direct involvement of spiritual leaders.

8. Specific measures should be taken to involve Native Americans in the research. This may include hiring Native Americans as part of the staff.

9. Researchers should be required to present their research to American Indians in a format that would be of interest to them. This would mean that any research should be presented in terms of what the research tells us about how people lived at the site in the past and what we learned that we did not know before.

10. There should also be outreach to the general public.

For the most part, these principles define the relationship between the Nanticoke Lenni-Lenape Tribe and potential archaeological researchers in terms of a *process* for collaboration. Even principle number 7, which deals with ritual contexts, is as much concerned with allowing the tribe's spiritual leaders to participate in decisions about those contexts as with placing those leaders in the role of informant in identifying such contexts. It is also clear that to implement these principles effectively, there must be ongoing communication between the parties to the process.

In the end, the local government declined to sell the Black Creek site to the Archaeological Conservancy, so these principles have not been put into practice at the site. Nonetheless, they provide a framework for future collaborative archaeology involving the Nanticoke Lenni-Lenape of New Jersey. Certainly, they have informed my own efforts to establish collaborative archaeology as standard practice in the Delaware Department of Natural Resources and Environmental Control and elsewhere.

Collaborative Archaeology at the Killens Pond Adena Site

Not long before I became involved with the efforts to preserve the Black Creek site in June 2001, the Delaware state historic preservation officer, an archaeologist, reported that archaeological deposits at the Killens Pond Adena site, in Killens Pond State Park, Kent County, Delaware, had been exposed by erosion. Sand-mining operations in 1938 had destroyed most of the site, exposing in the process one or more burials containing at least six individuals. The artifacts recovered from the burials (Cubbage 1941) indicated that the burials were associated with the Delmarva Adena complex (Custer 1984:118–121). Test excavations in 1983 (Wise 1984:32–33) demonstrated that a fairly intensively occupied settlement had also been present at the site at about the same time that the burials had taken place (ca. 2,500 years ago).

The deposits threatened by erosion were located on the narrow rim between the sand pit and the slope down to an ephemeral stream. They consisted of large numbers of fire-cracked rock fragments with occasional flakes and fragments of ceramics dating to about the same time period as the burials. Although these deposits most likely represented domestic debris, I was concerned that spiritual issues might be involved because of the burials that had been disturbed earlier at the site. This meant that tribal consultation was essential. I also wanted to make sure that the Lenape community was not excluded from these discussions, because the site fell within the territory that has been defined as Lenape; but I wanted to do this in an inclusive way that would not be interpreted as siding with the Lenape against the Nanticoke. Fortunately, a change in administration within one of the tribes in 2002 made it possible to explore ways that we could work cooperatively with all three of the tribes that represent Indian people indigenous to Delaware (some enrolled members of the Nanticoke Lenni-Lenape Tribe are from the Cheswold Lenape community). This took the form of a series of meetings with the chiefs of all three tribes along with other tribal members.

The first meeting was held toward the end of June 2002. In advance of the meeting, I prepared an outline of the issues involved, from both an archaeological and an Indian perspective (Blume 2002, 2003). The archaeological reasons for excavating the remaining deposits were fairly straightforward and included the kinds of information that might be recovered (Blume 2002:2):

1. If intact, the fire hearths might provide charcoal that could be used to provide new dates for the associated ceramic types.
2. If intact, the fire hearths might provide information about activity areas at the site.
3. If intact, the fire hearths might provide information, in the form of charred organic remains, which is not preserved elsewhere.
4. Like any other archaeologist, I hate to allow any recoverable information to be destroyed.

The Indian perspective was framed as two series of questions that might be of importance to the three tribes. These questions were developed in conversations with Urie Ridgeway, a Nanticoke Lenni-Lenape Tribal Council member who was the tribe's primary representative in the effort to preserve the Black Creek site. The first group of questions, paraphrased below, was intended to help me as an archaeologist learn how to proceed in a respectful and collaborative way and was influenced in part by the research conducted with Charles Clark IV and referred to earlier in this chapter (Blume 2003:12):

1. Is there a possibility that the fire hearths represent sweat lodge or other ritual fires?
2. How could this be determined?
3. Should such features be handled differently than a cooking hearth?
4. How should the Indian communities be involved in the excavations, if the decision is made to excavate?
5. What could we do to make the excavations meaningful to the Indian community?

The second group of questions focused on issues that the tribes would probably want to resolve before deciding whether to participate in the excavations or even to encourage the excavations to proceed (Blume 2003:13):

1. Does the destruction of much of the site, especially the cemetery, change the spiritual character of the site?

2. Is there a possibility that human remains might be found?
3. How would human remains be handled if they were found?
4. Are there ways to handle spiritual issues that would allow excavation to proceed?

I had expected that the discussions around these issues might be intense, and I was prepared to address any questions that came up (even hostile ones) as honestly and forthrightly as I could. However, it seemed that the chiefs were primarily concerned about how burials would be handled. Once they were assured that I did not expect to find any burials, but would be willing to stop the excavations if we did, they turned the meetings into discussions of intertribal matters. The chiefs did, however, provide five important answers to my questions, paraphrased below (Blume 2003:13):

1. It might not be possible to differentiate between ritual fires and domestic fires.
2. The fire hearths (if that is what the fire-cracked rock deposits turned out to be) should be excavated because they would be destroyed otherwise.
3. The tribes wanted to be involved.
4. Working together was important.
5. A sunrise ceremony would be appropriate.

Again, it was clear that the process of collaboration was of greater importance to the participants in these discussions than the opportunity to provide specific information.

The excavations themselves took place over a weekend at the end of October 2002, beginning with a sunrise ceremony at the site attended by about 15 Nanticoke, Nanticoke Lenni-Lenape, and Lenape people; most stayed to help with the excavations, at least for a few hours. Throughout the two days of the excavation, many more members of the Indian communities of Delaware and southern New Jersey visited the site, a number of whom had never visited an archaeological site before. As might be expected, the archaeological results of a two-day excavation could hardly be considered momentous, though we were able to demonstrate that some of the deposits were intact and associated with artifacts dating to about the same time period as the burials that were disturbed in 1938. More important, American Indian communities that are the likely descendants of the people who lived and died at the site were included in the decision-making process as well as in the excavations themselves.

Concluding Remarks

The relationship between archaeologists and American Indian tribes is inherently unequal in many ways. We archaeologists are the members of our society who are perceived as having specific academic or political qualifications to make decisions about archaeological resources. In the past, there has been little emphasis on seeking the opinions of the descendants of the people who created the sites we study. Today, we may be required by regulation to "consult" with American Indian tribes, both local (as interested parties) and federally recognized. But the term "consult," as defined in the fourth edition of *The American Heritage Dictionary of the American Language* merely means "to seek advice or information of." There is no requirement that the consulter accept or act on the advice or information received. Thus, the power remains firmly in the hands of the person or agency doing the consulting.

Involving Indian people in archaeological research as informants may appear to be a step forward in sharing our profession's power over their past. Even in this case, however, we archaeologists remain in control of the process. For the most part, we determine what questions are asked and which answers are relevant to our research. We decide how the research is presented. Again, the power remains in the hands of the archaeologist.

The primary meaning of the term "collaborate," on the other hand, is "to work together." Working together implies a partnership—each partner bringing something of value to the process of collaboration and each partner receiving something of value from it. The process of working together also means that each party to the collaboration learns from the other. Only in this way can Indian people come to understand what archaeologists can tell them about the past. And only in this way can archaeologists come to understand what interests Indian people about their own past. In the end, I am convinced that we archaeologists will gain more from sharing our power over the past than we lose from giving up our control over the process of studying the past.

Acknowledgments

My views on the relationship between archaeologists and American Indian tribes are based on many experiences, formal and informal, with the Lenape, Nanticoke, and Nanticoke Lenni-Lenape people of Delaware and New Jersey, talking with and listening to many people on many subjects. Any list of acknowledgments I could compile would inevitably leave out someone who contributed to my understanding of this issue. There are, however, a number of Indian people who have been particularly supportive of my efforts and patient with my misunderstandings.

Dennis Coker, chief of the Lenape Indian Tribe of Delaware, and I have worked together on several projects with the goal of bringing together Indian people and archaeologists, particularly the Lenape Delaware Archaeology Month symposia, and have had many discussions on the challenges involved in bringing this about. Chief Coker's experiences with other archaeologists working in Delaware and with government agencies have informed my views on collaboration.

The invitation to participate in the effort to preserve the Black Creek site has been one of the greatest challenges of my career, but it has also been very gratifying, in part because of the personal relationships that have developed with the Nanticoke Lenni-Lenape people who were most active in the fight, including Chief Mark Gould, Urie Ridgeway, Pat Rossello, and Christy Pierce, as well as Earl Evans (Haliwa Saponi), who served as tribal administrator during that period. They gently challenged me to question many of my assumptions about archaeology and have supported my efforts to bring Indian people into dialogue with archaeologists. More recently, I have come to know and to respect the Nanticoke Lenni-Lenape anthropologist Tina Pierce Fragoso, who has helped me understand some of the issues involved in the archaeologist-informant relationship, and enlarged my understanding of the post-Contact history of her people and their cousins in Delaware. Her father, Lew Pierce, who is also the tribe's spiritual leader, has provided quiet support to all of these efforts.

The people who attended the meetings that led to the excavations at the Killens Pond Adena site were amazingly supportive of the process developed through the meetings and of the excavations themselves. They included Chief James Norwood, his wife Jean Norwood, Assistant Chief Larry Jackson, and Bill Daisey from the Nanticoke Indian Association, Chief Dennis Coker and Tribal Treasurer Anna Coker from the Lenape Indian Tribe of Delaware, and Chief Mark Gould from the Nanticoke Lenni-Lenape Indians of New Jersey, as well as my friend Nena Todd. The importance of these meetings is reflected in the number of Indian people who made the trek to Killens Pond State Park to take part in or simply visit the excavations.

All the people mentioned here and many more have taken the time to talk to me, to include me in social events and ceremonies, and to help me to understand the realities of the lives of Lenape and Nanticoke people in Delaware and New Jersey today. Where my understanding has failed, it is because I have not paid proper attention—they have certainly provided me the opportunity to learn. I thank all of them for their patience and friendship.

14. Native American Collaboration in the Delmarva
New Meanings and an Expanded Approach to Delaware Archaeology

MICHAEL D. PETRAGLIA AND KEVIN CUNNINGHAM

The past two decades have been filled with contentious debates between archaeologists and Native Americans, mainly over disagreements about the repatriation of human remains and the management of cultural properties. Yet, a corps of archaeologists, working in collaboration with Native American peoples, have shown the academic community that partnerships have substantial benefits, including an enhanced level of protection of cultural resources (e.g., Dongoske et al. 2000; Ferguson 1996; Nicholas and Andrews 1997; Swidler et al. 1997).

Although a number of worthwhile collaborative unions between archaeologists and Native Americans have been forged in recent years, a substantial proportion of the cooperative effort has been dedicated to improving communication methods (often within a federal regulatory format) and to managing cultural resource programs and sites (often on tribal lands) more effectively. Currently, there are too few examples in the mainstream literature demonstrating how such partnerships lead to a more meaningful interpretation of archaeological phenomena. Interpretation of the past through oral histories and performances are examples that have research benefits (e.g., Echo-Hawk 2000), although like most investigative pursuits, the use of oral traditions in archaeology is not without controversy (Mason 2000).

In addressing precisely how Native American partnerships can lead to new insights and alternate ways of investigating the archaeological record, this chapter describes particular circumstances that developed in 1998–1999 at the Hickory Bluff site in Dover, Delaware, and the learning process that resulted from the dialogue and collaboration. It is important to state at the outset that this chapter describes only the experiences of two archaeologists involved in the Hickory Bluff investigations. Our observations are not necessarily the perceptions of the Native peoples or of anyone in the state or federal government who participated in this process. The goal of our chapter is to share our personal experiences at Hickory Bluff and to demonstrate to the wider archaeological and Native communities, through a particular example, that partnerships with interested parties have substantial personal, public, and research benefits.

The Hickory Bluff Project

The Hickory Bluff investigations were a component of the 77-km State Route 1 Highway Project initiated in 1983 by the Delaware Department of Transportation (DelDOT). As part of federal and state regulatory planning procedures, background research and archaeological investigations were initiated which indicated that numerous archaeological sites were present in the region (Custer and Cunningham 1986). Intensive surveys, site evaluations, and excavations in the highway corridor were performed over a 20-year period, leading to the preservation of hundreds of sites and the retrieval of substantive information on paleoenvironments and Native American occupational history, settlement patterns, subsistence, and material culture. Many reports published as part of the Delaware Department of Transportation Archaeology Series are widely distributed, and some have recently been placed on the DelDOT Web site (http://www.deldot. gov/static/projects/archaeology/hickory_bluff/hickory.shtml).

Among a cluster of important archaeological localities, the Hickory Bluff site was recognized to be a significant cultural resource, eligible for listing on the National Register of Historic Places (Petraglia et al. 2002). The site was in close proximity to a number of well-known prehistoric sites on the St. Jones River, including a substantial mortuary site dating to the Adena period (ca. 550 B.C. to A.D. 1). As a result of planned road and bridge construction, a large-scale excavation effort was initiated at Hickory Bluff in October 1997, and the excavations lasted until September 1998.

At the outset of the Hickory Bluff investigations, it was realized that the project would be lengthy and complex, requiring the completion of many block excavation units. In the end, Hickory Bluff was one of the largest lateral excavations ever conducted in the Middle Atlantic region, consisting of the excavation of more than 800 1-x-1-m units. Given the results of preliminary fieldwork, we also realized that a rich collection of artifact assemblages would be retrieved, likely dating to a long range of prehistory. Hickory Bluff exceeded our expectations, producing over 300 features and 77,000 stone and ceramic artifacts spanning a 5,000-year period.

In keeping with DelDOT's two-decade-long community outreach efforts, we aimed to conduct a public education campaign at the Hickory Bluff site. The purpose of the public outreach effort was to disseminate knowledge about the prehistory of the state, to communicate the goals and practice of archaeology, and to allow people to visit the site and participate in the excavations.

DelDOT and Parsons, the archaeological consulting firm, strove to activate a flexible and adaptive outreach and involvement program that would continue to make archaeology and historic preservation common knowledge across the state. Our cultural resource outreach activities mirrored the wider-scale efforts undertaken as part of the transportation planning process. We devised a number of strategies to reach as many people as possible, including talks to a variety of organizations (e.g., nature centers, schools, scouts), the creation and installation of traveling exhibits and posters, the production and distribution of thousands of brochures and handouts, interviews with the media (newspapers, magazines, radio, television), and the production and sale of hundreds of specially designed T-shirts.

Native American Involvement

As a backdrop to the Hickory Bluff excavations, collaborative efforts had been taking place between state government officials and Native Americans for some time. The Delaware State Historic Preservation Office (SHPO) and the state-recognized Nanticoke Indian Association, Inc., had previously developed a relationship over the Delaware Unmarked Human Remains Act and other reburial issues. Since the inception of DelDOT's report publication and distribution efforts in 1983, the department often sent the Nanticokes and the Lenape Indian Tribe, Inc., copies of site brochures, public outreach documents, and final archaeological reports. Over the years DelDOT worked with the Lenape on road projects in their community of Cheswold (e.g., Heite 1984; Heite and Blume 1995; Heite 1999). On the whole, however, the great majority of archaeological projects conducted throughout the state of Delaware did not directly involve the participation of Native American tribes, in part because no regulatory apparatus was in place to coordinate with non-federally recognized tribes. This meant that although Delaware's tribes had the opportunity to participate in the federal compliance and review process as "interested parties," no regulatory procedure was in place for us as archaeologists to partner with Native Americans.

Although no concerns or objections had been raised about the archaeology conducted along the State Route 1 corridor since its beginning in 1983, controversy did surround the Hickory Bluff excavations. This was the result of a number of factors, including the complex history of political relationships that had developed between Delaware's tribes and the state, some negative and inaccurate press coverage about the nature of and circumstances behind the archaeological investigations, and the view that Hickory Bluff was a sacred place. Although the Lenape and Nanticoke tribal representatives approached the archaeologists and state agencies about the Hickory Bluff investigations, the two tribes expressed their interest in different ways. The involvement of the Lenape Tribe was based on both individual and group participation. Some members of the Cheswold community came to the site to discuss the archaeology and to participate in the excavations; later, members of the tribe conducted private on-site ceremonies and attended public ceremonies. The Nanticoke representatives strongly voiced their desire to review the cultural resource investigations conducted as part of the construction of State Route 1. The Delaware Department of Transportation and the project archaeologists, with the involvement of the Delaware SHPO, immediately began a dialogue with the Nanticoke representatives. When a formal expression on the part of the Nanticoke was recognized, a variety of activities were arranged to update the tribe on efforts underway at Hickory Bluff in compliance with the National Environmental Policy Act (NEPA) and Section 106 of the National Historic Preservation Act. The first of these activities included field meetings between the archaeologists and Nanticoke representatives.

During the first meetings on-site in 1998, it was apparent that the archaeologists and the Native American representatives had divergent opinions about the meaning and interpretation of Hickory Bluff. In leading one of the first tours of the site with the Nanticoke, the archaeologists described the excavation methods, stratigraphy, features, and the scientific and analytical approaches. They reported the typical field interpretations and findings concerning site ecology, tool manufacture, feature formation, and activities. In sharp contrast, walking and peering around the excavated basins and gazing at the large oak, hickory, and pine trees, and the quiet tidal waters, the Native Americans talked about the "special feel" of the site and the "sacred" nature of the setting.

In the first field meeting, and in subsequent exchanges, the assistant Nanticoke chief spoke about the uncovered surfaces as the "ground my ancestors walked on" and where "my ancestors carried out their daily lives." We were reminded that as excavators we had a "moral obligation to tell meaningful stories" about their predecessors, since we were the ones who brought "the spirits back from long forgotten and dead things." In a discourse based on the Nanticoke Skeleton Dance—a burial process that involves placement of a body in a pit, later exhumation, bone defleshing, and bundling—it was opined that some of our archaeological basin features might have been cemetery related. The Nanticokes considered the basin features and associated artifacts as elements in sacred ceremonies.

Following such exchanges, we recognized that while the Nanticoke and the archaeologists had some divergent opinions about the archaeological record and its meaning, we all appreciated that past, and we held many ideas in common that needed to be developed. While all agreed that rapprochement was a good idea, the lack of mutually shared histories kept the sides somewhat separated. Symbolic of this disjuncture, when we archaeologists were asked whether we had ever been to the annual Nanticoke powwow, we had to say no. While the lack of interaction with Native peoples may be considered perplexing, this negative response is probably not too unusual, since professional archaeologists have a history of working on prehistoric sites with little communication with descendant communities. In order to learn more about Native Americans and their interests, we attended the Nanticoke powwow in September 1998. We found that the powwow was a major social event, consisting of the gathering of many regional tribes and large public crowds interested in celebrating Native American heritage.

Apart from the initial field exchanges and conversations initiated by the Nanticoke, meetings were held with representatives of the Advisory Council on Historic Preservation, the Federal Highway Administration, Delaware's federal Congressional offices, DelDOT, and the Delaware SHPO to discuss a variety of topics with the Nanticoke, including the past history of State Route 1 projects and future Native American involvement in cultural resource projects. One initial response to these discussions was a three-day workshop held in 1998 at DelDOT headquarters to review cultural resource projects and compliance procedures for the State Route 1 NEPA project. Representatives from the Nanticoke, DelDOT, and Parsons attended, and discussions and activities addressed Section 106, archaeology, laboratory methods, and the Hickory Bluff site itself. The three-day event succeeded in exchanging a great amount of information among all those involved.

During the postworkshop review meetings, the road building schedule at Hickory Bluff was discussed, and the Nanticoke were informed that construction would begin in early fall of 1998. The Nanticoke asked to conduct two on-site ceremonies before the destruction of Hickory Bluff. With the approval of federal and state officials, a sweat lodge and public blessing ceremony were held at Hickory Bluff in October 1998, just before construction began. The sweat lodge ceremony involved a small group of invited participants, whereas the blessing ceremony was an open public event. Among the attendees at the Nanticoke blessing ceremony were federal and state officials, archaeologists, Lenape representatives, and other members of the interested public. After the field investigation portion of the Hickory Bluff project was completed in September 1998, the involved parties maintained continual dialogue and monthly meetings to ensure that Nanticoke coordination continued through the analysis and report writing phases.

Before and after the Nanticoke meetings, discussions continued with the chief of the Lenape, and several community members from Cheswold participated in the excavations. The Lenape chief told us that a private pipe ceremony was held on the Hickory Bluff site. We were invited to give talks at the Nanticoke and Lenape community centers as part of Delaware Archaeology Month activities, and in 2000 we participated in the Nanticoke powwow, providing an exhibit of artifacts and demonstrating stone-tool manufacturing techniques.

Although we archaeologists were impressed with the interesting and often compelling arguments raised by the Native Americans, we were especially influenced by our direct participation in the sweat lodge ceremony. Since the sweat lodge ceremony led to a reshaping of our intellectual approach, altering our perspective of archaeological phenomena, it is necessary to describe briefly the significance of sweats and the event that took place at Hickory Bluff. In reviewing this ceremony, we aim to show archaeologists and others that collaboration can enhance and shape our learning experiences.

The Sweat Lodge Ceremony
The Sweat Lodge: Background and Meaning

The sweat lodge was a widespread custom in North America (Bruchac 1997), and these ceremonies are reported among groups as culturally and geographically diverse as the Klamath and Yurok of the Pacific Northwest, the Crow and Blackfoot on the Plains, and the historic Cherokee in North Carolina (e.g., Drucker 1955; Lowie 1954; Oswalt 1978). The sweat lodge was also used by some East Coast Algonquian groups, including the Powhatan of southeastern Virginia. As documented in Contact-period accounts, each village contained at least one "sweat house" (Rountree 1989).

But while the sweat lodge was common to many Native American tribes, its purpose and procedure varied greatly. "Sweats" could be taken informally for reasons of personal hygiene, or they could constitute elaborate ritual affairs with major spiritual implications. Participation in a sweat lodge ceremony could socially integrate the participants, bestow medicinal benefits, and serve as a test of endurance or stamina. Even within an individual group, a sweat lodge could be employed for multiple purposes ranging from elaborate purification rituals to providing sleeping quarters on cold nights (Oswalt 1978).

The sweat lodge is still used by some Native Americans, including those who wish to maintain elements of traditional customs. The Lakota Sioux, for example, have maintained their sweat lodge tradition despite the best efforts of the U.S. government to eradicate the practice during the nineteenth and twentieth centuries (Bruchac 1997). The Hickory Bluff lodge structure was constructed in the Lakota *Inipi* style, which includes hot rocks to produce steam (e.g., Brown 1953; Bruchac 1997; Lowie 1954). While sweat lodge ceremonies are conducted according to a general format established by tradition, it is important to recognize that each ceremony is a variation on a theme (e.g., Bucko 1998; Fields 2000).

The Sweat Experience

The sweat lodge ceremony held at Hickory Bluff was conducted by eight participants (three Nanticoke representatives and five archaeologists, including both coauthors of this chapter) over 14 hours, beginning at about noon on October 25, 1998, and ending at two o'clock the next morning. The ceremony began with construction of a domed shelter of tree saplings and the building of a large ceremonial fire to intensively heat the rock. After ceremonial prayers and offerings were completed, a four-hour-long sweat was held—a physically and mentally demanding experience. Once the participants were seated in the lodge, the fire tender brought in glowing red stones from the ceremonial fire basin. The facilitator ladled water onto the rocks, at which point the lodge filled with hot steam. The effects of fasting, preparatory events, and the lodge experience itself (replete with pitch darkness, overwhelming heat and smoke, pitched singing and drumming, personal revelations and reflections, and the pulsating view of red-hot stone) integrated in a mind-altering fashion. At the completion of the sweat, the participants exited the lodge, where a pipe ceremony was

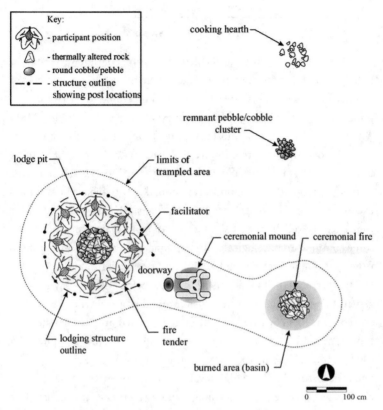

Key:
- participant position
- thermally altered rock
- round cobble/pebble
- structure outline showing post locations

cooking hearth

remnant pebble/cobble cluster

lodge pit

limits of trampled area

facilitator

ceremonial mound — ceremonial fire

doorway

lodging structure outline

fire tender

burned area (basin)

0   100 cm

Figure 14.1 Layout of the ceremonial sweat lodge site (Prepared by Michael Petraglia). Note the spatial distinction between the features inside the sacred circle and those lying outside.

held, followed by a feast. A separate cooking hearth was built, and care was taken to keep the lodge area free of any cooking debris or other refuse. At the public ceremony on October 26, several thermally altered stones from the sweat lodge basin were selected and buried in an excavated basin some distance from the sacred area.

As was evident to us at the conclusion of the Hickory Bluff ceremonies, we now had the opportunity to study the archaeological manifestations of a ceremonial behavior that had direct roots in traditional Native American life. With the permission and cooperation of our Nanticoke hosts, all material residues of the sweat lodge ceremony were documented (Figure 14.1).

Insights of the Sweat

The participation in, observation of, and recording of the sweat lodge provided a greater appreciation of the material manifestations of ceremonial activity in archaeological sites. Ceremonial meanings and material components of the archaeological record are not often considered in Middle Atlantic archaeology, since most researchers confine themselves to ecological and economic interpretations (e.g., Custer 1989; Gardner 1982). In fact, few Middle Atlantic archaeological sites or material patterns have been interpreted as containing symbolic, ceremonial, or ritual behaviors, with the exception of such obvious locations as burial sites. Our sweat lodge experience led us to believe that some archaeologists may be misinterpreting some common archaeological features, which may have not only economic functions but also ceremonial, social, and symbolic functions.

The ceremonial site that was produced during the two-day event had structural parameters that were visible and discernible (Figure 14.1). The site components consisted of a discrete trampled area, an earthen ceremonial mound, a ceremonial fire, a sweat lodge structure and pit, a cooking hearth, and a remnant cluster of unused stones. The spatial relations between features and the high level of feature integrity was clearly indicated, since the site resulted from a single two-day event conducted on a swept and artifactually clean surface.

There was a spatial distinction between the features in the sacred circle (e.g., lodge pit and ceremonial fire) and those outside the space (e.g., cooking hearth and remnant pebble/cobble cluster). The collection and accumulation of the pebbles and cobbles for use in the ceremonial fire was deliberate. The peripheral placement of the cooking hearth is noteworthy, since this feasting feature was intentionally segregated a distance away from the sacred circle behaviors. In contrast with other ritual features, the cooking hearth was the only feature that had organic, subsistence-related refuse materials associated with it.

From an archaeological perspective, the two sweat lodge features (Features 1 and 3) were defined by the presence of thermally altered stones. Other features would also be preserved archaeologically, including the cooking hearth (Feature 6) and the remnant pebble/cobble hearth (Fea-

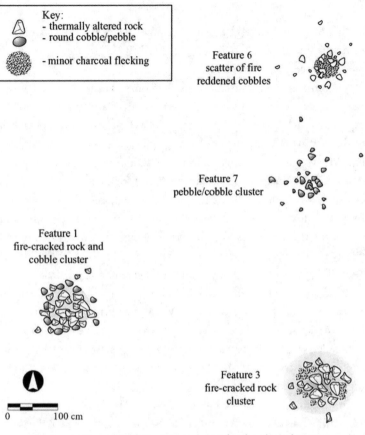

Figure 14.2. Ceremonial features in conjectural archaeological context
(Prepared by Michael Petraglia).

ture 7). To better understand how these might appear in archaeological
context, the features were simulated in plan view (Figure 14.2). Since the
lodge pit (Feature 1) and the ceremonial fire (Feature 3) are set in basins
and have dense rock concentrations, these would likely be well preserved
archaeologically. Behavioral relations between the ceremonial fire and the
sweat lodge pit could be archaeologically inferred, since some of the fractured rock would likely refit among the two features. As a surface manifestation, the cooking hearth feature (Feature 6) would presumably be
vulnerable to some horizontal scattering by postdepositional processes.
Upon burial of the feature, the cluster would be preserved, although some

of the stones would likely be dispersed some distance. The heavy charcoal component of the cooking hearth would likely be preserved to some degree as remnant charred pieces.

A significant point raised during the course of the sweat lodge ceremony concerned the value of material resources and the notion of "sacredness." Each and every act, whether it be the cutting down of saplings or the heating of stones in a fire, was conducted in a manner that recognized that nature was being subjected to alteration. It has long been recognized by anthropologists that traditional societies, in their daily actions, often did not divorce the spiritual, social, and economic realms. In this context, ceremonial and religious acts are extremely difficult to infer, and archaeologists working in the Delmarva have tended to favor purely utilitarian interpretations for any given finding. Given this situation, it is probable that the symbolic and ceremonial purposes of thermally altered stone features have been misinterpreted. The challenge for us, as archaeologists, is to better understand cultural, social, and cognitive situations and to develop ways to assess the relative contributions of such factors. Until such an approach is developed, it is likely that we will continue to misinterpret significant aspects of site structure and patterning on Native American sites.

To this point, the ceremonial residues of the Hickory Bluff sweat lodge are reminiscent of many common feature types encountered in the Northeast. The configuration of the ceremonial fire and the sweat lodge pit closely resemble features often referred to by contemporary archaeologists as various "hearth" types. Moreover, the behavior that resulted in the creation of the remnant stone pile might be incorrectly interpreted as some sort of technological or economic activity (e.g., cached material for use in anticipated stone tool reduction), whereas in reality this was material intended for incorporation into a ceremonial fire. This suggests that archaeologists are sometimes missing symbolic and ceremonial events, favoring instead economic or technological interpretations for a given set of material remains. It is noteworthy that all the feature types mapped from the ceremonial site showed some degree of similarity with prehistoric features encountered at Hickory Bluff. While no direct analogy was made with the sweat lodge, it is interesting to note that the Hickory Bluff archaeological site contained basin features with fractured rock, features with discolored but unfractured rock, and clusters of unaltered river pebbles and cobbles (http://www.deldot.gov/static/projects/archaeology/hickory_bluff/hickory.shtml).

Discussion

Collaboration with Native Americans opened up new ways of interpreting the material culture of Hickory Bluff. Collaboration led us to reexplore the ethnohistorical and ethnographical literature in order to examine traditional belief systems. Armed with such information, we looked at the archaeological record in different ways, examining artifact color, decoration, and breakage; the recycling and reuse of artifacts and features; social and ceremonial roles of archaeological features; and the symbolic nature of the site environment and its natural resources (Petraglia et al. 2002). Such an approach also inspired us to design the 2001 Delaware Archaeology Month poster integrating Native American beliefs with archaeological phenomena (www.delawarearchaeology.org/2001_poster_notes.htm).

As a tangible example of our expanded approach, we investigated the position of Hickory Bluff on the St. Jones River and saw how the cultural landscape can contain spiritual aspects of site location and ritual activity. Ethnohistorical research on the Algonquian worldview indicates that spiritual beliefs were correlated with a spatial logic organizing the cosmos, where directions were lined with different deities, powers, and sacred locations, and the cosmos were conceived of as multileveled worlds (e.g., Harrington 1921; Rountree 1989; Strachey 1953 [1612]). Indeed, archaeologists have found that Woodland ossuaries in Maryland were located in prominent high spots with excellent visibility and facing open water, which is often viewed to the west (Curry 1999). Although site patterning in the middle reaches of the St. Jones River may be biased by preservation conditions, the existing site locations, including the location of the St. Jones Adena mortuary complex, indicate preferential activity areas on the east side of the river (Figure 14.3). Research indicates that location of sites, such as Hickory Bluff north of the St. Jones Adena site, may be tied to locations north or east of burial locations, implying unobstructed paths for departing spirits. In further examining the position of Hickory Bluff, we found

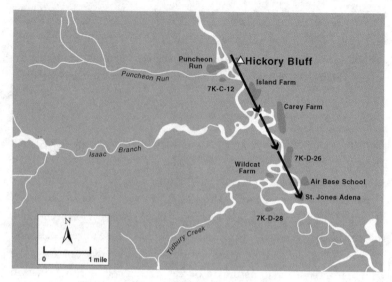

Figure 14.3. Alignment of sites along the St. Jones River
(Prepared by Michael Petraglia).

that the site offers the maximum view shed of the upstream and down-stream bend of the St. Jones River (Figure 14.4). In addition, at the site the sun sets in a west to southwestern direction, the direction dependent on the season. Modern-day views and sunsets are often unobstructed and spectacular, and it was probably no less so during the past. Taken together, the directionality, the riverine view shed, the sunsets, and the preferential site settings may be important factors in reinforcing, and perhaps conditioning, occupations at Hickory Bluff.

Close interactions with Native Americans at Hickory Bluff had a profound effect on the way in which we investigated and interpreted the archaeological record. Close interactions, discussions, and participation in ceremonies at Hickory Bluff made us more cognizant of the limitations of our interpretive paradigm, and it left us with a better understanding of, and sensitivity to, contemporary Native American beliefs. For the Native Americans, we hope that the collaboration at Hickory Bluff offered a venue to convey their interests and concerns and an opportunity to share their views. While much remains to be done to build and strengthen collaborations in the future, we believe that increased communication be-

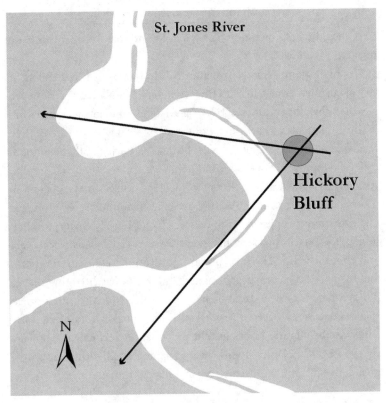

Figure 14.4. Hickory Bluff view shed (Prepared by Michael Petraglia). Note that the site occurs at a position that affords maximum view sheds upstream and downstream. The site is also in a position to view spectacular sunsets.

tween Native Americans and archaeologists can only result in a richer understanding of the past.

A goal of this chapter was to demonstrate that collaborative efforts between archaeologists and Native Americans can have personal, intellectual, and academic benefits. Our experiences at Hickory Bluff suggest that collaborative efforts can have real and direct benefits to archaeological practice. One of the critical points to emerge from our collaboration with Native Americans was the need to think about sites in ways not often considered by archaeologists. Additionally, the perspectives of Native Americans will help us expand on environmental and economic models so that the entire range of past ways of life and behaviors are considered, including the integration of symbolic and social elements into our research.

Two main points emerge from our collaborative experience. First, archaeologists have much to learn from contemporary Native American peoples in the Northeast, and second, we need to reformulate the way in which we investigate sites. On the first point, we have a long way to go. Both informal and formal methods need to be devised to ensure that communication is improved. On the second point, we argue in the Hickory Bluff report (Petraglia et al. 2002) that archaeologists need to expand our approach, not only asking big-picture questions that underscore processual and evolutionary approaches to culture change but also incorporating a humanities-based approach that is sensitive to social and historical events and contingencies. The incorporation of Native American viewpoints and the use of the ethnographical and ethnohistorical literature that explores tribal histories and culture have great value. Moreover, an approach that evaluates and incorporates oral tradition, tribal histories, and Native American beliefs and values has the potential to yield new insights into the nature of social interactions. Such an approach will ultimately provide greater insights into how societies were shaped through time.

Acknowledgments

The Federal Highway Administration and the Delaware Department of Transportation supported the archaeological excavations performed at Hickory Bluff. We would especially like to thank Bob Kleinburd of FHWA and Joe Wutka of DelDOT for supporting the archaeology program and our public outreach efforts over the years. Personnel from these agencies supported the archaeological excavations and participated in meetings, workshops, and the closing ceremony. We would like to thank Dan Griffith, state historic preservation officer, and Gwen Davis of the Delaware Historic Preservation Office for their guidance and expertise throughout the entire course of this project. The Nanticoke shared much of their personal time with the project archaeologists, and we are particularly indebted to Chief Kenneth Clark, Assistant Chief Charles Clark, Cecilia Harman, Pocita Lonewolf, Trantino Norwood, and Odette Wright. We thank Charlie Clark, Avery Harmon, and Joe McElwee for the gratifying and memorable sweat lodge experience. We thank the Lenape chief, Dennis Coker, for several meetings on-site and for sharing his perspectives. The archaeological investigations would not have been completed without the dedication of dozens of Parsons' archaeologists and researchers in the field, lab, and office. For their assistance on the Hickory Bluff Project, we especially wish to thank Susan Bupp, Virginia Busby, Chris Egghart, Sean Fitzell, Dennis Knepper, John Rutherford, Carter Shields, and Diane Halsall Woodley. Nicole Boivin, Chris Espenshade, Danica Ziegler, and Jordan Kerber provided useful comments on an earlier draft of this chapter. The views expressed in this chapter are entirely our own and do not necessarily reflect those of the FHWA, DelDOT, the Delaware SHPO, or other individuals and organizations.

Voluntary Collaboration
Research and Education

15. Case Studies in Collaborative Archaeology
The Oneida Indian Nation of New York and Colgate University

JORDAN E. KERBER

With the passage of the Native American Graves Protection and Repatriation Act (NAGPRA) in 1990 and the 1992 amendments to the National Historic Preservation Act of 1966, an increasing number of situations and projects across the United States have arisen in which archaeologists and American Indians have collaborated in the mutual pursuit of learning about the past. Several of these instances are well documented in Dongoske et al. (2000), Ferguson (1996), Klesert and Downer (1990), Swidler et al. (1997), Watkins (2000a), and now this volume. Indeed the majority of Native American–archaeologist cooperative ventures are mandated by these two federal laws, which require, among several things, consultation with federally recognized Native American groups and tribal historic preservation officers in specific circumstances. There are other instances, however, that are not legislated. This article discusses two case studies in collaborative archaeology between the Oneida Indian Nation[1] and nearby Colgate University in central New York State. The first involves a summer workshop in archaeology for Oneida youth, and the second concerns the repatriation and curation of Oneida archaeological remains in Colgate's Longyear Museum of Anthropology. The former is the focus of the chapter, while the latter is discussed briefly.

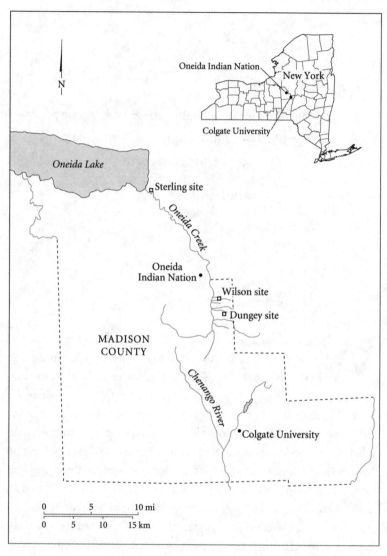

Figure 15.1. New York State map, showing the location of Colgate University and the Sterling, Dungey, and Wilson sites.

Summer Workshop in Archaeology

Between 1995 and 2003, Colgate University, located in Hamilton, New York, has offered an annual workshop in archaeology to members of the Oneida Indian Nation (Figure 15.1). Held each summer for two weeks, the program has been directed by the author with assistance from several Colgate students and recent alumni, as well as other individuals. So far, more than 100 Oneida teenagers have participated in nine offerings of the workshop and have gained direct archaeological and laboratory experience in learning about their ancestors and other Native Americans who once occupied central New York.

The three primary goals of the workshop are (1) to strengthen the relationship between Colgate University and the Oneida Indian Nation by bringing together members of both communities in important educational experiences, (2) to provide a hands-on opportunity in archaeology for Oneida youth that involves the limited excavation and laboratory processing of prehistoric and historic nonhuman remains from nonsacred Native sites in the region, and (3) to identify, manage, and protect significant archaeological resources located in central New York.

The idea for the archaeological workshop developed in 1992 when I was director of the Native American Studies Program at Colgate. At that time, faculty in the program drafted a grant proposal for a three-year project to improve community relations between the university and neighboring Native American groups. One of the proposal's initiatives was a summer workshop in archaeology that I envisioned for Iroquois youth living in the vicinity of the campus. Although I had no experience working with American Indians in this manner, I am strongly committed to public education in archaeology and had successfully directed previous archaeological workshops for a lay audience in Rhode Island (see Kerber 1997). In 1994 the John Ben Snow Foundation awarded a matching grant to fund the summer workshop from 1995 until 1997. The university provided the match, which was viewed as "seed money" to help start this innovative project.

I selected the Oneida Indian Nation, a small but growing Native American community of just over 1,000 members, as the particular audience for this workshop because of its geographical proximity to the Colgate campus. Simply put, there is no other Native American group living closer to the university. In the process of writing the grant proposal, I called a few members and employees of the Oneida Indian Nation with whom I had previously developed an informal relationship to discuss the possibility of my offering an archaeological workshop to nation members. After receiving a favorable response, it was suggested by the Oneida Indian Nation that participants in the nation's Youth Work/Learn Program be the target group for the workshop if funding were obtained. The Youth Work/Learn Program employs Oneida Indian Nation teenagers in various summer projects, including landscaping and working in nation facilities and offices.

The emphasis of the program on the nation's young members seemed appropriate, since many American Indian communities have been concerned about their youth "losing touch" with their heritage. I hoped (perhaps naively or somewhat romantically, in retrospect) that by recovering artifacts used in the daily lives of their ancestors, especially on tribal land, the adolescents would feel a connection to their historic roots. For some workshop students, this was probably not the case, at least during their immediate involvement. But for others, as will be discussed below, I believe the workshop functioned in this way, despite the participants resembling more "generic" teenagers than Native Americans, listening to rap music and wearing the latest style clothing during the excavation. Several may not realize the positive effect of the program for years to come.

The workshop consisted of two five-day sessions during July and August, and each session involved between 3 and 15 participants; larger numbers of students participated in the first three summers than more recently, as the Youth Work/Learn Program has decreased somewhat in size. In the earlier workshops, two separate groups participated in both sessions, while later workshops involved the same group per session. Nevertheless, every workshop focused on the limited archaeological excavation of one or two nonsacred Native American sites and the laboratory processing of the recovered cultural remains. On the first day of a session, an orientation was held in order to introduce the students to the field of archaeology and to dispel some common misconceptions. As is typical of a lay public, most of the participants had no firsthand experience in an archaeological excavation. They knew about the subject primarily through films and television programs and erroneously believed that archaeologists excavate dinosaur fossils. Authentic historic and prehistoric cultural materials were presented during the orientation so that the participants could become familiar with the various types of objects they might later recover from the sites. Also, I emphasized that we would deliberately not excavate human burials or human skeletal remains during the workshop. I added that if any were to be accidentally discovered, the excavation would stop, and I would contact the Oneida Indian Nation for direction.

This point warrants further discussion, since I believe it is the principal reason why the Oneidas have permitted me to offer this program. Because I specify in each workshop proposal submitted to the Oneida Indian Nation's Men's Council and Clan Mothers that I will not knowingly excavate human skeletal remains during the project, a solid foundation of mutual trust and respect has developed between me and a number of members of the nation. It is no secret that relations between archaeologists and Native Americans are still often strained, largely owing to the excavation and analysis of Native American skeletal remains (see, e.g., Biolsi and Zimmerman 1997; Bray 2001; Mihesuah 2000). Since 1995 very few human skeletal remains have been accidentally discovered during the workshop. Only isolated human teeth and a few disarticulated bones from nonburial contexts were recovered at two sites. In both situations, following my notifying the Oneida Indian Nation about these remains, we stopped the excavation of the test units containing the human skeletal material, as instructed by the Oneidas, but the fieldwork continued elsewhere at the sites.

Fieldwork for each five-day workshop session lasted three days (weather permitting), followed by a day of laboratory work at Colgate University to clean the recovered archaeological materials. For every workshop, I received indispensable assistance in the field and the lab from two or three people with previous experience. Most of the assistants were Colgate undergraduates or recent alumni, including two who were of Iroquois descent. Some have pursued graduate work in anthropology and employment in contract archaeology. As I tell my assistants, it is rare, especially in the Northeast, to be able to supervise American Indian youth in archaeological projects on their own land. In addition, at least one staff member of

Figure 15.2. Oneida Youth Work/Learn Program participant rejoices at finding a seventeenth-century glass trade bead during the archaeological workshop at the Wilson site in August 2003 (Photo courtesy of Tim Sofranko).

the Oneida Youth Work/Learn Program was present throughout the entirety of each workshop session.

For the first three summers, from 1995 to 1997, under funding from the John Ben Snow Foundation and Colgate University, the workshop sessions were conducted near campus at three prehistoric sites situated on private property (not Oneida territory).[2] I had been conducting archaeological research with Colgate students in field methods classes at these sites for a few years before the first workshop session. The sites contain primarily stone tools and chipping debris, dating to between about 4,000 and 1,000 years ago. All archaeological materials recovered and cleaned by the participants in the 1995–1997 workshop sessions were stored in the archaeology laboratory at the university for subsequent cataloging, analysis, interpreting, and reporting by Colgate students in my field methods classes during the fall term (e.g., Kerber et al. 1996).

The completion of the 1997 workshop marked the end of the three-year matching grant from the Snow Foundation and Colgate. Because of the success of the program and what I believed to be its unrealized potential, I decided to approach the Oneidas for funding and permission to hold the workshop on their territory (as close as 24 km north of Colgate). It was not that the three prehistoric sites adjacent to campus were unimportant or unproductive, but rather that known sites on nation land were more recent. Many of these sites date to between the sixteenth and eighteenth centuries and were inhabited by the direct ancestors of the workshop participants, as opposed to some distant prehistoric Native American groups who may not be directly related to the Oneida people. It was (and still is) my hope that finding artifacts from these historic sites would ignite the interest and curiosity of Oneida youth in their heritage. In 1998 I submitted the proposal to the Oneida Indian Nation Men's Council and Clan Mothers. In addition to requesting nation funding for the 1998 summer workshop on Oneida territory, I stipulated that all recovered artifacts from this land would be curated at the nation's Shako:wi Cultural Center following their cataloging, analysis, and reporting at Colgate.[3]

The Oneidas provided 100 percent funding of my 1998 proposal, and they permitted me to offer the workshop at the Sterling site, a multicomponent site dating between about 6,000 and 200 years ago, located on nation territory in Verona, New York (Figure 15.1).[4] Between 1998 and 2003, I submitted a similar proposal each year to the Oneida Indian Nation Men's Council and Clan Mothers, and each year they approved it. Beginning in 1999 and continuing until 2003, the Oneidas contributed the bulk of the financial support of the workshop, while Colgate provided a smaller portion of the funds. I intend to direct the workshop each summer for the foreseeable future, as long as joint funding is provided from the nation and the university and the workshop goals are met.

Between 1999 and 2001, the workshop sessions were held at the Dungey site in Stockbridge, New York, located to the south of the Sterling site (Figure 15.1). This village dates to about the 1660s–1670s and was settled by the Oneida people, who lived in longhouses and practiced hunting, fishing, gathering, and horticulture, all the hallmarks of traditional Iroquois culture. Despite many years of previous collecting and excavating at the site by avocational archaeologists and other individuals, Oneida workshop participants and Colgate students recovered more than 4,000 historic remains from more than 100 test units completed between 1999 and 2001. The majority of the objects are Euroamerican in origin and represent trade goods (e.g., shell and glass trade beads, clay smoking-pipe fragments, cassock buttons, and metal objects). Other remains consist of stone tools and chipping debris, pottery, charcoal, animal bone, and a charred maize kernel.

In 2002 and 2003, the workshop shifted to the nearby Wilson site, just north of the Dungey site, also in Stockbridge (Figures 15.1 and 15.2). This site dates to approximately the 1590s to the 1620s and contains many of the same kinds of remains as found at the Dungey site, but with fewer artifacts of Euroamerican origin and more of indigenous manufacture (e.g., stone and pottery artifacts) and domesticated plant remains (e.g., maize, beans, and squash). Analysis and interpretation of the cultural materials recovered from the Sterling, Dungey, and Wilson sites are not discussed here but are presented in five unpublished reports, completed by Colgate students in my field methods classes, based on research that they and the workshop participants conducted at these Oneida sites (Kerber et al. 1998, 1999, 2000, 2002, 2003). I have also given numerous presentations of this research, both with my Colgate students and separately, to members and employees of the Oneida Indian Nation and to members of the New York State Archaeological Association, among other groups. Further, former workshop assistants, both Colgate alumni, have used this work in the completion of a Ph.D. dissertation (Henry 2001) and an undergraduate honors research paper (Danielson 2001).

The success of the workshop can be evaluated on the basis of the more than 100 Oneida adolescents who have participated during the nine consecutive summers since 1995 and the fact that both the nation and the university have financially supported the program. In addition, several quotations from participants and nonparticipants alike reflect the importance of the experience. For instance, one workshop student commented that "it was interesting to learn about what archaeologists do, but the best thing was holding the materials used by my ancestors. I learned more about my cul-

ture and our past" (Malone and Hanks 1999/2000:23). As a Youth Work/
Learn Program staff member and schoolteacher stated, "You can't get a
better history class than this. The kids are learning more than they'd ever
learn in public school" (McCarroll 2001:14). This person added, "These
kids had hands-on discovery. They had a connection to history" (Walters 2003:14). In a similar vein, an Oneida clan mother remarked: "Walking over the land where our ancestors walked . . . thinking 'Our people
were here' . . . helps us to bring our ancestors back into our souls, into our
hearts, and the artifacts are real. They add so much to the knowledge and
understanding that we have of our very own people" (personal communication to Dixie Henry in 1999, cited in Henry 2001:10).

Perhaps most telling is the statement from a member of the nation's
Men's Council and Clan Mothers: "Everyone has studied our people, but
not with cultural sensitivity. We revere those who have gone before us.
We have our oral tradition, but to be able to provide our children with
an actual hands-on experience with our past, that is invaluable" (Cronin
2001). Although this person admitted that "archaeology used to be a bad
word among the Oneidas" (Corbett 2000), the workshop has changed
this perception, while also helping to shape the identity of the participants. In his words, referring to the workshop: "It gives our people a connection with their past and a greater understanding of who they are. It is
one thing to say 'I am Native American' and another to say 'I am Oneida
and I know who I am.' That's one thing the nation and Colgate can provide" (Hubbard 1997).

There are other collaborative programs in archaeology with an emphasis on Native American youth that have been introduced in the United
States and Canada. One that has had a similar effect on its young participants is the Red Earth Summer Archaeology Program for high school students, developed in cooperation with the Gila River Indian Community's Employment and Training Office in south-central Arizona (Ravesloot
1997:177). The primary goal of the program, which lasts eight weeks, is to
introduce high school students to archaeology. The parallels in expectations and outcomes between these two programs are clear:

> While it is our hope that one or more of the high school stu-
> dents who have participated in the Red Earth Archaeology

Program will elect to pursue a career in archaeology, that result is not absolutely necessary for the program to be a success. More important is the fact that the program has provided Native American students with an opportunity to participate in the study of their past and that it has introduced some to higher education who most likely would not have had the experience. In the process of introducing Native American students to archaeology, I also believe we have managed to change some perceptions about archaeology and archaeologists [Ravesloot 1997:177].

Another indication of the success of the workshop came in 2000. Before the nation's planned removal of two small structures adjacent to the Dungey site, the Oneidas asked that this area be tested as part of the 2000 workshop. They wanted to determine whether any important archaeological remains existed at that location so that they could be protected from any impact from the removal. Fortunately, no significant cultural materials were encountered.

Over the past few summers in particular, there has been a substantial amount of favorable local, regional, and national media coverage by newspapers (including the *Christian Science Monitor)* and television and radio stations (including programs on the local pbs affiliate and interviews on a local npr affiliate). This publicity has been mutually beneficial for both Colgate and the Oneidas, and it has helped to increase public awareness about archaeology, the Iroquois people, and the benefits of involving a Native American descendant community in archaeology. As a member of the nation's Men's Council and Clan Mothers stated, "The more people know about Oneidas, the more they will respect us" (Walters 2003:14).

I often talked informally in the field and in the lab about the significance of the findings and asked the participants what the objects, as well as the workshop experience, meant to them. Occasionally, some individuals were willing to share their thoughts, while others remained silent, perhaps feeling uncomfortable about speaking to a group or to me as a person not of Oneida descent. One student, however, offered this personal insight during an interview with a newspaper reporter:

I see this as an opening to many other things, not just archaeology. This is an opportunity that kids shouldn't overlook. It
opens the door to religion and other issues around us. People
need to get involved in our culture. We have lost a lot of people. . . . This makes me think about history and what's happened right here in Stockbridge, Munnsville, and Oneida. I
think about how our people were separated when these lands
were settled, and I dream about us [Oneidas] uniting again
one day. When I'm out here, I can dream and think. When I
find a bead, that is special to me . . . I still bead . . . when I find
a bead, I feel good, and I feel a connection with my ancestors
. . . and I feel hope for our future. I dream of my people coming together again [Cronin 2001].

Thus, from various perspectives, the workshop has clearly been successful, even if, as with the Red Earth Summer Archaeology Program, no participants become archaeologists. The goals have been met, and important
information and objects pertaining to Oneida heritage have been recovered. Further, mutual respect and trust have been fostered among those
associated with this program at Colgate and the Oneida Indian Nation.

Repatriation and Curation

In addition to the workshop in archaeology, collaboration between the
university and the Oneidas is ongoing in other ways. Since the mid-1990s,
members of both communities have continued to work together in compliance with NAGPRA and in reaching agreements concerning the exhibition and curation of certain objects in Colgate's Longyear Museum of Anthropology. While the repatriation process is required by federal statute,
decisions regarding the exhibition and curation of Oneida archaeological
remains were reached voluntarily.

The Longyear Museum of Anthropology contains a relatively small
archaeological and ethnographic collection of objects from around the
world. The museum takes its name from John Longyear, an emeritus professor and Mesoamerican archaeologist who began to build the collection
shortly after arriving at Colgate in 1948. Longyear continued to acquire

materials for the collection until he retired in 1978, when the museum was named in his honor. Since its inception, the museum's collection has been used principally for teaching purposes, providing numerous opportunities over the years for students to work with professors in studying the materials and creating exhibits in the gallery.

The largest part of the collection consists of more than 7,000 objects of Iroquoian ancestry. The vast majority come from Oneida archaeological sites, dating to between about 1,000 and 300 years ago. These materials were excavated in the 1950s and 1960s by avocational archaeologists, who later sold or donated their extensive collections to the university while Longyear was curator. The Oneida objects in particular make up one of the largest extant repositories of this people's heritage, and it is safe to say that much of what is known about Oneida archaeology is based on these artifacts in the museum's collection (see Pratt 1976). Included among the objects were Oneida skeletal remains, which were also excavated by collectors and eventually obtained by the university. None of the sites from which the human and artifactual remains were excavated was owned at the time by the Oneida Indian Nation, although the nation has recently purchased property on which some of these sites are located.

In the mid-1990s Professor Gary Urton, then curator of collections at the museum, worked with Colgate students to inventory the Oneida remains and add the collectors' provenience information to the newly created electronic database, which would store additional descriptive information (e.g., accession numbers, collectors' catalog numbers, object types and raw materials, etc.). A student generated a summer research report and an undergraduate honors research paper based on her experience in the museum (Henry 1995, 1996). The inventory included the Native American skeletal remains, representing at least six individuals, and more than 10 associated funerary objects that were removed from six archaeological sites by collectors in the 1950s and 1960s.

After the inventory was made, consultation was initiated with NAG-PRA representatives of the Oneida Indian Nation, who were given a list of the skeletal remains and associated funerary objects. On June 26, 1995, all of these remains and objects were repatriated to the nation, and "the Oneida feasted their ancestors, burned tobacco to carry their thoughts and prayers, spoke words to the Creator then laid their people back to rest" (Hubbard 1997). One of the NAGPRA representatives spoke eloquently about the experience:

> It helps to think these are my people, my ancestors housed in these institutions. To do the right thing, repatriations, can be strenuous and painstaking. It was quite straining, and quite rejuvenating at the same time. The nation is thankful for the approach the university has taken to correct a great wrong. Colgate has been very cooperative in working to resolve this sensitive issue [Hubbard 1997].

When I became curator of collections in 2001, I continued to work with Colgate students on the laborious task of inventorying and updating the electronic database of the museum's entire holdings; this task has now been completed. As a result of this process, I have identified in the collection more than 1,000 unassociated funerary objects that were excavated from Oneida sites by the avocational archaeologists. The Oneida Indian Nation possesses this list of materials, along with the electronic database. At the time of this writing, they have not requested repatriation of these items, perhaps because of our relationship of mutual trust and respect. There may be another reason as well. For the past several years, the museum has no longer displayed artifacts in its collection that are known to have come from human burials. The grave objects curated in the museum may now be viewed only by appointment. These decisions were made voluntarily as a sign of good faith and out of respect for the sensitivity of the sacred objects.

It is possible, however, that future requests may be made to repatriate some or all of these unassociated funerary objects, in compliance with NAGPRA. In light of this possibility, three retired individuals with strong ties to the New York State Archaeological Association recently asked me whether they could volunteer to take digital photographs of the museum's objects that are subject to NAGPRA, in order to preserve images of these items before their possible repatriation. I thought this was a wonderful idea that would result in a significant and lasting contribution both to the museum's database and to the archaeology of the Iroquois.

After receiving a grant from the Lincoln Financial Group Foundation, the volunteers purchased a Nikon digital camera and other equipment to undertake the digital imaging project. Over the course of nearly four months, they took more than 1,000 digital photographs of over 1,500 objects in the museum; some of these items did not pertain to the Oneida Indian Nation but were photographed because of their potential for repatriation. With assistance from staff in Colgate's Collaboration for Enhanced Learning, the volunteers also created 39 QuickTime digital "movies" of pots (mostly Oneida), which provide 360-degree rotating views of the objects. All the digital photographs and movies were archived and also linked to the electronic database of the collection so that the images of certain items may be viewed. Other museums have made similar use of technology to document skeletal remains and artifacts subject to NAGPRA. At the University of Texas at Austin, for example, a scanning and replication project, begun in 1993, has utilized both a computerized tomography scanner to print high-resolution illustrations and to store detailed measurements of remains and another computer-controlled laser to sculpt precise nylon replicas of objects in advance of repatriation (Bower 1994:186).

Shortly after completion of the Longyear Museum digital imaging project in 2001, I met with a few members of the Oneida Indian Nation Men's Council and Clan Mothers and nation employees to inform them of this accomplishment and to discuss ways they might use the digital images and the electronic database. We talked about the possibility of transferring this information to a computer for public viewing at the nation's Shako:wi Cultural Center, as well as the possibility of downloading some of the images onto the nation's Web site. I posed several questions at the meeting: Are the images themselves considered by the nation to be sacred, since the objects that they represent are sacred? Should access to the images be restricted in any way, since access to the sacred objects in the museum is restricted? Lastly, am I permitted by the nation to show these images in professional presentations and to my students? No one in the meeting responded to my questions, perhaps because they considered them to be rhetorical and thus not requiring a specific answer. These are new issues raised by technology, with very little discussion in the literature (e.g., Milun 2001).

My point in asking these questions was not only to demonstrate my sensitivity concerning the treatment of images of sacred Oneida objects but also to seek guidance from the nation as to the proper use of such images. Simply put, I was uncertain about what the Oneidas would deem inappropriate for viewing, and I did not want to use the images in a manner they would consider offensive. My questions remain unanswered, and I am still unclear whether these images are part of Oneida cultural property, in the manner that other indigenous peoples have redefined their heritage as a protected resource (see Brown 2003). I have shown the images at conferences and in classes but have not posted them or the electronic database on the museum's Web site. Also, I have incorporated the images in my Museum Studies course as the basis for student-designed electronic presentations of virtual exhibits, thereby avoiding displays of actual sacred objects.

Summary and Conclusion

In this chapter I have discussed two case studies in collaborative archaeology between the Oneida Indian Nation and Colgate University. The first case study consisted of a two-week summer workshop in archaeology that Colgate offered nine times between 1995 and 2003 to members of the nation's Youth Work/Learn Program. The workshop, directed by me and funded largely by the Oneidas, provided more than 100 Native American teenagers with hands-on experiences in the limited excavation and laboratory processing of prehistoric and historic nonhuman remains in central New York State. The other case study focused on ongoing collaboration between the nation and the university over the repatriation and curation of Oneida archaeological remains in Colgate's Longyear Museum of Anthropology. This cooperation stemmed from experiences in which both groups have continued to work together in compliance with NAGPRA and in voluntarily reaching agreements concerning the exhibition and curation of certain museum objects.

Such instances of cooperation and consultation over the past 10 years have created a strong relationship between the university and the Oneidas, built on mutual respect and trust. But like many relationships, it is fragile and requires nurturing and commitment. I am hopeful that with continued positive experiences this relationship will strengthen. Indeed collaborative archaeology can be a powerful tool for American Indians, while it may also bring together Native and non-Native communities in ways imagined and unimagined.

Acknowledgments

This chapter is a much expanded version of a previously published article (Kerber 2003). I wish to thank the Oneida Indian Nation Men's Council and Clan Mothers, particularly Richard Lynch, Brian Patterson, and Dale Rood, for permitting me to offer this archaeological workshop since 1995 and for providing the majority of funding since 1998. I am also grateful for the support of Randy Phillips, director of the Youth Work/Learn Program, and Anthony Wonderley, Oneida Indian Nation historian. I am indebted to Colgate University and the John Ben Snow Foundation for their financial support of the workshop, and to the Lincoln Financial Group Foundation for providing funding to complete the digital imaging project. I extend heartfelt gratitude to the more than 100 participants in nine years, as well as to Dixie Henry and all the other archaeological assistants who provided invaluable help. I thank Tim Sofranko for permission to use his photograph in Figure 15.2. Lastly, I thank Barbara and Gordon DeAngelo and Vicky Jane, assisted by Ray Nardelli of Colgate's Collaboration for Enhanced Learning, for their monumental and voluntary effort for more than three months in taking over 1,000 digital photographs of objects in Colgate's Longyear Museum of Anthropology; and Stenny Danielson and Seth Bidder for their long hours spent inventorying the museum's collection and updating its electronic database.

Notes

1. The Oneidas call themselves Onyota'a:ka, which means "the People of the Standing Stone." They are members of the Six Nations Iroquois Confederacy (also known as the Haudenosaunee, an indigenous term meaning "the People of the Longhouse"). For purposes of this article, the "Oneida Indian Nation," the "nation," and the "Oneidas" refer only to the Oneida Indian Nation of New York (i.e., people of Oneida descent living in central New York State), and not the Oneidas who live in Wisconsin or Ontario.

2. "Oneida territory" and "Oneida land" refer specifically to the more than

6,800 ha of property in central New York State owned by the Oneida Indian Nation, as opposed to a much larger tract of about 101,000 ha representing the current land claim case.

3. Until recently, all the recovered remains from Oneida territory have been curated at the Shako:wi Cultural Center, in accordance with this proposal. Some of the objects also have been displayed there. The materials are now kept in a new archive storage facility in the nation's Children and Elders Center.

4. It should be pointed out that the Oneida Indian Nation runs a lucrative casino (Turning Stone Casino), as well as other successful business enterprises.

16. Research and Dialogue
New Vision Archaeology in the
Cayuga Heartland of Central New York

JACK ROSSEN

I took a long road to investigating Cayuga settlements in the Finger Lakes region of central New York State, along with a "new vision" approach to doing archaeology. I worked for 20 years in Peru, Chile, and Argentina. However, it was my experience in two U.S. projects that was central to my political repositioning within archaeology. The first was the 1978 Carrier Mills Project in southern Illinois, where hundreds of burials were removed ahead of Peabody Coal Company strip miners (Jefferies and Butler 1982). The second was a brief experience at the Slack Farm Project in western Kentucky in 1988, where archaeologists were brought in to clean up and analyze the mess when looters tore up hundreds of burials in a Late Mississippian (Caborn-Welborn) cemetery (Pollack 1998). Slack Farm in particular became a media circus with looters, artifact traffickers, FBI investigators, archaeologists, and site-occupying Native Americans (Arden 1989; Fagan n.d.). It became clear to me that archaeology was not a dispassionate science, and that some Native people considered archaeologists to be villains who aided and abetted the destruction of sacred places and landscapes (Theft from the Dead 1986).

Over the last several years, I have developed a version of collaborative archaeology that is tailored to a local social, cultural, and political situation. The area of central New York in which I work includes a Native American land claim, both traditional and nontraditional Native groups, and a strident anti–land claim citizens organization. In this chapter, I describe my attempts to collaborate with Native people, including conducting sensitive and meaningful archaeological research while working with a not-for-profit community organization that promotes friendship and respect and is attempting to return land to Native peoples, all within a complex landscape of cultures and political issues. I offer this story not so much as a model, but as an example of the process of gradually making archaeology a positive force for Native people.

Background

On moving to Ithaca, New York, in 1996, I began to teach and do research in an area with a large Native population that was politically visible and culturally revitalizing. I found that the Cayuga Nation heartland, specifically the eastern shore of Cayuga Lake, was neglected by professional archaeologists. The area contains several of the largest historic Cayuga villages and towns, including the very largest of them all, Goi-o-gouen, or Cayuga Castle, described by Sergeant Major George Grant (Cook 2000 [1887]:113) in 1779 as having 50 well-built houses. There are other professionals working around Cayuga Lake (Baugher and Clark 1998; Levine 2003), but not in this eastern shore heartland. William Ritchie worked there in the 1940s, when he excavated the Frontenac Island cemetery (Ritchie 1945). Marian White briefly investigated in the area from 1969 to 1971 (Niemczycki 1984:18–19), but most of her research was conducted in the Niagara frontier area of western New York (White 1961, 1977).

The eastern Cayuga Lake shore heartland is a landscape of hills, sprawling farms with rolling fields, deep wooded gorges, and cliff lines. The view of the 64-km-long lake is present from nearly every bluff and ridgetop. Historical markers dot the roadways, with many glorifying the Sullivan-Clinton campaign of August and September 1779, when George Washington sent the Continental Army north to burn 43 Seneca and Cayuga towns and villages at the height of the Revolutionary War. The campaign was ostensibly conducted to punish the Haudenosaunee nations that backed the British and to protect frontier settlements, but historians have argued that it was instead conducted against the Cayugas as a training project to shore up the suspect supply lines and chain of command of the army (Fischer 1997) and to provide land as payment for soldiers. Markers placed in 1929 discuss the campaign "against the hostile aggressions" of the Cayugas (Ford 2002). Also commemorated are the many towns, villages, crop fields, and fruit tree orchards that were destroyed. After the Revolutionary War, the Cayugas were the only one of the six nations in the Haudenosaunee (Iroquois) Confederacy not to retain a land base.

In Aurora Village, the home of Wells College and its 500 students, a marker remembers the Cayuga village of Chonodote, known as "Peachtown" to the British and Americans, and the destruction of its unique 1,500-tree peach orchard during the Sullivan campaign. Nearby, in Springport, the historic Cayuga burial mound imposingly sits by the side of State Route 90, alongside the 36-m-deep gorge and waterfalls of Great Gully, both sites of tremendous spiritual importance for the Cayugas.

The local political climate is a significant factor for practicing collaborative, new vision archaeology in the area. There is a proliferation of signs stating "No Sovereign Nation, No Reservation," placed by a group called Upstate Citizens for Equality (UCE), who protest the Cayuga land claim, which has been in the courts since 1980 (Figure 16.1). The goals and ideology of UCE are complex, but a few basics may be stated for the record. The term "equality" in their name is used as a euphemism for assimilation, in that this group wants all people living in the area, non-Native and Native, to be politically equal tax-paying citizens of the United States. They fear that an increased Native presence in the area and a land claim settlement will bring a lower tax base once reconstituted reservation lands and businesses come off the tax rolls, and they fear the potential consequences of gaming in the area. For their part, Native people in the Finger Lakes, who claim national sovereignty and often do not accept U.S. citizenship, view UCE as being generally hostile to Native people. In 2003 the New York Cayugas bought two locations in the land claim area, Union Springs and Seneca Falls, where they sell gas and cigarettes, paying federal but not state taxes. The State of New York promised to enforce state tax collection by March 2004, then backed off in order to continue negotiations. In response, UCE called for the impeachment of Governor George Pataki (Kriss 2004). The

Figure 16.1. Anti-Native American sentiments of some people are visible on the landscape of the Cayuga heartland (Photo courtesy of Jack Rossen).

periodic protests and motorcades of UCE are noisy and angry affairs (Stith 2003; 200 UCE Vehicles 2003).

Members of UCE are farmers and business people living in the depressed economy of rural New York State. Sovereignty, taxes, and gaming are all complex issues, made more complex by the number of factions and sub-groups of Cayugas from New York, Canada, and Oklahoma that all stake a claim in the region. For archaeologists, the historic revision that accompanies the anti-Indian protests is notable. UCE states on its Web site, "The Cayuga Indians came to the area of New York in the 1500s, a wandering nomadic tribe that traveled around the northeast, never having a permanent settlement" (Upstate Citizens for Equality 2003). In a similar vein, a local historian wrote that when white settlers arrived at the future site of Aurora Village, they found "an empty wilderness" (Edmunds 2000:1).

Communities and families have been divided by the issues surrounding the long-standing land claim and the increasing Native presence in the area. In 1999 Julie and Jim Uticone, lifelong residents in the land claim area, began SHARE (Strengthening Haudenosaunee American Relations through Education) to promote friendship and mutual respect between local non-Native and Native people. Julie Uticone is a self-employed businesswoman, and Jim works at a local business. A major catalyst for the Uticones to begin SHARE was a public threat made around Thanksgiving of 1999 to bomb the Turning Stone Casino of the Oneida Indian Nation of New York and to murder a Native person every three days. SHARE was born modestly, with friends and neighbors gathering at a park for a peace circle. The Uticones recruited a small circle of people, including academics like me; Brooke Olson, a cultural anthropologist at Ithaca College; and Ernie Olson, a cultural anthropologist at Wells College. A local Seneca family was also central to the original SHARE group. Together we put out a quarterly newsletter, held gatherings, and visited local schools to discuss Native people and contemporary issues.

In 2001 we heard that a friend's organic farm was going up for sale near Union Springs in the claim area. The 28-ha farm is next to both Cayuga Castle, the largest Cayuga settlement site, and Great Gully. A few of us pondered the thought of who should really own that land. We ended up pooling money to buy the place, and the nonprofit SHARE Farm was born. (For a longer version of the story, see www.share.clarityconnect.com.) We have operated the farm as an educational center, an advocating voice for Native people, and a friendly place for people of all kinds to reconnect with each other and the land (Figure 16.2). The ultimate goal is to turn the land over to traditional Cayuga and Haudenosaunee people. Our Native friends have expressed interest in having community gardens and other environmental projects at the farm.

Immediately after its purchase in April 2001, the SHARE Farm was repeatedly visited by large and small groups of Native and non-Native people. There are many stories to tell about Native returns to the heartland, impromptu socials, heirloom crop projects, medicinal herb gardens, bridges built between people (after all, the SHARE slogan is "build a bridge and get over it"), student internships, and support from groups and organizations as diverse as the Onondaga Nation (the closest existing Native nation), the Haudenosaunee Environmental Task Force (HEFT), and Cultural Survival in Boston. SHARE also coorganized with Wells College the Peachtown Native American Festival, which provided a day of Native dance, music, food, and crafts for local people. SHARE became a social experiment and cul-

Figure 16.2. Volunteers from Ithaca College and Cultural Survival working at the SHARE Farm (Photo courtesy of Ernie Olson).

tural success that astounded us, although like most small organizations, it has also undergone financial struggle. My involvement on the board of directors of SHARE strengthened my relations with local Native people and helped me better understand their concerns about cultural presentation, resource management, and archaeology.

Principles of a New Vision Archaeology

My archaeological research in the area began in 2000. I followed a path toward communication and collaboration with the local Native nations and communities, but I believe there is no blueprint. Every region and researcher must follow his or her own path toward the "new vision," but the principles are clear. The new vision requires that archaeologists understand the historical, political, and community contexts of their research. With these contexts in mind, each archaeologist must strive toward a discipline that is a positive force for Native people, instead of the negative and destructive force it has so often been (Jemison 1997; Theft from the Dead 1986). Archaeologists must actively seek out Native leaders to help archaeologists decide what is acceptable or inappropriate to excavate. Excavation of burials and sacred sites must be avoided whenever possible, and these activities are acceptable only in extenuating circumstances and in close consultation with official Native representatives.

More specifically, archaeologists should try to find out what topics or research issues are interesting or important to Native people. When I asked one local Native leader this question, he paused and said, "I have to think about that. No one ever asked me before." In the Finger Lakes area at least, Native people are interested in knowing what the heart of the Cayuga Nation was like before and just after the scorched earth destruction of the Sullivan campaign. Thus, understanding the Cayuga heartland landscape in all its diversity of settlement size and type, roads, crop fields, and fruit tree orchards has become my overarching research concern. I want to recapture a picture or feeling of the grandeur of that nation and pass those images on. It seems to me that Native people in this region are not against archaeology per se, but against archaeologists running excavations without their knowledge or advice.

Archaeologists already recognize the power of the past: archaeology has the potential to help or to harm, to disenfranchise or to empower, to destroy relationships between people or to build bridges. Cooperation between Native people and archaeologists can result in common goals, particularly in the areas of site preservation and public education. At Ganondagan State Park, near Rochester, archaeological research led not only to site preservation but to the development of cooperative park administration and the reconstruction of a longhouse in its original location (Dean 1986).

An important aspect of new vision archaeology for me is the use of the archaeological site as a place for public dialogue on historical and contemporary issues. Excavations attract visitors of all political views and offer chances to discuss the nature and grandeur of the Cayuga Nation and the long archaeological sequence. People cannot help gaining a sense of history when gazing into an excavation block, along with a deeper understanding of the Cayuga attachment to the heart of their ancestral homeland. I try to convey a sense that while this is the Cayuga history, it is also a shared history for all people who live in the region.

My current research is done with archaeological field schools. Thus, I am not under the pressure of having to decide about imminent site destruction. I can also cultivate students who are sensitive to issues or have volunteered at the SHARE Farm (sometimes even lived there), and I can recruit Native students with free tuition scholarships. I have been fortunate to have Native students participate in three of the four field seasons.

Building relationships between archaeologists and Native people is a continual process of forward and backward steps, and the process will be different in every region (Swidler et al. 1997). I believe that archaeologists should be advocates and activists on contemporary Native American issues, including but reaching beyond the archaeological issues of site preservation and repatriation. Just as archaeologists recognize that the past is not dead and gone but a continuing influential backdrop to the present, we must be involved in that present. I will describe how this "new vision" developed in the specific case of my research over the last four years in the eastern Cayuga Lake region of central New York.

Research and Dialogue in a Land Claim Area

As stated above, my goal is to have a clan mother or other leader come to visit a site before excavation to decide whether the site feels positive or negative. During the 2000 survey we thought we were able to pinpoint a portion of the original site of Peachtown (now known as the Wells Barn site), based on soldiers' journals (Cook 2000 [1887]) and shovel test surveys. A historical marker for the site had once stood on Route 90 below the area, but had been moved a mile away to the center of Aurora Village. A visiting clan mother respectfully corrected me when I stated that I had found the site. She said that the site had chosen to reveal itself now because the time was right, maybe socially or politically. A similar example concerns the Tutelos, who were an adopted tribe from the southeast that settled in Ithaca before being burned out with the Cayugas in 1779. Archaeologists have been continually frustrated in their attempts to locate the village site (Baugher and Quinn 1995). Clan mothers have told us the time is just not yet right for its revelation. When it is ready, perhaps when the community is ready to appreciate it and protect it properly, it will be revealed. Or maybe the general cultural climate and attitudes of people toward Native Americans need to progress before certain stories can be told. In this way, the clan mothers are telling archaeologists to contemplate the unintended consequences of finding and investigating archaeological sites.

From my investigations, we are learning about the specialization of Cayuga villages. Excavations at the Wells Barn site revealed a pottery manufacturing area of thick, undecorated waster sherds from large storage vessels, including sherds that were fired multiple times. Many were probably broken sherds used to position pots during firing. The site was described in soldiers' journals as consisting of 12 or 14 older houses not as well kept as other settlements. According to the journal of Thomas Grant, it took all day for several hundred soldiers to destroy the site and its unique 1,500-tree peach orchard in September 1779 (Cook 2000 [1887]:143). The site is the only discovered Cayuga village on the eastern lakeshore; most villages were located along the cliff lines ranging from a mile or two from the lake (Niemczycki 1984).

Aurora Village is indeed a uniquely warm microenvironment: a sheltered, low-lying basin next to the lake where it often rains in the winter while it snows everywhere else. My surveys throughout the village have encountered lots of flood silt (there is a levy and heavily managed lake-level controls today), and also eighteenth-century Cayuga ceramics in secondary contexts or jumbled with more recent historic materials. Based on all the above observations, the working hypothesis is that the Wells Barn site was a specialized peach growing and processing site. One may imagine the enormous task and time pressure of fire drying and storing the ripe peaches of 1,500 trees. Except as an unusually warm spot for growing peaches, the site is otherwise not an optimal or typical Cayuga settlement location. The old, poorly kept houses described in the soldier journals may indicate a temporary seasonal occupation.

A second example of possible village specialization is still speculative but worthy of brief mention. Village X, a pseudonym given to the site at the landowner's request, is an impressive locale on the edge of a deep gorge and its tributaries, with three sides facing precipices. A portion of the site has a double earthen wall and ditch along the steepest gorge edge. Even before visiting it, one clan mother told me she felt it might be a powerful place, and she asked me whether it was triangular in shape, an area where

Figure 16.3. Students mapping the midden near the cliff edge of Village X (Photo courtesy of Jack Rossen).

energy converged. Indeed it is. Excavations at this sixteenth-century site were confined to a relatively deep (80 cm) trash midden near the site's edge to avoid damaging a wheat field (Figure 16.3). Prominent among the incised pottery sherds (smaller, thinner, and distinctive from the thick Wells Barn site sherds) were many fragments of small groundstone pallets, many with rims, and small grinding stones. I puzzled over the presence of so many small grinding artifacts, until my colleague Brooke Olson brought her students for a site visit. Olson and her students were conducting a regional inventory of wild medicinal plants throughout the area in cooperation with an Onondaga healer and midwife. Their trip into the deep gorge next to the site was provocative. They found the greatest number and variety of women's medicinal herbs present anywhere in the area, including extensive stands of endangered species and unusually large individual specimens of particular species (Keemer and Williams 2003). I had already wondered why trash and broken artifacts were not tossed over the edge of the site but were deposited in a midden near the steep drop-off. We ponder whether that area was indeed an area where medicinal herbs were encouraged or grown, and whether the groundstone pallets currently under analysis are evidence of a specialized healers' village.

Figure 16.4. The Patrick Tavern site on Main Street, Aurora, New York, provided a location for many discussions with townspeople of historical and contemporary Native issues (Photo courtesy of Jack Rossen).

I raise these speculations and working hypotheses as examples of potential archaeological findings that involve the excavation of nonsacred sites, such as manufacturing zones and trash middens, that produce ideas that are interesting to Native people as well as to archaeologists. I have not always been so lucky. While excavating at the site of another village destroyed in 1779, we unexpectedly disturbed human remains. We were surprised, because Haudenosaunee villages and cemeteries are usually well separated, and only domestic debris was observed on the site surface. The black matt layer of the burning of the site was clear in the excavations, and one rock-chinked posthole was excavated. It appears that we found a Sullivan campaign casualty in a burned house. The discovery led to a collaborative discussion with the clan mother. We decided together that it was not the best time to excavate this site, so we backfilled and left the site the next day.

Another example is my excavations at the Patrick Tavern site. The 1793 tavern building, recognized as the earliest Euroamerican structure in Aurora Village, still stands on Main Street (Figure 16.4). Doing archaeological excavation on a village Main Street is one of the best examples of public archaeology. Over two summers, excavations were conducted to illuminate the nature of the area's transition from the center of the Cayuga Nation to the periphery of a new expanding nation. During the excavations, I met many residents of Aurora, all interested in the archaeology and wanting to discuss historic and contemporary issues, including the land claim. In this way, the Patrick Tavern was as much a valuable context for dialogue about local preoccupations as it was an interesting and significant place for research.

Taverns were the bustling economic and social hubs of frontier towns and are great places for archaeologists to study the economic pathways and communication routes of the central New York frontier (Hayes 1965). A variety of fascinating assemblages of ceramics, glass, and fauna have produced or are leading to student senior theses (Moragne 2001). There were also unexpected results that make this site special. For example, the rich 1790s and early nineteenth-century assemblages were peppered with Native American pottery. This addresses an issue raised at the Cayuga land claim hearings of 1999, questioning whether a group of Cayugas stayed behind on the eastern lakeshore rather than flee to Canada after the 1779 destruction and the 1805 sale of their last land parcel. The Patrick Tavern deposits reflect a continued Cayuga presence in the area well into the nineteenth century, along with trade relations with the Euroamerican community of Aurora. Rather than abdicate the homeland after its scorched earth destruction and subsequent land sales, a faction of Cayugas stayed behind, demonstrating their attachment to the region.

Discussion

Being a public archaeologist with a new vision of archaeology is a professional and personal commitment. It is increasingly clear to me that archaeologists can no longer do archaeology in a cultural and political vacuum in areas such as central New York. My work and collaborative vision were shaped by my decision to investigate in and near a land claim area, where I met activist citizens like Julie and Jim Uticone and cultural anthropologists like the Olsons who were developing medical anthropology projects. The SHARE Farm project is an example of an opportunity that arose to build bridges between Native and non-Native people. For me, it is also an opportunity to continually connect history and contemporary issues.

As mentioned previously, I came into Haudenosaunee studies recently, and I am not a part of its establishment. The sad history of cemetery excavation and dispersal of artifact collections is changing, but archaeologists still retain a poor reputation with local Native people. I have learned that archaeology should be incorporated into a broader activism that advocates friendship, mutual respect, communication, and cooperation with Native people. It helps that through SHARE I have an identity that is more multidimensional than simply being an archaeologist. Similarly, it helps that I live near the region and spend a good deal of time there, visiting schools, organizing workshops, and presenting exhibits of artifacts. In these venues, I can raise awareness of the time depth, scope, and scale of Native occupation in the area; the destructiveness of the Sullivan campaign; the presence of significant archaeological sites throughout the area; the value of site preservation; and the importance of repatriation. I can also promote the various educational programs of my Native friends and colleagues at the SHARE Farm. I often conduct a tour of archaeological sites and locales that within a few miles includes sites like the Patrick Tavern, Wells Barn, Great Gully, Eagle Cottage (discussed below), and the Cayuga Burial Mound. This tour impresses on people the grandeur of the Cayuga homeland and the importance of the local archaeology and history; every site has a unique story to tell. These stories implicitly help people understand the Cayuga passion for their homeland. In comparison, it is more difficult to build and maintain good relations with Native people for out-of-state archaeologists who come in seasonally or send graduate students who are often unaware of the land claim or the controversy surrounding their work.

The goals of archaeological research in this climate become multifaceted and connected to the surrounding social and political situation. One goal is to demonstrate the absurdity of the "empty wilderness" and "wandering nomadic tribe" ideas that are still found in local publications and the literature of anti–land claim groups. This goal is accomplished by documenting and recapturing the complexity of the landscape, with its large and small settlements, quarries, occupationally specialized sites, crop fields, fruit tree orchards, and trade networks. Another goal is to make archaeology public, by exhibiting artifacts, giving talks and workshops, and making the archaeological site a place where people visit and discuss issues.

The results are subtle and cumulative, as people realize that the Cayugas are all around their homes, farms, and workplaces.

One excavation I conducted was in a yard in Aurora Village. The Eagle Cottage site produced eighteenth-century Cayuga artifacts and ash lenses heavily mixed with nineteenth-century historic materials. Yet the value of the site went far beyond its mixed archaeological integrity, as a steady stream of villagers stopped by to notice that the Cayugas had lived literally in their backyards. Eagle Cottage demonstrates the importance of the *process* of doing archaeology, which is equal in importance to the published products. What is important on a daily basis is that an archaeologist pursuing these goals is here and visible in the community. To local people, this means that there must be an important history here. In contrast, the thirty-year absence of an archaeologist imparted a sense that the area's history was unimportant, which is the first step to historical revision, representing an underlying component of hostility to Native people.

I began this essay by discussing my road to Cayuga archaeology, the nonprofit organization SHARE, and a new vision of archaeology. I claim no absolute blueprint, only a positive attitude, a patient approach to developing relationships, and a respect for the beliefs and instructions of Native leaders. There is also a need to work locally toward (1) education on contemporary issues, (2) active support for repatriation and site protection, and (3) collaboration not just with Native people but also with local farmers and businesspeople. The archaeology provides a necessary historic backdrop to SHARE's work to provide a place of friendship, mutual respect, and collaboration (and, we hope, part of a permanent land base for Native people). This work emphasizes the process of doing, discussing, and exhibiting archaeology, and it is driven by a commitment to maintaining dialogue and involvement in contemporary issues that reach beyond, but are informed by, the archaeology. In this atmosphere, the old product-driven, noncollaborative, contemporarily uninvolved archaeology seems barren and sterile in comparison.

Acknowledgments

I gratefully acknowledge the guidance of numerous friends, especially Bernadette Hill and Tim Twoguns of the Cayuga Nation, Norman Hill of the Tonawanda Band of Senecas, Freida Jacques and Oren Lyons of the Onondaga Nation, and Rick Hill of the Tuscarora Nation. Brooke Olson and Ernie Olson made important comments on an early draft. Kim Milling administered the Ithaca College archaeological field schools, and Terry Martinez coordinated the Wells College participation. This cooperative project would not have occurred without Julie and Jim Uticone, the founders of SHARE, who brought me into the organization. I also thank the more than 30 Ithaca College and Wells College students who enthusiastically participated in politically and socially conscious field schools.

17. Indigenous Archaeology in Southern New England
Case Studies from the
Mashantucket Pequot Reservation

BRIAN D. JONES AND KEVIN A. MCBRIDE

In the fall of 1982, shortly before the Mashantucket Pequot Tribe received federal recognition, Tribal Chairman Richard "Skip" Hayward approached Kevin McBride, then a University of Connecticut graduate student, to assist in identifying collections and gathering research materials for the creation of a Mashantucket Pequot Museum. Hayward noted to McBride that there was a lot of "interesting stuff" on the 87-ha reservation in which he might be interested. In the summer of 1983, with the aid of a National Park Service Survey and Planning Grant administered through the Connecticut Historical Commission, McBride confirmed the presence of numerous above-ground cultural features.

Since the tribe's federal recognition in the fall of 1983, the Mashantucket Pequot Reservation, in Ledyard, Connecticut, has grown to over 600 ha with an additional 2,023 ha held by the tribe in fee simple (Figure 17.1). Since 1983 over $300,000 have been provided by state and federal agencies to fund archaeological surveys and excavations on the reservation. Granting agencies have included the Bureau of Indian Affairs, the National Park Service, the Department of the Interior, and the Connecticut Historical Commission. The Mashantucket Pequot Tribe has also provided over $1 million in funding for archaeological surveys, conservation, and research. The tribe currently supports a full-time staff of archaeologists, conserva-

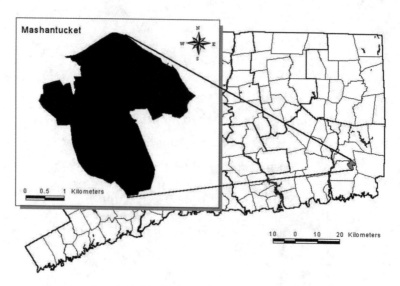

Figure 17.1. Location of the Mashantucket Pequot Reservation in Ledyard, Connecticut (Prepared by Brian Jones).

tors, and historical researchers at the Mashantucket Pequot Museum and Research Center (MPMRC). The University of Connecticut has conducted its annual summer field school in archaeology on the reservation since 1983, and the tribe continues to support academic research on a number of topics related to paleoenvironmental reconstruction, archaeology, and Native, African, and colonial history (e.g., Currie and McBride 2001; Forrest 1999; Jones 1997, 1998, 1999, 2002; Jones and Forrest 2003; McBride 1990, 1992, 1993, 1996, 1998; McWeeney 1994).

The Mashantucket Pequot Tribe values and supports archaeological research on a scale that has rarely been duplicated elsewhere in Indian country, with the possible exception of the Navajo and Zuni archaeological programs. This chapter outlines the numerous historical and contemporary factors that have led to the development of the archaeology program at Mashantucket and the tribe's ongoing support of archaeological and historical research.

Mashantucket Pequot Historical Context

The Mashantucket Pequot Reservation is one of the oldest continuously occupied cultural landscapes in the United States. The national significance of the Mashantucket Reservation was recognized in 1996 when it was designated the Mashantucket Pequot Reservation Archaeological District National Landmark (McBride 1998). The reservation is located in the geographic center of the traditional homeland of the Pequots and was used primarily for seasonal and temporary hunting and plant collecting by the Pequots during the early seventeenth century (McBride 1990). Archaeological surveys and excavations at Mashantucket have documented a continuous record of occupation from the Paleoindian period (ca. 10,500 B.P. [years before present]) through the twentieth century (Jones 1997, 1998, 1999, 2002; Jones and Forrest 2003; Forrest 1999; McBride 1990, 1992, 1993). Over 250 archaeological sites have been identified at Mashantucket over the last 20 years. They include more than 150 historic and 200 prehistoric components.

This unique archaeological record is the result of environmental and historical factors that have shaped the landscape and cultural history of Mashantucket. The Great Cedar Swamp, a 202-ha wetland in the center of the reservation, has been a focal point of Native American land use and settlement since the first human inhabitants arrived in the region over 10,000 years ago. Detailed palynological, plant macrofossil, and sediment analyses have documented regional and local environmental changes at Cedar Swamp over the last 15,000 years (McWeeney 1994, 1999; Thorson and Webb 1991). This research, combined with archaeological surveys and excavations, has resulted in one of the most comprehensive studies of human interaction with the physical and social environments compiled in the Northeast.

Ironically, the same factors that attracted Native peoples to Mashantucket for millennia diminished the usefulness of the area for Euroamerican settlers thousands of years later. The swampy, hilly, moraine-scarred environment at Mashantucket was not attractive to early Euroamerican settlers, but it was considered suitable for an Indian reservation. As a result, the Native presence at Mashantucket increased significantly in the seventeenth and eighteenth centuries, while it diminished and all but disappeared in most other areas of southern New England.

In the early seventeenth century, the Pequots inhabited an area of approximately 647 km² in what is now southeastern Connecticut (McBride

1990). Pequot villages were located adjacent to coastal and estuarine wetlands along Long Island Sound and the Thames and Mystic rivers. Pequot efforts to control the fur and wampum trade in coastal and near-interior areas of Long Island Sound resulted in the subjugation of many other Native groups in the region. Pequot political and economic control of southern New England stretched 129 km along the Connecticut and Rhode Island coast from New Haven in the west to Charlestown in the east, including eastern Long Island, Block Island, and the Connecticut River as far north as Massachusetts (McBride 1990).

Rising tensions with the English in the early 1630s led to the Pequot War of 1636–1637 and the annihilation of the Pequot Tribe as a viable political and social entity. Over 2,000 Pequots were killed, sold into slavery, or dispersed among the Mohegan and Narragansett tribes during and immediately following the war (McBride 1990).

At the end of the Pequot War, the Mashantucket band was one of many small groups of Pequots that were scattered throughout southern New England (McBride 1990). They were granted several parcels of land in the second half of the seventeenth century, the largest being the 1,012-ha reservation at Mashantucket in 1666 (McBride 1990). With Mashantucket, Noank (202 ha), and Walnut Hill (243 ha), the Mashantucket Pequots had a land base exceeding 1,416 ha in the early eighteenth century.

Reductions to this land base began during the second decade of the eighteenth century. The English demand for home lots, planting fields, pasture, and woodlots had an immediate impact on the tribe, which began to find it increasingly difficult to maintain its population on the ever-shrinking reservations. Within a 30-year period, from 1710 to 1740, tribal lands were reduced by 75 percent—more than 1,012 ha. In 1856 the State of Connecticut sold off all but 87 ha of the Mashantucket Reservation.

The continuous reduction in the Mashantucket land base and changing regional economies resulted in a steady emigration from Mashantucket throughout the eighteenth, nineteenth, and early twentieth centuries. Mashantucket families and individuals were forced to disperse to seek employment throughout rural and urban areas from New York City to Boston. By the mid-twentieth century, the reservation population had been reduced to only a handful of people.

In 1983 the Mashantucket Pequots were granted federal recognition and a land claim of 809 ha. The tribe immediately embarked on an aggressive economic, social, and political revitalization program to provide jobs, housing, and community infrastructure to encourage its members to return to the reservation. One of the key elements of the program was the planning and eventual construction of a museum and research center emphasizing the archaeology, history, and culture of the tribe. The tribe had long been frustrated and dismayed by its portrayal in history and textbooks, which described the Pequots as "extinct" after the Pequot War. In addition, many of the returning tribal members had no knowledge of many aspects of their history after the war. The Mashantucket leadership saw the reconstruction of Pequot history as vital to their efforts to inform tribal members of their own heritage and to redress the biases and misconceptions perpetrated in Euroamerican historical narratives. The leadership also recognized the importance of educating and informing the general public—particularly schoolchildren—of Pequot history and culture.

The tribal leadership immediately recognized the need to redress historical biases through an integrated research program that involved archaeology, historical research, and tribal perspectives as expressed through oral history, tradition, and folklore. Equally important were tribal perspectives on the past and their interpretations of the archaeological record. The Mashantucket leadership identified two principal ways in which these goals could be achieved: (1) ongoing support of historical and archaeological research on the Pequots and other Native groups in the region; and (2) construction of a museum and research center with innovative exhibits and educational programs.

Archaeologists and the Mashantucket Pequot Tribe

Until recently, relationships between archaeologists and Native Americans in southern New England (as elsewhere) were often characterized by distrust, animosity, misunderstanding, and lack of respect for the other's perspective. Generations of archaeologists excavated Native villages, camps, cemeteries, and sacred sites without informing or consulting Native people, and without including them in the analysis and interpretation of artifacts or in decisions about their final disposition. Although some archaeologists in the region developed relationships with Native peoples based on mutual respect and awareness of the necessity and importance of including Native viewpoints in decisions regarding their cultural heritage, they were the exception rather than the rule (Leveillee 2002b; McBride 1990; Poirier et al. 1985; Robinson 1990, this volume; Robinson et al. 1985; Rubertone 2001). Although the ultimate goals of both groups were often compatible (i.e., preservation and encouraging a broader understanding of Native history), long-term relationships were rarely developed between archaeologists and Native people.

This situation has changed in recent years, particularly in southern New England, because of three primary factors: (1) the passage of the Native American Graves Protection and Repatriation Act (NAGPRA), (2) the increasing number of Native groups who have acquired federal recognition and settled land claims, and (3) federal and state laws and regulations requiring consultation with Native groups. Over the last few decades, Native groups throughout the Northeast and elsewhere have become increasingly vocal about how research is conducted on archaeological sites, objects, and places of traditional and cultural importance.

As newly recognized tribes, such as the Mashantucket Pequot, Mohegan, and Eastern Pawcatuck Pequot, plan and initiate economic and social development projects on reservation lands, they are faced with a variety of issues related to the identification, assessment, preservation, and management of archaeological resources under Section 106 of the National Historic Preservation Act. In recent years, archaeologists have collaborated on a number of archaeological and historic preservation projects with the Mashantucket Pequots (McBride 1998), Narragansetts (Brown and Robinson, this volume; Leveillee 2002b; Robinson 1990;) and Gay Head (Aquinnah) Wampanoag (Chilton, this volume; Herbster and Cherau, this volume; McBride and Cherau 1996), identifying and assessing cultural resources on their reservations and developing historic preservation plans. Although initially forced to work together out of necessity, archaeologists and Native communities in the region have established solid relationships with each other as understanding and mutual respect for the other's perspective have developed.

Since 1982 the Mashantucket Pequot Tribe has worked with federal, state, and local governmental agencies, including the Connecticut Historical Commission, the Bureau of Indian Affairs, the National Park Service, the University of Connecticut's Department of Anthropology, and the Town of Ledyard, to develop a comprehensive research and cultural management plan on the reservation and adjacent lands. Since 1995 these functions have been subsumed and coordinated by archaeologists of the MPMRC's Research Department in coordination with the Mashantucket Pequot Tribal Council, and with tribal departments, committees, and individuals. Collectively, this effort—known as the Mashantucket Pequot Ethnohistory Project—integrates archaeological and historical research and cultural resource management objectives.

The Mashantucket Pequot Ethnohistory Project has four major goals which were identified through discussions with the Tribal Council and tribal archaeologists: (1) to reconstruct Mashantucket Pequot tribal history from the prehistoric period through the twentieth century, integrating archaeology, historical sources, and oral history; (2) to use this information to plan and construct exhibits on tribal history and culture for the MPMRC; (3) to develop and implement a cultural resource management plan for trust and fee lands held by the tribe; and (4) to train tribal members in archaeological field techniques, ethnohistorical methods, and historic preservation.

The early relationship between members of the tribe and non-Native archaeologists could at best be characterized as one of wariness and suspicion. Each group entered the relationship with a considerable amount of misinformation about and bias toward the other. Some tribal members referred to archaeologists as "grave diggers" and were worried that they were not always forthcoming about the nature of their finds, particularly in the case of burials and cemeteries. Archaeologists often expressed the opinion that contemporary Pequots had no connection with their past, had been thoroughly assimilated, and had no information to aid in the interpretation of their history and culture. Despite this rocky beginning, over the years the relationship between the tribe and the archaeologists eventually developed into one of understanding and mutual respect. Archaeologists are now called on to assume a number of duties and responsibilities on the reservation well outside their original role. Ironically, it was the excavation of a Mashantucket Pequot cemetery that solidified the relationship between the archaeologists and the tribe.

A Case Study: Long Pond Cemetery

In 1990 a Mashantucket Pequot tribal cemetery (Long Pond) was discovered during the excavation of a house foundation on private land (Figure 17.2). The land had been part of the Mashantucket Pequot Reservation from 1666 until 1720 (McBride 1993). The discovery of human remains and funerary objects at the Long Pond Cemetery initiated the first test of a recently passed Connecticut state law, Public Act 89-368, that dealt with the treatment of Native American burials on state and private land. The act, drafted and passed with the involvement of the Mashantucket Pequot Tribe and non-federally recognized tribes in Connecticut, required the state archaeologist to consult with the newly formed Native American Heritage Advisory Council to determine cultural affiliation and whether in situ preservation was possible. It was quickly determined that the Long Pond Cemetery was culturally affiliated with the Mashantucket Pequot Tribe, and the site was turned over to the tribe to determine the best course of action and to negotiate with the landowner and town officials.

The tribe took a unique approach to the situation, influenced in part by their long association with archaeologists and the enduring memory of centuries of desecration of their graves and sacred places. The tribe recognized that most "invisible" or "unmarked" Native American graves are accidentally discovered during construction projects and subsequently ignored or destroyed by construction personnel and private property owners, who fear construction delays, reprisals, and potential loss of their land.

In a spirit of cooperation, and wishing to set a precedent for future discoveries of unmarked Native American graves, the tribe agreed to remove those graves remaining within the unexcavated portion of the house foundation, thereby allowing the landowner to proceed with construction in a timely manner. The tribe also agreed to assume all costs and, along with tribal archaeologists, accompanied the landowner to the Town of Ledyard's zoning board of appeals to acquire a necessary variance to build within a

Figure 17.2. Excavations of the Mashantucket Pequot tribal Long Pond Cemetery at a house construction site in 1990 (© Mashantucket Pequot Museum and Research Center; Photo courtesy of Kevin McBride.)

known cemetery. In return, the Pequots asked that all remaining burials within the property be protected and that the zoning variance contain a clause stipulating that any future owners of the property contact the tribe if any future subsurface disturbance took place.

Under the tribe's direction, a team of University of Connecticut archaeologists and conservators exhumed 25 graves containing 28 individuals and conducted limited, noninvasive analysis on human remains and associated funerary objects. Additional human remains and unassociated funerary objects were recovered over a two-year period from backdirt piles created during construction.

The primary concern of the Mashantucket Pequot Tribe was that proper respect be shown during the excavation and analysis of their ancestors. The University of Connecticut archaeological team had been conducting archaeological research on the Mashantucket Pequot Reservation since 1983, and many were on a first-name basis with tribal members. Over the years, the tribe and the archaeologists had established an excellent working relationship, and tribal members were present during the entire excavation, analysis, and reburial process.

Throughout the course of the excavation, tribal members would frequently express their appreciation for the care the archaeologists were taking, and their respect for the human remains, and many tribal members remarked on how much information on their history and culture the excavation and analysis could provide. For their part, the archaeologists were concerned with the emotional impact on the tribe and took great care to treat all human remains and funerary objects with the utmost sensitivity and respect, while at the same time gathering as much information as they could for the scientific and tribal communities. The archaeologists were well aware of their potentially conflicting roles in the process, balancing the needs and concerns of the tribe with the needs and concerns of the archaeological community. However, because of the tribe's pragmatic approach, its desire to learn as much of its history and culture as possible, the archaeologists' understanding of tribal concerns, and the long-working relationship of the two groups, these potentially competing concerns never came into conflict.

This cooperation was exemplified during the excavation of three graves that were characterized by an unusually high degree of preservation. Normally, the preservation of human remains and organic objects in New England's highly acidic soils is very poor. However, since the burials dated to the historic period (A.D. 1666–1720), many contained cuprous funerary objects such as spoons, beads, and kettles. During excavation, archaeologists noted that three graves had areas of unusually good preservation, as indicated by the identification of large fragments of woolen trade cloth preserved by the presence of cuprous materials underneath them.

The decision was made to block-lift these features to remove them intact for examination under laboratory conditions. Subsequent analysis revealed that the blocks contained the remains of three children, aged three, six, and eleven. The high degree of preservation noted in the field was due to several dozen necklaces, headbands, and belts containing thousands of copper, brass, and shell beads, as well as many other cuprous objects such as spoons and kettles. All three sets of remains were remarkably well preserved, as were the associated organic funerary objects, such as deerskins, woolen blankets, linen cloth, threads, and sinew.

The initial stages of the visual examination of the three burials revealed a complex but potentially discernible array of individual necklaces and wampum belts. Out of respect for the tribe and the three children, archaeologists immediately decided not to complete the excavation of the remains but to notify the tribe and suggest that noninvasive techniques such as X-ray and magnetic resonance imaging be employed to explore the contents of the graves (Currie and McBride 2001). These techniques proved highly successful and resulted in the identification and subsequent reconstruction of all associated wampum belts, headbands, and necklaces, reproductions of which are currently on display at the MPMRC (McBride 1993). After the reburial of the human remains and funerary objects, the tribe held a tribal meeting and social gathering to thank all of the archaeologists who had participated in the project.

The Mashantucket Pequot Museum and Research Center

The MPMRC is the largest Native American–owned museum in the United States (Figure 17.3). The tribe initiated the design process in 1992, and the museum opened to the public in 1998. The 28,613-m^2 structure houses 8,361 m^2 of exhibit space, a 929-m^2 library and archive, and 929 m^2 of collections and research space. The tribe's support and commitment to archaeological and historical research is reflected in over 1,394 m^2 dedicated to the research department, including offices; classrooms; photography, microscopy, and X-ray rooms; two archaeology labs; an herbarium; faunal lab; digital mapping lab; conservation lab; and 929 m^2 of compactor shelving.

Figure 17.3. The Mashantucket Pequot Museum and Research Center (© Mashantucket Pequot Museum and Research Center; Photo courtesy of Esto/Jeff Goldberg).

With the opening of the museum, all archaeological activities and historical research at Mashantucket shifted to its facilities, supported by ten permanent research staff including five full-time archaeologists, two historical researchers, a conservator, a curator, and a collections manager. In recognition of the ongoing commitment to archaeological and historical research, the majority of the staff have training in archaeology, and several have specialized training in one or more disciplines, including ethnobotany, soil micromorphology, faunal analysis, seventeenth- to nineteenth-century material culture, and geomorphology.

Through the MPMRC, the tribe is also involved in collaborative research efforts with several other institutions. These include the Mystic Aquarium (the cultural ecology of El Barill adjacent to the Sea of Cortez in Baja Mexico), the Institute for Exploration (archaeological potential of the continental shelf off Block Island), the University of Connecticut (early coastal adaptations in Long Island Sound), and the University of Massachusetts Boston (prehistoric and historic Native American plant use at Mashantucket). Most recently, in partnership with the Navajo and Zuni nations, the museum received a $1.8 million National Science Foundation informal

Figure 17.4. The caribou kill diorama at the Mashantucket Pequot Museum
and Research Center (© Mashantucket Pequot Museum and Research Center;
Photo courtesy of Bob Halloran).

science education grant, "Archaeological Pathways for Native Learners,"
to encourage science education among middle school children.

Archaeologists played a critical role in the research and design of the
MPMRC exhibits, which were drawn largely from archaeological data and
research collected by the tribe's archaeologists, historians, and curators.
Many of the exhibits are based on information from archaeological sites on
or immediately adjacent to the reservation. Of particular note is the caribou kill exhibit, which depicts a hunting scene ca. 11,000 B.P., as well as a
presentation and discussion of the Hidden Creek site, a Late Paleoindian
site at Mashantucket dating to approximately 10,000 B.P. (Figure 17.4). The
data for both exhibits were drawn directly from Brian Jones's research on
the reservation (Jones 1997, 1998). There are also several Archaic period
(ca. 8,000–3,000 B.P.) exhibits, again based directly on results from excavations conducted under the auspices of the MPMRC.

Anthropology graduate students, historians, and geologists from the
University of Connecticut and elsewhere were also heavily involved in
designing the museum's research program and exhibits. These individuals met on a regular basis with tribal members and other Native Americans from dozens of tribes from around the country to discuss content,

research, and replications of tools, clothing, and dwellings used in the exhibits. In many ways, this was the most interesting part of the museum design and construction process, which involved integrating and assessing sometimes conflicting information and perspectives from archaeology, historical records, and oral traditions.

The Tribal Council was concerned primarily with the accuracy and integrity of the information, and with presenting multiple perspectives on the past to both Native and non-Native museum visitors. The tribe recognized that many perspectives, disciplines, and voices are necessary to interpret the past, and that how we view the past today may not be how we will view it tomorrow. Therefore, all the individuals who worked on the project were encouraged to listen to and respect the variety of perspectives brought to the table. The results speak for themselves. The MPMRC is considered one of the finest museums in the United States, and the tribe takes great pride in the fact that over 250,000 people visit the museum each year, including 70,000 schoolchildren, whose understanding of the past is changed forever.

Native American Graves Protection and Repatriation Act

One of the most important tasks the Mashantucket Pequot Tribe assigned to staff archaeologists and historians of the MPMRC was to assist in the repatriation of Pequot human remains and funerary objects. This exemplifies not only the trust and evolving relationship between the tribe and the archaeologists but also the tribe's recognition of the importance of collaboration with individuals familiar with the language and culture of archaeologists, collection managers, and curators.

One of the primary motivations for the tribe's repatriation efforts was to identify and to recover individuals' remains that had been looted from the tribe's historic Fanning Road Cemetery. At the tribe's request, archaeologists surveyed an 8-ha parcel surrounding the current cemetery which contained graves dating from the seventeenth through twentieth centuries. Tribal elders recalled "archaeologists" digging up graves sometime in the early twentieth century. State and local officials of the time had ignored the tribe's complaints, and many tribal members harbored considerable resentment toward archaeologists for the desecration of their ancestors. The survey identified more than 400 looted graves dating to the late seventeenth through early eighteenth centuries. Historical research indicated that most of the graves were excavated in the late nineteenth century, but the whereabouts of the human remains and funerary objects remained a mystery.

In an effort to locate these and other Pequot human remains and funerary objects housed in museums and other institutions, the tribe asked staff archaeologists to submit a NAGPRA grant in the fall of 1998. The grant application, entitled "NAGPRA and Beyond: Locating Pequot Remains and Cultural Items by Using a New Methodology," was funded in 1999–2000. The grant developed more-comprehensive investigative strategies than simply a review of existing museum inventories. The tribe and staff archaeologists recognized that most NAGPRA inventories did not necessarily identify all the human remains and funerary objects housed in reporting institutions. Such omissions were not the result of purposeful deceit or underreporting on the part of the institutions, but rather their inability to interpret and analyze accession records for information or nuances that could reflect mortuary rituals or items. Tribal members and archaeologists identified and repatriated dozens of sets of human remains and associated funerary objects. These were documented and reinterred by the tribe in 2000.

Conclusion

The positive relationship between the archaeologists and the Mashantucket Pequot Tribe serves as a model of cooperation between Native groups and archaeologists. An attitude of cooperation and respect has benefited the tribe, the public, and the scientific community. However, it should be noted that there are many aspects to this relationship that are unlikely to be found elsewhere. In 1983 there were approximately 50 tribal members residing on the Mashantucket Pequot Reservation when Skip Hayward initiated the archaeology program. In the last 20 years, over 600 Pequots have returned to the reservation—many of whom then encountered archaeologists for the first time. Archaeologists were already an integral part of the Mashantucket Pequot social, cultural, economic, and political structure, and as such enjoyed unprecedented support by the resident population and Tribal Council. Many current tribal members have never known a reservation without the presence of archaeologists. Nonetheless, many of the issues that archaeologists encounter elsewhere in Indian country are still present at Mashantucket, if to a lesser degree—initial distrust, lack of understanding of the goals and aims of archaeology, and stereotypes of archaeologists as grave diggers and looters of Native sites.

David Hurst Thomas articulates the established relationship between archaeologists and tribal members at Mashantucket:

> One of the stated aims of the Mashantucket Pequot Museum is to break down false imagery, and the exhibits look far beyond the white-created stereotypes of Indian people. True to this aim, the Pequot have also put aside the stereotypical confrontations between Indians and professional archaeologists during the late twentieth century. Rather than replaying the stale archaeologist-as-enemy scenario, the Mashantucket Pequot recognized the potential of conducting archaeological excavations on their reservation land to bring their past alive [2000:266].

The positive relationship at Mashantucket can be replicated anywhere in the United States if archaeologists and Native groups are prepared to speak openly with one another and to listen intently. Ongoing dialogue and communication are the keys to building relationships that lead to a mutual understanding and respect for each other's perspectives and concerns. Thomas emphasizes the importance of such communication. As our ability to understand one another's needs matures, so too will the broader relevance of our work.

18. From the Ground Up
The Effects of Consultation on Archaeological Methods

ELIZABETH S. CHILTON

Since the passage of the Native American Graves Protection and Repatriation Act (NAGPRA) in 1990, there have been many changes to
the way archaeology is practiced in the United States. NAGPRA mandates consultations among anthropologists, museum curators, and Native groups and has thus led to fruitful collaboration that, in many cases,
goes well beyond what is legislated. Many archaeologists have reported on
the success of these collaborations, which have led to some much-needed
adjustment in the types of evidence that archaeologists use in their understandings and interpretations of cultural continuity (e.g., Echo-Hawk
2000), and their understanding of the connection between reconstruc-
tions of Native history and contemporary Native issues (see Swidler et al.
1997). Such collaborations offer archaeologists opportunities to address
past wrongs with respect to the historical colonialism of the discipline.
However, few archaeologists have discussed—at least in the published literature—how consultations and collaborations with Native groups have
affected what are often seen as standard, "scientific" archaeological methods: excavation, sampling, analysis, and curation techniques (although see
Herbster and Cherau, this volume).

In this chapter I review my collaboration with members of the Wampanoag Tribe of Gay Head/Aquinnah, on Martha's Vineyard. In 1998 and 1999 I directed excavations at the Lucy Vincent Beach site for the Harvard University archaeological field school. Because the site was seriously threatened by shoreline erosion, and because the site contained pre-Contact Native American human remains, my work at this site and my collaboration with the Aquinnah have had a very positive effect on (1) how I practice archaeology—literally from the ground up; (2) the educational experiences of the Native and non-Native students who took part in the field schools; and (3) my approach to the management of archaeological resources.

History of the Project

When I first arrived at Harvard University in 1996 as an assistant professor and recent Ph.D. recipient from the University of Massachusetts Amherst, I began to plan a field school for the summer of 1998. Most of my previous archaeological experience had been in western Massachusetts and New York. I knew that I wanted the field school to be located in eastern Massachusetts, in part because one of the goals of the archaeological field schools I direct is to teach students about the history of the town and the community within which they live or attend school. Also, much of my teaching and research have focused on pre-Contact Native American history and archaeology, primarily because this history has traditionally been undervalued and largely silenced in American tellings of history.

A few months after my arrival in Cambridge, I made an appointment to meet with Brona Simon, the state archaeologist. I asked her to suggest possible site locations for a field school, qualifying my request by saying that I was interested in sites that were threatened in some way, whether by imminent construction, erosion, or artifact looting. The reason that most of my field schools have focused on threatened sites is that I believe that field school students should be trained in cultural resource management (CRM), and they should be aware of the social and political contexts of archaeological fieldwork. I also believe that field schools should benefit the communities in which we work. Since field schools are not necessarily the most efficient way to conduct archaeological research, I believe that the contribution of such work is greatly increased if there is a strong community service component, whether that community includes the town, Native tribes, local schools, or other constituencies.

Of the sites and projects that Brona Simon suggested, it seemed to me that the Lucy Vincent Beach site was the one most in need of some serious archaeological attention. The site is located on the western end of the island of Martha's Vineyard, in the traditional homeland of the Aquinnah, currently the only tribe in Massachusetts with federal recognition (for a brief history of the Aquinnah Tribe and archaeological research on the island, see Herbster and Cherau, this volume). The site is on a 12-m cliff overlooking the ocean and is eroding at a rate of approximately 2 m per year (Chilton and Doucette 2002a).

The site was discovered in the winter of 1995, when beachcombers found human remains on this town beach. The discovery was eventually reported to the Chilmark police, who then informed the state archaeologist (at the Massachusetts Historical Commission [MHC]) and the Aquinnah Tribe. The remainder of the skeleton was found to be eroding out of the cliff face, and the remains were determined to be ancient. The MHC sent two archaeologists to salvage the remains at the cliff face. Another burial was salvaged from the same site under similar conditions by MHC archaeologists one year later, in 1996.

Because the MHC excavations at the site were limited to recovering the two burials, very little was known about the site when I initiated the project in early 1997. For example, the artifacts recovered in the grave fill were apparently from the pre-Contact period, but they were not securely dated. Also, neither the size nor the function of the site was known: Was it a habitation with associated burials? Or was this site primarily a burial ground? At the time I began the project, the human remains and associated objects were being analyzed by the MHC for repatriation to the Aquinnah, which took place soon after. It was my understanding that the MHC, the Town of Chilmark, and the Aquinnah Tribe were all anxious about the possibility of more burials eroding from the cliff onto the town beach, and were interested in creating a long-term plan to manage the site.

Early in 1997 I made inquiries with the Aquinnah Tribe to see whether they would be supportive of an archaeological survey and, possibly, a future field school at the site. Because there was no tribal historic preservation officer (THPO) at that time, I dealt almost exclusively with the Aquinnah's Natural Resources Department, which was handling all their cultural resource issues.

I initially sought approval from the Aquinnah for a small-scale survey in the summer of 1997. My main goal was to determine how much of the site remained intact. The proposal was sent to the Natural Resources Department and was eventually presented to the Tribal Council. Because the site is located on town land, a similar proposal was made to the Chilmark Board of Selectmen and the Conservation Commission, and a permit was sought from the MHC.

Initial Archaeology Survey

With the approval from all parties, I directed an archaeological survey from August 12 to 14, 1997. The survey was funded by Harvard University, and I was assisted by graduate student volunteers. The purpose of the initial survey was to determine the site boundaries, the stratigraphy at the site, and whether there were still intact archaeological features. The subsurface testing consisted of eight test units (50 cm x 1 m in size), which were excavated at 8-m intervals across the site to a depth of approximately 50 cm. A total of 10 features were encountered, including 6 post molds. All post molds were cross-sectioned, and profiles were drawn. Other features were mapped but were not excavated. A total of 248 lithic artifacts, 3 pottery sherds, 4 historic period artifacts, 27 pieces of animal bone, 200 fragments of shell, 1 maize kernel, and wood charcoal were recovered.

As a result of this initial survey, I decided to seek permission for a larger investigation in the form of an archaeological field school in the summer of 1998. Again, we needed first to obtain approval and support from the Tribal Council, the Board of Selectmen, the Chilmark Conservation Commission, the MHC, and (since this was a field school) the Harvard University Summer School. Detailed proposals were sent to all parties. These proposals included an explication of what would happen in the event of the discovery of human remains, as per the Massachusetts Unmarked Burial Law (Massachusetts General Laws Chapter 7, Section 38A). The details of our field and laboratory methodologies were changed somewhat as a result of feedback from all parties, but the most serious concerns were raised by the town Board of Selectmen and the Conservation Commission. The selectmen were, rightly, concerned that our excavations might contribute to further erosion of the site, and also about the logistics of the five-week excavation, given that it would take place during the height of the summer season at Lucy Vincent Beach, a beautiful and exclusive town beach. With some changes to the field logistics, we were ready to begin.

1998 Archaeological Field School

The overall goal of the 1998 field school was to obtain as much information as we could about the site in order to assist the tribe and the state in their attempts to protect or to salvage the site. The specific objectives of the field school were to (1) determine the site boundaries; (2) locate all or most of the archaeological features—especially those in most imminent danger from soil erosion; and (3) partially excavate features in order to determine their age and function. In the interest of full collaboration with the Aquinnah, I was able to offer tuition waivers for up to two tribal students from the Harvard Summer School. Randy Jardin accepted one of the tuition waivers, and he has since worked on numerous projects with the Public Archaeology Laboratory, Inc. (PAL) (Herbster and Cherau, this volume).

Over the course of the field school, we had several visits from tribal representatives, primarily from the Natural Resources Department. Because we were excavating on the cliffs—which are normally off-limits to everyone—security was very tight, and the town beach guards were very diligent in that respect. We also received quite a bit of attention from the press, including a surprise visit from a *Boston Globe* reporter (see MacQuarrie 1998). Our experiences with the press turned out to be our biggest source of consternation in both 1998 and 1999, as I discuss below.

The field school ran for five weeks in the summer of 1998, with 14 students and three teaching assistants. We spent most of those five weeks in the field at the Lucy Vincent Beach site. I will not provide details of our findings here, since these have been published elsewhere (Chilton and Doucette 2002a, 2002b; Largy et al. 2002). Suffice it to say that we excavated 20 2-x-2-m test units over the course of the summer and identified archaeological features (including post molds) in nearly every test unit excavated. Our results indicated that the site was utilized by Native people from the Late Paleoindian period (ca. 10,000 years B.P.) through at least the late seventeenth century A.D.. The most intensive use of the site was during the Late Woodland and early Contact periods (ca. A.D. 1000–1700).

In the summer of 1998, as per our proposal to all parties, we excavated only those features that were in most imminent danger from erosion, that is, those that were closest to the cliff edge. However, at the urging of the Conservation Commission (and for the sake of the safety of our students), we had agreed not to excavate within 2 m of the cliff edge. Therefore, we clearly were not in a position to locate *all* the features that were likely to erode in the near future. Likewise, the Conservation Commission had urged us not to excavate contiguous units: they requested we excavate in a checkerboard fashion, so as to mitigate the effects of erosion. This caused us a great deal of concern over what might be contained within unexcavated units. We complied with the commission's request as much as possible, while also attempting to ensure that important features—especially burials—were not missed.

On the last day of the field school in 1998, we were furiously attempting to finish the excavation of several of the features we had encountered. The last feature to be profiled was a large hearth found at the topographic high point of the site, and only a few meters from the cliff edge. This was the only intact hearth encountered at the site. It contained large fire-cracked and fire-reddened rocks, lithic debitage, a few stone tools and pottery sherds, animal bone, shell, wood charcoal, and charred plant remains. At the very bottom of the feature, underneath all the fire-cracked rock— and on the last day, as the sun was setting—we uncovered a partial human skull. We left the skull in place and immediately contacted representatives from the Aquinnah Tribe, the MHC, and the town. It was agreed by all parties that the burial should be left in place, and the site backfilled as planned, so that a detailed agreement and plan could be worked out, and so as not to call further attention to the site by the island's tourists and curiosity seekers.

It was at this point that my perspectives on archaeology began to change. In my previous 14 years of archaeological experience, I had not encountered human remains while working in the field in the Northeast. Therefore, I had never been in a position to consider the dying wishes of the deceased, or of living descendants. Had I not been working so closely with the Aquinnah on a day-to-day basis, I do not think the discovery and eventual excavation of this burial would have had such an emotional impact on me. The few visits to the site by Wampanoag tribal members after the discovery of the burial were emotional, spiritually charged, uncomfortable, and somber, and these interactions set the stage for the rest of the project (see Peters, this volume).

Over the next couple of months, we worked on a proposal with the tribe and the MHC, and we returned to excavate the burial in September 1998. The reason for excavating the burial was that it was clearly in imminent danger from erosion. Our excavation uncovered evidence of a secondary burial consisting of half of a human cranium. All analysis was done in the field and in a temporary lab on the Vineyard, and all human remains and funerary objects were left with the Aquinnah at the tribal headquarters. Apparently, and understandably, the excavation of this burial made many tribal members uncomfortable, and we had only a few visits or interactions with representatives from the tribe during this time.

1999 Archaeological Field School

Because many more features had been recorded than were excavated, we wanted to continue work at the site in 1999. Initially, the people we talked with at Aquinnah were supportive of our return and suggested we submit another proposal to the Tribal Council. It was the Town of Chilmark Board of Selectmen that was not initially enthusiastic about our possible return. From their perspective, there were several concerns. First, the *Boston Globe* article in the summer of 1998 had drawn an enormous amount of attention to the site, and this presented a security risk. Under normal conditions, admittance to the beach is closely controlled, since it is a popular and exclusive beach. The publicity—and our presence in general—put extra strain on the beach guards and their supervisors. Second, the town was not completely satisfied that we had done enough to stem further erosion; although we had worked with the USDA Natural Resources Conservation Service to reseed the site after we backfilled our excavations, much of the soil had settled and not much of the vegetation had grown back. It was clear that if we returned we were going to have to try replanting our backfilled units. In order to address the town's concerns, we wrote a detailed proposal, and we were asked to appear before a meeting of the Board of Selectmen in April 1999. After I made my presentation to the board, including details on the importance of the site and our previous findings, a board member asked me, publicly, if I knew there was a member of the local press present at the meeting. My heart sank. I said something like, "No, but if it's all right with you, it's all right with me, since public education is an important component of our field school." After the meeting, I asked the reporter if he would follow up with me on the details before publishing the article, and I asked him to contact the Aquinnah Natural Resources Department to make sure they would support this kind of story. I explained how sensitive this issue was, and he seemed to understand. Nonetheless, without contacting me or the tribe, the story was printed in the local newspaper—with gross inaccuracies.

As a result of that particular newspaper article, many members of the Aquinnah Tribe were justifiably angry, and their support of the field school was nearly rescinded. For one thing, the story made it seem as if I were being self-aggrandizing and purposefully attempting to call attention to the site. Since site protection was paramount to the tribe (as well as to the town, and to us), the tribe was understandably concerned about my motivations and trustworthiness. Certainly, this was the highest crisis point of the project. I remember feeling a complete loss of control over my responsibilities to the tribe, to the town, to my students (who would arrive on the Vineyard in just a few weeks), to the larger Vineyard community, to the university, and to the archaeological site itself, which continued to be in danger from the roaring waves and casual passersby.

I appeared before the Tribal Council a few weeks later, along with a few of the graduate students with whom I had been working. I expressed my dismay over the recent press attention and tried to clarify our goals, objectives, and priorities in working at the Lucy Vincent Beach site. There was much discussion by the Tribal Council, and we answered several questions. In the end, the tribe was supportive, and we were granted permission to return to the site for two weeks in July 1999.

In the summer of 1999, we worked at Lucy Vincent Beach for only two weeks and spent our other two weeks in the field at another site on the Vineyard. We did not excavate any new test units at Lucy Vincent; instead we focused our attention on features that had been recorded during the 1998 field school but had not been excavated. Since we did not have time to excavate all the features identified at the site, we concentrated our efforts near the cliff edge.

Most of these features were apparently food storage or composting pits, but on the last field day we uncovered another burial at the bottom of a pit feature. This burial was approximately 5 m from the cliff edge, on a section of the cliff that had been undercut by wind erosion. As in 1998, I notified the tribe, the MHC, and town officials, and we backfilled the site. Our original plan was to return to the site to excavate the burial in the fall of 1999, but our tribal contacts were not receptive to this idea. Instead, they expressed the desire to monitor the level of erosion at the site, and to delay burial excavation until or unless it became apparent that the burial was in imminent danger.

From my perspective, this approach was unsettling, for two reasons. First, since I was teaching full-time at Harvard University, I would not be able to be on-call for a salvage operation in the event of a storm or other type of disturbance. Any emergency salvage would have to be conducted by MHC archaeologists. The MHC archaeologists are highly competent, but for the sake of continuity I felt it was important that we somehow be involved. Second, I was not sure we could predict the pace of erosion at the site, since the undercutting of the cliff edge had led to some large blocks of earth breaking off the edge onto the beach below.

Nevertheless, the Aquinnah were ultimately the ones who would decide whether this burial would be excavated in advance of a potential salvage operation. During the interim, I kept in close communication with tribal members. Nearly two years later, in June 2001, we agreed on a plan to excavate the burial. Similarly to the burial excavation in 1998, we conducted all analysis of human remains and burial objects on the Vineyard and left them at the tribal headquarters. All feature sediment was screened over tarps to make sure that any human remains and artifacts were kept together, and the sediment was rebagged for possible inclusion in a future reburial. It is my understanding that the tribe reburied both of the Lucy Vincent Beach individuals in the fall of 2001. At that time, we assisted them in ensuring that the individuals were reburied with the artifacts that were originally interred with them. I have not returned to the Vineyard since resuming my work in western Massachusetts. However, both the tribe and the MHC continue to monitor the site.

Collaboration and the Practice of Archaeology: What Did We Learn?

So how did this collaboration affect the on-the-ground practice of archaeology? The entire project, including the initial survey and both field schools, required that I relinquish a certain amount of control over the research design. For example, the town and the tribe wanted me to concentrate my efforts at the cliff edge (although not too close) and not to dig too deep. The town officials did not want us to dig below about 1 m because they were concerned that it would weaken the integrity of the hill with respect to erosion. The tribe, too, was worried about erosion, and expressed concern over both the depth and the location of our test excavation. The tribe also communicated a general sense that features (and potential burials) should be disturbed only if they were in imminent danger.

If I had been excavating this site from a purely CRM or research perspective, I would have done several things differently. First, not only would I have concentrated excavations on the cliff edge, I would have attempted to get a better idea of the larger site context. I would have excavated contiguous units all along the cliff edge. While this may have led to more erosion, the site and the features we did not excavate are ultimately going to erode completely within 20 years or so regardless. Also, I would have excavated all test units deeper than 1 m. Even though we were reasonably sure that we excavated to the bottom of each pit feature, excavating deeper overall would have ensured that we did not miss anything.

My collaboration with the Aquinnah also affected the analysis of human remains, since this had to be done quickly. We were able to complete a basic documentation of all the recovered human remains, but there was no time or support by the tribe for a paleopathology analysis, dietary analysis, or other studies. There was no radiocarbon dating or other sampling of the burial in 1999. We did obtain one radiocarbon date from a piece of wood charcoal in 1998, before the Aquinnah told us they did not want more samples taken. I believe the decision about sampling in 1999 was, in part, a result of the tribe's collaborations with PAL (see Herbster and Cherau, this volume).

This project also challenged my own feelings about the importance of public education. Public education has been a large part of my archaeological fieldwork since 1986, when I worked at the New York State Bureau of Historic Sites as their public interpretation coordinator. For the two field schools at Lucy Vincent Beach, we had planned to have an open field lab so that people from the town or Vineyard tourists could learn about the great antiquity and complexity of Native history of the island. However, because of the tribe's and the town's concerns about the security of the site, we did very little public education in 1998, and virtually none in 1999. Public education is still a priority for me, but I am much more sensitive to the social and political contexts of such education and of publicity in general.

Overall, these effects of consultation were, from my perspective, very positive, with the benefits far outweighing the so-called concessions. Many of my colleagues, in hearing about this project, have offered condolences that I chose a project that required so much compromise and attention to contemporary sociopolitical relationships. From my perspective, however, no other project would have taught me and my students more about the ever-present contemporary social and political contexts of archaeology. Without a vigilant, self-conscious assessment of these contexts, archaeologists will never be able to leave behind the colonial history of the discipline.

Aside from simply learning how to be more flexible in our research designs and methodologies, our work at Lucy Vincent Beach made me aware of a number of false dichotomies in our thinking and in our methodologies, such as the distinction between "historic" and "prehistoric" objects (Hart 2004), and the distinction between a "ceremonial" site and a "domestic" site. It is clear that no such mutually exclusive definitions apply at the Lucy Vincent Beach site. Native peoples used the site for at least 10,000 years, and it is still a very special place for the Wampanoag people today. Having students in both 1998 and 1999 who were tribal members really brought this point home to everyone involved. The archaeological evidence from this site, and others on Martha's Vineyard (see Herbster and Cherau, this volume) and in coastal New England in general, provides us with a clear opportunity to demonstrate long-term cultural continuity before, during, and after European colonization. This kind of information can and should be used for NAGPRA cases and other issues of Native sovereignty.

It is also important to discuss how this collaborative experience with the Aquinnah has affected the way I practice archaeology on projects that may not involve such complete or formal Native collaboration, and that do not involve burial excavation. Even though I have taught students for years that "archaeology is not just about studying the past," this experience brought that point home in a way that more "traditional" CRM or academic archaeology would certainly not have done. It has sensitized me to the relevance of archaeological fieldwork and interpretation to contemporary Native issues, such as NAGPRA, land claims, and federal recognition. Therefore, whether I or my students are choosing research, or laboratory or fieldwork projects, I am far more attuned to the implications of that work for contemporary Native peoples, and the ways in which archaeological research might either help or interfere with tribal initiatives and priorities. In general, this has strengthened my commitment to what would traditionally be called a "resource management perspective," except that instead of prioritizing the preservation of archaeological resources for future archaeologists, the emphasis is on being a part of a larger effort to protect, to respect, and to celebrate the Native past by and for people living in the present. There is a lot of support and inspiration for this perspective at the University of Massachusetts Amherst, where my colleagues on the Department of Anthropology's Repatriation Committee have been working for many years to build alliances and collaborations among all the Native groups with connections to the Connecticut Valley, given that there is no federally recognized tribe resident in western Massachusetts. In the process, the archaeologists here have learned—and will continue to learn— far more about regional histories (including oral histories), genealogies, landscapes, and traditions than we would have from a strictly archaeological perspective (see Bruchac 2005; Bruchac and Chilton 2003).

To conclude, archaeological field schools are still the keystone for the continuation of archaeology as a profession and for training students for CRM, which is now the most prevalent type of archaeology practiced in this country. But if the goal were simply to have students learn the basics of archaeological fieldwork, they could excavate test units on college campuses or in simulated digs designed by field school directors. I strongly believe that field schools should be tied into the current research of the professional archaeologists who direct the schools, and that students should learn about the social contexts of archaeology. As this project demonstrates, when one moves beyond the academic and research priorities of field schools, there are other, more important constituents to consider, such as the landowners, the community, and, in many ways most important, Native American or other descendant populations. By including and discussing these other constituencies as part of the core mission of field schools, we teach our students to be sensitive to the social and political implications of all archaeological research. Field schools are formative experiences for training future generations of archaeologists, and our primary responsibility is to instill in our students a commitment to respect the archaeological record and Native history, and their importance to present and future generations.

Acknowledgments

Dianna Doucette was the field director in 1998 and 1999 and worked with me every step of the way through this project from 1997 to the present. I am greatly indebted to Brona Simon for suggesting this project in the first place, and for all her assistance and guidance throughout. Matthew Vanderhoop (former THPO) and Mark Harding (former deputy THPO) have been helpful to us throughout this project, and they have also taught us the importance of these kinds of special places in the landscape to the Aquinnah today. Irv and Nancy DeVore kindly provided us with housing during two of our shorter stays on the Vineyard. Brett Sterns of the Aquinnah Natural Resources Department, and Rusty Walton of the Chilmark Conservation Commission were both very helpful in making the site physically and logistically accessible for us to excavate. Randy Jardin (field school student in 1998 and Aquinnah tribal member) educated us, helped us, challenged us, and serves as a staunch protector of archaeological resources on the island. I wish to thank all the field school students, volunteers, and teaching assistants for their hard work. I wish to thank Charles Cobb for his not-so-anonymous prepublication review of the complete volume and for helping me to push the envelope a bit further. A special thanks goes to Jordan Kerber for comments on an earlier draft of this chapter and for initiating this edited volume and bringing it to fruition.

19. Constructing Alliances along the Northern Border
Consultations with
Mi'kmaq and Maliseet Nations

BERNARD JEROME AND DAVID E. PUTNAM

Many current collaboration and consultation activities between archaeologists and Native American groups occur as government-to-government relationships that are initiated and guided by formal policy. This chapter, however, describes an informal collaborative relationship between the two authors—one, Bernard Jerome, a respected Mi'kmaq leader, and the other, David Putnam, a non-Native archaeologist. We came together to address in separate voices issues of concern regarding archaeology, but the results of the ensuing partnership have been much more far-reaching. Rather than considering this a new and innovative approach, we believe that it follows the pattern of traditional protocol with centuries of precedent.

The case study discussed in this chapter focuses on archaeological consultation with Mi'kmaq and Maliseet nations in Maine and New Brunswick about a field school excavation of a prehistoric site in northern Maine that raised a variety of contentious issues. The problems were resolved through a series of traditional councils in which tribal elders and archaeologists arrived at consensus on a procedural outline for the work. The project resulted in archaeologists, Mi'kmaqs, and Maliseets working together to recover information about the past and to find common ground for the future.

Although we are friends and partners in this collaborative relationship, we have very different backgrounds and perspectives. Jerome is a member of the Aroostook Band of Micmacs and former chief of the Mi'kmaq community of Gesgapegiag, in Maria, Quebec, at the mouth of the Cascapedia River, the premier Atlantic salmon river in North America. He negotiated with the late prime minister of Canada, Pierre Trudeau, during the Mi'kmaq Salmon Wars of the 1970s. Mi'kmaq is his first language, but he is also fluent in English and French. He is a traditionalist and a highly respected cultural and spiritual leader and teacher. Putnam is a non-Native professional archaeologist and an assistant professor in science and anthropology at the University of Maine at Presque Isle.

Our situation is somewhat different from others described in this volume. The geography, climate, and culture history of northern Maine are closely akin to what is now eastern Canada, and, as a consequence, collaborative efforts cannot be limited by the arbitrary and recent construct of the international boundary. Two indigenous nations occupy the northern Maine/Canadian Maritimes region (Figure 19.1): the Maliseet (Wolastuqiyik, Wulustuqweig, Malecite) and Mi'kmaq (Micmac, Mi'gmag). Both nations retain significant elements of traditional culture, and many elders continue to speak their native languages on a daily basis. Although the Passamaquoddy Tribe in eastern Maine is comparable in this regard, other indigenous groups in the northeastern United States have experienced greater degrees of assimilation and loss of language and traditional perspective.

Long-standing intertribal political differences are particularly evident between Mi'kmaq and Maliseet elders. These animosities have deep historical roots stemming from the European fur trade and resulting "Beaver Wars" that began in the early sixteenth century. Mi'kmaqs from the central Maine coast killed the Maliseet/Abenaki leader Bashaba in 1615 (Prins 1996). During the struggle by the Aroostook Band of Micmacs for U.S. federal recognition, granted in 1991, they were actively opposed by Maliseets, who claimed the Mi'kmaqs were recent interlopers into Maliseet territory.

The two tribes also have a long history of alliances against common enemies. The Wabanaki Confederacy, which in Maine currently consists of the Aroostook Band of Micmacs, the Houlton Band of Maliseet Indians,

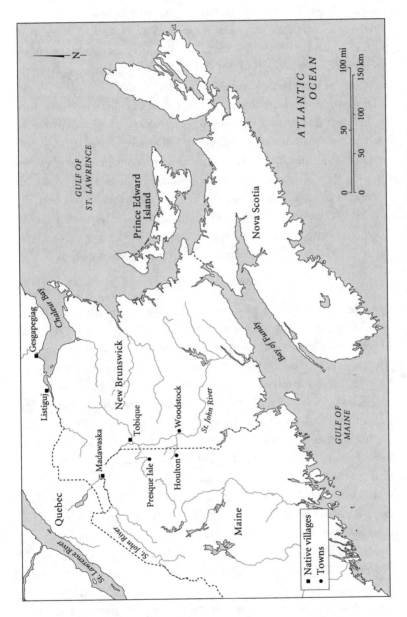

Figure 19.1. Map of the Maine-Maritimes region, showing the location of the St. John River basin.

the Penobscot Nation, and both divisions of the Passamaquoddy Tribe, grew out of an alliance of Algonquian peoples against Iroquois raids in the early 1600s. In contemporary Maine archaeology, these same allies stand unified in conflicts with New England museums concerning the Native American Graves Protection and Repatriation Act (NAGPRA) and the repatriation of human remains and ceremonial objects.

Differing U.S. and Canadian federal government tribal relations policies complicate this situation. The provinces of New Brunswick and Quebec and the State of Maine all contribute an additional array of regional policies. The multitiered and often conflicting government approaches create a variety of difficulties for Native people and the archaeologists who attempt to collaborate with them. In our situation, these issues were addressed in the context of numerous traditional councils before we could develop a common shared vision of the appropriate form of archaeological discovery, artifact treatment, and information dissemination.

Geography and History

The northern half of the modern state of Maine is an infrequently visited cul-de-sac of the United States. It is a sparsely populated region that includes more than nine million acres of uninhabited forest, drained by tributaries of the St. John River. It is bounded on the east by the Canadian province of New Brunswick, and on the north and west by Quebec.

Glacial ice persisted in the form of an isolated and independent ice cap in northern Maine and adjacent Quebec until at least 10,200 years ago (Borns et al. 2004). Forest colonization and subsequent succession lag behind southern New England by at least 4,000 years. Headwater tributaries of the St. John River flow through refugia of classic spruce-fir boreal forest. The climate is poorly documented in those uninhabited areas, but the annual mean temperature is almost certainly lower than the legendary northeastern cold spots in northern New York, Vermont, and New Hampshire.

The St. John River drains an area of 55,167 km² and tumbles 673 km from its source to the Bay of Fundy. The Connecticut River, considered the largest river in New England, is 660 km long and drains 28,490 km². Well into the historic period, the St. John River canoe routes provided an essential inland connective link between the Gulf of St. Lawrence, the St. Lawrence River, the Bay of Fundy, and the Gulf of Maine. The original Maliseet name for the St. John River is Wulustuq (beautiful river), now modified to Aroostook and applied to the largest tributary. The modern Aroostook River was called Mus iyik, or Moosiec, roughly translated as "river of many moose."

Europeans have largely defined the ethnicity of Native people of this region. Early accounts of Gaspesians, Souriquois, Etchemin, Sokokis, and Canibas reflect the European need to define polities and territories. Prins (1996) describes a more fluid relationship in which individuals moved freely between and among the defined groups. It is likely that kinship ties and association with a seasonal village may have initially been more important than clearly defined tribal boundaries. Many archaeologists have come to accept the riverine model (Snow 1980) in which boundaries between large drainages and cultural entities are the same. This approach is convenient and somewhat logical in the sense that difficult canoe carries between drainages form barriers to communication and exchange. However, such a useful archaeological model can dangerously structure our thinking about the nature of cultural systems.

The name Malecite is thought to be derived from a Mi'kmaq word meaning "slow or bad talkers." The Maliseet people now generally prefer to be called Wolastoqiyik (or Wulustuqweig or Wulustukwiyik), referring to "people of the beautiful river," or "people of the St. John River." Traditional villages along the St. John River included Meductic, Tobique, and Madawaska (Figure 19.2). The Houlton Band of Maliseet Indians, located in Houlton and Littleton, Maine, represent a band that seasonally used the Meduxnekeag River basin and was originally associated with the village at Meductic. The remaining people of Meductic were relocated to the contemporary Woodstock Reserve in Woodstock, New Brunswick. Other contemporary Maliseet reserves include Gagetown, Oromocto, St. Mary's, Kingsclear, and Tobique. Both traditional villages and contemporary reserve locations reflect a seasonal dependence on annual runs of Atlantic salmon. The traditional village of Madawaska, located on the New Brunswick bank of the St. John River across from the present town of Madawaska, Maine, offered a strategic location above the anadromous fish bar-

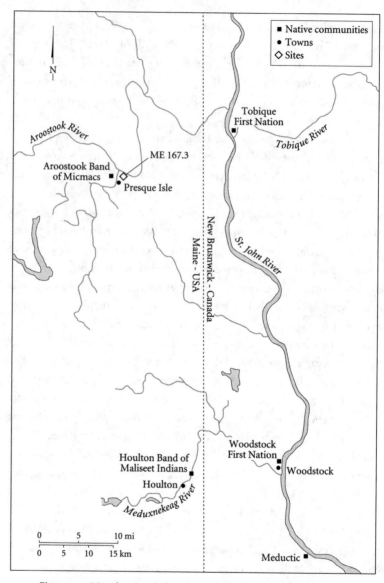

Figure 19.2. Map showing the location of archaeological site ME 167.3 and Native American/First Nation Reserves.

rier of Grand Falls (see Figure 19.2). The Madawaska River provided access to the St. Lawrence River and Quebec, but it was also quite convenient to the large Mi'kmaq village of Listiguj (Restigouche) at the mouth of that river on Chaleur Bay. Historic accounts suggest an integrated community of Maliseet and Mi'kmaq people at Madawaska.

Maliseet ethnicity grades into their close relatives, the Passamaquoddy Tribe, of southeastern New Brunswick and Maine. The linguistic dialects are quite similar, and intermarriage is very common. The most significant distinction is probably linked to the primarily marine-based economy of the Passmaquoddies as opposed to a traditional interior food foraging strategy of the Maliseets.

The Mi'kmaqs represent affiliated villages in seven districts including the Gaspé Peninsula of Quebec, New Brunswick, Prince Edward Island, Nova Scotia, and Newfoundland. Historically, Mi'kmaqs occupied areas as far west as Penobscot Bay in Maine and extended eastward into erstwhile Beothuk Newfoundland. They interacted with the Innu (Montagnais) north of the St. Lawrence River and occasionally traveled or raided far up the Labrador coast and most likely had contact with Inuit people. Early European accounts document the presence of Souriquois (Mi'kmaqs) in Etchemin (Maliseet) villages along the St. John River.

The history of intertribal and intratribal relations in prehistoric Maine is difficult to glean from the archaeological record. The ethnographic record indicates animosity between Wabanaki and Iroquoian groups that likely existed before the arrival of Europeans, as well as intratribal conflicts between Wabanakis themselves. Both Mi'kmaqs and Maliseets came into contact with Iroquoian people along the lower St. Lawrence River. Both groups may have played a role in the disappearance of the St. Lawrence Iroquois shortly after the arrival of early French explorers.

The U.S.-Canadian border presents problems for archaeologists. An American archaeologist must keep abreast of the Canadian research, and much of the work conducted in Quebec is published in French. Contemporary archaeologists carry the historical burden of the perceptions, attitudes, and practices of their predecessors. In the nineteenth and early twentieth centuries, archaeologists largely conformed to a "tomb raider" model, supported by wealthy patrons or institutions. Politically, they represented an extension of powerful interests and demonstrated their value by returning to their benefactor with trophy relics. With the onset of public archaeology in the 1970s, archaeologists became associated with government policy. Funded with public money, they found it necessary to justify their work for the first time. Only very recently have North American archaeologists been challenged to defend their goals and methods to the indigenous descendants of the people they study.

Archaeology has become politically vulnerable to reductions in government funding or to changes in legislated regulatory policies. Concurrently, a resurgence of political, litigious, and social justice awareness has been growing within Native communities. Owing to the political vulnerability of archaeology, and the legacy of archaeological practices, methods, and goals, the field is a predictable flashpoint of contention with Native people.

Progressive archaeologists have become increasingly concerned with the ethics of research and interpretation of one culture by another. These progressives acknowledge the relationship between understanding traditional Native thought and the ability to substantively interpret archaeological data. It is surprising, though not unprecedented, that progressive archaeologists and traditional Native elders often find fertile common ground.

We present the following sections from our individual viewpoints. Although we agree on many issues, our perspectives are different and should not be blended into a single voice. In our opinion, American archaeologists have a common interest in association with waning political clout, or, more accurately, the need for political clout is increasing while influence is not. Native nations, especially those that are federally recognized, also constitute a common interest group, whose political fortunes are on the rise. Both groups need allies and have many interests in common. To achieve a constructive alliance between archaeologists and Native people, effective communication is essential to the process of finding compromises acceptable to both groups.

The history of Native American and western European negotiations is replete with examples of cultural misinterpretation and misunderstanding. Now that archaeology has become a significant area of contention and negotiation, anthropologists find themselves on the front line of that process. One would think that practitioners in the field would revel in this opportunity to apply knowledge of culture to real-world conflict. To date, however, many archaeologists have taken the same rigid cultural stance as their military and political predecessors and continue to communicate in an ethnocentric manner objectionable to Native people.

An Archaeologist's View (by David Putnam)

My relationship with Native people of northern Maine is both personal and historical. My ancestors were guided to the present-day town of Houlton, Maine, by a Maliseet Indian whose name was not considered worthy of mention (Putnam 1958). My grandfather worked as a sporting guide on the Allagash and St. John rivers (Sleeper 2002). His friendships with Maliseet hunters resembled those between blacks and whites in the American South. My personal experience was contradictory, reading romanticized accounts of Native people but seeing the Houlton Band of Maliseet Indians relegated to living in shacks along the road to the town dump.

By the time I entered graduate school, I had become an avowed disciple of Karl Butzer's environmental archaeology. My fellow students often chanted the refrain "American archaeology is anthropology or it is nothing" (Willey and Phillips 1958:2), only to hear my predictable burst of long-practiced expletives. Ironically, I have since learned that consulting with Native people infuses anthropology into the otherwise sterile process of archaeology. It provides fresh insight and a human element into the interpretation of dry and dusty data (e.g., bits of stone scattered along a riverbank). Eloquent Native expressions of cultural perspective define through contrast that blind spot within us from which our own worldview emanates.

Over the past 20 years, I have participated in many collaborative archaeological and educational efforts with Native people in the United States and Canada. Perhaps most enlightening were those in such areas as Alaska, the Rocky Mountains, and Canada where prehistory occupies the recent past, and traditional culture remains a vibrant part of contemporary community life.

These experiences raise a number of unsettling questions. By what authority do I claim the right to interpret the Native past through a filter of ethnocentric cultural and academic judgment? If I attempt to convince Native people to accept my view, am I not simply promoting assimilation? If I compromise in negotiations over the methods or goals of archaeology, am I selling the field short, or building a bridge that will ultimately enrich it? What benefit do Native people derive from my archaeological study?

Each collaborative effort involves a unique set of circumstances and goals. While I cannot claim to have found a formula for success in these endeavors, there are some factors that can facilitate the process. In my opinion, archaeologists should meet with Native people on their own turf and never summon them to ours. Allow elders to officiate the meetings and adhere to their rules of protocol. Enlist respected members of the community as active participants in the project and listen to what they offer. Form a real partnership in which all participants have a voice in the process, rather than the hierarchical approach traditional to field archaeology.

During the winter of 2001, I began planning an archaeological field school to be offered as a summer course for students at the University of Maine at Presque Isle. The site I chose for the project, ME 167.3, was located in the town of Presque Isle on the south bank of the Aroostook River. It was one of three prehistoric sites identified during an archaeological survey that I conducted with Dariel McKee and Luke Joseph of the Houlton Band of Maliseet Indians (Putnam 1996). The sites were significant in that they were the first prehistoric sites documented in the entire U.S. Geological Survey 15-min Presque Isle quadrangle. The land was owned by the Aroostook Centre Mall and had been plagued by rumors of an "Indian burial ground" before, during, and following construction in the 1970s. Until our identification of prehistoric cultural material along the riverbank, no such evidence had been recorded in the area. Local myths persist that no Native people ever lived in the area, and they only relocated here for work in the past 100 years.

Oral accounts of Maliseet use of the Aroostook River indicate that in the early historic period, the Bear (Muin or Mu win) Clan from the village at Tobique in New Brunswick used the drainage from late summer through spring for dispersal into winter hunting camps (Nicholas and Prins 1989; Andrea Bear-Nicholas, personal communication 1999). The Tobique First

Nation is located in New Brunswick at the mouth of the Tobique River on the St. John River, just below the mouth of the Aroostook River.

The Houlton Band of Maliseet Indians were aware of the sites and my fieldwork through a collaborative relationship developed over many years. However, their traditional use areas are located well south of the site location, and my contact with them was in the context of a regular informal dialogue. The Aroostook Band of Micmacs, based in Presque Isle, is composed of people from many of the Mi'kmaq communities scattered across the Canadian Maritimes, and some families with long roots in the local community. I first contacted the Aroostook Band of Micmacs through Bernard Jerome, the director of cultural programs. It also seemed appropriate to approach the Maliseets of Tobique in advance of excavation. The Tobique First Nation is a political entity with links to the Canadian government. I was concerned at the prospect of involving issues of U.S. and Canadian sovereignty, while at the same time recognizing the sovereignty of Native nations that span the international boundary.

I contacted the Wulustuk Grand Council, a grassroots organization of Maliseet (Wulustukweig) people from all of the reserves along the St. John River. Their goal is to regain a traditional form of self-governance and to counter what they perceive as a strategy by the provincial and federal Canadian government to divide the reserves. I attended a Grand Council meeting convened in Tobique by Chief Daniel Ennis. Patrick Paul introduced me to the council, and I requested permission to excavate portions of the site. A number of members of the Bear Clan voiced concerns about the possibility of encountering graves or other sensitive features. I suggested that members of the Wabanaki Repatriation Committee—formed from the Penobscot Nation, Passamaquoddy Tribe, Maliseet, and Micmac bands in Maine to negotiate NAGPRA issues in that state—could provide a logical advisory body for our project. I received permission from the council to proceed with planning, with the provision that those issues be resolved before excavation began.

I felt that I had made the appropriate contact with Maliseets in New Brunswick, in addition to those in Houlton, and the Micmacs in Presque Isle. Irvin Polchies, a revered Maliseet elder and spiritual leader from the Woodstock First Nation, graciously agreed to conduct a ceremony at the site before our work began. Sixteen students had enrolled in the course; several were members of the Aroostook Band of Micmacs and Tobique First Nation, including Deborah Bear, of the Tobique Muin Clan.

On the first day of the course, Mi'kmaqs, Maliseets, students, and I gathered at the site for the blessing ceremony led by Irvin Polchies. Many of the Tobique Maliseets objected to a Mi'kmaq role in the proceedings, since they believed that the site was emplaced by Maliseets in Maliseet territory. A circle had been formed with joined hands for the ceremony. Some of the Mi'kmaqs broke contact and stepped out of the circle, in symbolic protest over the infusion of politics into a spiritual ceremony. As we dispersed in dismay, I was approached by Karen Perley, a member of the Maliseet Advisory Committee on Archaeology, formed to advise the Province of New Brunswick on archaeological issues in Maliseet tribal territories in the province. She suggested that I address that committee, since the site fell within traditional Maliseet tribal territory, even though its location was in Maine.

The New Brunswick provincial government had endeavored to solve consultation issues with First Nations by assigning contemporary territorial boundaries to the tribes. Any archaeological site located within Maliseet territory would require consultation with Maliseet First Nations, and any site located within Mi'kmaq territory would require Mi'kmaq consultation. This arrangement was in part a response to the controversy that had erupted over the archaeological site at Jemseg, New Brunswick, at the proposed location of a bridge on a realigned portion of the Trans-Canada Highway. The purpose was to simplify the process of Native consultation, but the concept does not reflect the complexity of cultural expression through time and space, so fundamental to archaeological theory.

In Maine, little effort has been made by archaeologists to consult with the tribes about archaeological issues at all. The most notable exception has been NAGPRA consultations. The NAGPRA requirement that tribes demonstrate their descent from specific human remains held by museums in order to claim them or the grave goods recovered with them has resulted in the reemergence of the Wabanaki Confederacy in the form of the Wabanaki Repatriation Committee. Representatives of the Houlton Band of Maliseet Indians, the Aroostook Band of Micmacs, the Penobscot Nation, and the two divisions of the Passamaquoddy Tribe claim a common ancestry and request the return of disputed materials on behalf of all Wabanaki people.

The injection of the New Brunswick territorial model into the Maine common ancestry strategy imposed an intractable difficulty on the process of collaboration and the attempt to build a strong partnership among the interested parties. Initially I was asked to determine whose territory it was, which I declined to do. First, I argued that it was inappropriate for me to make such a determination. Furthermore, neither I nor any other archaeologist can review the available data and make a defensible statement about the nature of prehistoric Wabanaki tribes, their territories (if such existed), or their relations with each other.

The field school students were distraught and feared that the project would not proceed. Bernard Jerome, Irvin Polchies, Daniel Ennis, and Patrick Paul agreed to meet to discuss the problem. The students and I attended a series of councils in which the pertinent issues were discussed. The issue of territory was raised first. The elders spoke at length and listened carefully to the statements of others. Eventually, they agreed that territorial issues were based on use rather than ownership. Bernard acknowledged that Maliseets had used the Aroostook River drainage, although it was impossible to rule out the possibility that Mi'kmaqs had also used it. Irvin suggested that it was simply an issue of protocol: the polite request by one group to enter an area currently used by another. When everyone agreed that the site in question fell within the area generally used by Maliseets, the issue of territory was resolved.

The next issue concerned which group would have oversight of the archaeological work. The difficulty here involved convenient proximity to the work, and ultimately the problems involved in transporting prehistoric artifacts across an international boundary. Faced with these difficulties, the Maliseets (i.e., Daniel Ennis and Irvin Polchies representing all Maliseets) respectfully requested that Bernard Jerome, as the Mi'kmaq representative to the Wabanaki Repatriation Committee, oversee the work on behalf of all Wabanaki people.

A general procedural outline for the project was discussed and formalized. I was directed to stop excavation immediately and to contact Bernard if concentrations of red ocher or other indications of graves or ceremonial features were encountered. I was granted one year to study any recovered artifacts, which would then be given to the Wabanaki Repatriation Committee for eventual reburial, an arrangement to which the landowner agreed. I attended a meeting of the Maliseet Advisory Committee on Archaeology in Fredericton, New Brunswick, and reported the details of the arrangement. Irvin is held in high esteem, and his role as a principal architect of the plan eliminated any concerns that the committee may have harbored.

The field school commenced, and we ultimately excavated 22 m² to a basal substrate of channel lag cobbles. Several projectile points diagnostic only to late prehistory were recovered from disturbed contexts. At one point, we did encounter some red ocher and halted our work. Bernard arrived at the site within an hour, and we determined that it did not represent a ceremonial or mortuary feature. The site ultimately produced copious fire-cracked rock, many lithic flakes, and a few flaked stone tools, most from a largely disturbed context. We submitted two radiocarbon samples for assay, but both returned disappointing modern dates. Ironically, the best temporally diagnostic artifact that we recovered was a black English gunflint of ca. 1760.

Many people from the Tobique First Nation, the Aroostook Band of Micmacs, the Houlton Band of Maliseet Indians, and the non-Native community visited the project. Visits were daily, and many friendships grew out of them. Several of the non-Native field school students attended sweats, feasts, and other cultural gatherings. The students learned the skills and methods of field archaeology, but also emerged from the experience permanently enriched by the process of cross-cultural collaboration. They had the opportunity to participate in the councils held on the Aroostook Band of Micmacs Reserve and to observe the civil approach that the elders used to resolve differences.

Native visitors also expressed great interest and satisfaction in the project. Several individuals who had initially been opposed to the work became frequent visitors who assisted with screening and developed a keen interest in the process. Many people in the broad Native community became enthusiastic supporters of the work and expressed interest in conducting additional projects. It was more than scientific inquiry; it was a spiritual connection to a deep ancestral history.

From an archaeological standpoint, the units we excavated were somewhat disappointing. The context was disturbed, and the radiocarbon dates were equivocal. However, the implications of the partnership that excavated this unremarkable archaeological site are enormous.

Our Shadows (by Bernard Jerome)

When I conduct a ceremony, I refer to my ancestors as *eng'i jamig*. This translates into English as "spirit" and also as "shadow." This concept in the Mi'kmaq language indicates our spiritual nature, and the conviction that we carry our ancestors with us, and they provide us with guidance. We are never alone. We have a deep respect for our ancestors who have passed on.

Older Mi'kmaq culture had a creation story. The sun is life itself, and its rays, or sunbeams, had intercourse with the moon and reflected down upon the earth, and life began. All life has purpose, and the purpose of humans is to act as a guardian of Mother Earth.

We believe that all life is sacred. Life has both a physical and a spiritual aspect that cannot be separated and that combine to form an integrated whole. A healthy life must continually balance the physical and spiritual components.

Science is concerned only with the physical nature of life. While I see my ancestors as my shadow who are always with me, science describes this relationship through DNA. My children and grandchildren have my DNA. I have the DNA of my ancestors from many thousands of years ago. I also carry much of the belief, language, and tradition of my ancestors, and I try to pass these things down to my children and grandchildren, from our ancestors to grandchildren. Respect for our ancestors and the willingness of our children to learn the language and traditions cannot be separated.

When an artifact is found in this region, no one knows whether it was made by a Mi'kmaq or a Maliseet. But Wabanaki people are all relatives. Different groups split off in the past, but we share the same ancestors. In archaeology, many things have happened that were disrespectful to Native people. It is wrong for anyone to excavate burial grounds for personal benefit. All people consider burial grounds to be sacred, and they should all be protected.

Sometimes we inadvertently discover burials, and then actions should be taken to protect them. We can learn from whatever is found, but those things must be respectfully returned. When an archaeological site such as an ancient encampment is recognized, we do not know what will be found there. We approach it in a good way. We conduct a ceremony and apologize in prayer to our ancestors for any disturbance that we might cause. We smudge, and the smoke goes into the spirit world. All smoke and air goes upward, just as our spirits go up.

We know that digging might uncover something that would otherwise be lost or destroyed. When an artifact is found, it was meant to be found. I see the artifact as a physical and spiritual link between me and my ancestors. When our ancestors placed an ax in a grave, they knew that the physical ax would not go to the spirit world with them. The spirit of the ax goes with them, just as part of their spirit remains with the ax.

Most people have curiosity about the past. I am a curious person and wish to learn from discoveries. The issue comes down to having respect for other people. Many of the artifacts that are found are everyday tools that were just lost or discarded, and some have a more significant spiritual meaning. I do not condemn the science, only the way that it is sometimes done. It depends on who is doing it and how it is done.

When a child is born, it begins life in a good way. Nothing is born evil or angry, but it must be nurtured in a good way. Relationships between people are the same. I do not know the dates, but people have robbed graves. We have lost many artifacts and objects placed in the graves of our ancestors. Those people who have passed on have rights also. Those objects belong to them forever. It is our obligation to protect and defend their rights. The most important thing is to respect those who have passed on. Those people who abuse this basic rule should be stopped.

I have learned much from examining the artifacts found through archaeology. When I handle them, I can feel the entity or person from the past. The experience brings me closer to my ancestors and reaffirms my physical and spiritual connection to them. I cannot say for sure whether an artifact is a normal camp tool or a funeral piece. Perhaps the funeral piece would be heavier. Because I do not know for certain, it is important always to act respectfully.

When David Putnam wished to study the archaeological site along the Aroostook River, he contacted the Native community. He acknowledged that Native people have an interest in learning about their ancestors and in how the work is done. Even if you want to do it respectfully, you may not know the protocol. If you ask, they will tell you and help you to do it. When you need something or want something, you always give first. Then you will get even more in return.

In that project, the first thing was to establish trust. A proper ceremony was conducted to ask the ancestors for forgiveness and permission. The elders were invited to the work and asked for their advice. They felt a connection to their ancestors. When a test hole reveals charcoal from an ancient campfire, they will say, "My ancestors were here, camping and cooking." You are reconnecting people to their past. You are doing a good thing.

If a burial is found, we will do whatever we can to preserve that. But we first need to know what it is, or we cannot protect it. The archaeology can be used to locate things so that we can protect them. If some things need to be transplanted or covered over so they will not be destroyed by a construction project, then it must be done with respect. But we can also learn about those things. If we do not know where things are or what they are, we cannot learn anything from them or protect them from destruction. Evidence must be found to demonstrate what things are, and the science of archaeology can do that. Sometimes things are found, such as burials, which should not be disturbed at all. The solution then is to avoid them or find some other way to complete the project.

In an old site, I cannot tell whether the people were Mi'kmaq or Maliseet, but I am convinced that they were Wabanaki. Mi'kmaq and Maliseet people should all be concerned about how the archaeology is done. By having so many people involved, no one is left out, and we come to consensus. Our cultures were all nomadic people, so who can say who camped in one spot a thousand years ago?

Because we were all part of the archaeological work, the door was always open for comment. I feel no guilt in being a part of that work. Those wooden artifacts that were found there might have been wigwam cover fasteners. They give us insight into how our ancestors lived and how they might have constructed their wigwams.

The university students experienced the steps that we took and learned about protocol. When they go out later, they will do it the same way because it worked. It is a beginning of something that will grow. Everyone involved learned an important lesson from this project. If you start right, in a respectful way, people will come together as a group, and that is something we do not see often. It was a good thing, and we felt a part of that.

We cannot stop change. Native people have always adapted to change as they needed, and we will continue to adapt in our time. When our ancestral sites are in places where progress is occurring, compromises must be made on all sides. We wish to retain our identity and our connection to our ancestors through tradition, language, and spirituality. Archaeology can contribute to this in a good way, but we must approach it as partners, willing to listen and to learn from each other.

Conclusions

We accomplished a number of significant goals in this project. We brought together several Native nations and the non-Native community to explore a previously unknown, but shared, history. An unofficial process for the conduct of archaeology in northern Maine was piloted, and we encourage others who may work here to adopt it. Connections established between people of different ethnic and cultural backgrounds have persisted and grown in other community systems. Non-Native students experienced the civility of traditional Native conflict resolution and developed a solemn respect for the culture they were studying. Native people participated in scientific archaeology that enhanced their own cultural heritage. School groups visited the excavation and were guided by Native interpreters. Deborah Bear, a Tobique Maliseet, is currently writing her senior thesis on the nature of floodplain archaeological sites in the St. John River valley.

Through this process, other faculty members at the University of Maine at Presque Isle were introduced to the Native community. Those connections resulted in additional course offerings such as a sociology course, Native American Holocaust. The university has since hired two Maliseet professors to offer teacher education courses in Wabanaki Education, and recently both Mi'kmaq and Maliseet language courses were approved. With additional faculty interest, the number of Native students from both Maine and Canada continues to grow at the University of Maine at Presque Isle.

At the request of the Mi'kmaq community of Gesgapegiag, my wife, JoAnne Putnam, Bernard and his wife, Ramona, and I collaborated on an eighth grade curriculum for Wepgwajniag School. The curriculum, *Plamu Wesit* (Leaping Salmon), introduces Atlantic Salmon biology and conservation utilizing a blend of modern science, traditional knowledge, and Mi'kmaq language.

In the summer of 2003 we conducted an archaeological survey of the remote headwaters of the St. John River on a huge tract of land recently acquired by the Maine chapter of the Nature Conservancy. In consultation with tribal elders, the Nature Conservancy requested that artifacts discovered along the riverbank be left in place rather than collected. Our team consisted of Mi'kmaq and Maliseet participants, as well as individuals of St. John Valley Acadian community. Although we retained archaeological material from test pit excavation for analysis and eventual disposition to the Wabanaki Repatriation Committee, we photographed and described artifacts found on the surface and left them there.

This project in turn led to a new relationship with the large forest landowners and furthered their commitment to protect and manage the archaeological resources on their lands. One concept that has been discussed involves the development of cultural tourism, in which the archaeological sites become an economic resource that would stimulate archaeological site protection within the local community. This could additionally provide culturally compatible employment for Native people as cultural guides, and an opportunity to present Native culture and language to interested clients in a wild, beautiful, and yes, spiritual setting.

20. Passamaquoddy Homeland and Language
The Importance of Place

DAVID SANGER, MICAH A. PAWLING,

AND DONALD G. SOCTOMAH

Places exemplify our worldview.
Wayne Newell, Passamaquoddy elder

Introduction

Although the study of place-names has a long history in the Maine-Maritimes area, only recently have scholars systematically recorded, translated, and then analyzed them in their cultural context. This chapter recounts a collaborative effort by an archaeologist (David Sanger), an ethnohistorian (Micah Pawling), and a Passamaquoddy tribal member and tribal historic preservation officer (Donald Soctomah). In keeping with the theme of this volume, we focus on the collaborative process, and what each of us "brings to the table" in terms of background and interest. Although the accompanying maps depicting Passamaquoddy homeland and place-names are a primary product of the research, the long-term ramifications are considerable in helping to document and sustain for Passamaquoddy tribal members their rich traditions and ties to their homeland.

The Passamaquoddy Tribe has two recognized reservations in Washington County, Maine (see Figure 20.1 for traditional homeland). Although no complete ethnography—in a traditional anthropological sense—exists, Erickson (1978) provided a basic description and history, titled "Maliseet-

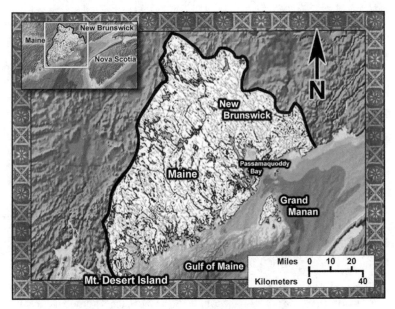

Figure 20.1. Passamaquoddy homeland in eastern Maine and western New Brunswick (Prepared by Edward Bassett).

Passamaquoddy," in *Northeast*. In the same volume, Goddard (1978b) gives their language as Maliseet-Passamaquoddy, one of several Eastern Algonquian languages. Collectively, the term "Wabanaki" is employed to refer to the Passamaquoddy, Mi'kmaq, Maliseet, and Penobscot tribes, but it can also include other Abenaki groups. Today, many community members speak Passamaquoddy despite the almost continual proximity of Europeans for at least 400 years. Language survival, commonly regarded as integral to cultural retention, lies behind the current project. Our project, the study of Passamaquoddy place-names, complements the Passamaquoddy-Maliseet Dictionary Project, which brings together Native speakers and non-Native linguists. Recognizing an opportunity, Soctomah presented place-names for incorporation in the dictionary.

The Study of Places

The study of place has assumed many meanings in anthropology. One form of spatial analysis was made famous in archaeology by the seminal study of the Virú Valley, Peru (Willey 1953). Where large monumental buildings and elaborated settlement organization are found, it may be possible to infer certain social implications. But when working in the domain of hunter-gatherer archaeology in the Maritime peninsula (defined as most of Maine, the Gaspé region of Quebec, and the Maritime Provinces), where above-ground remains are few and site preservation problematic, a different methodology is needed. In this region, archaeological analyses of space became largely devoid of sociocultural context. Analyses of sites with respect to compass orientation, land characteristics, access to food and other resources, season of occupation, and so on, discern patterning, sometimes referred to as the "settlement pattern" (for examples in the region, see Kellogg 1987, 1994; Sanger 1996a, 1996b). It is not that these archaeologists deny the social element in the pattern; the problem is how to identify it in a cultural context that extends back for millennia and where linkages with descendants of those creating the pattern may be fragile. One revealing example in the Northeast demonstrates the value of ethnographic research combined with concepts of space. Tanner's (1979) book *Bringing Home Animals* integrates the physical and cultural space of Quebec Mistassini Cree in a study informed by people for whom place and cultural memories were current in the 1960s.

Recently, anthropologists and ethnohistorians have combined place with cultural context by soliciting information from those who used space and named it to reflect its significance in their lives, thereby making place dynamic and relevant to how Native peoples view the land (Hirsch 1995; Potter 2004). Various scholars have lamented that anthropologists have been slow to recognize the potential of such an approach. Recently, Ashmore claimed that "the *still-growing appreciation* that space is actively inhabited, and that social relations and spatial structure are linked recursively, has transformed our understanding of the past" (2002:1172; emphasis added). Nevertheless, without information from community members, interpretation runs the risk of being mere speculation or worse. Carson noted that Basso's 1996 publication *Wisdom Sits in Places: Landscape and Language among the Western Apache* is "by far the most sophisticated reconstruction of an ethnogeography" (2002:782). After spending two decades with Western Apache community members, Basso "stumbled onto places" (1996:xiv) as a direct result of his intimacy with the people.

Basso (1996) used the term "place-worlds" to encompass both the physical places and the cultural places of the Western Apache. The place-worlds concept is not static. Place-names may change through time or in response to subsequent events. Place-names may relate to seemingly mundane events, but they can also incorporate traditions and spiritual occurrences kept alive by place-worlds. In Australia, landscapes and place-worlds mediate between the present and the past, because people "absorb their identity from the ancestral past and transmit that identity to new generations" (Morphy 1995:205). This is as valid for Passamaquoddy homeland as it is for aboriginal Australia.

The Passamaquoddy Homeland

Figure 20.1 depicts the Passamaquoddy homeland, a landscape perceived as borrowed from the Creator and on which ancestral Passamaquoddy people lived. The heart of the homeland lies between the Union River in Maine and Point Lepreau, New Brunswick. Within this area is a much smaller region, the Passamaquoddy tribal lands, created by a 1794 treaty with the Commonwealth of Massachusetts and Native petitions. Oral and written accounts reveal regular movements beyond reservation boundaries and into lands occupied by other Wabanaki groups, which routinely interacted and intermarried with Passamaquoddies. Traditionally, homeland borders were porous; individuals and families moved freely to good hunting and fishing places in a cycle determined largely by social relationships and the seasonal availability of food. Thus, Passamaquoddy place-names and place-worlds extend far beyond present tribal lands. Not surprisingly, place-names are not evenly distributed across the traditional homeland. The heavy concentration in and around the modern reservation lands reflects both the modern political reapportionment and the transient nature of culturally affiliated place-worlds (Figures 20.2 and 20.3). However, the persistence of place-names well beyond reservation lands is testimony to the continued importance of these places to the Passamaquoddy people.

Without the benefit of written records, archaeologists working in the Passamaquoddy homeland have depended on excavated sites and regional synopses. Abundant sites in Passamaquoddy Bay and its environs resulted in several studies that demonstrated a mixed economy using ma-

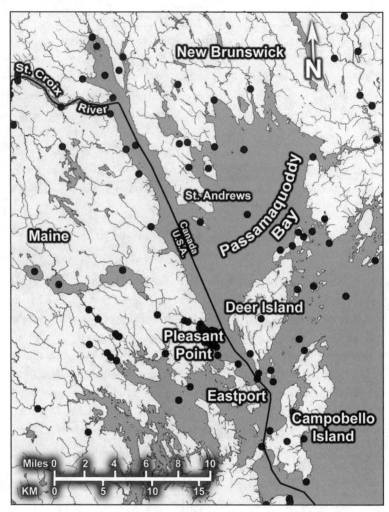

Figure 20.2. A selection of place-names in Passamaquoddy Bay in proximity to Pleasant Point Reservation, Perry, Maine (Prepared by Edward Bassett).

rine and terrestrial resources (e.g., Black 1992; Sanger 1987). The large number of sites attests not only to the eclectic nature of the economy but also to a substantial population. However, in the absence of any census data, credible population estimates are impractical. Archaeological sites in the area have been eroding for years (Sanger and Kellogg 1989), and historical developments have taken a heavy toll. The first documented Eu-

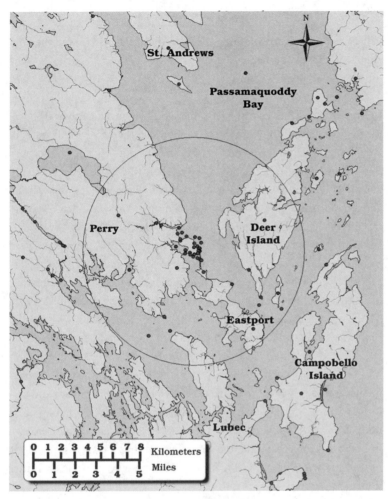

Figure 20.3. Place-names in an 8-km radius of Pleasant Point Reservation, Perry, Maine
(Prepared by Edward Bassett).

ropean contact in Passamaquoddy homeland occurred in 1604 with the
short-lived French settlement of de Monts and Champlain on St. Croix
Island. Thereafter, Europeans settled parts of the area, and in the after-
math of the American Revolutionary War, the influx compelled Passamaquoddies to petition administrators for their own lands within their
traditional homeland in an attempt to avoid frictional contact with settlers (Pawling 1999). These secured tracts of land also reflect family band

values that include maintaining access to the coast as well as to the interior river and lake systems.

Place-Name Research History

In the late eighteenth century, Passamaquoddy homeland fell in the middle of a contentious boundary dispute between the new United States of America and Britain. Both American and British officials interviewed Passamaquoddies in hopes of bolstering their respective claims (Carroll 2001; Demeritt 1997). Early surveyors hired Native guides and learned about canoe routes and portages (e.g., Ganong 1891, 1896). Anthropological interest in Passamaquoddy place-names dates to the efforts of Albert Gatschet (1897a, 1897b), a Bureau of Ethnology linguist. He was followed by William Ganong, professor of botany at Smith College and a "renaissance scholar" who spent years in multifaceted studies of New Brunswick, his native province. Ganong established a long-term correspondence with Maine resident Fanny Hardy Eckstorm, part of which dealt with aboriginal place-names and their interpretation (Sanger 1980). Eckstorm (1941) later published *Indian Place-Names of the Penobscot River Valley and the Maine Coast*, in which she used Wabanaki informants, historical documents, and survey maps to access the multiple names for a place and various spellings through time. Speck (1940) made use of place-names in his book *Penobscot Man*. As used by these early scholars, place-names aided in historical interpretation and in understanding the English meaning of well-known geographical features identified by variations on Native nomenclature.

The Passamaquoddy-Maliseet Dictionary

The Place-Names Project parallels the Passamaquoddy-Maliseet Dictionary (P-MD) Project, codirected by Passamaquoddy elder David Francis Sr. and linguist Robert Leavitt (Francis and Leavitt 2003). The P-MD follows on a shorter dictionary (only 3,000 words) compiled by Philip LeSourd (1984), *Kolusuwakonol: Passamaquoddy-Maliseet and English Dictionary*. As noted above, Maliseet-Passamaquoddy is classified as an Eastern Algonquian language (Goddard 1978b). According to the directors of the P-MD, fewer than 2,000 people speak the language with any ability, and most of these are over the age of 40; only 400 people are considered to be fluent. In recognition of the key nature of language retention, the P-MD is supported in large part by the National Science Foundation. It has progressed through two phases—Phase I (1996–1999) and Phase II (2000–2004). To date, the project has compiled more than 26,000 words, most of which have been entered into a computerized database, where they can be edited further. Native speakers of nine communities assisted with pronunciations and translations, in addition to providing oral histories and other expressive media such as story and song.

Plans for the P-MD call for a published book, in addition to a Web site and a CD-ROM for educational use. With the protocol established, it should be relatively easy to update and revise the dictionary as new words and translations appear.

Place-Names Project

Donald Soctomah, a resident of Motahkomikuk, or Indian Township, Maine, became interested in recent Passamaquoddy tribal history and published two volumes, *Passamaquoddy at the Turn of the Century, 1890–1920* (Soctomah 2002), and *Hard Times at Passamaquoddy, 1921–1950* (Soctomah 2003). Formally trained as a forester, Soctomah returned to his homeland as an adult, served as the Passamaquoddy tribal representative to the Maine State Legislature (1998–2001), and engaged in a number of tribal activities, many associated with culture history, interpretation, and retention of tribal traditions. As he writes:

> Searching for my Tribe's past is a journey many Passamaquoddy people are taking and learning about a unique history that was kept from us. Growing up on the Pleasant Point Indian Reservation in eastern Maine was my most cherished memory of my youth. . . . There were strong connections within the community, I would visit families all around the reservation and it felt like I was part of each family. Each family had stories to tell, of legend[s] from the past and stories of a grandfather or grandmother and their adventures. . . . One day an elder said to me that my ancestors came from the

Table 20.1. Selected Geographical Place-names, Passamaquoddy Place-names, and Meanings

Place-name	Passamaquoddy	Meaning
Oak Bay	Wehgayik	At head of bay
Waweig River	Wehgapigek	At tide's head
Devil's Head	Qaqocuhs	Dirty mountain
St. Croix Island	Mehtonuwekoss	Little out of food place
Red Beach	Mehqamkesk	At the small red beach
Liberty Point	Wapsamkuk	White quartz place
St. Andrews	Qonasqamkuk	Sandy point bar
Navy Island	Kuwi-kanis	Small particular bark wigwam location
Reardon Island	Monhikkatik	Peeling place for wigwam poles
Campobello Island	Epakuwitk	Floating between
Friar's Head	Wskitapq	Giant rock man
Deer Island	Othuhki elenk	Deer-his-island
Indian Island	Mocinikoss	Little bad current
Mcmaster Island	Nekkopahamk	Landing place Glooscap
Chamcook Beach	Cemkuk	Big gravel beach
White Horse Island	Oqonsapsq	Place of shags (cormorants)
Mcmaster's Lookout Hill	Skuwasutik	Looking for the returning canoe
Minister's Island	Qonasqamqi Monihkuk	Sand point island
St. Andrews Brook	Motehehsimtik	Place of splashing ducks
Oak Point Creek	Kiulatmakek	Look out or waiting place
Cherry Island	Monosapskuhsisk	Little rock island of trees
Dunn Island	Pqapitossisk	Red tooth place
Simpson's Island	Pkuwahqi monihkuhsis	Bog on little island
Welchpool	Wehqayik	Enclosed area of water
Cummings Cove	Walamkuk	At a hollow sand beach
Carlow Island	Kalusaylon	Carlow's place
Bliss Island	Sissepsekuk	3 land points divided into island

Kennebec River area, [and] I never forgot those words. That may have been the statement that started my search back in time. . . . Finding family roots and following the footsteps left by my ancestors would help me find my connections to my other tribal roots and the connection between peoples [Soctomah 2003:preface].

Soctomah recalls that as a boy he heard of places not spoken of when he returned to the reservation as an adult. So when he could find only the occasional place-name in the ongoing P-MD, he decided to expand the list. As he made inquiries, he realized that place-names provided access to much more than simply a name. In brief, he "discovered" for himself a whole series of place-worlds (cf. Basso 1996) that offered an entrée into tribal history and culture, information that would be lost with the passing of the older generation. As a community member, Soctomah could interview people and learn not only place-names but the "legends" related to place, which provided a rich cultural context to accompany the physical place (Table 20.1). Some legends spoke of common things, such as a place "to dry fish," but interwoven were spiritual accounts of Glooskap, the culture hero who created much of Passamaquoddy homeland.

Because such stories may constitute privileged information, and thus be considered appropriate only for community members, Soctomah's role in the project was crucial. Soctomah's involvement enabled tribal people to have confidence that these privileged accounts would not be publicly or otherwise inappropriately displayed. He talked with Native guides who hunted and fished on tribal lands, and with fishermen and others working on the coast. On occasion, Soctomah enlisted the help of young people who would then ask older relatives to tell them the stories that would normally be passed down intergenerationally. The technique was highly effective, perhaps because it appealed to the traditional method of passing along information. Community members were taken to land and water locations and asked to recall place-names. Tape-recorded interviews permitted the P-MD research team to evaluate the place-names, to decide jointly on appropriate translations, and to document the legends. Finally, once the team members had decided on the best rendition and translation, they submitted their work to an advisory group consisting of community elders.

Soctomah realized that a potential additional source of place-names lay outside the knowledge held by modern community members, in part simply because time had passed, and in part because traditional Passamaquoddy homeland extended far beyond the current tribal boundaries. Recent history restricted most of the known place-names to current tribal lands—those landscapes most often visited. His own historical research had made him aware of early written history and archaeological work in Passamaquoddy homeland. Soctomah learned that the University of Maine System has a collaborative Cultural Heritage Research Grant Program. Accordingly, he approached David Sanger, a University of Maine faculty member, and suggested that they apply together. In 2002 the project, titled "Landscapes and Language: A Passamaquoddy Place Name Project," was awarded a small pilot-study grant to incorporate into the P-MD a limited number of place-names derived from historical and archaeological research. The proposal also listed Micah Pawling, a Ph.D. candidate in the University of Maine's History Department and a specialist in the ethnohistory of the region, and various Passamaquoddy community members, also part of the P-MD. Soctomah then applied to the U.S. National Park Service Tribal Preservation Program, which gave money to help defray research expenses, including travel funds, compensation for informants' time, linguistic help, and computer programming and data entry.

In his previous historical research, Pawling had seen a number of documents that provided Passamaquoddy place-names beyond those already published (e.g., Eckstorm 1941; Ganong 1891, 1896; Gatschet 1897a, 1897b; Speck 1940). Often these place-names were found on maps and in reports made by early surveyors guided by Passamaquoddies. As expected, given the presence of sounds not found in French or English, the words had been recorded with varying degrees of accuracy. Native speakers in the P-MD analyzed what the writer thought he had heard and then, by taking into account the place itself, rendered the term into modern Passamaquoddy. The plan was to submit up to 50 place-names; in fact, the list grew to include many more. Pawling's rationale for cooperation in the Place-Names Project was both personal and professional. During his research involving Native land petitions, he had observed that even after treaties had formally defined a new Passamaquoddy homeland—the reservation—people routinely traveled beyond its rigid boundaries to procure traditional items for food and other cultural activities. Thus, even after the establishment of reservations, traditional aspects of the flexible settlement pattern persisted, keeping alive the larger homeland through place-worlds. Pawling's earlier work had put him in close touch with Soctomah and other community members whose willingness to talk about homeland issues had greatly informed his research. When Soctomah extended the invitation to participate in the Place-Names Project, Pawling enthusiastically accepted.

David Sanger has worked for many years in the Passamaquoddy homeland on both sides of the international boundary. For the Place-Names Project, rather than simply provide all known site locations, he recommended a pilot study to analyze a handful of relatively late pre-European sites (Late Ceramic period, mostly dating to around A.D. 1000 and later), particularly those where excavation had recovered a considerable amount of cultural material. Tribal members would be shown locations, sometimes taken to archaeological sites, and then asked to recall what they knew. For Sanger, it was gratifying to contribute to Passamaquoddy cultural retention and also to gain insights into behavior and nonmaterial culture unobtainable from archaeologically recovered data. Like Pawling, he felt greatly honored to be included in the project.

Results of the Place-Names Project

One result of the project has been the addition to the P-MD of a number of new words (over 400 entries) and several oral traditions that accompany the place-names. In some areas, the increase is dramatic: around Indian Township, for example, the number of place-names went from 1 to 20. The place-names will be published in various formats and will provide invaluable data for language and culture retention programs. In particular, the Place-Names Project has resulted in a computerized map (Figures 20.1, 20.2, and 20.3) that depicts Passamaquoddy homeland. This map integrates distinct Canadian and U.S. digital mapping methods in a single map that spans the international boundary. Named places appear on the map as red dots. By clicking on a dot, the viewer can hear the Passamaquoddy name, as spoken by David Francis Sr., and the English translation (Soctomah and Bassett 2004). Access to oral traditions may be restricted for privacy and spiritual reasons. For security reasons, archaeological site locations are also limited. The first public viewing of the new map took place in May 2004, in a new facility—the Downeast Heritage Center, located in Calais, Maine—honoring Passamaquoddy tribal traditions together with land and water resources. The opening was timed for ceremonies to commemorate the 1604 settlement of Pierre Du Gua Sieur de Monts and Samuel de Champlain on nearby St. Croix Island. The winter of 1604 was a severe one in which many men died from malnutrition, especially scurvy. Quite conceivably, the toll would have been much worse were it not for the assistance Passamaquoddy people rendered the ill-prepared Europeans.

Beyond the acquisition of new data, the Place-Names Project has demonstrated the effectiveness of integrating Native community knowledge with the formal methodologies of history and archaeology contributed by non-Native scholars.

Discussion and Conclusions

The Passamaquoddy Place-Names Project offers a blueprint for one kind of cross-cultural collaboration leading to cultural preservation; direct application to other regions in the Northeast may require different strategies. One variable is the pace of European settlement, which varied considerably in the Northeast. For the first two centuries of interactions with the French and British, the Passamaquoddies did not experience direct resettlement of their homeland. Between the first written accounts of European contact on St. Croix Island in 1604 and the final conflicts in the American Revolution, the Passamaquoddies' perception of their homeland prevailed. They had traded with small populations of Acadians and English fishermen who had come and gone. Life on the fringe of empires may have offered some advantages in that the Passamaquoddy could trade with the newcomers, but they were far enough away that resettlement—and the consequent renaming of places to accommodate European place-worlds—was slowed. In contrast with Algonquian groups in southern New England, where numerous European settlers farmed the land and replaced most of the Native place-names with their own toponymy (Harley 1994; Krim 1980; O'Brien 1997; Pearce 2004), the Passamaquoddy retained many of their original place-names, some of which are still commonly used for rivers, lakes, islands, and wetlands. Language retention, combined with continuous occupation on comparatively sizable reservations, also helped the community's ability to retain Passamaquoddy place-names.

Modern borderlands, such as the Maine–New Brunswick border area, represent distinctive geographical and cultural regions where local events and interests may supersede national policies. However, there is a deterrent to scholarship when nationalism focuses and constrains research interests (Hornsby et al. 1989; Pawling 1999; Sanger 2002:6; Taylor 2000). Reconstruction of the Passamaquoddy homeland through place-names requires that the research traverse the Canadian-American borderland region, whether it involves searching for historical documents, archaeological sites, or the recollections of community members.

The Place-Names Project has fulfilled many of its goals. Although most of the place-names are concentrated in and around present tribal reservation lands, the general dispersal of place-names reflects a much broader distribution of Passamaquoddy peoples in the past. Place-worlds (Basso 1996) represent cultural heritage, and their documentation is key to preserving Passamaquoddy culture and self-awareness. Future generations of Passamaquoddies will depend on the Passamaquoddy-Maliseet Dictionary as a basis for language teaching and retention. In addition, we anticipate that they will use the place-name data to gain further insights into their past.

Finally, the Passamaquoddy-Maliseet Dictionary and the Place-Names Project demonstrate how Natives and non-Natives can collaborate in ways that are mutually reinforcing and beneficial. It may well be that a Native initiator is crucial under certain circumstances. In this case, the cultural sensitivity of place-worlds, potentially so fundamental to a people's identity, meant that the material was best approached by a community member. This project has demonstrated that scholarship does not have to split into a Native way and a non-Native way of knowing about the past. Rather, research can involve both perspectives in a synthesis, from multiple "voices" through time, that leads to a better understanding of culture and history. In the final analysis, a synergy develops from mutual trust and respect.

Acknowledgments

The authors appreciate the invitation to participate in this volume and the opportunity to synthesize the Passamaquoddy Place-Names Project. To the Passamaquoddy-Maliseet Dictionary team headed by David Francis Sr. and Robert M. Leavitt, we owe many thanks for translations, computer programming and data entry, interviews, recordings, and hours of analysis trying to make sense out of poorly recorded words. Many tribal members shared their memories and stories with Donald Soctomah. To them, we owe a huge debt. The illustrations were prepared by Edward Bassett. We would also like to acknowledge the cooperation of the Passamaquoddy Environmental Department, the Cobscook Bay Resource Center, and Heidi Leighton. We are grateful to Ann Acheson, who made us aware of Keith Basso's place-names research. The Passamaquoddy-Maliseet Dictionary Project was made possible in part by National Science Foundation Grant (Number SBR-960 1540). We are grateful to Robert Leavitt, for reading a draft of the manuscript and for making some helpful suggestions. Finally, we are grateful to the University of Maine System's Cultural Heritage Research Grant and to the National Park Service's Tribal Preservation Program for financial support.

References

Adams, Roxana (series editor)
  2001 *Implementing the Native American Graves Protection and Repatriation Act*. Professional Practice Series. American Association of Museums, Washington DC.
Advisory Council on Historic Preservation (ACHP)
  1986 *Fact Sheet: Section 106 Participation by Indian Tribes and Other Native Americans*. Advisory Council on Historic Preservation, Washington DC.
Allen, Susan
  1986 UVM Wants to Study Indian Bones for Two More Years. *Burlington Free Press* 14 September:1A.
American Indian Ritual Object Repatriation Foundation
  1996 *Mending the Circle: A Native American Repatriation Guide*, edited by B. Meister. American Indian Ritual Object Repatriation Foundation, New York.
Arden, Harvey
  1989 Who Owns Our Past? *National Geographic* 175(3):376–393.
Ashmore, Wendy
  2002 "Decisions and Dispositions": Socializing Spatial Archaeology. *American Anthropologist* 104(4):1172–1183.
Axtell, James
  1981 *The European and the Indian: Essays in the Ethnohistory of Colonial North America*. Oxford University Press, New York.
Babcock, William H.
  1899 The Nanticoke Indians of Indian River, Delaware. *American Anthropologist* 1:277–282.
Baker, Jane S.
  1976 *Report to Governor Thomas P. Salmon of the State of Vermont Regarding the Claims Presented by the Abenaki Nation*. On file at the Office of Governor, State of Vermont, Montpelier.
Basso, Keith H.
  1996 *Wisdom Sits in Places: Landscape and Language Among the Western Apache*. University of New Mexico Press, Albuquerque.

Baugher, Sherene, and Sara Clark
1998 *An Archaeological Investigation of the Indian Fort Road Site, Trumansburg, New York*. On file at the Department of Landscape Architecture, Cornell University, Ithaca NY.

Baugher, Sherene, and K. Quinn
1995 *An Archaeological Investigation of Inlet Valley, Ithaca, New York*. On file at the Department of Landscape Architecture, Cornell University, Ithaca NY.

Beck, Lane A. (editor)
1995 *Regional Approaches to Mortuary Analysis*. Plenum Press, New York.

Beckerman, Ira
2003 Tribal Consultation in Pennsylvania—A View from PennDOT. Paper presented at the Annual Meeting of the Society for Pennsylvania Archaeology, State College PA.

Bell, Edward L.
1994 *Vestiges of Mortality and Remembrance: A Bibliography on the Historical Archaeology of Cemeteries*. Scarecrow Press, Metuchen NJ.

Bell, Edward L., and Brona G. Simon
1993 Dedication of Historic Native American Cemetery on Nantucket. *Preservation Advocate* 20(4):6. Newsletter of the Massachusetts Historical Commission, Boston.

Bernstein, David J.
1993 *Prehistoric Subsistence on the Southern New England Coast: The Record from Narragansett Bay*. Academic Press, San Diego CA.

Binford, Louis R.
1971 Mortuary Practices: Their Study and Their Potential. In *Approaches to Social Dimensions of Mortuary Practices*, edited by J. A. Brown, pp. 6–29. Memoir 25. Society for American Archaeology, Washington DC.

Biolsi, Thomas, and Larry J. Zimmerman (editors)
1997 *Indians and Anthropologists: Vine Deloria, Jr., and the Critique of Anthropology*. University of Arizona Press, Tucson.

Birchfield, Jim
1989 *Negotiations on the Reburial of the Boucher Collection, May 22, 1989*. A video filmed at the University of Vermont, Department of Anthropology.

Black, David W.
1992 *Living Close to the Ledge: Prehistoric Human Ecology of the Bliss Islands, Quoddy Region, New Brunswick, Canada*. Occasional Papers in Northeastern Archaeology 6. Copetown Press, Dundas, Ontario.

Blom, Deborah E.
2002 *Final Report on Human Remains from Monument Road, Highgate,*

Vermont. On file at the Department of Anthropology, University of Vermont, Burlington.

2003 Repatriation and Monument Road: Working with the Abenaki to Find a Solution. Paper presented at the 43rd Annual Meeting of the Northeastern Anthropological Association, Burlington VT.

Blom, Deborah E., and Chief April St. Francis Merrill

2002 Steps Forward and Steps Back: Repatriation and DNA Legislation in the State of Vermont. Paper presented at the 101st Annual Meeting of the American Anthropological Association, New Orleans.

Blume, Cara Lee

2001 Archaeological Conservancy meeting, electronic communication, December 19.

2002 *Proposed Excavations at the Killens Pond Adena Site (7K-E-3), Killens Pond State Park.* On file at the Delaware Division of Parks and Recreation, Dover.

2003 Working with the Keepers of the Land: Creating Partnerships for Preservation and Management. Paper presented at the 5th World Archaeological Congress, Washington DC.

Blume, Cara Lee, and Tina Pierce Fragoso

2003 The People Who Stayed Behind: Delaware and Nanticoke Indian Communities in the States of Delaware and New Jersey. *Native American Policy Network Newsletter* 14(1):Spring. Electronic document.

Bordewich, Fergus M.

1996 *Killing the White Man's Indian: Reinventing Native Americans at the End of the Twentieth Century.* Anchor Books, New York.

Borns, Harold W., Jr., Christopher C. Dorion, George L. Jacobson Jr., M. R. Kaplan, K. J. Kreutz, Woodrow Thompson, Thomas K. Weddle, and Thomas Lowell

2004 The Deglaciation of Maine, USA. In *Quaternary Glaciations—Extent and Chronology, Part II: North America*, edited by J. Ehlers and P. L. Gibbard. Developments in Quaternary Science, Vol. 2b. Elsevier, Amsterdam.

Bower, Bruce

1994 Fossils on File: Computerized Preservation May Give Reburied Bones Back to Science. *Science News* 145(12):186–187.

Bray, Tamara L. (editor)

2001 *The Future of the Past: Archaeologists, Native Americans, and Repatriation.* Garland Publishing, New York.

Briggs, L. Cabot

1971 Prehistoric Indian Skeletons from New Hampshire. *Man in the Northeast* 1:51–53.

Brown, John
    2001 Letter to Edward F. Sanderson, Deputy State Historic Preservation Officer and Executive Director, Rhode Island Historical Preservation and Heritage Commission, Providence. 26 June.

Brown, Joseph E. (editor)
    1953 *The Sacred Pipe: Black Elk's Account of the Seven Rites of the Oglala Sioux.* University of Oklahoma Press, Norman.

Brown, Michael F.
    2003 *Who Owns Native Culture?* Harvard University Press, Cambridge MA.

Bruchac, Joseph
    1997 *The Native American Sweat Lodge History and Legends.* The Crossing Press, Freedom CA.

Bruchac, Margaret M.
    2005 Earthshapers and Placemakers: Reflections on Algonkian Indian Stories and the Landscape. In *Indigenous Archaeologies: Decolonising Theory and Practice,* edited by C. Smith and H. M. Wobst, pp. 56–80. Routledge, London.

Bruchac, Margaret M., and Elizabeth S. Chilton
    2003 From Beaver Hill to Bark Wigwams: Reconsidering Archaeology and Historical Memory in the Connecticut River Valley. Paper presented at the 36th Annual Meeting of the Society for Historical Archaeology, Providence RI.

Bucko, Raymond A.
    1998 *The Lakota Ritual of the Sweat Lodge: History and Contemporary Practice.* University of Nebraska Press, Lincoln.

Byers, Douglas S., and Frederick Johnson
    1940 *Two Sites on Martha's Vineyard.* Papers of the Robert S. Peabody Foundation for Archaeology 1. Phillips Academy, Andover MA.

Calloway, Colin G.
    1989 *The Abenaki.* Chelsea House, New York.
    1990 *The Western Abenakis of Vermont, 1600–1800: War, Migration, and the Survival of an Indian People.* University of Oklahoma Press, Norman.

Carlson, Catherine Carroll, Elizabeth A. Little, D. Richard Gumaer, Leonard W. Loparto, and Brenda J. Baker
    1992 *Archaeological Survey and Historical Background Research for the Miacomet Indian Village and Burial Ground, Nantucket, Massachusetts.* On file at the Massachusetts Historical Commission, Boston.

Carroll, Francis M.
    2001 *A Good and Wise Measure: The Search for the Canadian-American*

Boundary, 1783–1842. University of Toronto Press, Toronto.

Carson, James T.

2002 Ethnogeography and the Native American Past. *Ethnohistory* 49(4):769–788.

Casjens, Laurel

1978 *A Cultural Resource Overview of the Green Mountain National Forest, Vermont.* Institute for Conservation Archaeology Report No. 72. Harvard University, Cambridge MA.

Champagne, Duane

1999 Part I: Native Identity. In *Contemporary Native American Cultural Issues*, edited by D. Champagne, pp. 11–12. AltaMira Press, Walnut Creek CA.

Charrier v. Bell

1986 *Leonard Charrier v. Louise Lessely Bell et al.*, 496 So. 2d 601 (La. App. 1 Cir.).

Cherau, Suzanne Glover. See also Glover, Suzanne

1998 *Historic Preservation Plan, Tribal Trust Lands, Wampanoag Tribe of Gay Head (Aquinnah), Gay Head, Massachusetts.* Public Archaeology Laboratory, Inc., Report, Pawtucket RI.

2001 Native Building Traditions in Southern New England: A Study of the Aquinnah Wampanoag Community, Martha's Vineyard. Paper presented at the Annual Meeting and Conference, Vernacular Architecture Forum, Mashantucket Pequot Museum and Research Center, Mashantucket CT.

Chilton, Elizabeth S., and Dianna L. Doucette

2002a The Archaeology of Coastal New England: The View from Martha's Vineyard. *Northeast Anthropology* 64:55–66.

2002b Archaeological Investigations at the Lucy Vincent Beach Site (19–DK-148): Preliminary Results and Interpretations. In *A Lasting Impression: Coastal, Lithic, and Ceramic Research in New England Archaeology,* edited by J. E. Kerber, pp. 41–69. Praeger, Westport CT.

Cissna, Paul B.

1986 The Piscataway Indians of Southern Maryland: An Ethnohistory from Pre-European Contact to the Present. Unpublished Ph.D. dissertation, Department of Anthropology, The American University, Washington DC.

Clark, Charles C., IV, and Jay F. Custer

2003 Rethinking Delaware Archaeology: A Beginning. *North American Archaeologist* 24(1):29–81.

Clark, Meggan

2002a Whose Bones? Archaeologist Claims Claremont Skeleton May Not

Belong to Abenakis. *Eagle Times* 18 November:A1, A14. Claremont NH.

2002b 35 Years Later, Claremont Skeleton Back with Abenaki. *Eagle Times* 17 November:A1, A16. Claremont NH.

Clifford, James

2004 Looking Several Ways: Anthropology and Native Heritage in Alaska. *Current Anthropology* 45(1):5–30.

Cook, Frederick

2000 [1887] *Journals of the Military Expedition of Major General John Sullivan against the Six Nations of Indians in 1779 with Records of Centennial Celebrations.* Heritage Books, Bowie MD.

Corbett, R. Patrick

2000 Nation Students Dig into Their Culture. *Utica Observer-Dispatch* 1 August:1C.

Crimmins, Rob

2002 Keepers of the Land. *Delaware Today* September:68–72.

Cronin, Michelle

2001 Local Archaeological Dig Continues to Unearth Artifacts. *Oneida Daily Dispatch* 1 August:14.

Cubbage, William O.

1941 Killens Mill Pond. *Bulletin of the Archaeological Society of Delaware* 3(4):23–24.

Currie, Douglas R., and Kevin A. McBride

2001 Respect for the Ancestors: New Approaches for the Recovery and Analysis of Native American Burials. In *Human Remains: Conservation, Retrieval and Analysis,* edited by E. Williams, pp. 61–68. BAR International Series 934. Archaeopress, Oxford.

Currier, Trisha

1989 Indians, State Strike Balance on Remains. *Cape Cod Times* 6 November:1, 10.

Curry, Dennis C.

1999 *Feast of the Dead: Aboriginal Ossuaries in Maryland.* The Archeological Society of Maryland, Inc., and Maryland Historical Trust Press, Crownsville.

Custer, Jay F.

1984 *Delaware Prehistoric Archaeology: An Ecological Approach.* University of Delaware Press, Newark.

1989 *Prehistoric Cultures of the Delmarva Peninsula: An Archaeological Study.* University of Delaware Press, Newark.

Custer, Jay F., and Kevin W. Cunningham

1986 *Cultural Resources of the Proposed Route 13 Corridor: An Overview Prepared for the Draft Environmental Impact Statement.* Delaware

Department of Transportation Archaeology Series 40. Dover.

Danielson, Stentor

2001 Oneida-Archaeologist Relations: A Utilitarian Perspective on Cooperation between American Indians and Archaeologists. SOAN 452 Honors Research Paper, Department of Sociology and Anthropology, Colgate University, Hamilton NY.

Davidson, Iain, Christine Lovell-Jones, and Robyne Bancroft (editors)

1995 *Archaeologists and Aborigines Working Together.* University of New England Press, Armidale, New South Wales, Australia.

Davis, Paul, and Katie Mulvaney

2003 A Fight as Old as America. *Providence Sunday Journal* 20 July:A1, A12.

Day, Gordon M.

1965 The Indian Occupation of Vermont. *Vermont History* 33:365–374.

Dean, Richard L.

1986 Archaeology at Ganondagan. In *Art from Ganondagan, the Village of Peace*, pp. 11–15. New York State Office of Parks, Recreation, and Historic Preservation, Bureau of Historic Sites, Waterford NY.

Demeritt, David

1997 Representing the "True" St. Croix: Knowledge and Power in the Partition of the Northeast. *The William and Mary Quarterly,* 3rd Series LIV(3):515–548.

Dempsey, Jack (editor)

1999 [1637] *The Essential New England Canaan by Thomas Morton of "Merrymount" 1637.* Digital Scanning, Inc., Scituate MA.

Dent, Richard J.

2003 Excavations at a Late Woodland Village in the Middle Potomac Valley: Theory and Practice at the Winslow Site. *Journal of Middle Atlantic Archaeology* 19:3–24.

Dhody, Anna N., and Harley A. Erickson

2001 *Osteological Analysis of Human Remains from the Smyth Site, Manchester,* NH. On file at the Department of Anthropology, Franklin Pierce College, Rindge NH.

Dincauze, Dena F.

1976 *The Neville Site: 8000 Years at Amoskeag.* Peabody Museum Monographs 4. Harvard University, Cambridge MA.

Dincauze, Dena F., H. Martin Wobst, Robert J. Hasenstab, and David M. Lacy

1980 *Retrospective Assessment of Archaeological Survey Contracts in Massachusetts, 1970–1979.* On file at Massachusetts Historical Commission, Boston.

Dongoske, Kurt E., Mark Aldenderfer, and Karen Doehner (editors)

2000 *Working Together: Native Americans and Archaeologists.* Society for American Archaeology, Washington DC.

Doucette, Dianna L.

   1997 *Annasnappet Pond: 9,000 Years in Carver, Massachusetts: A Popular Report on the Archaeology in Carver, Massachusetts for the Route 44 Reconstruction Project.* Public Archaeology Laboratory, Inc., Report, Pawtucket RI.

   2003 Unraveling Middle Archaic Expressions: A Multidisciplinary Approach Towards Feature and Material Culture Recognition in Southeastern New England. Unpublished Ph.D. dissertation, Department of Anthropology, Harvard University, Cambridge MA.

Doucette, Dianna L., and John R. Cross

   1997 *Annasnappet Pond Archaeological District: An Archaeological Data Recovery Program, North Carver, Massachusetts.* Vols. I, II, and III. Public Archaeology Laboratory, Inc., Report No. 580, Pawtucket RI.

Drucker, Philip

   1955 *Indians of the Northwest Coast.* Natural History Press, Garden City NY.

Echo-Hawk, Roger C.

   2000 Ancient History in the New World: Integrating Oral Traditions and the Archaeological Record in Deep Time. *American Antiquity* 65(2):267–290.

   2002 *Keepers of Culture, Repatriating Cultural Items Under the Native American Graves Protection and Repatriation Act.* Denver Art Museum, Denver CO.

Echo-Hawk, Roger C., and Walter R. Echo-Hawk

   1994 *Battlefields and Burial Grounds: The Indian Struggle to Protect Ancestral Graves in the United States.* Lerner Publications Company, Minneapolis MN.

Echo-Hawk, Walter

   1996 Preface to *Mending the Circle, A Native American Repatriation Guide,* edited by B. Meister, pp. 1–2. American Indian Ritual Object Repatriation Foundation, New York.

Eckstorm, Fanny H.

   1941 *Indian Place-Names of the Penobscot Valley and the Maine Coast.* University of Maine Press, Orono.

Edmunds, Sheila

   2000 *Aurora: Time Well Spent.* © Sheila Edmunds, published for Aurorafest 2000, Aurora NY.

Ehrlich, Arlene

   1989 The Right to Rest in Peace: Native Americans Are at Odds with Collectors and Archaeologists over the Disturbance of Their Ancestors' Graves. *Baltimore Sun, Sun Magazine* 22 October:Cover, 9–13.

Ehrlich, Robert L., Jr.

2003 Letter to Maryland Commission on Indian Affairs. 24 September.

Elia, Ricardo J., and Al B. Wesolowsky (editors)

1989 *Archaeological Excavations at the Uxbridge Almshouse Burial Ground in Uxbridge, Massachusetts.* Office of Public Archaeology Report No. 76. Boston University, Boston.

1991 *Archaeological Excavations at the Uxbridge Almshouse Burial Ground in Uxbridge, Massachusetts.* BAR International Series 564. British Archaeological Reports, Tempus Reparatum, London.

Erickson, Vincent O.

1978 Maliseet-Passamaquoddy. In *Northeast*, edited by Bruce G. Trigger, pp. 123–136. Handbook of North American Indians, Vol. 15, W. C. Sturtevant, general editor. Smithsonian Institution Press, Washington DC.

Fagan, Brian M.

n.d. The Tragedy of Slack Farm. Electronic document, http://mc.maricopa.edu/dept/d10/asb/lost_tribes/Slack Farm.html, accessed January 5, 2004.

Fenton, William N.

1968 Introduction to *Parker on the Iroquois*, edited by W. N. Fenton, pp. 1–47. Syracuse University Press, Syracuse NY.

Ferguson, T. J.

1996 Native Americans and the Practice of Archaeology. *Annual Review of Anthropology* 25:63–79.

Ferguson, T. J., Joe Watkins, and Gordon L. Pullar

1997 Native Americans and Archaeologists: Commentary and Personal Perspectives. In *Native Americans and Archaeologists: Stepping Stones to Common Ground*, edited by N. Swidler, K. E. Dongoske, R. Anyon, and A. S. Downer, pp. 237–252. AltaMira Press, Walnut Creek CA.

Fields, Gregory P.

2000 *Inipi*, the Purification Rite (Sweat Lodge) and Black Elk's Account in the *Sacred Pipe*. In *The Black Elk Reader*, edited by C. Holler, pp. 169–187. Syracuse University Press, Syracuse NY.

Fine-Dare, Kathleen S.

2002 *Grave Injustice: The American Indian Repatriation Movement and NAGPRA.* University of Nebraska Press, Lincoln.

Fischer, Joseph R.

1997 *A Well-Executed Failure: The Sullivan Campaign against the Iroquois, July–September 1779.* University of South Carolina Press, Columbia.

Folger, George Franklin

1910 Remembers Last Indian Who Lived on Nantucket. *Boston Globe*.

Reprinted in *Nantucket Inquirer and Mirror*, September.

Ford, Howard S.

2002 *Sure Signs: Stories behind the Historical Markers of Central New York.* First Books Library, Bloomington IN.

Forrest, Daniel T.

1999 Beyond Presence and Absence: Establishing Diversity in Connecticut's Early Holocene Archaeological Record. *Bulletin of the Archaeological Society of Connecticut* 62:79–98.

Foster, Donald, Victoria B. Kenyon, and George P. Nicholas

1980 *The Smyth Site Report.* On file at the New Hampshire Division of Historical Resources, Concord.

1981 Ancient Lifeways at the Smyth Site, NH 38–4. *New Hampshire Archeologist* 22(2):1–91.

Fragoso, Tina Pierce

2003 Oral Histories: Documenting the Survivals of East Coast Native Americans. Paper presented at the 33rd Middle Atlantic Archaeological Conference, Virginia Beach VA.

Francis, David, Sr., and Robert M. Leavitt

2003 *Project Summary: Passamaquoddy-Maliseet Dictionary Phase I (1996–1999) and Phase II (2000–2003).* On file at the Passamaquoddy Tribal Office, Pleasant Point, Perry ME. See also http://www.lib.unb.ca/Texts/Maliseet/dictionary, accessed May 10, 2004.

Gallagher, Nancy L.

1999 *Breeding Better Vermonters: The Eugenics Project in the Green Mountain State.* University Press of New England, Hanover.

Ganong, William F.

1891 The St. Croix of the Northeastern Boundary. *Magazine of American History* XXVI(4):261–265.

1896 A Monograph of Place-nomenclature of the Province of New Brunswick. *Transactions of the Royal Society of Canada* Section II:175–289.

Gardner, William M.

1982 Early and Middle Woodland in the Middle Atlantic: An Overview. In *Practicing Environmental Archaeology*, edited by R. W. Moeller. Occasional Papers of the American Indian Archaeological Institute 3:53–87. Washington CT.

Gatschet, Albert S.

1897a All Around the Bay of Passamaquoddy: With the Interpretation of its Indian Names of Localities. *National Geographic Magazine* VII(1):16–24.

1897b All Around the Bay of Passamaquoddy, Second Article. *Eastport Sentinel* 15 September:1.

Glover, Suzanne, and Kevin A. McBride

1991 *Intensive (Locational) Archaeological Survey, Parcel I, Tribal Trust Lands, Gay Head, Massachusetts*. Public Archaeology Laboratory, Inc., Report No. 404. Pawtucket RI.

1992 *Intensive (Locational) Archaeological Survey and Additional Testing, Parcels I, IIA, IIB, and III—Tribal Trust Lands, Gay Head, Massachusetts*. Public Archaeology Laboratory, Inc., Report No. 434–1. Pawtucket RI.

1994 *Old Ways and New Ways, 7,000 Years Along the Old South Road: An Archaeological Study. Gay Head, Martha's Vineyard, MA*. Wampanoag Tribe of Gay Head/Aquinnah, Gay Head MA.

Goddard, Ives

1978a Delaware. In *Northeast*, edited by B. G. Trigger, pp. 213–239. Handbook of North American Indians, Vol. 15, W. C. Sturtevant, general editor. Smithsonian Institution Press, Washington DC.

1978b Eastern Algonquian Languages. In *Northeast*, edited by B. G. Trigger, pp. 70–77. Handbook of North American Indians, Vol. 15, W. C. Sturtevant, general editor. Smithsonian Institution Press, Washington DC.

Gonsalves, Sean

2002 Solemn Wampanoags Lay Ancestors' Remains to Rest. *Cape Cod Times* 11 June:1, 14.

Goodby, Robert G.

1995 Native American Ceramics from the Rock's Road Site, Seabrook, New Hampshire. *New Hampshire Archeologist* 35(1):46–60.

1999 *Phase I-A Preliminary Archaeological Reconnaissance, Project (13197), Holderness, New Hampshire*. Victoria Bunker, Inc., Report. Alton NH.

2000 *Draft Technical Report, Phase I-B Archaeological Testing and Phase II Intensive Archaeological Survey, Holderness Projects 13197, 12289*. Victoria Bunker, Inc., Report. Alton NH.

2001 *Draft Technical Report, Phase III Archaeological Data Recovery Davison Brook Site (27GR201), Holderness, New Hampshire, Holderness Projects 13197, 12289*. Victoria Bunker, Inc., Report. Alton NH.

2002a Defining the Dynamic Late Archaic Period at the Davison Brook Site, 27GR201. *New Hampshire Archeologist* 41(1):1–87.

2002b Native American Remains from the Smyth Site, Manchester, New Hampshire. *New Hampshire Archeological Newsletter* 18(1):9–11.

Goodby, Robert G., Dennis Howe, and Victoria Bunker

2001 *Technical Report: Archaeological Subsurface Testing Monitoring, Squam Lakes Natural Science Center*. Victoria Bunker, Inc., Report. Alton NH.

Grand Council of the Haudenosaunee
2002 *Building Relationships between Federal Agencies and the Haudenosaunee*. On file at the Public Archaeology Facility, Binghamton University, Binghamton NY.

Guernsey, Samuel J.
1916 Notes on Explorations of Martha's Vineyard. *American Anthropologist* 18(1):81–97.

Harjo, Susan Shown
1996 Introduction to *Mending the Circle, A Native American Repatriation Guide*, edited by B. Meister, pp. 3–7. American Indian Ritual Object Repatriation Foundation, New York.

Harley, J. B.
1994 New England Cartography and the Native Americans. In *American Beginnings: Exploration, Culture, and Cartography in the Land of Norumbega*, edited by E. W. Baker et al., pp. 287–313. University of Nebraska Press, Lincoln.

Harrington, Mark R.
1921 *Religion and Ceremonies of the Lenape*. Indian Notes and Monographs 19. Museum of the American Indian, Heye Foundation, New York.

Harrison, Barbara
2001 *Collaborative Programs in Indigenous Communities: From Fieldwork to Practice*. AltaMira Press, Walnut Creek CA.

Harrison, Rodney, and Christine Williamson (editors)
2004 *After Captain Cook: The Archaeology of the Recent Indigenous Past in Australia*. AltaMira Press, Walnut Creek CA.

Hart, Siobhan M.
2004 Mixed Assemblages and Indigenous Agents: Decolonizing Pine Hill. *Northeast Anthropology* 68:57–71.

Haviland, William
1973 All Wrong. *Vermont Freeman* Early June:19.
1986 It's My Turn—Anthropologists Would Return Indian Bones. *Burlington Free Press* 20 June:15A.

Haviland, William A., and Marjory W. Power
1981 *The Original Vermonters: Native Inhabitants, Past and Present*. University Press of New England, Hanover NH.
1994 *The Original Vermonters: Native Inhabitants, Past and Present*. 2nd ed. University Press of New England, Hanover NH.

Hayes, Charles F., III
1965 *The Orringh Stone Tavern and Three Seneca Sites of the Late Historic Period*. Research Records 12. Rochester Museum of Arts and Sciences, Rochester NY.

Heath, Dwight B. (editor)

1963 [1622] *A Journal of the Pilgrims at Plymouth (Mourt's Relation: A Relation or Journal of the English Plantation Settled at Plymouth in New England, by Certain English Adventurers both Merchants and Others).* Corinth Books, New York.

Heckenberger, Michael J., James B. Petersen, and Louise A. Basa

1990a Early Woodland Period Ritual Use of Personal Adornment at the Boucher Site. *Annals of Carnegie Museum* 59(3):173–217.

Heckenberger, Michael J., James B. Petersen, Ellen R. Cowie, Arthur E. Spiess, Louise A. Basa, and Robert Stuckenrath

1990b Early Woodland Period Mortuary Ceremonialism in the Far Northeast: A View from the Boucher Cemetery. *Archaeology of Eastern North America* 18:109–144.

Heckenberger, Michael J., James B. Petersen, Frances B. King, and Louise A. Basa

1996 Fiber Industries from the Boucher Site: An Early Woodland Cemetery in Northwestern Vermont. In *A Most Indispensable Art: Native Fiber Industries from Eastern North America,* edited by J. B. Petersen, pp. 50–72. University of Tennessee Press, Knoxville.

Hecker, Howard M.

1981 Preliminary Physical Anthropological Report on the 650 Year Old Skeleton from Seabrook, New Hampshire. *Man in the Northeast* 21:37–60.

Heite, Edward F.

1999 *The Nathan Williams Archaeological Site.* Delaware Department of Transportation Archaeology Series 169. Dover.

Heite, Edward F., with Cara L. Blume

1993 *A Community on McKee Road.* Delaware Department of Transportation Archaeological Series 109. Dover.

Heite, Edward F., and Cara L. Blume

1992 *Archaeological and Historical Discoveries in Connection with Scarborough Road, Dover, Kent County, Delaware.* Delaware Department of Transportation Archaeological Series 91. Dover.

1995 *Data Recovery Excavations at the Blueberry Hill Prehistoric Site.* Delaware Department of Transportation Archaeology Series 130. Dover.

n.d. *Mitsawokett to Bloomsbury: Archaeology and History of an Unrecognized Indigenous Community in Central Delaware* (Draft). Delaware Department of Transportation Archaeological Series 154. Dover.

Heite, Louise B.

1984 *Archaeological Investigations at the Mudstone Branch Site, Saulsbury*

Road. Delaware Department of Transportation Archaeology Series 26. Dover.

Heite, Louise B., and Edward F. Heite

1985 *Fork Branch/duPont Station Community Archaeological Investigations on Denney's Road, Dover, Kent County, Delaware*. Delaware Department of Transportation Archaeology Series 37. Dover.

Hemingway, Sam

2003 Abenaki Rap Dean: Stump Speech Contrary to his Vt. Position, They Say. *Burlington Free Press* 20 September:2A.

Henry, Dixie L.

1995 Bringing Our Ancestors Home . . . The Controversy over Repatriation. Summer Research Report, Department of Sociology and Anthropology, Colgate University, Hamilton NY.

1996 "The Tomb of the Red Man": Repatriation and Its Impact on the Role of the Museum. SOAN 490 High Honors Research Paper, Department of Sociology and Anthropology, Colgate University, Hamilton NY.

2001 Cultural Change and Adaptation among the Oneida Iroquois, AD 1000–1700. Unpublished Ph.D. dissertation, Department of Anthropology, Cornell University, Ithaca NY.

Herbster, Holly, and Suzanne Glover

1993 *Archaeological Investigations at Squibnocket Ridge, Chilmark, Massachusetts*. Public Archaeology Laboratory, Inc., Report No. 458. Pawtucket RI.

Hill, Richard

1996 Reflections of a Native Repatriator. In *Mending the Circle, A Native American Repatriation Guide*, edited by B. Meister, pp. 81–96. American Indian Ritual Object Repatriation Foundation, New York.

Hirsch, Eric

1995 Landscape: Between Place and Space. In *The Anthropology of Landscape: Perspectives on Place and Space*, edited by E. Hirsch and M. O'Hanlon, pp. 1–30. Clarendon Press, Oxford.

Hornsby, Stephen J., Victor A. Konrad, and James J. Herlan (editors)

1989 *The Northeastern Borderlands: Four Centuries of Interaction*. Acadiensis Press, Fredericton, New Brunswick.

Hubbard, John D.

1997 An Ancient Wrong Righted. *The Colgate Scene* May:6.

Hutt, Sherry

1994 Overview of NAGPRA, the Law. In *Native American Graves Protection and Repatriation Act: Implications and Practical Applications* (with T. McKeown). Cultural Resource Management, University of Nevada, Anthropology Department, Historic Preservation Department,

Division of Continuing Education, Reno.

Ignorant Savages

1973 *Vermont Freeman* 5(9):9.

Jacobs-Carnahan, Eve

2002 *State of Vermont's Response to Petition for Federal Acknowledgement of the St. Francis/Sokoki Band of the Abenaki Nation of Vermont.* On file at the Office of Attorney General, State of Vermont, Montpelier.

Jefferies, Richard, and Brian M. Butler (editors)

1982 *The Carrier Mills Archaeological Project: Human Adaptation in the Saline Valley, Illinois.* Center for Archaeological Investigations Research Paper No. 33. Southern Illinois University, Carbondale.

Jemison, G. Peter

1997 Who Owns the Past? In *Native Americans and Archaeologists: Stepping Stones to Common Ground*, edited by N. Swidler, K. E. Dongoske, R. Anyon, and A. S. Downer, pp. 57–63. AltaMira Press, Walnut Creek CA.

2000 Sovereignty & Treaty Rights—We Remember. In *Treaty of Canandaigua 1794, 200 Years of Treaty Relations between the Iroquois Confederacy and the United States*, edited by G. P. Jemison and A. M. Schein, pp. 149–161. Clear Light Publishers, Santa Fe NM.

Jones, Brian D.

1997 The Late Paleo-Indian Hidden Creek Site in Southeastern Connecticut. *Archaeology of Eastern North America* 25:45–80.

1998 Human Adaptation to the Changing Northeastern Environment at the End of the Pleistocene. Unpublished Ph.D. dissertation, Department of Anthropology, University of Connecticut, Storrs.

1999 The Middle Archaic Period in Connecticut: The View From Mashantucket. *Bulletin of the Archaeological Society of Connecticut* 62:101–123.

2002 Continuity Versus Change During the Last Three Millennia at Mashantucket. *Northeast Anthropology* 64:17–29.

Jones, Brian D., and Daniel T. Forrest

2003 Life in a Postglacial Landscape: Settlement-Subsistence Change during the Pleistocene-Holocene Transition in Southern New England. In *Geoarchaeology of Landscapes in the Glaciated Northeast*, edited by D. L. Cremeens and J. P. Hart, pp. 75–89. New York State Museum Bulletin 497. Albany.

Jones, Lisa

2000 Real Estate vs. Respect for Dead: Construction Fuels Abenaki Battle for Land, Recognition, Protection of Ancient Burial Ground in Highgate. *Burlington Free Press* 19 November:1A, 6A.

Keemer, Kelly, and Amanda Williams

2003 *Medicinal Herb Resource Guide: SHARE Farm,* 2003. SHARE, Union Springs NY.

Kelley, Marc A., Paul S. Sledsik, and Sean P. Murphy

1987 Health, Demographics and Physical Constitution in Seventeenth-Century Rhode Island Indians. *Man in the Northeast* 34:1–25.

Kellogg, Douglas C.

1987 Statistical Relevance and Site Locational Data. *American Antiquity* 52(1):143–150.

1994 Why Did They Choose to Live Here? Ceramic Period Settlement in the Boothbay, Maine, Region. *Northeast Anthropology* 48:25–60.

Kenny, Kathleen M., James B. Petersen, John G. Crock, Geoffrey A. Mandel, and Chris K. Slesar

2003 *Life and Death in the Northeast Kingdom: Archaeology and History at the Old Burial Ground in St. Johnsbury, Vermont, ca. 1790–1853.* Consulting Archaeology Program Report No. 303. University of Vermont, Burlington.

Kerber, Jordan E.

1997 *Lambert Farm: Public Archaeology and Canine Burials along Narragansett Bay.* Case Studies in Archaeology. Harcourt Brace College Publishers, New York.

2003 Community-Based Archaeology in Central New York: Workshops Involving Native American Youth. *The Public Historian* 25(1):83–90.

Kerber, Jordan E., Bridget Benisch, and Terrence Zinn (editors)

2000 *Archaeological Investigations in Central New York: Colgate University Field Methods Project.* Vol. 3. Department of Sociology and Anthropology, Colgate University, Hamilton NY.

Kerber, Jordan E., Seth Bidder, and Michael Wild (editors)

2003 *Archaeological Investigations in Central New York: Colgate University Field Methods Project.* Vol. 5. Department of Sociology and Anthropology, Colgate University, Hamilton NY.

Kerber, Jordan E., Bryan Deegan, and Christen Monk (editors)

2002 *Archaeological Investigations in Central New York: Colgate University Field Methods Project.* Vol. 4. Department of Sociology and Anthropology, Colgate University, Hamilton NY.

Kerber, Jordan E., Megan Glennon, and Thomas Palmer (editors)

1996 *Archaeological Investigations in the Chenango Valley: Colgate University Field Methods Project.* Vol. 5. Department of Sociology and Anthropology, Colgate University, Hamilton NY.

Kerber, Jordan E., and Dixie L. Henry (editors)

1998 *Archaeological Investigations in Central New York: Colgate University*

Field Methods Project. Vol. 1. Department of Sociology and
Anthropology, Colgate University, Hamilton NY.

Kerber, Jordan E., Corrine Ochsner, and Helen Saul (editors)

1999 *Archaeological Investigations in Central New York: Colgate University
Field Methods Project.* Vol. 2. Department of Sociology and
Anthropology, Colgate University, Hamilton NY.

King, Thomas S.

1998 *Cultural Resource Laws and Practice, an Introductory Guide.* AltaMira
Press, Walnut Creek CA.

2002 *Thinking About Cultural Resource Management, Essays from the Edge.*
AltaMira Press, Walnut Creek CA.

Kingsley, Robert G., and Billy R. Roulette Jr.

1990 *The Joyner Site: Late Archaic–Early Woodland Adaptations and
Cultural Dynamics in Conanicut Island, Rhode Island.* John Milner
Associates, Inc., Report. Philadelphia PA.

Klesert, Anthony L., and Alan S. Downer (editors)

1990 *Preservation on the Reservation: Native Americans, Native American
Lands, and Archaeology.* Navajo Nation Papers in Anthropology No.
26. Navajo Nation Archeology Department and the Navajo Nation
Historic Preservation Department, Window Rock AZ.

Kraft, Herbert C.

2001 *The Lenape-Delaware Indian Heritage: 10,000 B.C. to A.D. 2000.*
Lenape Books, Stanhope NJ.

Krim, Arthur J.

1980 Acculturation of the New England Landscape: Native and English
Toponymy of Eastern Massachusetts. In *New England Prospect:
Maps, Place Names, and the Historical Landscape,* edited by P.
Benes, pp. 69–88. Dublin Seminar for New England Folklife Annual
Proceedings. Boston University Press, Boston.

Kriss, Erik

2004 UCE Wants Pataki Impeached. *Syracuse Post-Standard* 14 February:
A-1.

Lacy, David M.

1989 A "Human Remains Policy": Observations from the Green Mountain
National Forest, Vermont. Paper presented at the Conference on New
England Archaeology, Sturbridge MA.

1994 Prehistoric Land-Use in the Green Mountains: A View from the
National Forest. *The Journal of Vermont Archaeology* 1:92–102.

1999a Myth Busting and Prehistoric Land Use in the Green Mountains of
Vermont. In *The Archaeological Northeast,* edited by M. A. Levine,
K. E. Sassaman, and M. S. Nassaney, pp 115–124. Bergin & Garvey,
Westport CT.

1999b Establishing Government to Government Relations: Identifying and Incorporating Abenaki Concerns in the Federal Planning Process. Paper presented at the Conference "Reflections on Remembering and Forgetting: Revisiting 'The Original Vermonters,' " University of Vermont, Burlington.

Lacy, David M., and Cheryl Bluto-Delvental

1995 Common Ground: Joint Stewardship of Abenaki Heritage Sites on the Green Mountain National Forest. Paper presented at the 35th Annual Meeting of the Northeastern Anthropological Association, Lake Placid NY.

Lacy, David M., John Moody, and Jesse Bruchac

1992 *Preliminary Heritage Resources Reconnaissance Report: Pico/ Killington "Preferred" and "No Action" Alternatives.* Green Mountain National Forest. Submitted to the National Park Service Eastern Team, Applied Archaeology Center, Denver CO.

LaFantasie, Glenn W. (editor)

1988 *The Correspondence of Roger Williams.* Published for the Rhode Island Historical Society by Brown University Press/University Press of New England, Hanover NH.

LaFantasie, Glenn W., and Paul R. Campbell

1978 *Land Controversies and the Narragansett Indians, 1880–1938.* On file at the Office of Attorney General, State of Rhode Island, Providence.

Largy, Tonya, Peter Burns, Elizabeth S. Chilton, and Dianna L. Doucette

2002 Lucy Vincent Beach: Another Look at the Prehistoric Exploitation of Piscine Resources off the Coast of Massachusetts, U.S.A. *Northeast Anthropology* 64:67–73.

Lassiter, Luke Eric

2004 Collaborative Ethnography. *AnthroNotes* 25(1):1–9.

LeSourd, Philip S.

1984 *Kolusuwakonol: Passamaquoddy-Maliseet Dictionary.* Micmac-Maliseet Institute, University of New Brunswick, Fredericton.

Leveillee, Alan

1998 *"An Old Place, Safe and Quiet": Program of Archaeological Data Recovery Millbury III Cremation Complex, Millbury Massachusetts.* Vols. I and II. Public Archaeology Laboratory, Inc., Report No. 396. Pawtucket RI.

1999 *A History Written in Stone: Six Thousand Years of Native American Land Use in the Narragansett Bay Region.* Public Archaeology Laboratory, Inc., Report. Pawtucket RI.

2002a *An Old Place, Safe and Quiet: A Blackstone River Valley Cremation Burial Site.* Bergin & Garvey, Westport CT.

2002b Applied Archaeology Influencing Native Traditions: A Case From Rhode Island. *Archaeology of Eastern North America* 30:1–28.

Levine, Mary Ann
2003 The Cayuga Lake Archaeology Project: Surveying Marginalized Landscapes in New York's Finger Lakes Region. *Archaeology of Eastern North America* 31:133–150.

Little, Elizabeth A.
1994 *Abram Quary of Abram's Point, Nantucket Island.* Nantucket Algonquian Studies No. 16. Nantucket Historical Association, Nantucket MA.

Little, Elizabeth A., and Margaret J. Schoeninger
1995 The Late Woodland Diet on Nantucket Island and the Problem of Maize in Coastal New England. *American Antiquity* 60(2):351–368.

Lounsbury, Floyd G.
1978 Iroquoian Languages. In *Northeast*, edited by B. G. Trigger, pp. 334–343. Handbook of North American Indians, Vol. 15, W. C. Sturtevant, general editor. Smithsonian Institution Press, Washington DC.

Lowenthal, David
2000 *George Perkins Marsh: Prophet of Conservation.* University of Washington Press, Seattle.

Lowie, Robert H.
1954 *Indians of the Plains.* The Natural History Press, Garden City NY.

McBride, Kevin A.
1990 The Historical Archaeology of the Mashantucket Pequot. In *The Pequots: The Fall and Rise of an American Indian Nation*, edited by L. M. Hauptman and J. D. Wherry, pp. 96–116. University of Oklahoma Press, Norman.
1992 Prehistoric and Historic Patterns of Wetland Use in Eastern Connecticut. *Man in the Northeast* 43:10–24.
1993 "Ancient & Crazie": Pequot Lifeways During the Historic Period. In *Algonkians of New England: Past and Present*, edited by P. Benes and J. M. Benes, pp. 63–75. Annual Proceedings of the 1991 Dublin Folklife Seminar. Boston University Press, Boston.
1996 The Legacy of Robin Cassacinamon: Mashantucket Leadership in the Historic Period. In *Northeastern Indian Lives, 1632–1816*, edited by R. S. Grumet, pp. 74–93. University of Massachusetts Press, Boston.
1998 The Mashantucket Pequot Reservation Archaeological District National Landmark. *Bulletin of the Archaeological Society of Connecticut* 63:32–43.

McBride, Kevin A., and Suzanne G. Cherau
1996 Gay Head (Aquinnah) Wampanoag Community Structure and Land

Use Patterns. *Northeast Anthropology* 51:13–39.

McCarroll, Christina
2001 Oneida Teens Unearth Layers of Their History. *Christian Science Monitor* 14 August:14–15.

McKeown, C. Timothy (guest editor)
1995 Special Report: The Native American Graves Protection and Repatriation Act. *Federal Archaeology* 7(3).

McManamon, Francis P., James W. Bradley, and Ann L. Magennis
1986 *The Indian Neck Ossuary. Chapters in the Archeology of Cape Cod, V.* Cultural Resources Management Study No. 17. National Park Service, Division of Cultural Resources, North Atlantic Regional Office, Boston.

MacQuarrie, Brian
1998 Scoop by Scoop, Team Unearths Vineyard's Past. *Boston Globe* 5 July: B1.

McWeeney, Lucinda J.
1994 Archaeological Settlement Patterns and Vegetation Dynamics in Southern New England in the Late Quaternary. Unpublished Ph.D. dissertation, Department of Anthropology, Yale University, New Haven CT.
1999 A Review of Late Pleistocene and Holocene Climate Changes in Southern New England. *Bulletin of the Archaeological Society of Connecticut* 62:3–18.

Malone, Jena, and Stephen Hanks
1999/2000 What I Dug on My Summer Vacation. *Dig: The Archaeology Magazine for Kids* December/January:22–23.

Marks, Jonathan M.
2002 *What it Means to be 98% Chimpanzee: Apes, People, and Their Genes.* University of California Press, Berkeley.

Marsh, George Perkins
1998 [1864] *Man and Nature—Or, Physical Geography as Modified by Human Action.* Seventh printing of 1965 edition, edited by David Lowenthal, Harvard University Press, Cambridge MA.

Mason, Ronald J.
2000 Archaeology and Native North American Oral Traditions. *American Antiquity* 65(2):239–266.

Massachusetts Historical Commission (MHC)
n.d. *Guidelines for the Analysis of Human Skeletal Remains.* On file at the Massachusetts Historical Commission, Boston.

Mattfeld, William H.
1980 *Guidelines for the Protection of Ancient Indian Burials for the*

Massachusetts Historical Commission. On file at the Massachusetts Historical Commission, Boston.

Medaglia, Christian C., Elizabeth A. Little, and Margaret J. Schoeninger
1990 Late Woodland Diet on Nantucket Island: A Study Using Stable Isotope Ratios. *Bulletin of the Massachusetts Archaeological Society* 51:49–60.

Mihesuah, Devon A. (editor)
2000 *Repatriation Reader: Who Owns American Indian Remains?* University of Nebraska Press, Lincoln.

Mills, Barbara J.
2003 Review of *Indigenous Archaeology: American Indian Values and Scientific Practice*, by J. Watkins. *American Anthropologist* 105(2):473–474.

Milun, Kathryn
2001 Keeping-While-Giving-Back: Computer Imaging, Native American Repatriation, and an Argument for Cultural Harm. *PoLAR: Political and Legal Anthropology Review* 24(2):39–57.

Moragne, Steven
2001 Faunal Analysis of the Patrick Tavern Site, Aurora, New York. Senior honors thesis, Department of Anthropology, Ithaca College, Ithaca NY.

Morenon, E. Pierre
2003 Nagged by NAGPRA: Is There an Archaeological Ethic? In *Ethics and the Profession of Anthropology: Dialogue for Ethically Conscious Practice*, edited by C. Fluehr-Lobban, pp. 107–140. 2nd ed. AltaMira Press, Walnut Creek CA.

Morgan, Lewis Henry
1969 [1851] *League of the Iroquois*. Corinth Books, New York.

Morphy, Howard
1995 Landscape and the Reproduction of the Ancestral Past. In *The Anthropology of Landscape: Perspectives on Place and Space*, edited by E. Hirsch and M. O'Hanlon, pp. 184–209. Clarendon Press, Oxford.

Murphy, Tim
1986 Indian Remains, Artifacts Returned to Narragansetts. *Providence Journal-Bulletin* 16 January:B3.

Nassaney, Michael S.
1989 An Epistemological Enquiry into Some Archaeological and Historical Interpretations of Seventeeth-Century Native American-European Relations. In *Archaeological Approaches to Cultural Identity*, edited by S. Shennan, pp. 76–93. Unwin Hyman, London.

New York Archaeological Council (NYAC)

1994 *Standards for Cultural Resource Investigations and the Curation of Archaeological Collections in New York State.* On file at the New York State Office of Parks, Recreation, and Historic Preservation, Waterford.

New York State Education Department (NYSED)

1998 *Work Scope Specifications for Cultural Resource Investigations.* New York State Education Department, New York State Museum, Albany.

Nicholas, Andrea Bear, and Harald E. L. Prins

1989 Spirit in the Land: The Native People of Aroostook. In *The County: Land of Promise: A Pictorial History of Aroostook County, Maine,* edited by A. F. McGrath, pp. 25–26. Donning Company, Norfolk VA.

Nicholas, George P.

1997 Education and Empowerment: Archaeology with, for, and by the Shuswap Nation, British Columbia. In *At a Crossroads: Archaeology and First Peoples in Canada,* edited by G. P. Nicholas and T. D. Andrews, pp. 85–104. Publication No. 24, Department of Archaeology, Simon Fraser University. Archaeology Press, Burnaby, British Columbia.

Nicholas, George P., and Thomas D. Andrews (editors)

1997 *At a Crossroads: Archaeology and First Peoples in Canada.* Publication No. 24, Department of Archaeology, Simon Fraser University. Archaeology Press, Burnaby, British Columbia.

Niemczycki, Mary Ann Palmer

1984 *The Origin and Development of the Seneca and Cayuga Tribes of New York State.* Research Records 17. Rochester Museum and Science Center, Rochester NY.

O'Brien, Jean M.

1997 *Dispossession By Degrees: Indian Land and Identity in Natick, Massachusetts, 1650–1790.* Cambridge University Press, Cambridge.

O'Shea, John M.

1984 *Mortuary Variability: An Archaeological Investigation.* Academic Press, Orlando FL.

Oswalt, Wendell H.

1978 *This Land Was Theirs: A Study of North American Indians.* John Wiley and Sons, New York.

Parker, Arthur C.

1968 The Constitution of the Five Nations. In *Parker on the Iroquois,* edited by W. N. Fenton, pp. 8–64. Syracuse University Press, Syracuse NY.

Patterson, Rick

2001 *Black Creek Site National Register Nomination.* On file at the New Jersey Historic Preservation Office, Trenton.

Pawling, Micah A.

1999 Petitions, Kin, and Cultural Survival: The Maliseet and Passamaquoddy Peoples in the Nineteenth Century. M.A. thesis, Department of History, University of Maine, Orono.

Pearce, Margaret W.

2004 Encroachment by Word, Axis, and Tree: Mapping Techniques from the Colonization of New England. *Cartographic Perspectives* 48:24–38.

Perrelli, Douglas J., Ellen Biederman, and Mary F. Hofmeier

1998 *Archaeological and Architectural Reconnaissance Survey for the Replacement of the Cotton Road Bridge (Route 951) over the Allegheny River, Town of Allegany, Cattaraugus County, New York.* Reports of the Archaeological Survey 30(18). Department of Anthropology, State University of New York, Buffalo.

Perrelli, Douglas J., James E. Hartner, and Ellen Biederman

2001 *Archaeological and Architectural Reconnaissance Survey for the Replacement of the US Route 20/NY Route 5 Bridge over Cattaraugus Creek, Town of Hanover, Chautauqua County, New York.* Reports of the Archaeological Survey 33(4). Department of Anthropology, State University of New York, Buffalo.

Petraglia, Michael D., Susan L. Bupp, Sean P. Fitzell, and Kevin W. Cunningham

2002 *Hickory Bluff: Changing Perceptions of Delmarva Archaeology.* Vols. I and II. Delaware Department of Transportation Archaeology Series, No. 175. Dover.

Philbrick, Nathaniel

1998 *Abram's Eyes: The Native American Legacy of Nantucket Island.* Mill Hill Press, Nantucket MA.

Poirier, David, Nicholas Bellantoni, and Mikki Aganstata

1985 Native American Burials: The Ethical, Scientific and Bureaucratic Matrix. *Bulletin of the Archaeological Society of Connecticut* 48:3–12.

Pollack, David

1998 Intraregional and Intersocietal Relationships of the Late Mississippian Caborn-Welborn Phase of the Lower Ohio River Valley. Unpublished Ph.D. dissertation, Department of Anthropology, University of Kentucky, Lexington.

Porter, Frank W., III

1987 *The Nanticoke.* Chelsea House, New York.

Potter, James M.

2004 The Creation of Person, the Creation of Space: Hunting Landscapes in the American Southwest. *American Antiquity* 69(2):322–338.

Powless, Chief Irving

2000 Treaty Making. In *Treaty of Canandaigua 1794, 200 Years of Treaty Relations between the Iroquois Confederacy and the United States*, edited by G. P. Jemison and A. M. Schein, pp. 15–34. Clear Light Publishers, Santa Fe NM.

Pratt, Peter P.

1976 *Archaeology of the Oneida Iroquois*. Vol. I. Man in The Northeast, Inc., George's Mill NH.

Prewitt, Terry J.

2001 The Big House Described. In *Voices from the Delaware Big House Ceremony*, edited by R. S. Grumet, pp. 3–22. University of Oklahoma Press, Norman.

Price, H. Marcus, III

1991 *Disputing the Dead: U.S. Law on Aboriginal Remains and Grave Goods*. University of Missouri Press, Columbia MO.

Prins, Harald E. L.

1996 *Mi'kmaq: Resistance, Accommodation, and Cultural Survival*. Harcourt Brace Publishers, New York.

Prucha, Francis Paul

1962 *American Indian Policy in the Formative Years: The Indian Trade and Intercourse Acts 1790–1834*. Harvard University Press, Cambridge MA.

Putnam, Cora Carpenter

1958 *Story of Houlton*. House of Falmouth, Inc., Portland ME.

Putnam, David E.

1996 *Phase I Archaeological Survey of the Proposed Maine Department of Inland Fisheries and Wildlife Boat Landing, Presque Isle, Maine*. On file at the Maine Historic Preservation Commission, Augusta.

Ravesloot, John C.

1997 Changing Native American Perceptions of Archaeology and Archaeologists. In *Native Americans and Archaeologists: Stepping Stones to Common Ground*, edited by N. Swidler, K. E. Dongoske, R. Anyon, and A. S. Downer, pp. 172–177. AltaMira Press, Walnut Creek CA.

Rhode Island Historical Preservation and Heritage Commission (RIHPHC)

1988 *Guidelines for Indian Participation on Archaeological Surveys*. Rhode Island Historical Preservation and Heritage Commission, Providence.

Ritchie, William A.

1945 *An Early Site in Cayuga County, New York: Type Component of the Frontenac Focus, Archaic Pattern*. Researches and Transactions of the New York State Archaeological Association 10(1). Lewis Henry Morgan Chapter, Rochester.

1969 *The Archaeology of Martha's Vineyard*. Natural History Press, Garden City NY.

Robinson, Brian S., and Charles S. Bolian
  1987 A Preliminary Report on the Rock's Road Site (Seabrook Station):
      A Late Archaic to Contact Period Occupation in Seabrook, New
      Hampshire. *New Hampshire Archeologist* 28(1):19–51.
Robinson, Paul A.
  1990 The Struggle Within: The Indian Debate in Seventeenth-Century
      Narragansett Country. Unpublished Ph.D. dissertation, Department
      of Anthropology, Binghamton University, Binghamton NY.
  1994 Archaeology, History, and Native Americans: Preserving the Richness
      of the Past. In *Cultural Resource Management: Archaeological
      Research, Preservation Planning, and Public Education in the
      Northeastern United States*, edited by J. E. Kerber, pp. 87–95. Bergin &
      Garvey, Westport CT.
Robinson, Paul A., Marc A. Kelley, and Patricia E. Rubertone
  1985 Preliminary Biocultural Interpretations from a Seventeenth-Century
      Narragansett Indian Cemetery in Rhode Island. In *Cultures in
      Contact: The Impact of European Contacts on Native American
      Cultural Institutions, A.D. 1000–1800*, edited by W. W. Fitzhugh, pp.
      107–130. Smithsonian Institution Press, Washington DC.
Robinson, Paul A., and Charlotte C. Taylor
  2000 Heritage Management in Rhode Island: Working with Diverse
      Partners and Audiences. In *Cultural Resource Management in
      Contemporary Society: Perspectives on Managing and Presenting
      the Past*, edited by F. P. McManamon and A. Hatton, pp. 107–119.
      Routledge, London.
Robinson, Paul A., Charlotte C. Taylor, and Pamela Kennedy
  2002 *Native American Archaeology in Rhode Island*. Rhode Island
      Historical Preservation and Heritage Commission, Providence.
Rountree, Helen C.
  1989 *The Powhatan Indians of Virginia: Their Traditional Culture*.
      University of Oklahoma Press, Norman.
Rowland, Erin
  2003 Massachusetts Projects Advance National Tribal Lands Program. *The
      Trust for Public Land New England Newsletter* Spring:1, 10.
Rubertone, Patricia E.
  2001 *Grave Undertakings: An Archaeology of Roger Williams and the
      Narragansett Indians*. Smithsonian Institution Press, Washington DC.
Salisbury, Neal
  1982 *Manitou and Providence: Indians, Europeans, and the Making of New
      England, 1500–1643*. Oxford University Press, New York.
Sanger, David
  1987 *The Carson Site and the Late Ceramic Period in Passamaquoddy*

Bay, New Brunswick. Mercury Series 135. Canadian Museum of Civilization, Ottawa.

1996a An Analysis of Seasonal Transhumance Models for Pre-European State of Maine. *Review of Archaeology* 17(1):54–58.

1996b Testing the Models: Hunter-Gatherer Use of Space in the Gulf of Maine, USA. *World Archaeology* 27:512–526.

2002 Archaeological Taxonomy: Beyond Typology to Behavior. *Review of Archaeology* 23(1):5–11.

Sanger, David, and Douglas C. Kellogg

1989 Prehistoric Archaeology and Evidence of Coastal Subsidence on the Coast of Maine. In *Neotectonics of Maine*, edited by W. Anderson, and H. W. Borns Jr., pp. 107–126. Vol. 40. Maine Geological Survey, Augusta.

Sanger, Mary E.

1980 William Francis Ganong, Regional Historian. M.A. thesis, Department of History, University of Maine, Orono.

Santone, Lenore, Rhea J. Rogers, Henry M. R. Holt, and Ronald C. Kearns

1997 *Phase III Archaeological Data Recovery, Maple Grange Road Bridge Site (28–Sx-297): Maple Grange Road, Vernon Township, Sussex County, New Jersey*. The Cultural Resource Group, Louis Berger & Associates Report. East Orange NJ.

Schoch, Deborah

1986a Bones Give Secrets of Vermont Past. *Burlington Free Press* 1 June:1A, 18A.

1986b Abenakis Want Remains Back. *Burlington Free Press* 1 June:1A, 18A.

Seneca Nation of Indians

1986 *Archaeological Policy*. On file at the Seneca Nation of Indians Tribal Historic Preservation Office, Salamanca NY.

Shen, Fern

1989 Indian Bones Pit Religion Against Science: Tests on Maryland Find Opposed. *Washington Post* 17 October:B1, B7.

Simmons, William S.

1989 *The Narragansett*. Chelsea House, New York.

Simon, Brona G.

1988 *Preliminary Field Report: Miacomet Village Elderly and Family Housing/Miacomet Praying Indian Burial Ground, Nantucket*. On file at the Massachusetts Historical Commission, Boston. Revised 1990.

1990 Native American Culture Change and Persistence in Contact Period New England: Analysis of Mortuary Data from a Praying Indian Burial Ground in Massachusetts. Paper presented at the 55th Annual Meeting of the Society for American Archaeology, Las Vegas NV.

1995 Office of the State Archaeologist and Repatriation. *Massachusetts Archaeological Society Newsletter* 21(3):1.

Simon, Brona G., and Valerie A. Talmage

1989 The Status of State Programs Protecting Burial Sites in New England. *Conference on New England Archaeology Newsletter* 8(2):3–12.

Slattery, Richard G., and Douglas R. Woodward

1992 *The Montgomery Focus: A Late Woodland Potomac River Culture.* Archaeological Society of Maryland Bulletin 2.

Sleeper, Frank H.

2002 *Baxter State Park and the Allagash River.* Arcadia Publishing, Charleston SC.

Smith, Claire, and H. Martin Wobst (editors)

2005 *Indigenous Archaeologies: Decolonising Theory and Practice.* Routledge, London.

Snow, Dean R.

1980 *The Archaeology of New England.* Academic Press, New York.

Soctomah, Donald G.

2002 *Passamaquoddy at the Turn of the Century, 1890–1920: Tribal Life and Times in Maine and New Brunswick.* Passamaquoddy Tribe of Indian Township, Princeton ME.

2003 *Hard Times at Passamaquoddy, 1921–1950: Tribal Life and Times in Maine and New Brunswick.* Passamaquoddy Tribe of Indian Township, Princeton ME.

Soctomah, Donald G., and Edward Bassett

2004 *Landscapes, Legends and Language of the Passamaquoddy People: An Interactive Journey in the Land of the Passamaquoddy.* CD available from the Maine Indian Basketmakers Alliance, 240 Main St., Old Town ME 04468.

Speck, Frank G.

1915 The Nanticoke Community of Delaware. *Contributions from the Museum of the American Indian, Heye Foundation* 2(4). New York.

1940 *Penobscot Man: The Life History of a Forest Tribe in Maine.* University of Pennsylvania Press, Philadelphia.

1942 Back Again to Indian River, Its People and Their Games. *Bulletin of the Archaeological Society of Delaware* 3(5):17–24.

Stapp, Darby C., and Michael S. Burney

2002 *Tribal Cultural Resource Management: The Full Circle to Stewardship.* AltaMira Press, Walnut Creek CA.

Stetson, Frederick

1973 Highgate Indian Burial Site Offers Insights. *Burlington Free Press* 18 October:1A–2A.

Stith, John

    2003 Miles Apart on Cayugas: In Union Springs, a Protest; in Springport, a Festival. *Syracuse Post-Standard* 15 June:B1–B2.

Strachey, William

    1953 [1612] *The Historie of Travell into Virginia Britania.* Series 2, No. 103, edited by L. B. Wright and V. Freund. Hakluyt Society, London.

Swidler, Nina, Kurt E. Dongoske, Roger Anyon, and Alan S. Downer (editors)

    1997 *Native Americans and Archaeologists: Stepping Stones to Common Ground.* AltaMira Press, Walnut Creek CA.

Talmage, Valerie A.

    1982a The Violation of Sepulture: Is it Legal to Excavate Human Burials? *Archaeology* 35(6):44–49.

    1982b Massachusetts General Laws and Human Burials. *Bulletin of the Massachusetts Archaeological Society* 43(2):60–65.

    1984 New Legislation Protects Indian Burial Sites. *Massachusetts Historical Commission Newsletter* May:10.

Tanner, Adrian

    1979 *Bringing Home Animals: Religious Ideology and Mode of Production of the Mistassini Cree Hunters.* C. Hurst & Company, London.

Tantaquidgeon, Gladys

    1942 *A Study of Delaware Indian Medicine Practices and Folk Beliefs.* Pennsylvania Historical Commission, Harrisburg.

Taylor, Alan

    2000 Centers and Peripheries: Locating Maine's History. *Maine History* 39(1):3–16.

Theft from the Dead.

    1986 In *Art from Ganondagan, the Village of Peace,* p. 8. New York State Office of Parks, Recreation, and Historic Preservation, Bureau of Historic Sites, Waterford.

Thomas, David Hurst

    2000 *Skull Wars: Kennewick Man, Archaeology, and the Battle for Native American Identity.* Basic Books, New York.

Thomas, Matthew

    2004 Narragansetts Have Right to Their Dream: Still Fighting King Philip's War. *Providence Journal-Bulletin* 3 March:B7.

Thomas, Peter A.

    1994 Vermont Archaeology Comes of Age: Perspective on Vermont's Prehistoric Past. *The Journal of Vermont Archaeology* 1:38–91.

Thorson, Robert M., and Robert S. Webb

    1991 Postglacial History of a Cedar Swamp in Southeastern Connecticut. *Journal of Paleolimnology* 6:17–35.

Trust for Public Land
2002 Wampanoag Successes Inaugurate New England Region into Tribal Lands Program. *The Trust for Public Land Tribal Lands Program Newsletter* 1(3):1, 3.

Turnbaugh, William A.
1984 *The Material Culture of RI 1000: A Mid-Seventeenth-Century Narragansett Burial Site in North Kingstown, Rhode Island.* On file at the Department of Sociology and Anthropology, University of Rhode Island, Kingston.

200 UCE Vehicles Protest at Cayuga Nation Store.
2003 *Syracuse Post-Standard* 23 November:B-1.

Upstate Citizens for Equality
2003 The Cayuga Indians and Their Claim: Historic Perspective. Electronic document, http://upstate-citizens.org/cayugaclaim.htm, accessed January 5, 2004.

USDA Forest Service
2003 *Report of the National Tribal Relations Program Implementation Team, June 2003.* U.S. Government Printing Office, No. 2003–0–583–088/60009, Washington DC.

van Gelder, Sarah
1999 Corporate Futures. *Yes!* 10(Summer):40–45.

Vaughan, Jon
2002 *Coastal Effects: Cape Cod, Martha's Vineyard & Nantucket.* Yankee Ingenuity, Chatham MA.

Waller, Joseph N., Alan Leveillee, and A. Peter Mair II
2001 *Archaeological Monitoring: Southwest Avenue 3R Improvements Project, Jamestown, Rhode Island.* Public Archaeology Laboratory, Inc., Report. Pawtucket RI.

Walters, Jolene
2003 Oneidas' History Unearthed. *Oneida Daily Dispatch* 19 February:1,14.

Warfield, Ruth
1995 Talking Stick Discussions. *"Round Robbins" Newsletter of the Friends of the Robbins Museum/Massachusetts Archaeological Society* Winter:4–5.

Warner, Gene, and Barbara O'Brien
1988 1812 Repatriation Ceremony Stirs Memories, Emotions in Fort Erie. *Buffalo News* 1 July:C1.

Watkins, Joe E.
2000a *Indigenous Archaeology: American Indian Values and Scientific Practice.* AltaMira Press, Walnut Creek CA.
2000b Native Americans, Western Science, and NAGPRA. In *Working*

Together: Native Americans and Archaeologists, edited by K. E. Dongoske, M. Aldenderfer, and K. Doehner, pp. 91–96. Society for American Archaeology, Washington DC.

2003 Beyond the Margin: American Indians, First Nations, and Archaeology in North America. *American Antiquity* 68(2):273–285.

Weslager, C. A.

1943a *Delaware's Forgotten Folk: The Story of the Moors & Nanticokes.* University of Pennsylvania Press, Philadelphia.

1943b Indian Village of Lewes, Delaware. *Bulletin of the Archaeological Society of Delaware* 4(1):13.

1949 The Indians of Lewes, Delaware and an Unpublished Indian Deed Dated June 7, 1659. *Bulletin of the Archaeological Society of Delaware* 4(5):6–14.

1972 *The Delaware Indians: A History.* Rutgers University Press, New Brunswick NJ.

White, Marian E.

1961 *Iroquois Culture History in the Niagara Frontier Area of New York State.* Anthropological Papers 16. Museum of Anthropology, University of Michigan, Ann Arbor.

1970 Foreword to *Archaeological Salvage Work on New York State Highways, 1963–69*, edited by W. E. Engelbrecht, M. E. White, and E. Sidler, pp. 1–2. Department of Anthropology, State University of New York, Buffalo.

1977 The Shelby Site Reexamined. In *Current Perspectives in Northeastern Archaeology: Essays in Honor of William A. Ritchie*, edited by R. E. Funk and C. F. Hayes III, pp. 85–91. New York State Archaeological Association, Rochester NY.

White Deer, Gary

2000 From Specimens to SAA Speakers: Evolution by Federal Mandate. In *Working Together: Native Americans and Archaeologists*, edited by K. E. Dongoske, M. Aldenderfer, and K. Doehner, pp. 9–14. Society for American Archaeology, Washington DC.

Willey, Gordon R.

1953 *Prehistoric Settlement Patterns in the Virú Valley, Peru.* Bureau of American Ethnology 155. Smithsonian Institution, Washington DC.

Willey, Gordon R., and Philip Phillips

1958 *Method and Theory in American Archaeology.* University of Chicago Press, Chicago.

Williams, Paul

2000 Treaty Making: The Legal Record. In *Treaty of Canandaigua 1794, 200 Years of Treaty Relations between the Iroquois Confederacy and the United States*, edited by G. P. Jemison and A. M. Schein, pp. 35–42. Clear Light Publishers, Santa Fe NM.

Winter, Eugene

1999 An Early Woodland Date for the Smyth Site, NH 3–84. *Newsletter of the New Hampshire Archeological Society* 15(1):11.

Wise, Cara L.

1984 *Cultural Resources Management Plan for Killens Pond State Park.* Delaware Division of Parks and Recreation, Dover.

Wiseman, Frederick Matthew

2001 *The Voice of the Dawn: An Autohistory of the Abenaki Nation.* University Press of New England, Hanover.

Wright, Muriel H.

1979 *A Guide to the Indian Tribes of Oklahoma.* 7th ed. University of Oklahoma Press, Norman.

About the Contributors

IRA BECKERMAN, Cultural Resources Section Chief, Bureau of Design, Pennsylvania Department of Transportation.

DEBORAH E. BLOM, Associate Professor of Anthropology, Department of Anthropology, University of Vermont.

CARA LEE BLUME, Cultural Heritage Program Manager, Delaware Division of Parks and Recreation.

JOHN B. BROWN III, Tribal Historic Preservation Officer, Medicineman-in-Training, Tribal Council Member, Narragansett Indian Tribe, Rhode Island.

SUZANNE CHERAU, Senior Archaeologist, Public Archaeology Laboratory, Inc., Rhode Island.

ELIZABETH S. CHILTON, Associate Professor of Anthropology, Department of Anthropology, University of Massachusetts Amherst.

KEVIN CUNNINGHAM, Archaeologist, Delaware Department of Transportation.

ROBERT L. DEAN, Tribal Historic Preservation Office, Seneca Nation; and President, Heritage Preservation and Interpretation, Inc., New York.

ROBERT G. GOODBY, Associate Professor of Anthropology, Department of Anthropology, Franklin Pierce College, New Hampshire.

DIXIE L. HENRY, Preservation Officer, Maryland Historical Trust.

HOLLY HERBSTER, Project Archaeologist, Public Archaeology Laboratory, Inc., Rhode Island.

RICHARD W. HILL SR., Director, Haudenosaunee Resource Center, Tonawanda Seneca Nation; Chairperson, Haudenosaunee Standing Committee on Burial Rules and Regulations; and Member of the Tuscarora Nation at Six Nations in Ontario.

RICHARD B. HUGHES, Chief, Office of Archaeology, Maryland Historical Trust.

BERNARD JEROME, Director of Cultural Programs and Member, Aroostook Band of Micmacs, Maine.

BRIAN D. JONES, Senior Archaeologist, Public Archaeology Survey Team, Inc., Connecticut.

JORDAN E. KERBER, Associate Professor of Anthropology, Department of Sociology and Anthropology, and Curator of Collections, Longyear Museum of Anthropology, Colgate University, New York.

DAVID M. LACY, Forest Archaeologist, USDA Green Mountain National Forest, Vermont.

KEVIN A. MCBRIDE, Associate Professor of Anthropology, Department of Anthropology, University of Connecticut; and Director of Research, Mashantucket Pequot Museum and Research Center, Connecticut.

DONNA ROBERTS MOODY, Repatriation and Site Protection Coordinator, Abenaki Nation.

MICAH A. PAWLING, Ph.D. Candidate, Department of History, University of Maine at Orono.

DOUGLAS J. PERRELLI, Director, Archaeological Survey, University at Buffalo, State University of New York.

RAMONA L. PETERS, Repatriation Coordinator, Wampanoag Confederation; and Member of the Mashpee Wampanoag Tribe, Massachusetts.

JAMES B. PETERSEN (1954–2005), Professor of Anthropology, Department of Anthropology, University of Vermont.

MICHAEL D. PETRAGLIA, Lecturer, Leverhulme Centre for Human Evolutionary Studies, University of Cambridge, England.

DAVID E. PUTNAM, Assistant Professor of Undergraduate Research, Department of Science and Math, University of Maine at Presque Isle.

PAUL A. ROBINSON, Principal State Archaeologist, Rhode Island Historical Preservation and Heritage Commission.

JACK ROSSEN, Associate Professor of Anthropology, Department of Anthropology, Ithaca College, New York.

DAVID SANGER, Emeritus Professor of Anthropology, Department of Anthropology, University of Maine at Orono.

BRONA G. SIMON, State Archaeologist and Deputy State Historic Preservation Officer, Massachusetts Historical Commission.

DONALD G. SOCTOMAH, Member of the Passamaquoddy Nation, Maine.

NINA M. VERSAGGI, Director, Public Archaeology Facility, and NAGPRA Coordinator, Binghamton University, New York.

JOE WATKINS, Associate Professor of Anthropology, Department of Anthropology, University of New Mexico; and Member of the Choctaw Nation, Oklahoma.

FREDERICK WISEMAN, Associate Professor, Department of Humanities, Johnson State College; Director, Abenaki Tribal Museum and Cultural Center; and Member of the Abenaki Nation, Vermont.

Index

Page numbers in italic refer to illustrations.

Abenaki Nation: Boucher site, 79–84; Bushey site, 85–90; creation stories, 151–52, 156; Davison Brook site, 95, 99–104, 103, 105; "dialogue" with U.S. Forest Service, 151–58; Green Mountain National Forest collaboration, 158–64; intratribal politics, 164; and Massachusetts Commission on Indian Affairs (MCIA), 48; N'dakinna (homeland), 98, 151–53; recognition and sovereignty issues, 77–79, 90, 98–99, 108–10; Rock's Road site, 94, 95, 97–98, 99, 110; Smyth site, 95, 99, 104–8; structure of, 98, 150; and Wampanoag Confederation, 35. See also Wabanaki Confederacy
Abenaki Research Project (ARP), 159
Abrams Point II Burial Ground, 44–45, 56
Achushnet River, 41
Advisory Council on Historic Preservation (ACHP), 71–74, 114
affiliation. See cultural affiliation
AHLC (Archaeological and Historical Liaison Committee, Maryland), 119, 121
Algonquian worldview, 225
Allegany Reservation, 133, 136, 137–38
Allegheny National Forest, 136
Allegheny River, 138
Almalel, Suzanne, 122, 123, 124
Alves, Kenneth, 34, 35, 41
American Indian Heritage Month symposium (Maryland), 121

Amoskeag Falls, 104
analysis. See skeletal remains, analysis of
ancestors: Haudenosaunee connection with, 12–14; Mi'kmaq view of, 309–12; and Wampanoag, 33, 39–40
Andrews, Edith, 34
Andrews-Maltais, Cheryl, 181
Appalachian Trail/Long Trail, 159, 160
Aquinnah, Martha's Vineyard (town), 169
Aquinnah Natural Resources Department, 284, 285
Aquinnah Wampanoag. See Wampanoag Tribe of Gay Head/Aquinnah
Archaeological and Historical Liaison Committee, Maryland (AHLC), 119, 121
Archaeological Conservancy, 205
archaeological field schools and constituents, 293. See also Lucy Vincent Beach project; site ME 167.3
archaeological monitoring in contaminated homelands, 40–42
Archaeological Society of Maryland (ASM), 113, 122
archaeological theory, 8, 12–13
archaeology: and anthropology, 40, 303; benefits to Native Americans of, xxi–xxii, 56, 125–26; informant role vs. community relationships, 197–98, 201–4; new vision, 255–57, 261–63; political vulnerability of, 302; progressive, 302; public education, 56–57
archaeology, Native attitudes toward: Abenaki, 91; Haudenosaunee, 12–14; and information sharing, 51; Mashantucket Pequot, 279–80;

archaeology, Native attitudes toward
(*continued*)
and new vision archaeology, 262;
Piscataway, 118, 120, 124; Wampanoag,
38–40
Archaeology Month (MA), 56–57
"Archaic Indian" and Haudenosaunee,
13, 14
Aroostook Band of Micmacs, 296, 305–8
Aroostook River, 299. *See also* site ME 167.3
ARP (Abenaki Research Project), 159
Ashmore, Wendy, 316
Assonet Wampanoag, 33
Aurora Village NY, 257–58, *260*, 260–61,
263
authority, establishing areas of, 144

Babcock, William, 203
Basa, Louise, 80, 82
Basso, Keith H., 316–17
Bear, Deborah, 312
Bear (Muin or Mu win) Clan, 304, 305
Beckerman, Ira, 143
Binghamton University (SUNY), 19–21,
25–29, 134
Black Creek site, 204–6
Blume, Cara Lee, 145
Boisvert, Richard, 102, 103, 108, 110
Boston University, 54
Bouchard Tank Barge, 41
Boucher site (Abenaki), 79–84
Bragdon, Kathleen, 169
bridge replacement projects in western
New York, 136–41
Briggs, L. Cabot, 106
Brown, Gail, 69
Brown, Jim, 41
Bruchac, Marge, 109
burial grounds. *See* cemeteries and burial
grounds
burials: Haudenosaunee beliefs and
policy, 14–16; key-hole structures, 187–
88; marked vs. unmarked, 15–16; single
burials and Massachusetts policies,

50–51; soil matrix, importance of, 39.
See also graves, unmarked
"burnishing the silver chain," 193
Bushey site (Abenaki), 85–90
Buzzards Bay, 41

Canadian Maritimes. *See* Maine-
Maritimes region
Canadian-U.S. border, 301, 320, 327
Canandaigua Treaty (1794), 16, 23–24
canoe transport of remains, 81–82
Carrier Mills Project, 250
Carson, James T., 316
Cattaraugus Reservation, *133*, 140
Cayuga Nation: heartland and land
claim, 251–53, 256; and new vision
archaeology, 256–57, 261–63; and
SHARE, 253–55, 263; site excavations
in land claim area, 257–61, 263;
and US 15 project, 186, 190. *See also*
Haudenosaunee
cemeteries and burial grounds: Abrams
Point II Burial Ground, 44–45, 56;
Boucher site, 79–84; Bushey site,
85–90; Chapman Street Ponkapoag
Praying Indian Cemetery, Canton,
56; Davison Brook site, *95*, 99–104,
103, 105; Fanning Road Cemetery,
278–79; Jefferson Patterson Park and
Museum (MD), 114; Killens Pond
Adena site, 207; Long Pond, 272–75,
273; Maryland Eastern Shore ossuary
burial, 116–17; Mashpee Indian
Burial Ground, New Seabury, 55–56;
Massachusetts Historical Commission
studies on, 56; Massachusetts policies
on, 51; Miacomet "Praying Indians"
cemetery, 52, 56; Millbury III site, 55;
Narragansett Indian cemetery, 59–60;
ownership of artifacts in, 69–70; RI
1000 site, 59–60, 66–71; Rock's Road
site, 94, *95*, 97–98, 99, 110; Shawkemo
II Burial Ground, 53, 56; Smyth site,
95, 99, 104–8; at Squibnocket Ridge,

Martha's Vineyard, 175–79; at US 15 project, 187–88; Uxbridge Almshouse Cemetery (MA), 54. *See also* burials

CfMA (Council for Maryland Archaeology), 119, 121

Chadwick, William, 41

Champagne, Duane, 113

Chapman Street Ponkapoag Praying Indian Cemetery (Canton), 56

Chappaquiddick Tribe, 48, 167

Cheswold Lenape Community, 201, 203, 207, 216

Chonodote (Peachtown), 252, 257–58

Christian missionaries, 23, 56

circle of life, 156

Cissna, Paul, 115

Clark, Charles, IV, 202

Clark, William Russel, 200–201

coexistence policy of Narrangansett, 63–64

Colgate University: Longyear Museum of Anthropology, 243–47; summer workshop in archaeology, 234, 235–43

collaboration issues: Abenaki and Forest Service, 157–64; consultation vs. collaboration, 210–11; cooperation vs. collaboration, 145; definitions and connotations, 62, 145–46; Piscataway and Maryland, 125–28; reciprocal education, 127–28, 171; research benefits, 213–14, 227; resource management perspective, 292; spiritual dangers of excavation, 44–45

collaborative archaeology, defined, xxi

colonial period: grave robbery in, 36–38; King Philip's War, 63–66; Revolutionary War, 251–52, 256

Columbus, Christopher, 56–57

communication: and conflict, dealing with, 91–92; "dialogue" between Abenaki and Forest Service, 151–58; face-to-face vs. mediated, 82; naive attempts at, 158; and noncompliance interactions, 19, 30–31; and privacy

issues, 84; process of, 124, 127–28; regulatory context for, 144; and relationships, 163; and trust, 124; and understanding, 194. *See also* language

community relationships vs. informant role, 197–98, 201–4, 210–11

Conanicut Island, 65

condolence ritual, 11

Confederated Tribes of Maine, 107–8

conflicts of interest, 9

Connecticut (State), 268, 272. *See also* Mashantucket Pequot Tribe

Connecticut River (Kwanitewk), 152

conservationist ethic, 155

construction: and conflict at Bushey site (Vermont), 85–86; and Massachusetts law, 51; and Rhode Island law, 67–68

consultation: definitions of, xxi, 187, 210; expense of, 99; informant role vs. community relationships, 197–98, 201–4, 210–11; NAGPRA, negative impacts of, 27–29; Narrangansett assertion of right to, 73; in New Brunswick, 298, 306; nonfederal repatriations, negative impact of, 27–29; overview of legislation, xx–xxi; Pennsylvania guidelines, 190–95; and Pennsylvania highway projects, 186; as process, 18–19, 30–31; streamlining, 194; and tribal politics, 20, 24–25

consulting party status: and Narrangansett, 72, 74; and PennDOT, 191, 192

cooperation vs. collaboration, 143, 145–46

Covenant Chain of Peace, 11

creation stories, 151–52, 156, 309

Crist, Thomas, 178

Crock, John, 85

Cross, John R., 55

cultural affiliation: and Haudenosaunee, 8–14, 26–29; in Maryland, 119; and Massachusetts Unmarked Burial Law, 49; obstacles to, 8–9; and tribal politics, 28–29

cultural anthropology and archaeology,
40, 303
"culturally unidentifiable" remains,
39–40, 98
Cultural Resource Commission, 174
cultural resource management (CRM)
projects. *See* Lucy Vincent Beach
project; Martha's Vineyard; western
New York highway archaeology
cultural resource outreach, 215
Cultural Resources Geographic
Information System (GIS), 195
cultural resource surveys in western New
York, 136, 140
cultural sequencing as problematic, 8,
12–13, 40
cultural tourism, 313
culture, understandings of, 13, 194
Curry, Dennis, 123

Davison Brook site, *95*, 99–104, *103, 105*
Davison Brook site (Abenaki), *95*
Dean, Howard, 78–79, 86
Delaware (State): and informants vs.
community relationships, 197–98,
201–4, 210–11; Killens Pond Adena site,
206–10; recognition issues, 200; tribal
politics in, 203; tribes of, 198–201,
199. See also Nanticoke, Lenape, and
Nanticoke Lenni-Lenape tribes
Delaware Department of Transportation
(DelDOT), 214–15. *See also* Hickory
Bluff project
Delaware Nation and US 15 project, 186,
190. *See also* Nanticoke, Lenape, and
Nanticoke Lenni-Lenape tribes
Delmarva Adena complex, 207
Deloria, Vine, Jr., 198
demonstrated interest, 191, 196n3
Dent, Richard J. (Joe), 122, 123
desecration. *See* grave robbery and
desecration
detribalization of Narrangansetts, 66

Developments of Regional Impact (DRIS),
168
digital imaging, 245–46
Dillon, Scott, 85
DNA testing, 78, 86, 90
double standard in treatment of burials,
3–7, 16
Doucette, Diana L., 55
Douglas, Helen, 41
Dow, Judy, 109
Downeast Heritage Center, 325
Downs, Mary, 107
DRIS (Developments of Regional Impact),
168
Dungey site, *234*, 239–40, 242
Dutch in New York, 22–23

Eagle Cottage site, 263
Earth Mother (or Mother Earth):
Abenaki beliefs, 153; and burial,
14; business as destroyer, 42;
Haudenosaunee beliefs, 11–12, 14;
Mi'kmaq beliefs, 309; modern
disconnection with, 43; Wampanoag
views of, 39
Eastern Woodland tribes, 35
Eckstorm, Fanny Hardy, 320
education, reciprocal, 127–28, 171
Ehrlich, Robert L., Jr., 126
Eliot, John, 56
en'i jamig (ancestors as "spirit" or
"shadow"), 309
Ennis, Chief Daniel, 305, 307
Environmental Protection Agency (EPA)
Superfund sites, 41–42
erosion at Lucy Vincent Beach, 283,
285–90
expense of consultations, 99

*Fact Sheet: Section 106 Participation
by Indian Tribes and Other Native
Americans* (ACHP), 71–72
Fanning Road Cemetery, 278–79
Federal Highway Administration

(FHWA), Pennsylvania Division: future
prospects, 195; legislative history,
183–85; policy changes and guidelines,
190–95; US 15 project, *185*, 185–90
Federal Highway Administration (FHWA)
and Narragansett in Rhode Island,
72–73, 74
Ferguson, T. J., 112, 128
Field Museum (Chicago), 6
field schools and constituencies, 293. See
also Lucy Vincent Beach project; site
ME 167.3
fire hearths, 208–9, 224
Five Nations Constitution, 21
Fragoso, Tina Pierce, 201
Francis, David, Sr., 325
Franklin Pierce College, 104–7, 109, 110

Gagne, Paul Iron Turtle, 55
Ganong, William, 320
Gatschet, Albert, 320
Geographic Information System (GIS) of
cultural resources, 195
George, Doug, 6
Gila River Indian Community, 241–42
GMNF. See Green Mountain National
Forest
Grand Council (Haudenosaunee), 22, 24
Grant, George, 251
grave robbery and desecration: Abenaki
view of, 82–83, 84; Haudenosaunee
view of, 3–5, 7, 15–16; Mashantucket
Pequot experience of, 278–79; Mi'kmaq
view of, 310; by Pilgrims, 36–37;
Wampanoag view of, 36–38, 42–43
graves, unmarked: legal discrimination
against, 15–16, 47; New Hampshire
law on, 110; Pequot approach to,
272–73; as protection against looting,
42; in Rhode Island, 66–67. See also
cemeteries and burial grounds;
Massachusetts Unmarked Burial Law
Great Cedar Swamp, 267
Great Law of Peace (Kaianerekowa), 21, 22

Green, Geraldine, 6
Green, Judy, 6
Green Mountain National Forest
(GMNF): contacts and meetings with
Abenaki, 158–60; "dialogue" with
Abenaki, 151–58; future steps, 163–64;
history of, 153–54; lessons and benefits
of collaboration, 163; problems in
collaboration, 160–63
Greenwich Cove, 67–68
*Guidelines for Indian Participation on
Archaeological Surveys* (RIHPHC), 71–72
*Guidelines for the Analysis of Human
Skeletal Remains* (MHC), 48–49
Guswenta treaty (Two Row Wampum
belt), 22–23

Halftown, Clint, 6
Hall, Charlie, 120, 122–25, 127–28
Hamlin, Gina, 121–28
Harris, Doug, 60
Harvard archaeological field school. *See
Lucy Vincent Beach project*
Haudenosaunee (Six Nations Iroquois
Confederacy): and cultural affiliation,
10–14, 27–29; defined, 146n1;
geographic boundaries, 26, 26–27;
Iroquois Constitution and political
system, 21–22; meaning of name, 17n1;
nations within, 10; policy on human
remains, 14–16; and Revolutionary
War, 251; and Seneca Nation, 146n1.
See also Cayuga Nation; Oneida
Indian Nation of New York; Onondaga
Nation; Seneca Nation
Haudenosaunee Standing Committee
on Burial Rules and Regulations
(HSCBRR), 4–7, 23–25, 27–29
Haviland, William, 80, 82, 84
Hawken, Paul, 42
Hayward, Richard "Skip," 265, 279
Henry, Chief Leo, 6
Henry, Dixie L., 171
Henry, Ray, 6

Herring Creek, 172–73
Herring Pond Wampanoag, 33
Hiawatha belt, 22
Hickory Bluff project, *226, 227*;
    collaboration and results, 225–28;
    context, 213–14; Native American
    involvement, 215–19; project overview,
    214–15; sweat lodge ceremony, 219–28,
    221, 223
Highway Archaeology Program (NY),
    138, 141, 144. *See also* western New York
    highway archaeology
historic preservation, attitudes toward, 52
Holderness NH, *95*, 99–104, *105*
Houlton Band of Maliseets, 296, 299,
    304–8
Hughes, Richard B., 171
humanities-based approach, 228
human rights, 6–7, 15–16
Hume, Gary, 99, 104, 106, 107

identity conflicts in Maryland, 113
Indian Burial Policy Committee
    (Maryland), 116
informant role vs. community
    relationships, 197–98, 201–4, 210–11
intellectual property rights, 40
interested party status, 72, 216
intertribal politics. *See* politics, tribal
Iroquoian languages, 10
Iroquois Confederacy. *See*
    Haudenosaunee
Iroquois Constitution, 21

Jardin, Randy, 178, 180, 181, 285
Jefferson Patterson Park and Museum, 114
Jeffords, Jim, 78
Jemison, Peter, 5
John, Darwin, 6
John, Richard Johnny, 6
Johnson, Eric, 41
Jonas, Rosanna, 55–56
Joseph, Luke, 304
journey after life (Haudenosaunee), 14–15

Kaianerekowa (Great Law of Peace), 21, 22
Keepers of the Grand Council fire, 22
Kelley, Marc, 69
key-hole burial structures, 187–88
Killens Pond Adena site, 206–10
King, Thomas S., 18–19, 29
King Philip's War, 63, 65–66
Klein, Joel, 41
knowledge, traditional. *See* oral tradition
    and knowledge
Kwanitewk (Connecticut River), 152

LaFrance, Ron, 6
Lakota Sioux, 220
land, Euroamerican vs. Native American
    views of, 43, 155–57
language: academic, 89–90; as culturally
    conditioned, 194; Iroquoian, 10;
    Passamaquoddy-Maliseet Dictionary,
    320–21, 327; racist, 106. *See also*
    Passamaquoddy Place-Names Project
Lenape Tribe. *See* Nanticoke, Lenape, and
    Nanticoke Lenni-Lenape tribes
Leroy, Sharon, 6
LeSourd, Philip, 320
Leveillee, Allan, 55
Lischio, Paul, 68
loans, long-term, 192
Logan, Clayton, 6
Long Pond Cemetery (Pequot), 272–75,
    273
Longyear, John, 243–44
Longyear Museum of Anthropology
    (Colgate), 243–47
Louisiana Supreme Court, 69–70
Lounsbury, Floyd, 10
Lucy Vincent Beach project:
    archaeological field school, 38–39, 285–
    90; history of site and project, 282–84;
    initial survey, 284–85; lessons learned
    and effects on methods, 290–93

Madawaska village, 299–301, *300*
Maddox, Lee White Wolf, 55

Maine-Maritimes region: border issues, 301, 320, 327; field school at site ME 167.3 (Presque Isle), 303–9, 312–13; geography and history, 298–303; map, 297; Mi'kmaq and Maliseet in, 295–98; Mi'kmaq view of archaeology in, 309–12. *See also* Passamaquoddy Place-Names Project

Maliseet Advisory Committee on Archaeology, 306, 308

Maliseet Nation (Wolastoqiyik): geography and history, 298–303; and Mi'kmaq, 296–98, 306, 307; and site ME 167.3 field school, 303–9

Maliseet-Passamaquoddy language, 320–21

Malonson, Chief Donald, 171, 172

Manchester, New Hampshire, 95, 104–8

marginalization, 108–10. *See also* recognition and nonrecognition

Maritimes. *See* Maine-Maritimes region

Marks, Jonathan, 78

Marsh, George Perkins, 154

Martha's Vineyard (Noepe): Aquinnah town bylaw surveys, 179–80; construction outside of Aquinnah, 180–81; environmental and cultural context, 167; future opportunities, 181–82; historic preservation plan (HPP), 173–74; history of archaeology on, 167–68; map, 166; and Massachusetts Commission on Indian Affairs, 53; overview, 165–67; Squibnocket Ridge project, 174–79; Vineyard Open Land Foundation, 174–75. *See also* Lucy Vincent Beach project

Martha's Vineyard Commission (MVC), 168

Maryland: dialogue and relationship with Indians, 114–21, 124, 125–28; Eastern Shore ossuary burial, 116–17; legislation, 117; and Piscataway Indian Nation, 115, 115, 126; tribal conflict

in, 113; Winslow site, 121–25. *See also* Piscataway Indian Nation

Maryland Commission on Indian Affairs (MCIA): annual symposium, 121; establishment of, 114; and relationship between archaeologists and Indians, 114, 115–19; and Winslow site, 123, 124

Maryland State Historic Preservation Office (SHPO), 116–19, 122–23, 127

Mashantucket Pequot Ethnohistory Project, 271

Mashantucket Pequot Museum and Research Center, 265–66, 275–78, 276, 277, 280

Mashantucket Pequot Reservation, 265, 266, 266–69

Mashantucket Pequot Tribe: and archaeologists, 269–72, 279–80; historical context, 266–69; Long Pond Cemetery excavation, 272–75, 273

Mashpee Indian Burial Ground, New Seabury (MA), 55–56

Mashpee Wampanoag, 33

Maslack, Fred, 78, 86

Massachusetts. *See* Martha's Vineyard; Wampanoag Confederation; Wampanoag Tribe of Gay Head/ Aquinnah

Massachusetts Archaeological Society, 52

Massachusetts Commission on Indian Affairs (MCIA): and Massachusetts Unmarked Burial Law, 47, 48–49; and John Peters Sr., 44, 52; and NAGPRA, 52; and Wampanoag Confederation, 34

Massachusetts Highway Department, 54–55

Massachusetts Historical Commission (MHC): collaborative work, 53–54; *Guidelines for the Analysis of Human Skeletal Remains*, 48–49; Lucy Vincent Beach excavations, 283; and Martha's Vineyard Commission, 168; and moratorium bill, 46

Massachusetts Military Reserve, 41–42

Massachusetts State Historic Preservation
Office (SHPO), 173–74
Massachusetts Unmarked Burial Law:
background and introduction, 44–47;
case examples, 52–56; description of,
47–49; implementation and results,
50–52, 57; and Martha's Vineyard, 168,
175, 176; and NAGPRA, 35
Massasoit, 43n2
McBride, Kevin, 169
MCIA. See Maryland Commission
on Indian Affairs; Massachusetts
Commission on Indian Affairs
McIntyre, Jamie, 184
McKee, Dariel, 304
medical examiner (ME) in Massachusetts,
47
medicinal herbs, 259
Merrill, Chief April St. Francis, 79, 83,
85–87
MHC. See Massachusetts Historical
Commission
Miacomet "Praying Indians" cemetery,
52, 56
Miantonomo, 64–65
Mi'kmaq Nation: geography and history,
298–303; and Maliseet, 296–98, 306,
307; and site ME 167.3 field school, 303–9
Millbury III site, 55
Mills, Barbara J., xx
Minthorn, Armand, 107
missionaries, Christian, 23, 56
Missisquoi, Abenaki Nation of. *See*
Abenaki Nation
Mitchell, Kathleen, 135
Mohegan Tribe, 64–65
Monadnock Institute of Nature, Place,
and Culture, 109
Monterio, Roque, 41
Moody, Chris, 97
Moody, Donna, 96–97, 102, 104, 106–7,
109, 110
Moody, John, 96–97, 102, 104, 109
moratorium bill in Massachusetts, 46

Morenon, Pierre, 68
Morgan, Lewis Henry, 26
Morton, Thomas, 37–38, 42, 43
Mother Earth. *See* Earth Mother
mountains, Abenaki: and Forest Service
views of, 154–55
Mourt's Relation (Pilgrim journal), 36–37
Mrozowski, Stephen, 169
museums: Field Museum (Chicago),
6; Jefferson Patterson Park and
Museum, 114; Longyear Museum of
Anthropology, 243–47; Mashantucket
Pequot Museum and Research Center,
275–78, *276, 277,* 280; Peabody Museum,
36, 39–40, 106; Robbins Museum, 52;
Seneca Iroquois National Museum, 135,
140. *See also* New York State Museum/
State Education Department
MVC (Martha's Vineyard Commission),
168

NAGPRA. *See* Native American Graves
Protection and Repatriation Act of
1990
Nanticoke, Lenape, and Nanticoke Lenni-
Lenape tribes: about, 198–201, *199;*
Black Creek site, 204–6; and Hickory
Bluff project, 215–19; and informant
role vs. community relationships, 197–
98, 201–4, 210–11; Killens Pond Adena
site, 206–10; powwow, 218; public
blessing ceremony, 218–19; recognition
of, 200; sweat lodge ceremony, 219–28,
221, 223. See also Delaware Nation and
US 15 project
Nanticoke Skeleton Dance, 217
Nantucket Island, 44–45, 52–53
Nantucket Wampanoag, 42–43
Naranjo, Tesse, 106
Narrangansett Indian Archaeological-
Anthropological Committee (NIAAC),
61–62, 71–73
Narrangansett Indian Tribal Preservation
Office (NITHPO), 60–61, 73–74

Narrangansett Indian Tribe: and colonists, 63–66; detribalization and later acknowledgment of, 66; relationship with Rhode Island, 60–61, 66, 71–74; and RI 1000 project, 59–60, 66–71

Nasseny, Michael, 69

National Advisory Council on Historic Preservation, 9

National Historic Preservation Act (NHPA) amendments, xx–xxi, 72, 73. See also Section 106, National Historic Preservation Act

Native American Archaeology in Rhode Island (Robinson et al.), 60–61

Native American Graves Protection and Repatriation Act of 1990 (NAGPRA): and Abenaki, 98, 106–8; and Binghamton University, 19–21, 25–29; and Green Mountain National Forest, 158; and Haudenosaunee, 4, 8, 16–17, 25–29; and highway archaeology in New York, 131–32, 134; in Maine, 306; and Maryland, 118, 119; and Mashantucket Pequot, 278–79; and Massachusetts Commission on Indian Affairs, 52; Massachusetts law compared to, 35; and nonrecognized Wampanoag tribes, 35–36; provisions of, xx, 18; and Wampanoag, 34. See also consultation; cultural affiliation

Native American Liaison Committee (Maryland), 119

Nature Conservancy, 313

N'dakinna (Abenaki homeland), 98, 151–53

New Brunswick, 298, 304–5, 306. See also Maine-Maritimes region

Newell, Beverly, 109

Newell, Don, 109

New Hampshire: Abenaki relationship with, 94–97; law on unmarked burials, 110; maps of sites in, 95; Smyth site, 99, 104–8. See also Abenaki Nation

New Hampshire Archaeological Society (NHAS), 104–5, 108

New Hampshire Division of Historical Resources (NHDHR), 96, 100–101

New Jersey: Black Creek site, 204–6; recognition by, 200; tribes of, 198–201, 199

Newman, Rico, 123

Newman, Savoy, 123

New Seabury (MA), 55–56

new vision archaeology, 255–57, 261–63

New York Archaeological Council, 25, 131, 138

New York Office of Parks, Recreation, and Historic Preservation (OPRHP), 131, 143–44

New York State: bridge replacement projects, 136–41; and Cayuga sovereignty, 252–53; Haudenosaunee frustration with, 5, 9; highway archaeology, 131–36; maps, 26, 133, 234; Seneca collaboration and cooperation, 141–45; and US 15 project, 186. See also Cayuga Nation; Haudenosaunee; Oneida Indian Nation of New York

New York State Archaeological Association, 245

New York State Department of Transportation (NYSDOT), 132, 133, 134, 136–37

New York State Indian Law 12A, 5

New York State Museum/State Education Department (NYSM/NYSED): and highway archaeology, 132–34, 136–39; and interagency cooperation, 143–44; and NYAC standards, 131

NHAS (New Hampshire Archaeological Society), 104–5, 108

NHDHR (New Hampshire Division of Historical Resources), 96, 100–101

NHPA. See National Historic Preservation Act (NHPA) amendments; Section 106, National Historic Preservation Act

NIAAC (Narrangansett Indian
Archaeological-Anthropological
Committee), 61–62, 71–73
Nipmuck Nation, 48, 54
Nipmuc Nation, 35, 48
NITHPO (Narrangansett Indian Tribal
Preservation Office), 60–61, 73–74
Noka, Bella, 63
nonprofit incorporation, 35
NYSDOT (New York State Department of
Transportation), 132, 133, 134, 136–37
NYSM/NYSED. *See* New York State
Museum/State Education Department

oil spills, 41
Oil Springs Reservation, *133*
Olson, Brooke, 254, 259
Olson, Ernie, 254
Oneida Children and Elders Center,
249n3
Oneida Indian Nation Men's Council and
Clan Mothers, 237, 239
Oneida Indian Nation of New York:
Colgate summer archaeology
workshop, 235–43; and cultural
affiliation, 29; Haudenosaunee and
sovereignty issues, 24; and Longyear
Museum of Anthropology (Colgate),
243–47
Oneida Tribe of Indians of Wisconsin, 29
Ongwe'o:we ("the Original, Real
People"), 8, 11–12, 14
Ongwe'o:weheka ("The Way of Life of the
Original, Real People"), 11–12
Onondaga Nation, 22. *See also*
Haudenosaunee
OPRHP (New York Office of Parks,
Recreation, and Historic Preservation),
131, 143–44
oral tradition and knowledge: Abenaki,
151–53; and cultural affiliation, 8–9;
Haudenosaunee (Iroquois), 8–9, 11–12,
13–14, 21–22; hesitancy to document,
9, 40

Original Instructions, 12
Original People: in Abenaki tradition,
157; in Haudenosaunee tradition, 8,
11–12, 14
osteological study. *See* skeletal remains,
analysis of
Owasco people, 14
ownership issues, 69–70, 139–40, 192

Paiva, Marcos, 41
PAL. *See* Public Archaeology Laboratory,
Inc.
"Paleoindians" and Haudenosaunee, 13,
14
Parker, Arthur C., 21
Parker, Chief Bernie, 6
Passamaquoddy-Maliseet Dictionary
(P-MD), 320–21, 327
Passamaquoddy Place-Names Project:
and homeland, 314–15, 317–20; maps,
315, *318*, *319*; and Passamaquoddy-
Maliseet Dictionary, 320–21; project
overview, 321–25; research history, 320;
results and conclusions, 325–27; and
study of place, 315–17
Passamaquoddy Tribe: homeland, 314–15,
315, 317–20, *318*, *319*; and Maliseet, 301;
and Wabanaki Confederacy, 298, 306–7
Patrick Tavern site, *260*, 260–61
Paul, Patrick, 305, 307
Peabody Museum (Harvard), 36, 39–40,
106
Peachtown (Wells Barn site or
Chonodote), 252, 257–58
Pennsylvania Department of
Transportation (PennDOT): future
prospects, 195; legislative history,
183–85; policy changes and guidelines,
190–95; US 15 project, *185*, 185–90
Pennsylvania Historical and Museum
Commission (PHMC), 192
Pennsylvania State Historic Preservation
Office (SHPO), 188, 189
Penobscot Nation, 298, 306–7

Pequots. *See* Mashantucket Pequot Tribe
Pequot War, 268, 269
Perez, Michael, 3
Perry, Laurie, 181
persistence, idea of, 71
Peters, John, Jr., 34, 55
Peters, John, Sr. (Slow Turtle):
 on archaeology, 51, 56–57; and
 Massachusetts Commission on Indian
 Affairs, 46, 52; and Massachusetts
 Unmarked Burial Law, 35, 44, 45, 47,
 53–55; and preservation, 53
Peters, Ramona, 55
Peterson, David, 41
photography, digital, 245–46
Piechota, Dennis, 69
Pinchot, Gifford, 155
Piscataway Conoy Tribe, 122–23, 126
Piscataway Indian Nation: archaeologists,
 view of, 118; map of communities, *115*;
 and Piscataway National Park, 115;
 site visits to learn about archaeology,
 120; and Winslow site, 122–25. *See also*
 Maryland
place, study of, 315–17
place-worlds concept, 317, 327
Pleasant Point Reservation, *319*, 321
P-MD (Passamaquoddy-Maliseet
 Dictionary), 320–21, 327
Point Peninsula people, 14
Polchies, Irvin, 305–6, 307–8
politics, tribal: Abenaki, 164; competing
 claims in Maryland, 113, 118, 127; and
 consultation process, 20; in Delaware,
 203; Mi'kmaq and Maliseet, 296, 306;
 recognition and representation among
 Haudenosaunee, 24–25, 27–29; Seneca,
 190
Pollard, Chief Paul, 55
Poodry, Ken, 6
Potomac River Archaeology Survey, 122
Power, Marjory, 80, 84
power sharing and collaboration, 70,
 210–11

Powless, Irving, Jr., 5, 6
powwow, Nanticoke, 218
"Praying Indians," 52, 56
"prehistoric" as problematic term, 12–13
Presque Isle. *See* site ME 167.3
Proctor, Natalie, 120
Public Archaeology Facility (PAF), 19
Public Archaeology Laboratory, Inc.
 (PAL): Aquinnah town bylaw surveys,
 180; Aquinnah Wampanoag trust lands
 surveys, 169–74; and Massachusetts
 Highway Department, 54–55; renewed
 Aquinnah partnership with, 181;
 Squibnocket Ridge project, 174–79
public awareness: Abenaki and Green
 Mountain National Forest, 160; and
 new vision archaeology, 256, 262; and
 privacy issues, 84
public blessing ceremony, Nanticoke,
 218–19
public education, social and political
 contexts of, 291
public input and the U.S. Forest Service,
 157
publicity: and Davison Brook site, 104,
 105; and Lucy Vincent Beach site,
 287–88, 291

Quary, Abram, 42–43, 45

racism, 106
recognition and nonrecognition: of
 Abenaki, 77–79, 90, 98–99, 108–10;
 and consulting party status, 191; of
 Haudenosaunee, 6, 23–25; in Maryland,
 113, 117–18, 119, 126; of Mashantucket
 Pequot, 269; of Nanticoke, Lenape,
 and Nanticoke Lenni-Lenape, 200; of
 Narragansett, 66; of Wampanoag,
 35–36
Recognition of Maryland Indian Status
 Act (1988), 117, 126
Red Earth Summer Archaeology
 Program, 241–42

"remains," confusion about definition of, 80, 83

repatriations: Abenaki, 81–82, 90, 98–99, 110–11; Haudenosaunee, 7, 27–28; in Maryland, 117; and Massachusetts Unmarked Burial Law, 49, 51–52; Oneida, 244–45; Pequot, 278–79; as return home, 111; in Rhode Island, 67; Wampanoag, 36, 39

representation, conflicts over, 24–25. *See also* politics, tribal

resource management perspective, 292

respect: and behavior at archaeological sites, 48, 274; building through noncompliance interactions, 19; and collector, presence of, 89; during colonial period, 65–66; and cross-cultural divide, 157; earning, 144; equal respect for white and Native burials, 3–4, 15–16, 82; mutual, 16, 20–21, 27, 30, 120, 128; process of, 124–25; and racist terminology, 106; and sovereignty, 193; for spiritual beliefs, 13; toward ancestors, 7, 11, 189; toward spirits, 83. *See also* grave robbery and desecration

Revolutionary War, 251–52, 256

Rhode Island: history of relations with Narragansett, 60–66, 71–74; legislation, 67; RI 1000 project, 59–60, 66–71, 72

Rhode Island Preservation and Heritage Commission (RIHPHC), 59, 60–61, 69

Rhode Island State Historic Preservation Office (SHPO), 61, 71–72

rights: to consultation, 73; of deceased, 310; human, 6–7, 15–16; intellectual property, 40; spiritual, 7, 15

RIHPHC (Rhode Island Preservation and Heritage Commission), 59, 60–61, 69

RI 1000 project, 59–60, 66–71, 72

Ritchie, William, 251

ritual contexts at Black Creek site, 205

riverine model, 299

robbery of graves. *See* grave robbery and desecration

Robbins Museum, 52

Rock's Road site (Abenaki), 95, 97–98, 99

Rose, Camille, 180, 181

Rossen, Jack, 144

Route 1 Highway Project (DE). *See* Hickory Bluff project

Rubertone, Patricia, 69

Ryan-Elderkin, Cindy Shining Star, 55

sacred circle and sweat lodge, 221, 222

sacredness of places, 154. *See also* Earth Mother

Sargent, Howard, 105, 106

Savoy, Mervin, 122

science, Mi'kmaq view of, 309

SCRAP (State Conservation Rescue Archaeology Program [NH]), 96, 102–3

Scutop, 65

Seabrook, New Hampshire, 94, 95, 97–98, 110

Section 106, National Historic Preservation Act (NHPA): legal overlap and conflicts with, 9; and New Hampshire projects, 99; and Pennsylvania projects, 184–85, 192; training in Onondaga NY, 187

Seneca Faith Keepers, 188

Seneca Falls (NY), 252

Seneca Iroquois National Museum (SINM), 135, 140

Seneca Nation, 186–89. *See also* Haudenosaunee

Seneca Nation of Indians (SNI) Tribal Historic Preservation Office (THPO): archaeological policy, 135, 146–49; bridge replacement projects, 136–41; collaboration and cooperation issues, 142–44; creation and recognition of, 131; and highway archaeology, 132, 134–36; map, 133; structure of, 146n1

Settlement Act (1874), 169

settlement pattern, 316

Shako:wi Cultural Center (Oneida), 239, 246, 249n3

SHARE (Strengthening Haudenosaunee American Relations through Education), 253–55, 263

SHARE Farm project, 254, 255

Shawkemo II Burial Ground, 53, 56

shore claims, 66

Simmons, William, 67

Simon, Brona, 35, 282–83

SINM (Seneca Iroquois National Museum), 135, 140

site ME 167.3 (Presque Isle): archaeologist's perspective, 303–9; and connections, 312–13; geographical and historical context, 298–303; Mi'kmaq perspective, 309–12

Six Nations. *See* Haudenosaunee

skeletal remains, analysis of: Bushey site (VT), 87; Massachusetts guidelines for, 48–49; sharing information from, 51; spiritual dangers of, 44–45, 83, 89

Skeleton Dance, Nanticoke, 217

Slack Farm Project, 250

Slattery, Richard, 121

Smithsonian Institution: and Winslow site, 124

smoke-shop raid, 63

smudging, 44–45, 86, 89

Smyth site (Abenaki), 95, 99, 104–8

SNI. *See* Seneca Nation of Indians (SNI) Tribal Historic Preservation Office

Snow Foundation, 235, 238–39

soil matrix in burials, 39

souls and afterlife, Haudenosaunee beliefs on, 14–15

Sovereign Abenaki Nation of Missisquoi. *See* Abenaki Nation

sovereignty: and Abenaki, 77–79, 90; and Cayuga land claim, 252–53; and Haudenosaunee, 22–23, 24–25; and Narrangansett, 63; and specialization of roles, 193

spatial logic, Algonquian, 225

specialization of Cayuga villages, 258–59

specialization of roles, 193

Speck, Frank, 201, 203, 320

spiritual beliefs: Algonquian worldview, 225; danger from disinterment and spirits, 44–45, 83; Mi'kmaq, 309; modern disconnection with Earth, 43; neglected by anthropology and archaeology, 13, 39

spiritual rights, 7, 15

Squam Lake Natural Science Center, 99–100, 103–4, 105

Squibnocket Ridge project, 174–79

St. Croix Island, 326

St. Francis, Chief Homer, 79, 81, 158

St. Johns River basin, 297, 298–99, 300, 313. *See also* site ME 167.3

St. Jones Adena site, 225

Stabler, Hugh, 121

State Conservation Rescue Archaeology Program (SCRAP), New Hampshire, 96, 102–3

Sterling site, 234, 239

Stinson, Wesley, 108

Stockbridge (NY), 239–40

Stockbridge Munsee Community, 48

stone features, thermally altered, 222–24, 223

Stony Brook University, 134

Sullivan-Clinton campaign, 251–52, 256

summer workshop in archaeology (Colgate), 235–43

Superfund sites, 41–42

Susquehanna Tribe, 55

sweat lodge ceremony, 219–28, 221, 223

Tadodaho of the Iroquois, 22, 24, 27

Talmage, Valerie, 46, 47

Tanner, Adrian, 316

Tantaquidgeon, Gladys, 203

taxes and sovereignty, 252–53

thermally altered stone features, 222–24, 223

Thomas, Chief Sachem Matthew, 60, 63

Thomas, David Hurst, 280
THPOS. *See* tribal historic preservation
 officers
time, Haudenosaunee view of, 12
Tobique First Nation, 304–5, 308
Tonanwanda Senecas, 146n1
TPL (Trust for Public Land), 56
Transfer of Human Remains Act (MD), 117
transport of remains by canoe, 81–82
treaties, 16, 22–24
Treaty of Canandaigua (1794), 16, 23–24
tribal historic preservation officers
 (THPOS): NHPA provisions, xx–xxi; in
 Rhode Island, 73–74; Wampanoag, 34,
 181. *See also* Seneca Nation of Indians
 (SNI) Tribal Historic Preservation
 Office
Tribal Lands Program (TPL), 56
tribal politics. *See* politics, tribal
"tribe," as term, 198–99
Trubowitz, Neal, 134
True, Charlie, 98, 102, *103*, 104
Trust for Public Land (TPL), 56
Tunica-Biloxi Tribe, 69–70
Turnbaugh, William, 69
Turning Stone Casino (Oneida), 249n4,
 254
Tutelos, 257
Two Row Wampum belt (*Guswenta*
 treaty), 22–23

UCE (Upstate Citizens for Equality),
 252–53
Union Springs (NY), 252, 254
University at Buffalo (UB) Archaeological
 Survey (SUNY): bridge replacement
 projects, 136–41; collaboration and
 cooperation, 141–45; and cultural
 resource management (CRM) projects,
 132; highway archaeology, 133–34, 136;
 overview of, 134
University of Connecticut, 273–74
University of Maine, 304, 312–13, 324
University of Massachusetts Amherst, 292

University of New Hampshire (UNH),
 96–97
University of Vermont (UVM), 79–84,
 85–90
unmarked graves. *See* graves, unmarked
Upstate Citizens for Equality (UCE),
 252–53
Urton, Gary, 244
U.S.-Canadian border, 301, 320, 327. *See
 also* Maine-Maritimes region
US 15 project, *185*, 185–90
U.S. Forest Service: mission and
 conservation ethic of, 155, 156. *See also*
 Green Mountain National Forest
Uticone, Julie and Jim, 253–54
Uxbridge Almshouse Cemetery, 54

Vandalia Bridge project, 137–40
Vanderhoop, Matthew, 181
Vanderhoop, Tobias, 38
Vermont: Abenaki and Forest Service
 descriptions of, 151–52; Abenaki
 homeland in, 150, 151–53; Abenaki
 recognition and sovereignty issues,
 77–79; misunderstandings about
 Native presence in, 84. *See also* Abenaki
 Nation; Green Mountain National
 Forest
Vernon Valley, 204
Verona, New York, 239
Versaggi, Nina, 127
Village X, 258–59, *259*
Vineyard Open Land Foundation, 174–75
voluntary collaboration: as complication
 for NAGPRA, 27–29; importance of, xxi,
 19. *See also* collaboration issues

Wabanaki Confederacy, 296–98, 306–7.
 See also Abenaki Nation; Aroostook
 Band of Micmacs; Houlton Band of
 Maliseets; Maliseet Nation; Mi'kmaq
 Nation; Passamaquoddy Tribe;
 Penobscot Nation

Wabanaki Repatriation Committee, 305, 306–8, 313

Wabanaki Tribes of Maine, 98

Wampanoag Confederation: and Abenaki, 98, 107–8; formation of, 33–34; and grave robbery, 36–38, 42–43; and honoring ancestors, 32–33, 40; and impacts of repatriation process, 39–40; and Massachusetts Unmarked Burial Law, 48, 53; and non-NAGPRA repatriations, 35–36; nonprofit incorporation of, 35. *See also* Assonet Wampanoag; Herring Pond Wampanoag; Mashpee Wampanoag; Nantucket Wampanoag; Wampanoag Tribe of Gay Head/Aquinnah

Wampanoag Confederation Repatriation Project, 33–35

Wampanoag Tribe of Gay Head/ Aquinnah: Aquinnah town bylaw surveys, 179–80; change in THPO of, 181; and construction elsewhere on the island, 180–81; federal recognition of, 167; future opportunities, 181–82; and grant from National Park Service, 43n3, 173; and Harvard archaeological field school, 38–39, 282–93; historic preservation plan (HPP), 173–74; and history of archaeology on the island, 167–68; and Massachusetts Commission on Indian Affairs, 53; Natural Resources Department, 284, 285; overview, 165–67; SHPO role, 173–74; Squibnocket Ridge project, 174–79; and Superfund site, 42; surveys on

trust lands, 169–74; and Wampanoag Confederation, 33, 34

Washburn, Arthur, 178

Washburn site, 140

Washington, George, 251

Watkins, Joe E., xxi, 127, 128

Webster, Chief Emerson, 6

Wellfleet Ossuary, 51

Wells Barn site (Peachtown or Chonodote), 252, 257–58

Wepgwajniag School, 313

Weslager, C. A., 201, 203

Western Abenaki, 98, 150. *See also* Abenaki Nation

western New York highway archaeology: bridge replacement projects, 136–41; collaboration and cooperation, 141–45; map, *133*; overview, 131–36

White, Marian, 134, 251

Williams, Paul, 20–21

Williamson, Frederick, 70

Wilson site, *234*, 240

Winslow site, 121–25

Wolastoqiyik. *See* Maliseet Nation

Woodstock First Nation, 305–6

Woodstock Reserve, 299

Work Scope Specifications for Cultural Resource Investigations (NYSED), 138

Wulustuk Grand Council, 305

Youth Work/Learn Program (Oneida), 236–43

Zobel, Melissa, 64–65